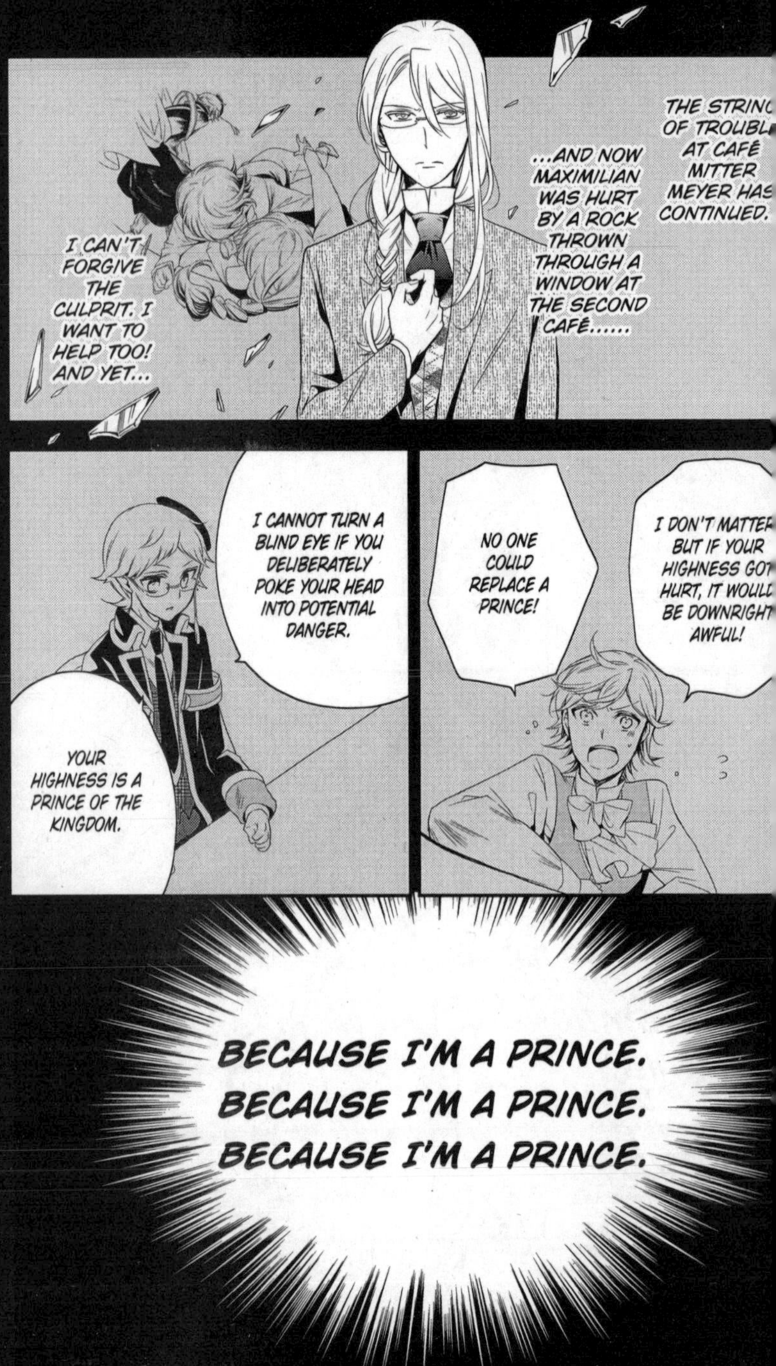
THE STRIN OF TROUBL AT CAFÉ MITTER MEYER HAS CONTINUED.
...AND NOW MAXIMILIAN WAS HURT BY A ROCK THROWN THROUGH A WINDOW AT THE SECOND CAFÉ......
I CAN'T FORGIVE THE CULPRIT. I WANT TO HELP TOO! AND YET...
I DON'T MATTE BUT IF YOUR HIGHNESS GO HURT, IT WOUL BE DOWNRIGHT AWFUL!
NO ONE COULD REPLACE A PRINCE!
I CANNOT TURN A BLIND EYE IF YOU DELIBERATELY POKE YOUR HEAD INTO POTENTIAL DANGER.
YOUR HIGHNESS IS A PRINCE OF THE KINGDOM.
BECAUSE I'M A PRINCE.
BECAUSE I'M A PRINCE.
BECAUSE I'M A PRINCE.

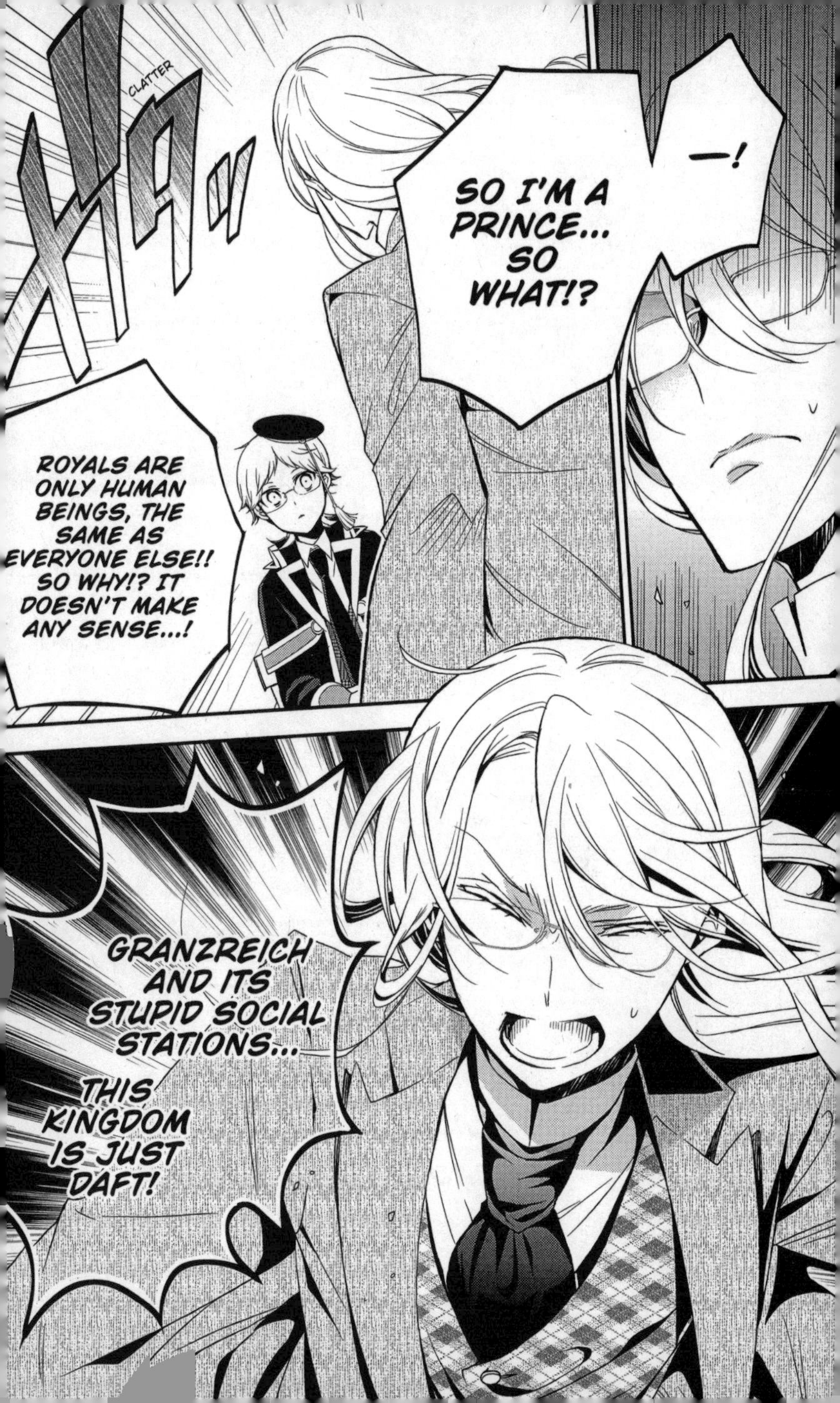
—!
SO I'M A PRINCE... SO WHAT!?
CLATTER
ROYALS ARE ONLY HUMAN BEINGS, THE SAME AS EVERYONE ELSE!! SO WHY!? IT DOESN'T MAKE ANY SENSE...!
GRANZREICH AND ITS STUPID SOCIAL STATIONS...
THIS KINGDOM IS JUST DAFT!

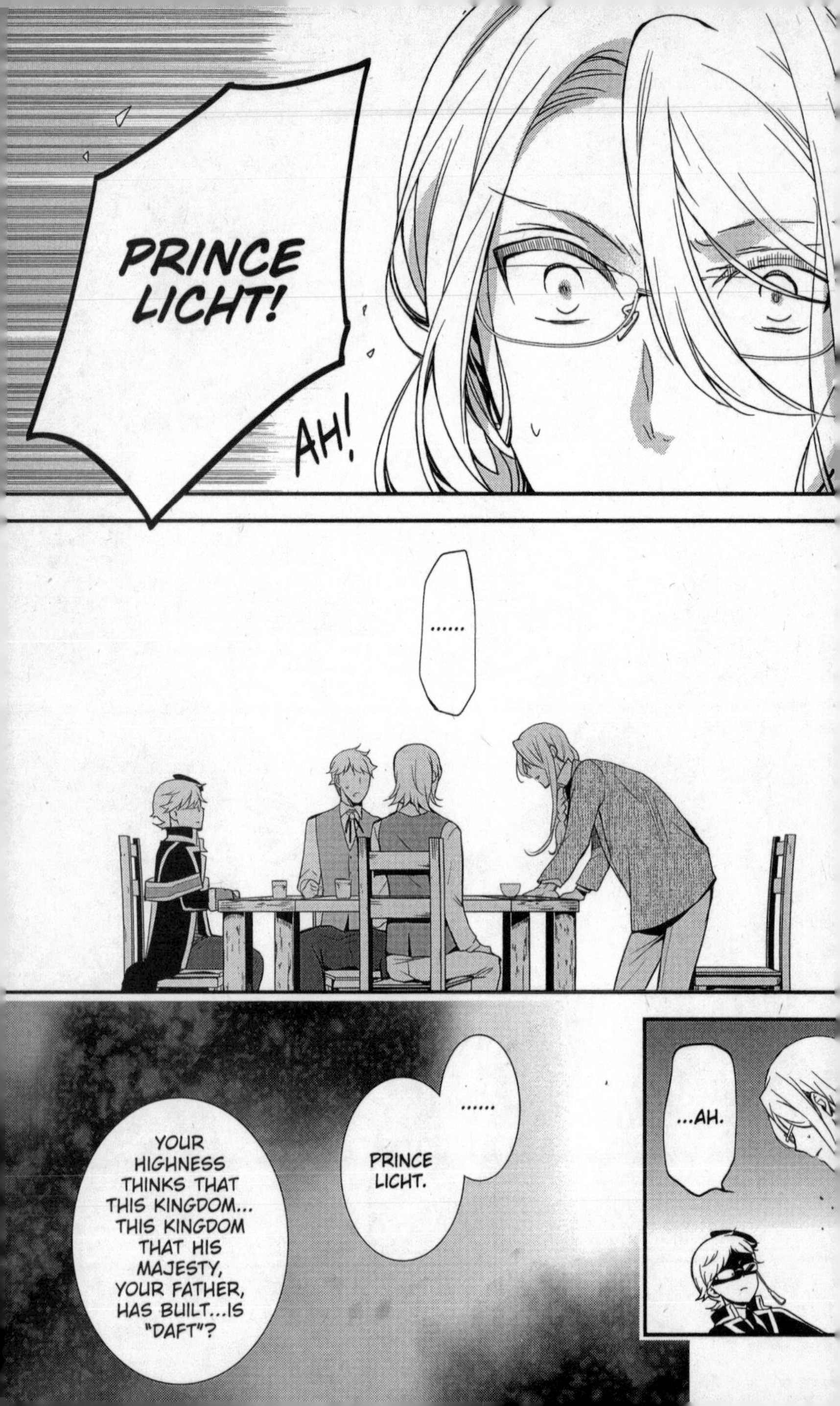
PRINCE LICHT!
AH!
......
...AH.
......
PRINCE LICHT.
YOUR HIGHNESS THINKS THAT THIS KINGDOM... THIS KINGDOM THAT HIS MAJESTY, YOUR FATHER, HAS BUILT...IS "DAFT"?

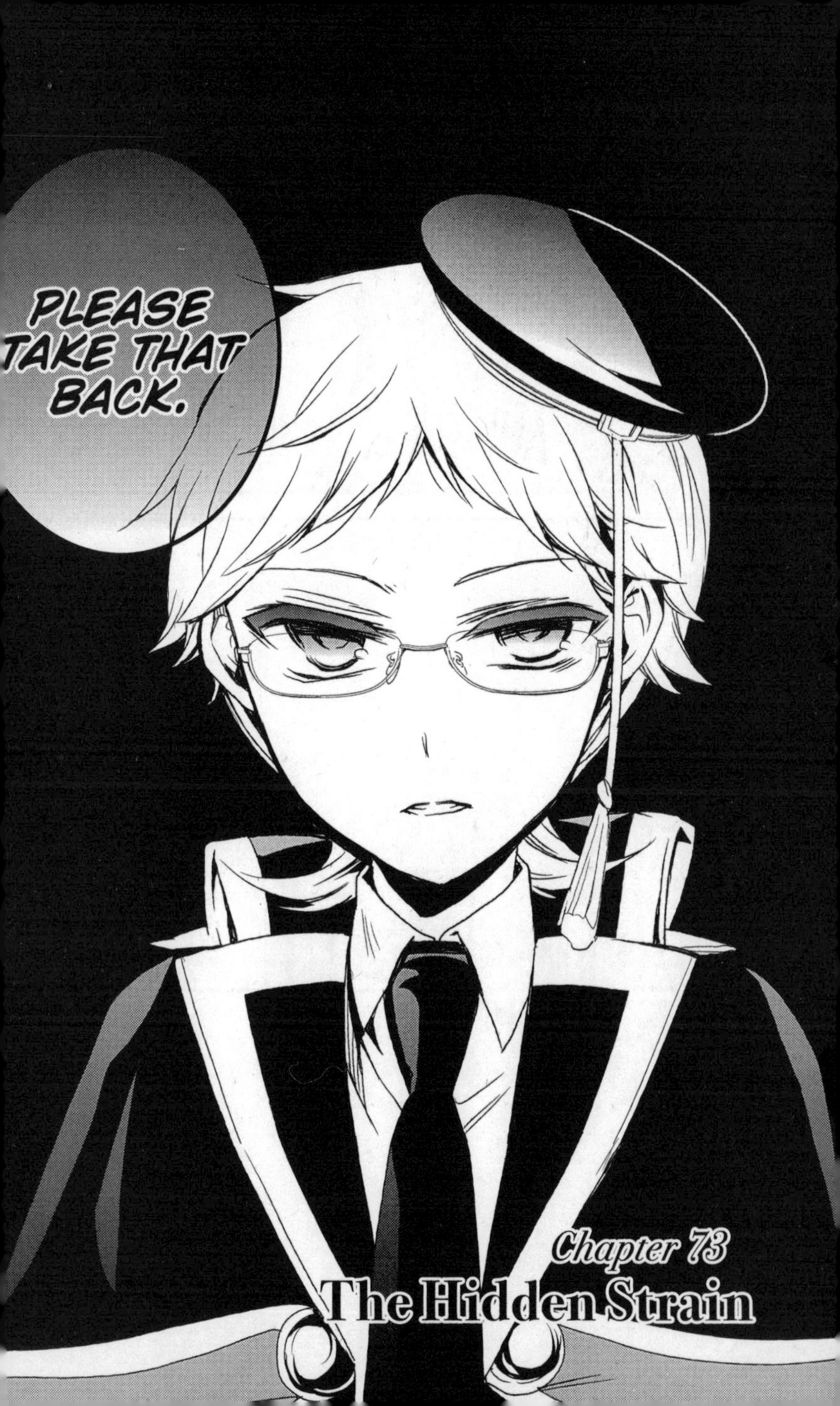
PLEASE TAKE THAT BACK.
Chapter 73
The Hidden Strain

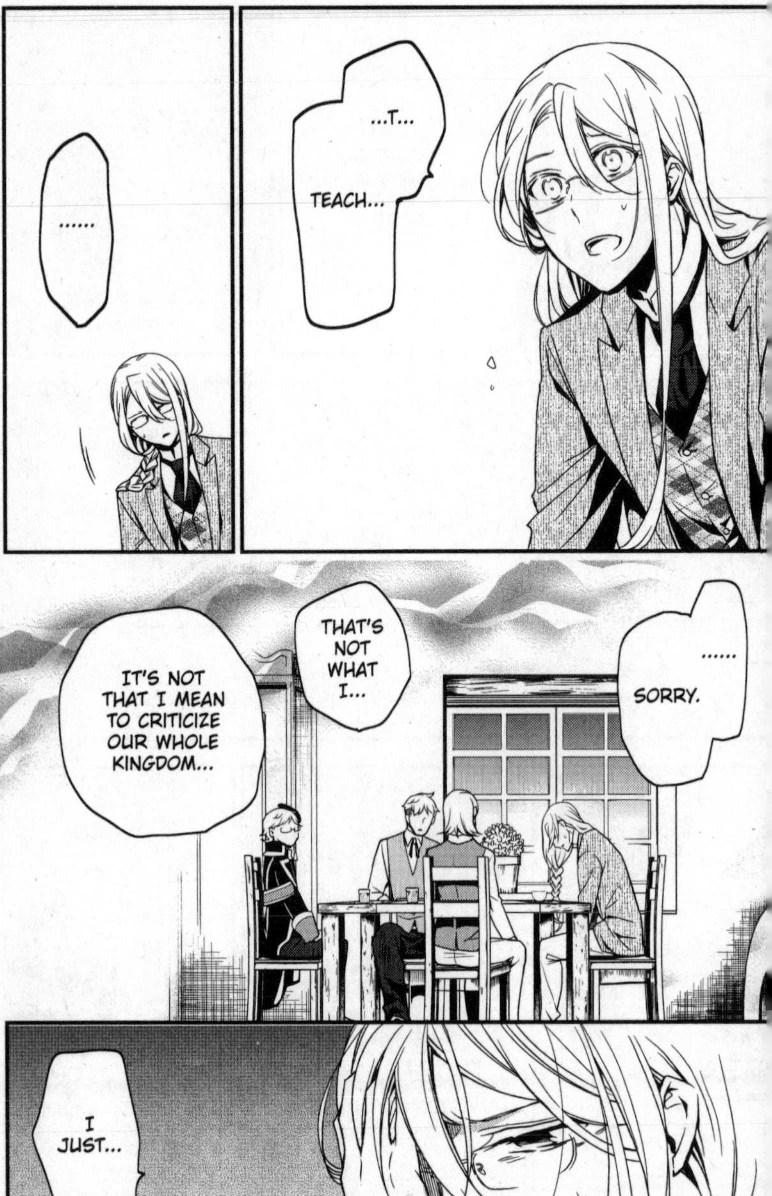

...T... TEACH...
......
...... SORRY.
THAT'S NOT WHAT I...
IT'S NOT THAT I MEAN TO CRITICIZE OUR WHOLE KINGDOM...
I JUST...

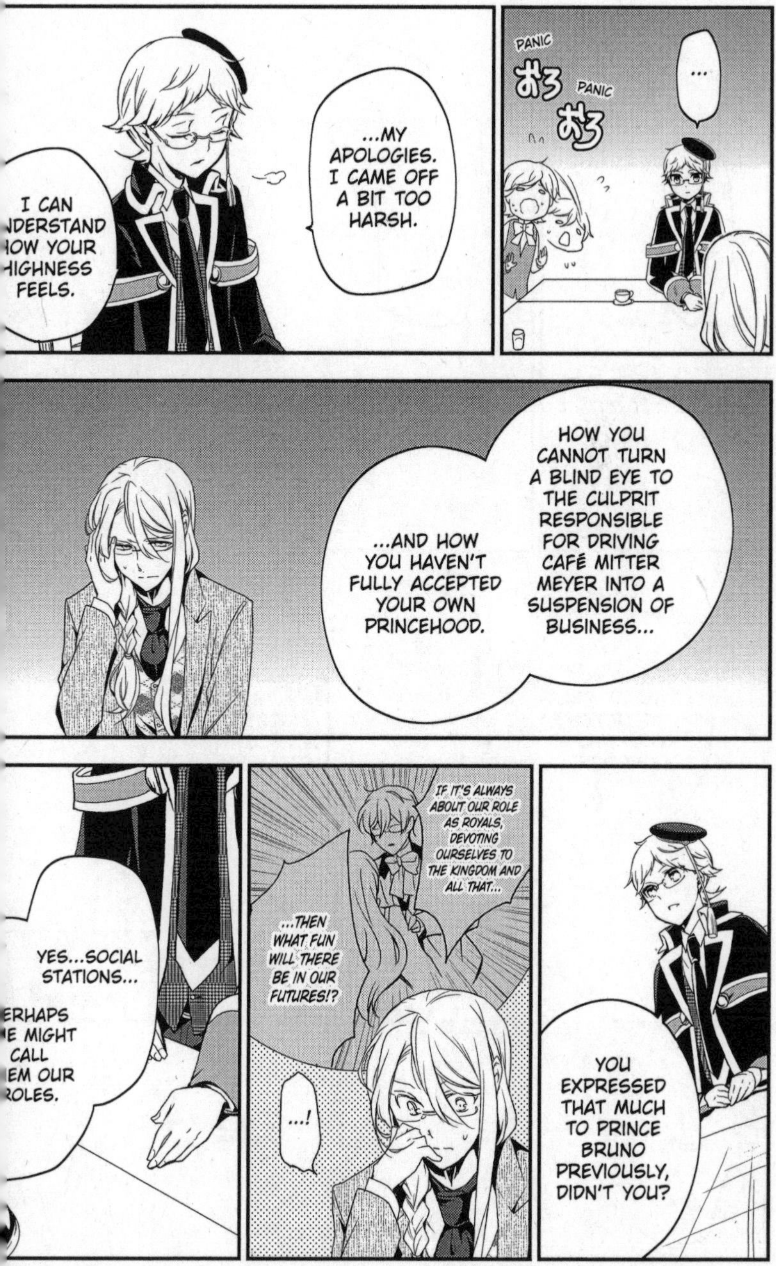
PANIC
おろ
PANIC
おろ
...
...MY APOLOGIES. I CAME OFF A BIT TOO HARSH.
I CAN NDERSTAND HOW YOUR HIGHNESS FEELS.
HOW YOU CANNOT TURN A BLIND EYE TO THE CULPRIT RESPONSIBLE FOR DRIVING CAFÉ MITTER MEYER INTO A SUSPENSION OF BUSINESS...
...AND HOW YOU HAVEN'T FULLY ACCEPTED YOUR OWN PRINCEHOOD.
YOU EXPRESSED THAT MUCH TO PRINCE BRUNO PREVIOUSLY, DIDN'T YOU?
IF IT'S ALWAYS ABOUT OUR ROLE AS ROYALS, DEVOTING OURSELVES TO THE KINGDOM AND ALL THAT...
...THEN WHAT FUN WILL THERE BE IN OUR FUTURES!?
...!
YES...SOCIAL STATIONS...
ERHAPS E MIGHT CALL EM OUR ROLES.

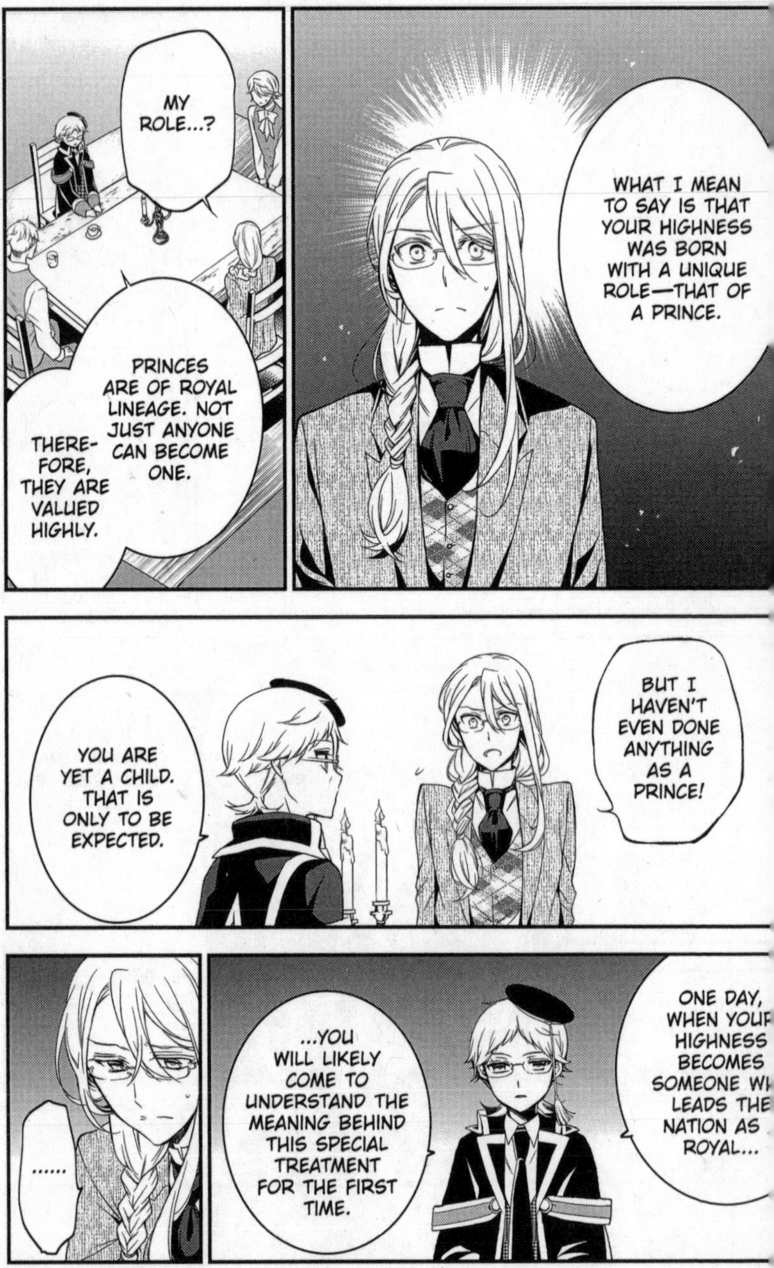
WHAT I MEAN TO SAY IS THAT YOUR HIGHNESS WAS BORN WITH A UNIQUE ROLE—THAT OF A PRINCE.
MY ROLE...?
PRINCES ARE OF ROYAL LINEAGE. NOT JUST ANYONE CAN BECOME ONE.
THEREFORE, THEY ARE VALUED HIGHLY.
BUT I HAVEN'T EVEN DONE ANYTHING AS A PRINCE!
YOU ARE YET A CHILD. THAT IS ONLY TO BE EXPECTED.
ONE DAY, WHEN YOUR HIGHNESS BECOMES SOMEONE WH LEADS THE NATION AS ROYAL...
...YOU WILL LIKELY COME TO UNDERSTAND THE MEANING BEHIND THIS SPECIAL TREATMENT FOR THE FIRST TIME.
......

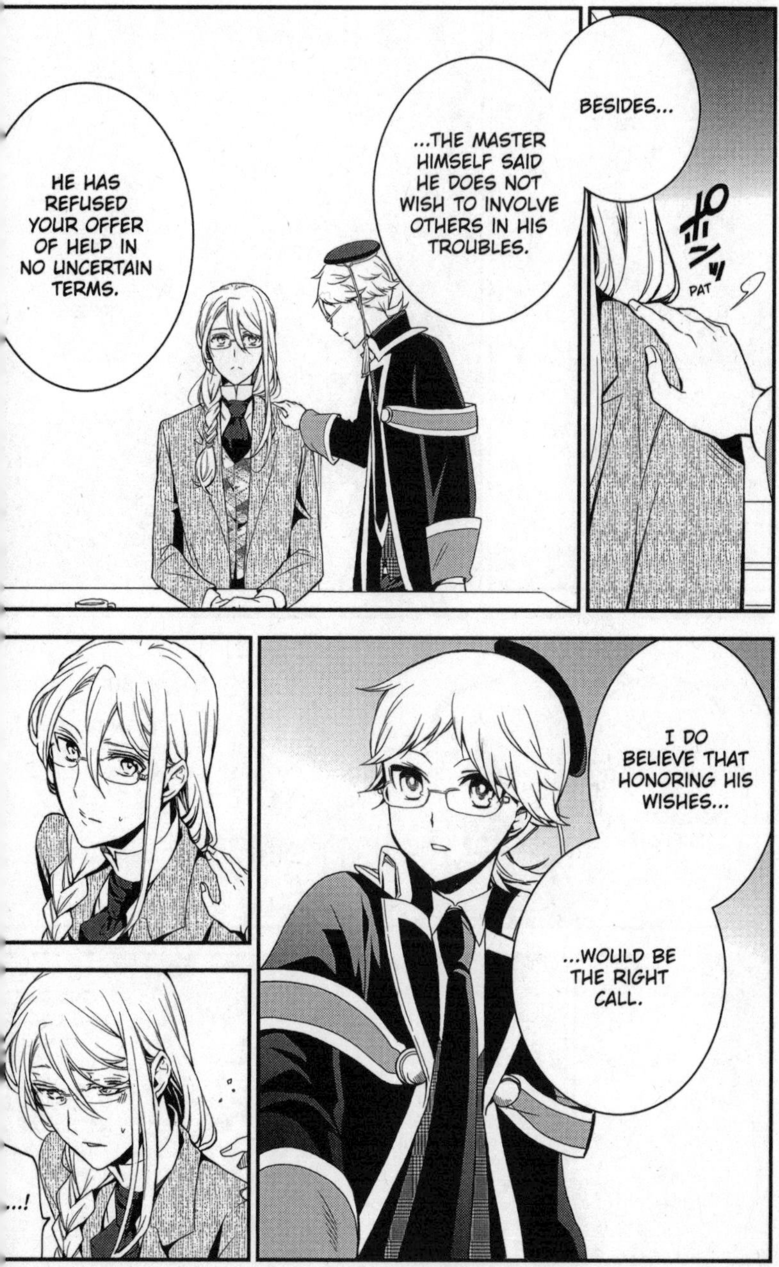
BESIDES...
PAT
...THE MASTER HIMSELF SAID HE DOES NOT WISH TO INVOLVE OTHERS IN HIS TROUBLES.
HE HAS REFUSED YOUR OFFER OF HELP IN NO UNCERTAIN TERMS.
I DO BELIEVE THAT HONORING HIS WISHES...
...WOULD BE THE RIGHT CALL.
...!

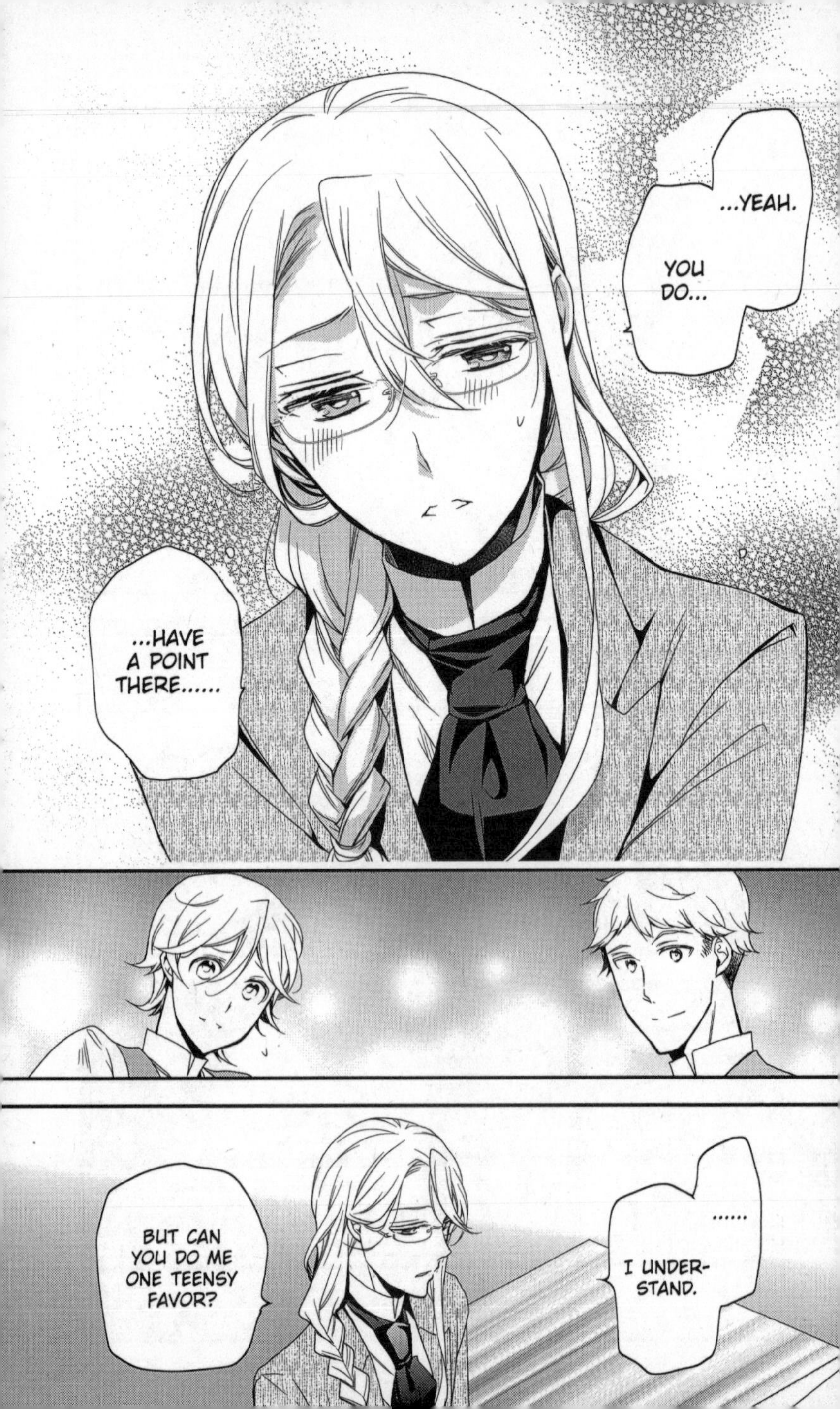
...YEAH. YOU DO...
...HAVE A POINT THERE......
...... I UNDER-STAND.
BUT CAN YOU DO ME ONE TEENSY FAVOR?

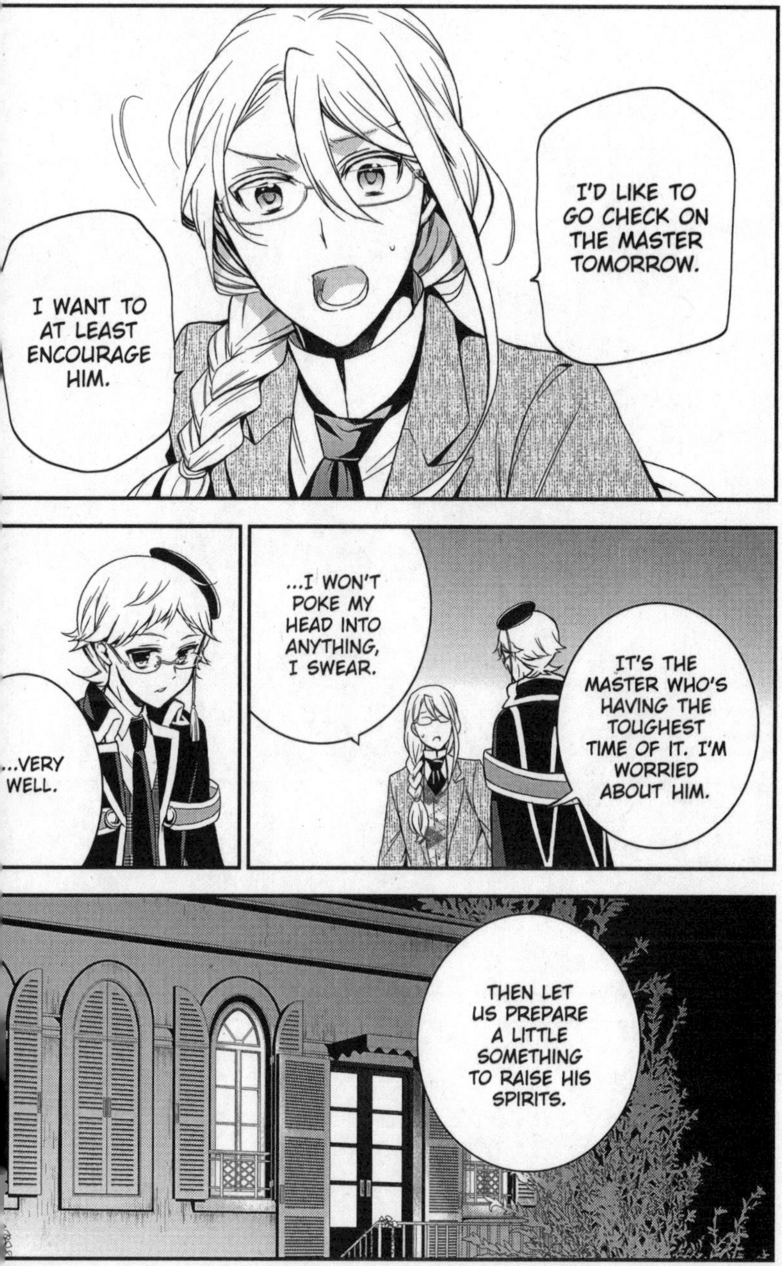
I'D LIKE TO GO CHECK ON THE MASTER TOMORROW.
I WANT TO AT LEAST ENCOURAGE HIM.
IT'S THE MASTER WHO'S HAVING THE TOUGHEST TIME OF IT. I'M WORRIED ABOUT HIM.
...I WON'T POKE MY HEAD INTO ANYTHING, I SWEAR.
...VERY WELL.
THEN LET US PREPARE A LITTLE SOMETHING TO RAISE HIS SPIRITS.

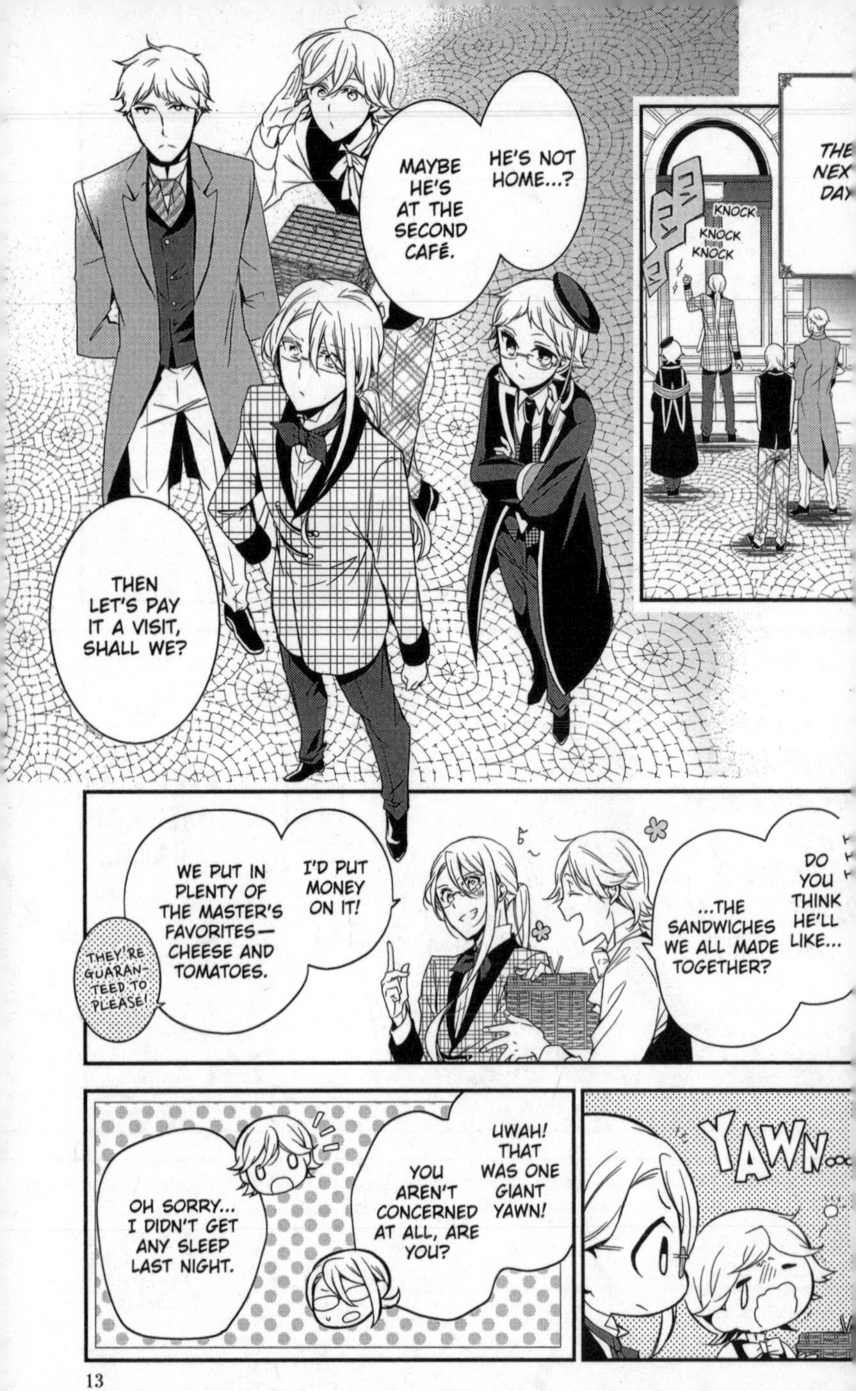
THE NEX DAY
KNOCK KNOCK KNOCK
HE'S NOT HOME...?
MAYBE HE'S AT THE SECOND CAFÉ.
THEN LET'S PAY IT A VISIT, SHALL WE?
DO YOU THINK HE'LL LIKE...
...THE SANDWICHES WE ALL MADE TOGETHER?
I'D PUT MONEY ON IT!
WE PUT IN PLENTY OF THE MASTER'S FAVORITES—CHEESE AND TOMATOES.
THEY'RE GUARANTEED TO PLEASE!
YAWN...
UWAH! THAT WAS ONE GIANT YAWN!
YOU AREN'T CONCERNED AT ALL, ARE YOU?
OH SORRY... I DIDN'T GET ANY SLEEP LAST NIGHT.

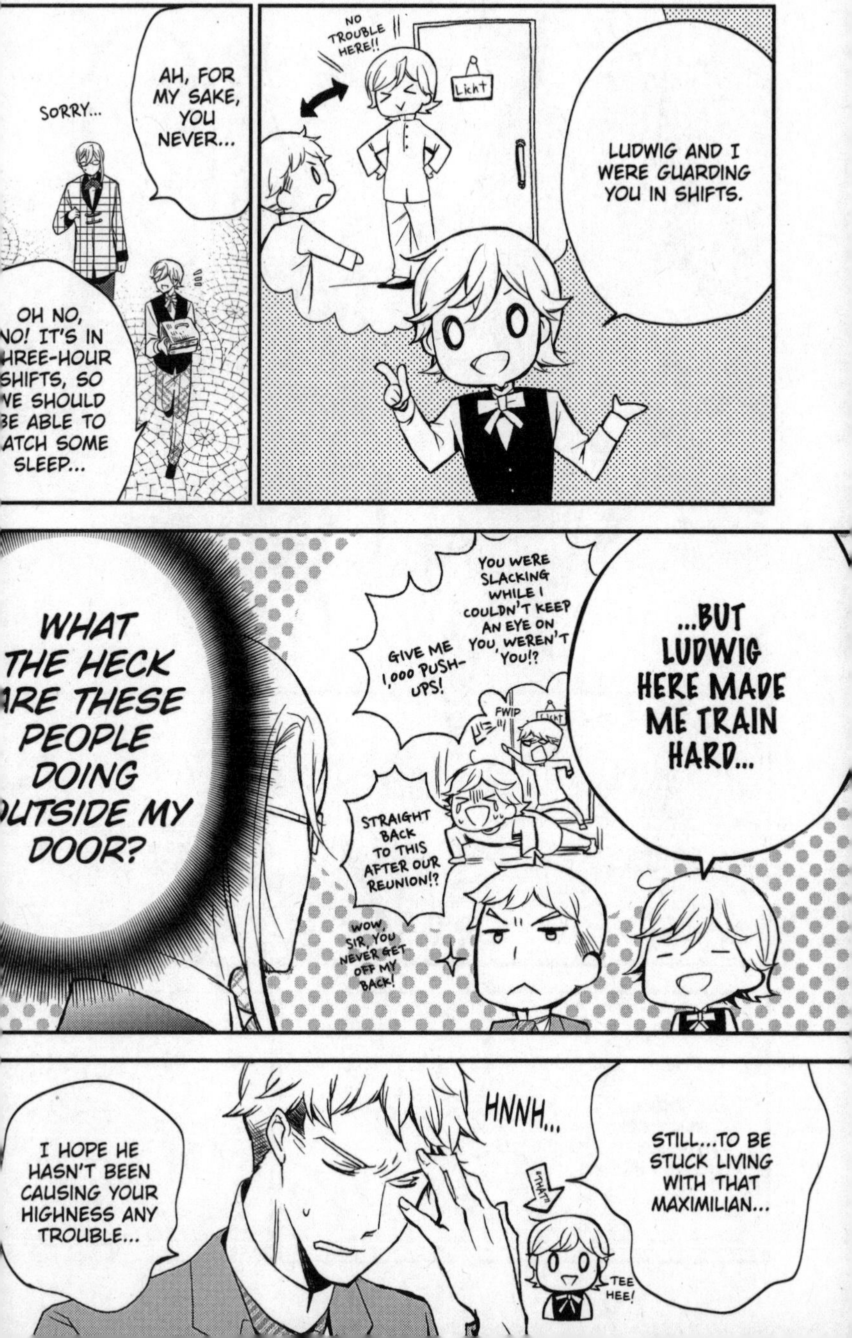
NO TROUBLE HERE!!
LUDWIG AND I WERE GUARDING YOU IN SHIFTS.
Licht
AH, FOR MY SAKE, YOU NEVER...
SORRY...
OH NO, NO! IT'S IN HREE-HOUR SHIFTS, SO VE SHOULD E ABLE TO ATCH SOME SLEEP...
...BUT LUDWIG HERE MADE ME TRAIN HARD...
YOU WERE SLACKING WHILE I COULDN'T KEEP AN EYE ON YOU, WEREN'T YOU!?
GIVE ME 1,000 PUSH-UPS!
FWIP
STRAIGHT BACK TO THIS AFTER OUR REUNION!?
WOW, SIR, YOU NEVER GET OFF MY BACK!
WHAT THE HECK RE THESE PEOPLE DOING UTSIDE MY DOOR?
STILL...TO BE STUCK LIVING WITH THAT MAXIMILIAN...
TEE HEE!
HNNH...
I HOPE HE HASN'T BEEN CAUSING YOUR HIGHNESS ANY TROUBLE...

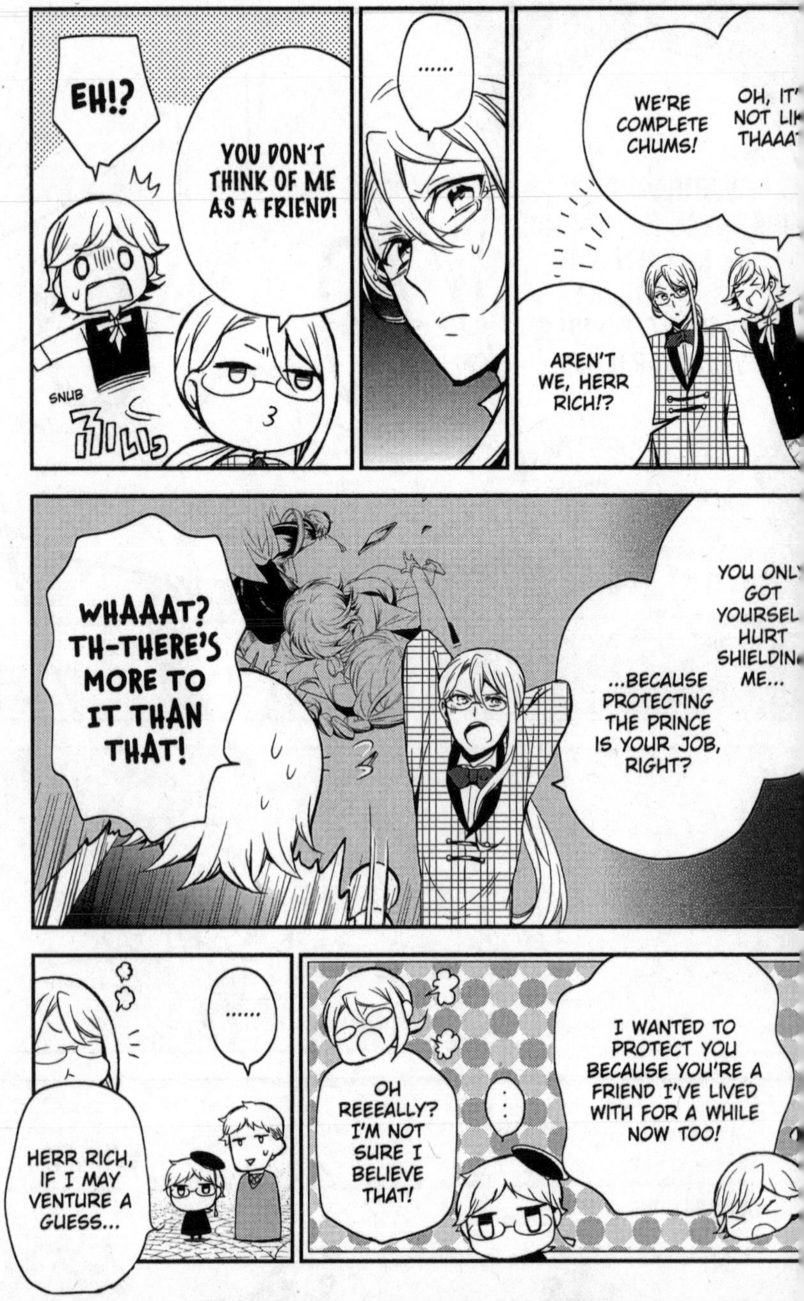
OH, IT' NOT LI THAAA
WE'RE COMPLETE CHUMS!
AREN'T WE, HERR RICH!?
......
EH!?
YOU DON'T THINK OF ME AS A FRIEND!
SNUB
YOU ONL GOT YOURSEL HURT SHIELDIN ME...
...BECAUSE PROTECTING THE PRINCE IS YOUR JOB, RIGHT?
WHAAAT? TH-THERE'S MORE TO IT THAN THAT!
I WANTED TO PROTECT YOU BECAUSE YOU'RE A FRIEND I'VE LIVED WITH FOR A WHILE NOW TOO!
...
OH REEEALLY? I'M NOT SURE I BELIEVE THAT!
......
HERR RICH, IF I MAY VENTURE A GUESS...

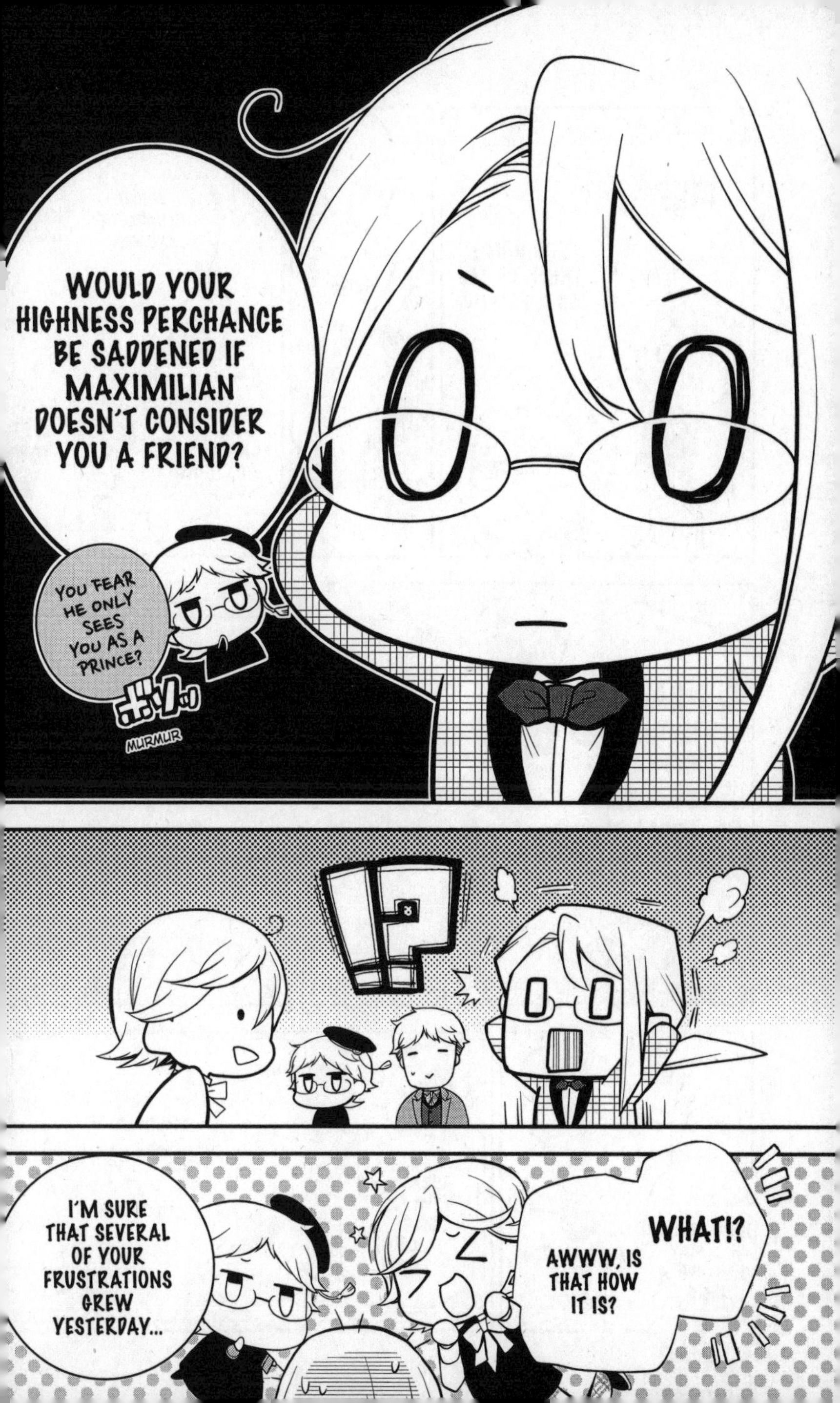
WOULD YOUR HIGHNESS PERCHANCE BE SADDENED IF MAXIMILIAN DOESN'T CONSIDER YOU A FRIEND?
YOU FEAR HE ONLY SEES YOU AS A PRINCE?
MURMUR
!?
WHAT!?
AWWW, IS THAT HOW IT IS?
I'M SURE THAT SEVERAL OF YOUR FRUSTRATIONS GREW YESTERDAY...

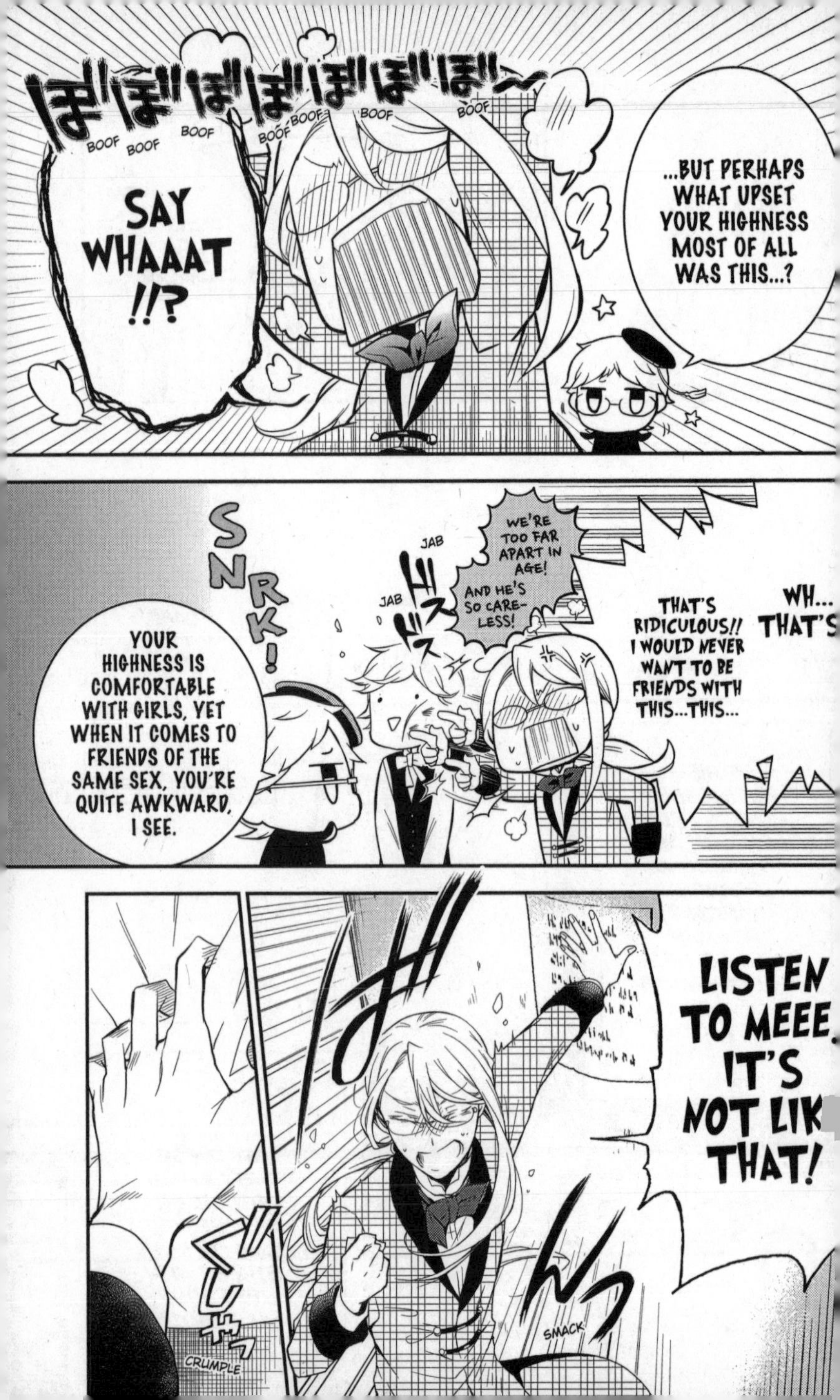
...BUT PERHAPS WHAT UPSET YOUR HIGHNESS MOST OF ALL WAS THIS...?
BOOF BOOF BOOF BOOF BOOF BOOF BOOF
SAY WHAAAT!!?
WH... THAT'S
THAT'S RIDICULOUS!! I WOULD NEVER WANT TO BE FRIENDS WITH THIS...THIS...
WE'RE TOO FAR APART IN AGE!
AND HE'S SO CARE-LESS!
JAB JAB
SNRK!
YOUR HIGHNESS IS COMFORTABLE WITH GIRLS, YET WHEN IT COMES TO FRIENDS OF THE SAME SEX, YOU'RE QUITE AWKWARD, I SEE.
LISTEN TO MEEE. IT'S NOT LIK THAT!
SMACK
CRUMPLE

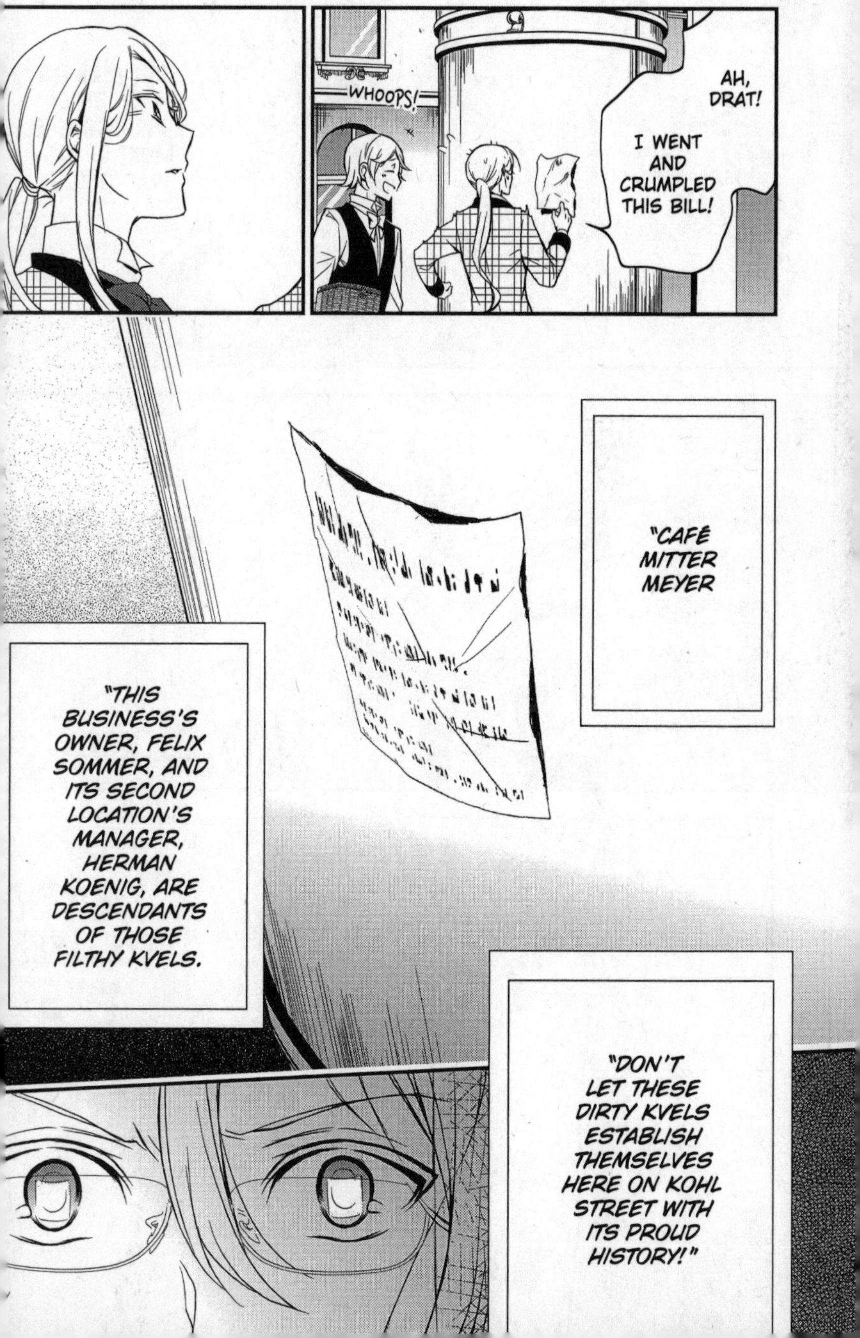
AH, DRAT!
I WENT AND CRUMPLED THIS BILL!
WHOOPS!
"CAFÉ MITTER MEYER
"THIS BUSINESS'S OWNER, FELIX SOMMER, AND ITS SECOND LOCATION'S MANAGER, HERMAN KOENIG, ARE DESCENDANTS OF THOSE FILTHY KVELS.
"DON'T LET THESE DIRTY KVELS ESTABLISH THEMSELVES HERE ON KOHL STREET WITH ITS PROUD HISTORY!"

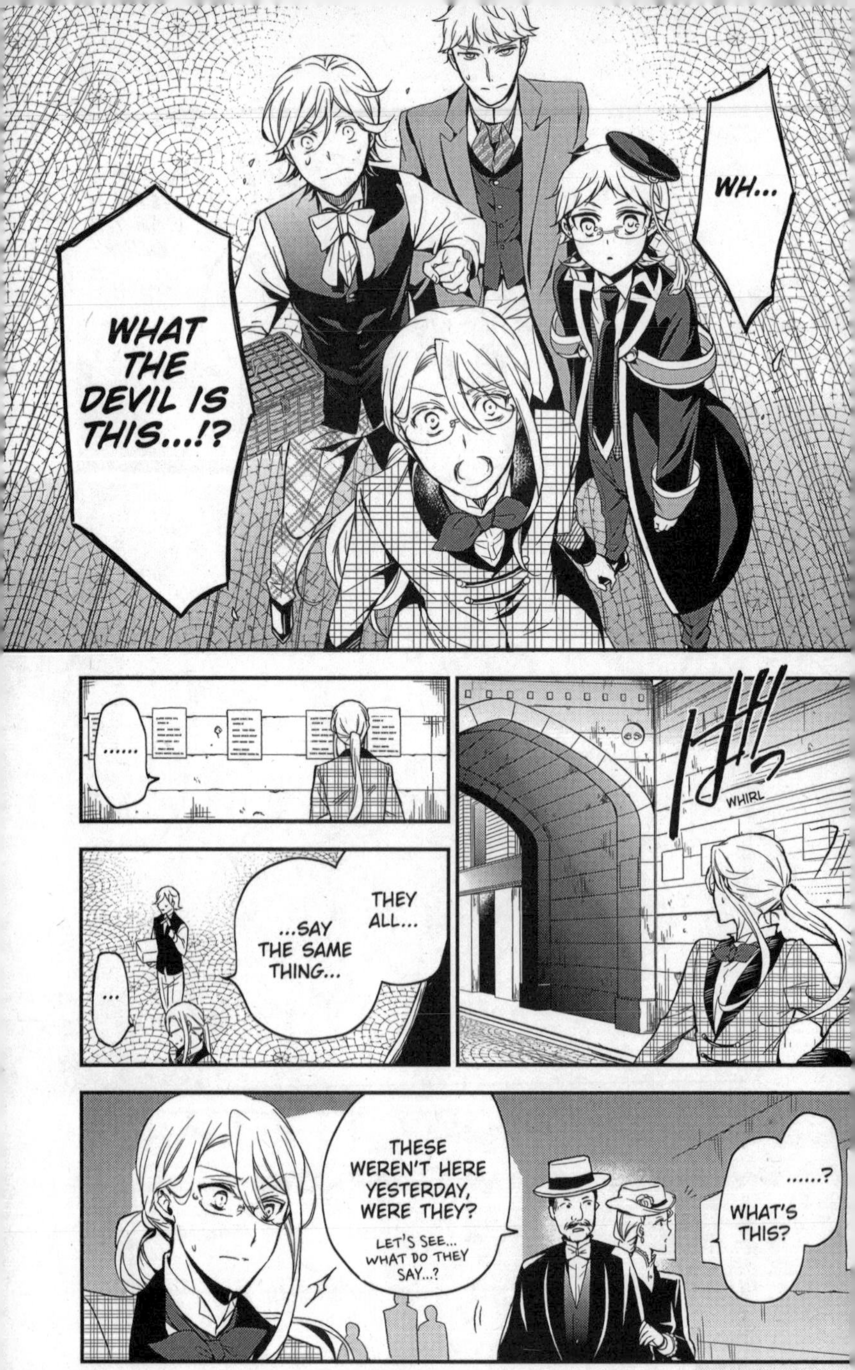
WH...
WHAT THE DEVIL IS THIS...!?
はっ
WHIRL
......
THEY ALL... ...SAY THE SAME THING...
...
......? WHAT'S THIS?
THESE WEREN'T HERE YESTERDAY, WERE THEY?
LET'S SEE... WHAT DO THEY SAY...?

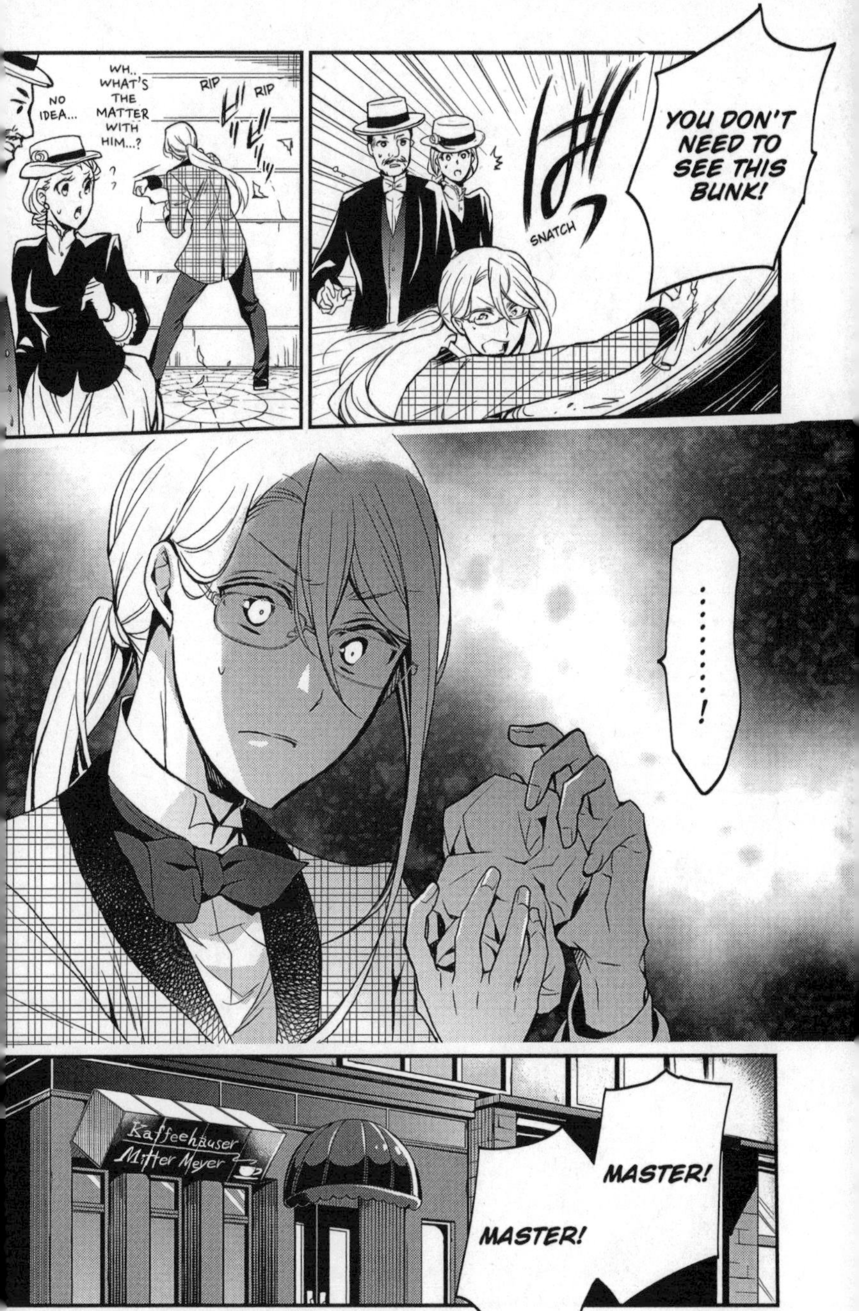
YOU DON'T NEED TO SEE THIS BUNK!
はっ
SNATCH
RIP
RIP
WH.. WHAT'S THE MATTER WITH HIM...?
NO IDEA...
........!
Kaffeehäuser Mitter Meyer
MASTER!
MASTER!

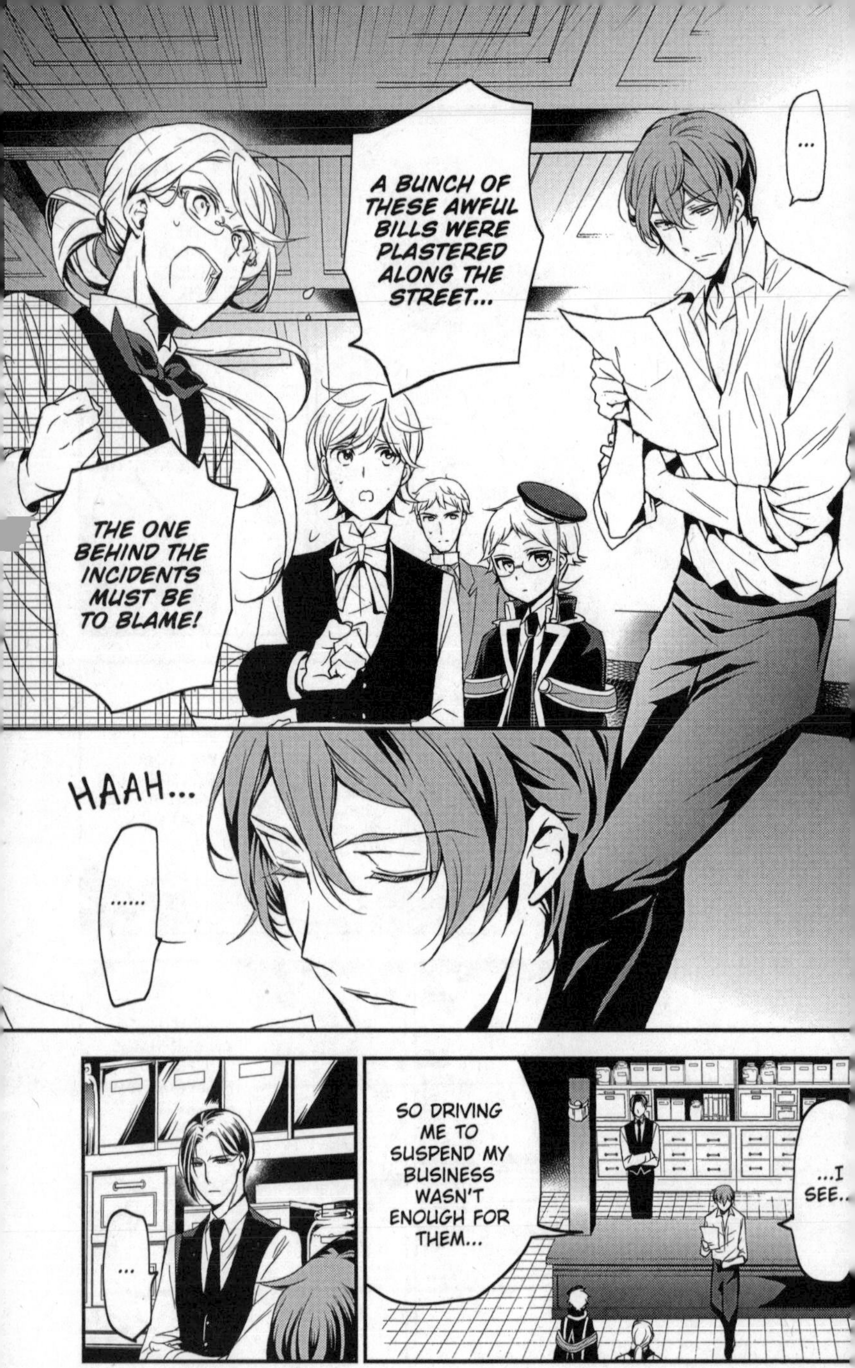
...
A BUNCH OF THESE AWFUL BILLS WERE PLASTERED ALONG THE STREET...
THE ONE BEHIND THE INCIDENTS MUST BE TO BLAME!
HAAH...
......
...I SEE..
SO DRIVING ME TO SUSPEND MY BUSINESS WASN'T ENOUGH FOR THEM...
...

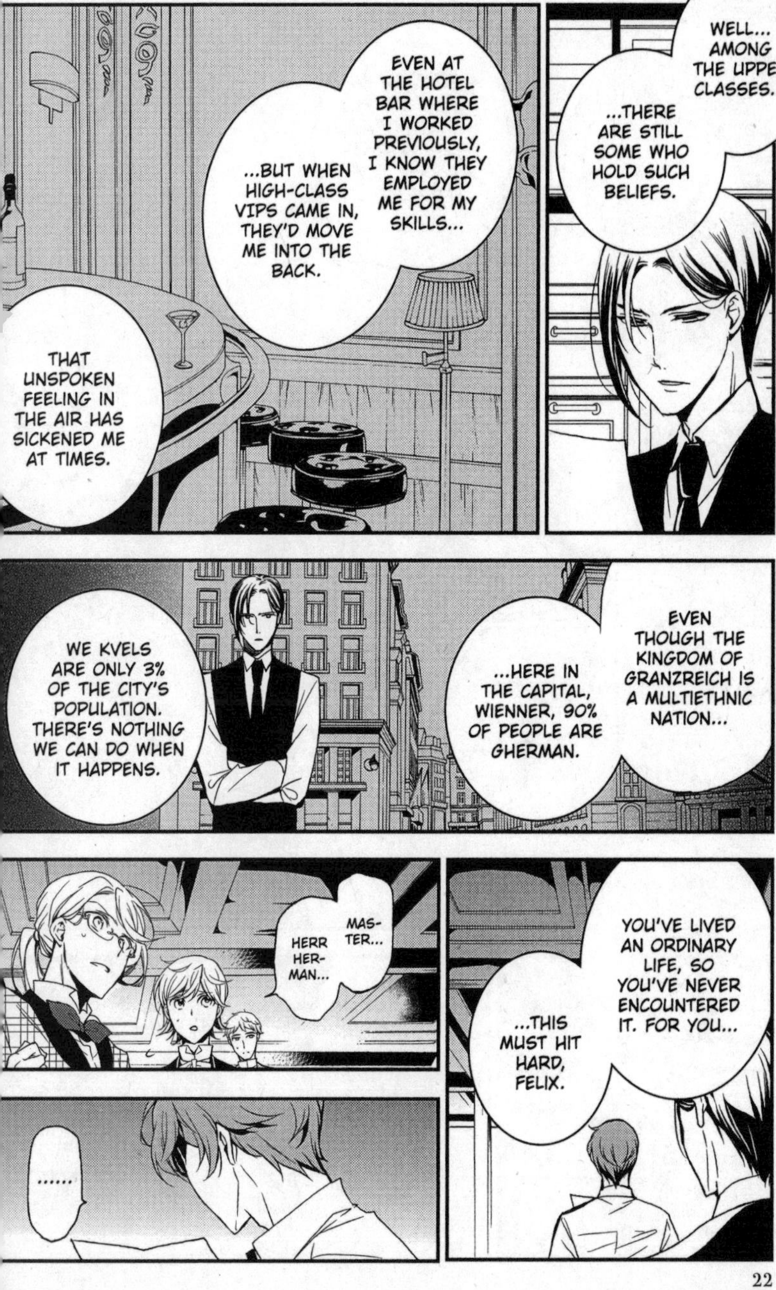
WELL... AMONG THE UPPER CLASSES...
...THERE ARE STILL SOME WHO HOLD SUCH BELIEFS.
EVEN AT THE HOTEL BAR WHERE I WORKED PREVIOUSLY, I KNOW THEY EMPLOYED ME FOR MY SKILLS...
...BUT WHEN HIGH-CLASS VIPS CAME IN, THEY'D MOVE ME INTO THE BACK.
THAT UNSPOKEN FEELING IN THE AIR HAS SICKENED ME AT TIMES.
EVEN THOUGH THE KINGDOM OF GRANZREICH IS A MULTIETHNIC NATION...
...HERE IN THE CAPITAL, WIENNER, 90% OF PEOPLE ARE GHERMAN.
WE KVELS ARE ONLY 3% OF THE CITY'S POPULATION. THERE'S NOTHING WE CAN DO WHEN IT HAPPENS.
YOU'VE LIVED AN ORDINARY LIFE, SO YOU'VE NEVER ENCOUNTERED IT. FOR YOU...
...THIS MUST HIT HARD, FELIX.
MAS-TER...
HERR HER-MAN...
......

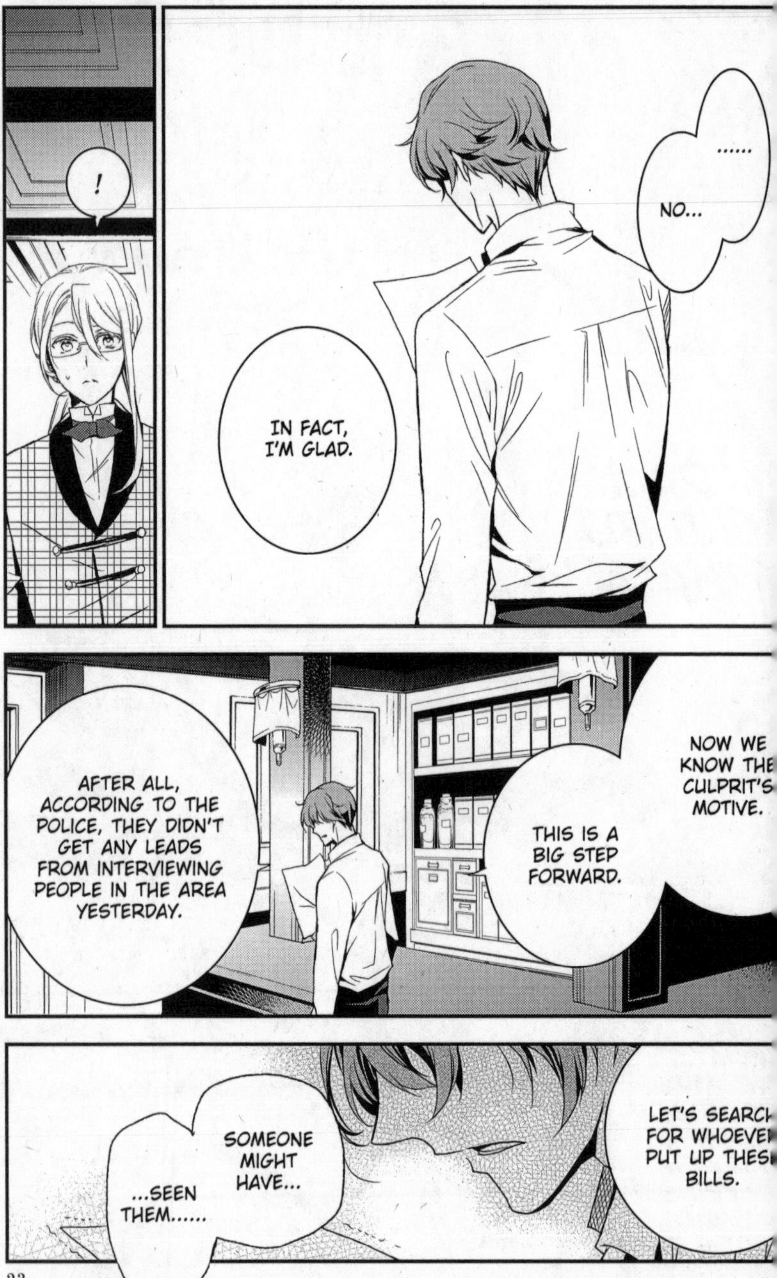
......
NO...
IN FACT, I'M GLAD.
!
NOW WE KNOW THE CULPRIT'S MOTIVE.
THIS IS A BIG STEP FORWARD.
AFTER ALL, ACCORDING TO THE POLICE, THEY DIDN'T GET ANY LEADS FROM INTERVIEWING PEOPLE IN THE AREA YESTERDAY.
LET'S SEARC FOR WHOEVE PUT UP THES BILLS.
SOMEONE MIGHT HAVE...
...SEEN THEM......

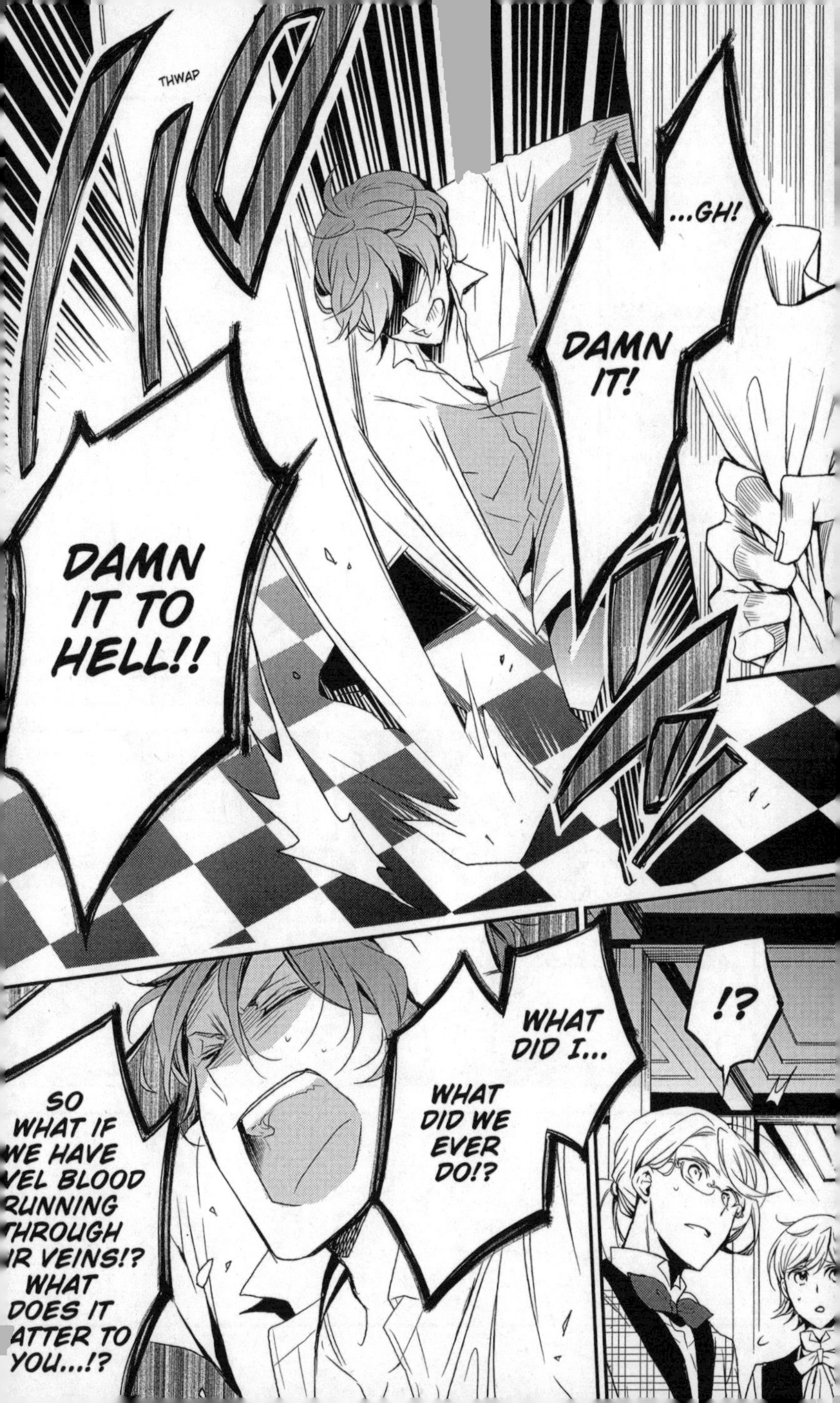
...GH!
DAMN IT!
THWAP
DAMN IT TO HELL!!
!?
WHAT DID I...
WHAT DID WE EVER DO!?
SO WHAT IF WE HAVE VEL BLOOD RUNNING THROUGH IR VEINS!? WHAT DOES IT ATTER TO YOU...!?

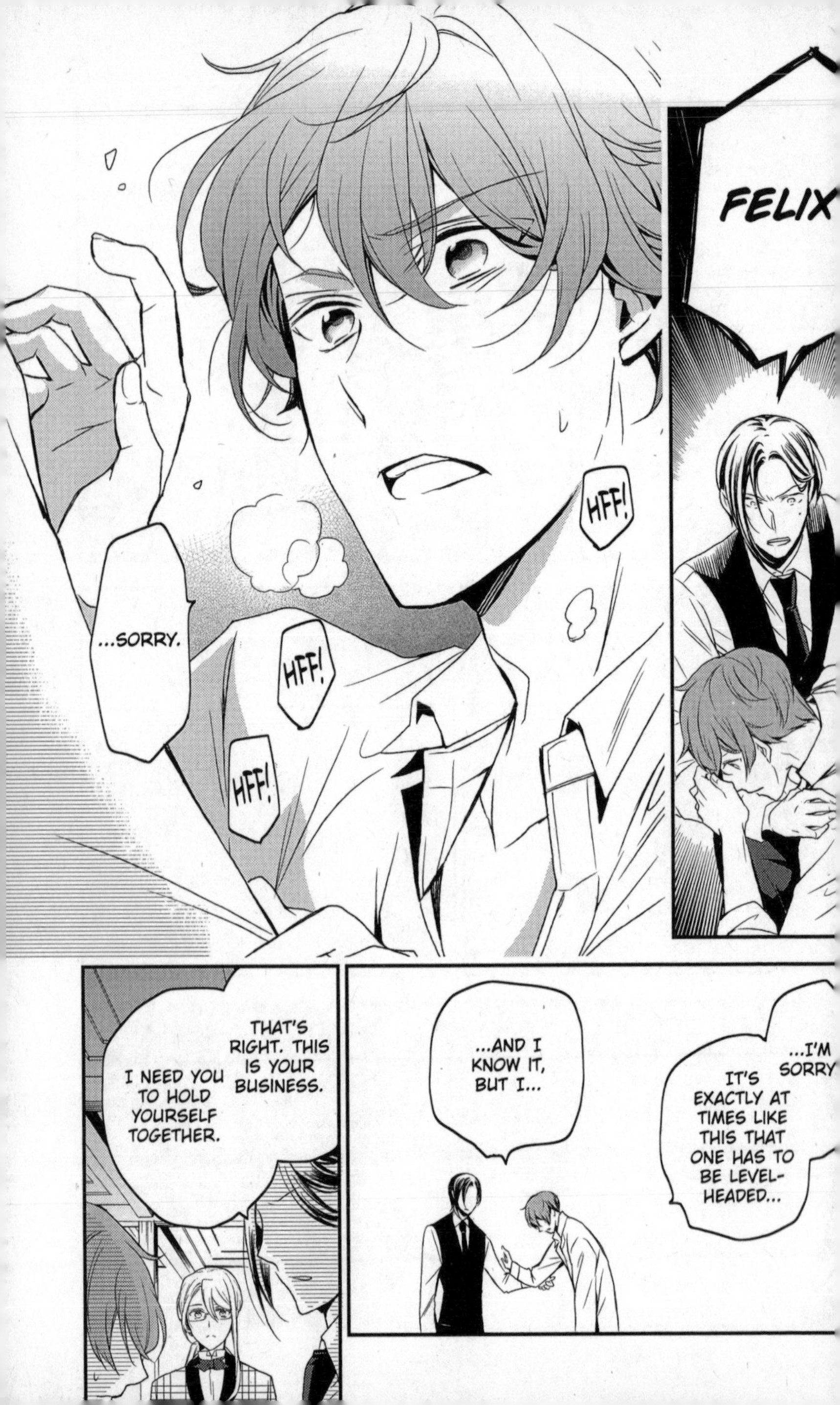
FELIX
HFF!
HFF!
...SORRY.
HFF!
...I'M SORRY
IT'S EXACTLY AT TIMES LIKE THIS THAT ONE HAS TO BE LEVEL-HEADED...
...AND I KNOW IT, BUT I...
THAT'S RIGHT. THIS IS YOUR BUSINESS.
I NEED YOU TO HOLD YOURSELF TOGETHER.

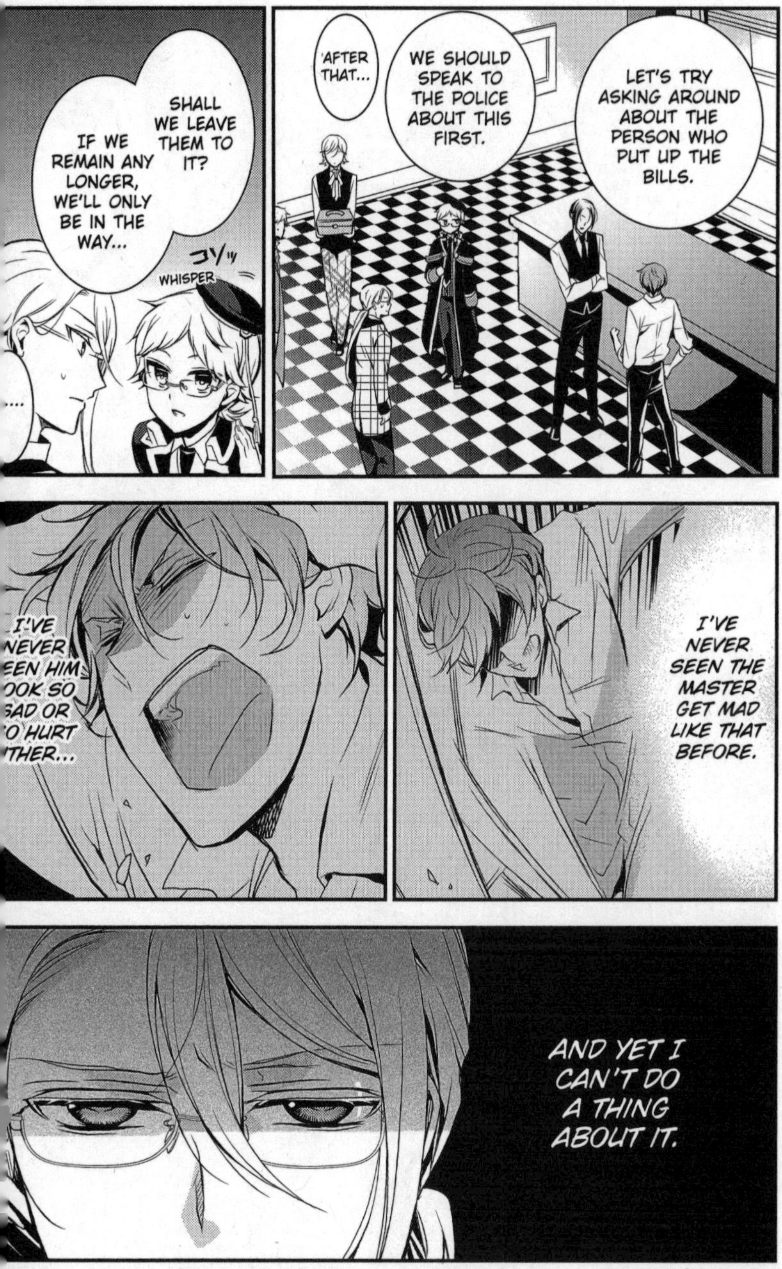
LET'S TRY ASKING AROUND ABOUT THE PERSON WHO PUT UP THE BILLS.
WE SHOULD SPEAK TO THE POLICE ABOUT THIS FIRST.
'AFTER THAT...
SHALL WE LEAVE THEM TO IT?
IF WE REMAIN ANY LONGER, WE'LL ONLY BE IN THE WAY...
コソッ
WHISPER
....
I'VE NEVER SEEN THE MASTER GET MAD LIKE THAT BEFORE.
I'VE NEVER EEN HIM OOK SO SAD OR O HURT THER...
AND YET I CAN'T DO A THING ABOUT IT.

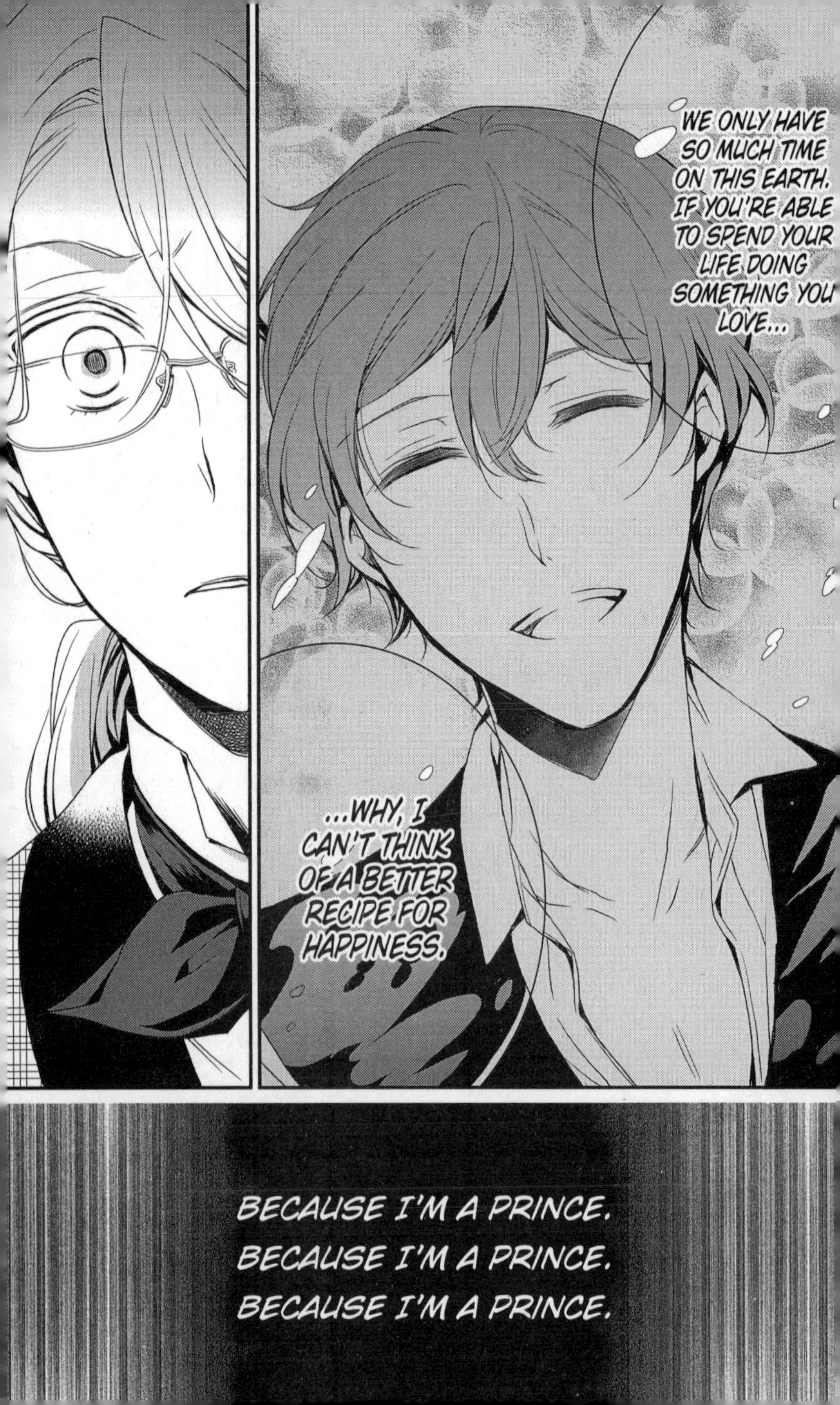
WE ONLY HAVE SO MUCH TIME ON THIS EARTH. IF YOU'RE ABLE TO SPEND YOUR LIFE DOING SOMETHING YOU LOVE...
...WHY, I CAN'T THINK OF A BETTER RECIPE FOR HAPPINESS.
BECAUSE I'M A PRINCE.
BECAUSE I'M A PRINCE.
BECAUSE I'M A PRINCE.

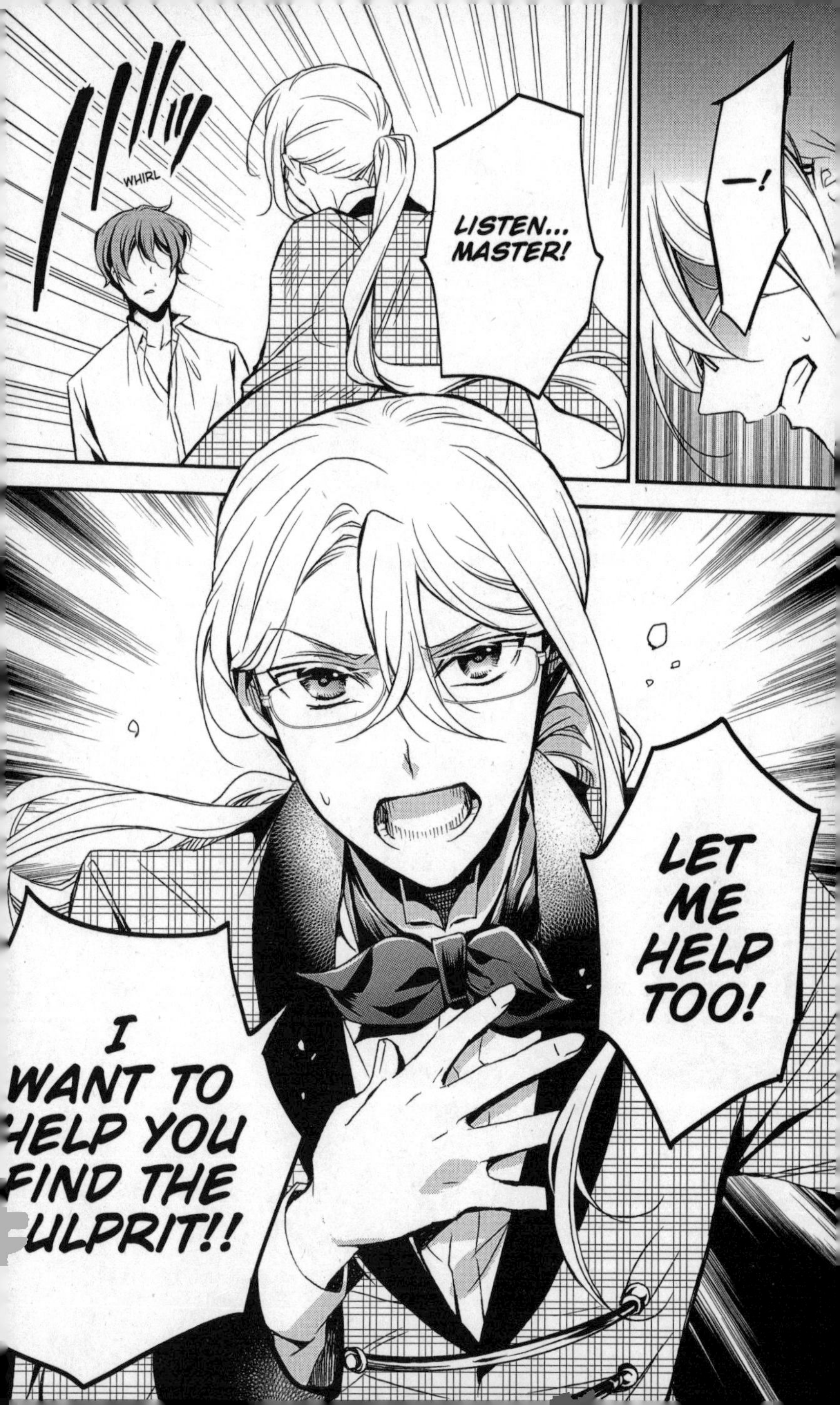
—!
WHIRL
LISTEN... MASTER!
LET ME HELP TOO!
I WANT TO HELP YOU FIND THE CULPRIT!!

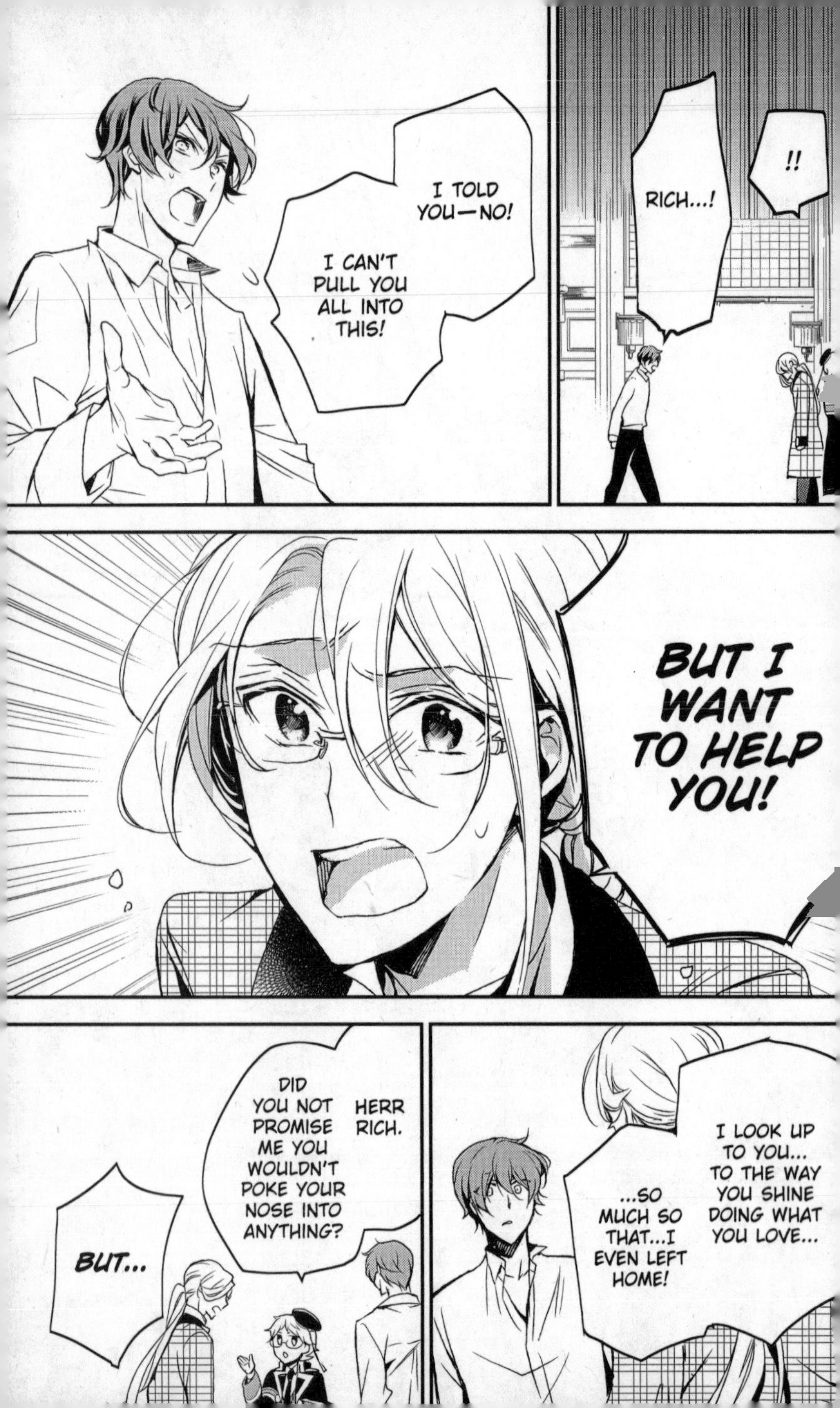
I TOLD YOU—NO!
I CAN'T PULL YOU ALL INTO THIS!
RICH...!
!!
BUT I WANT TO HELP YOU!
BUT...
DID YOU NOT PROMISE ME YOU WOULDN'T POKE YOUR NOSE INTO ANYTHING?
HERR RICH.
I LOOK UP TO YOU... TO THE WAY YOU SHINE DOING WHAT YOU LOVE...
...SO MUCH SO THAT...I EVEN LEFT HOME!

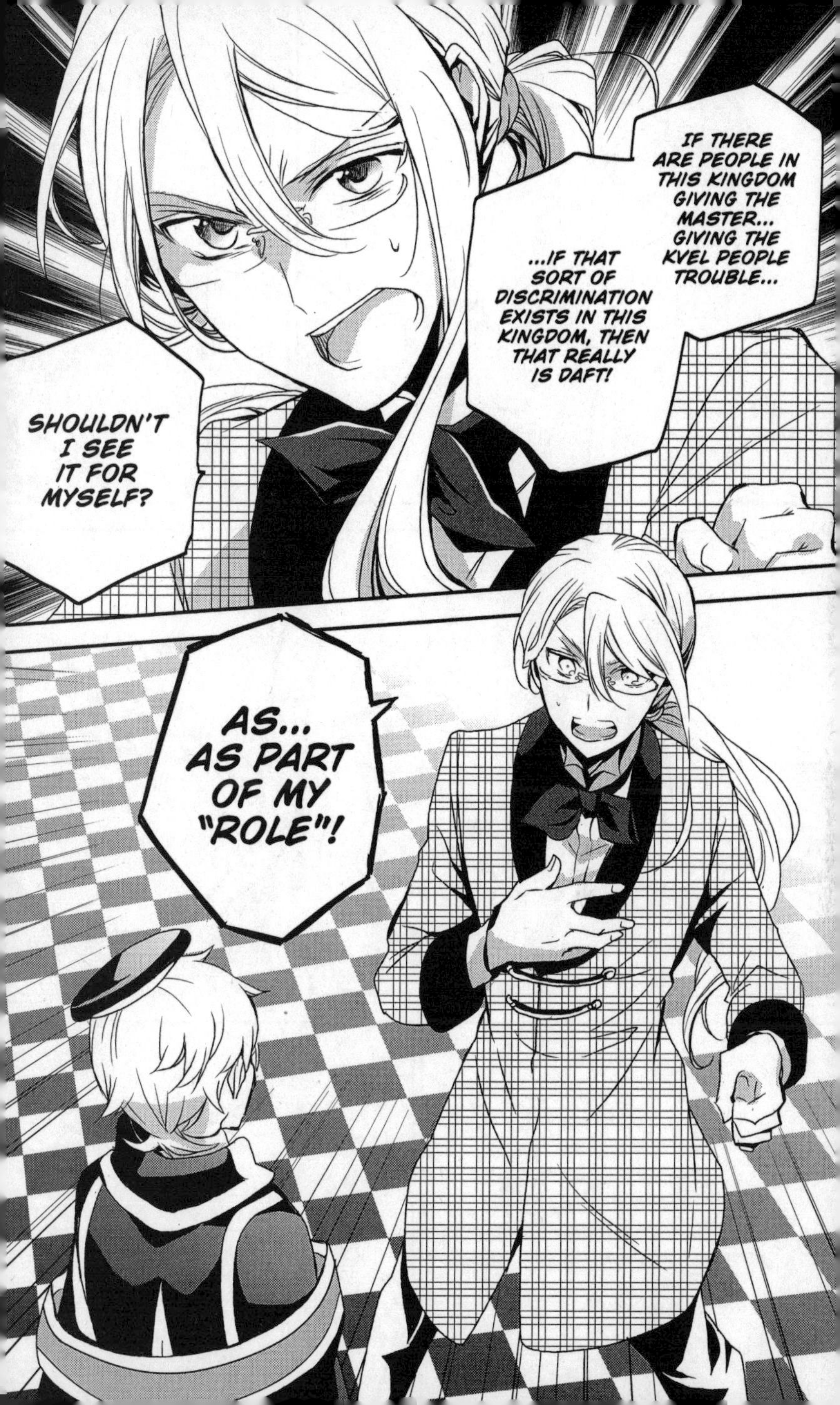
IF THERE ARE PEOPLE IN THIS KINGDOM GIVING THE MASTER... GIVING THE KVEL PEOPLE TROUBLE...
...IF THAT SORT OF DISCRIMINATION EXISTS IN THIS KINGDOM, THEN THAT REALLY IS DAFT!
SHOULDN'T I SEE IT FOR MYSELF?
AS... AS PART OF MY "ROLE"!

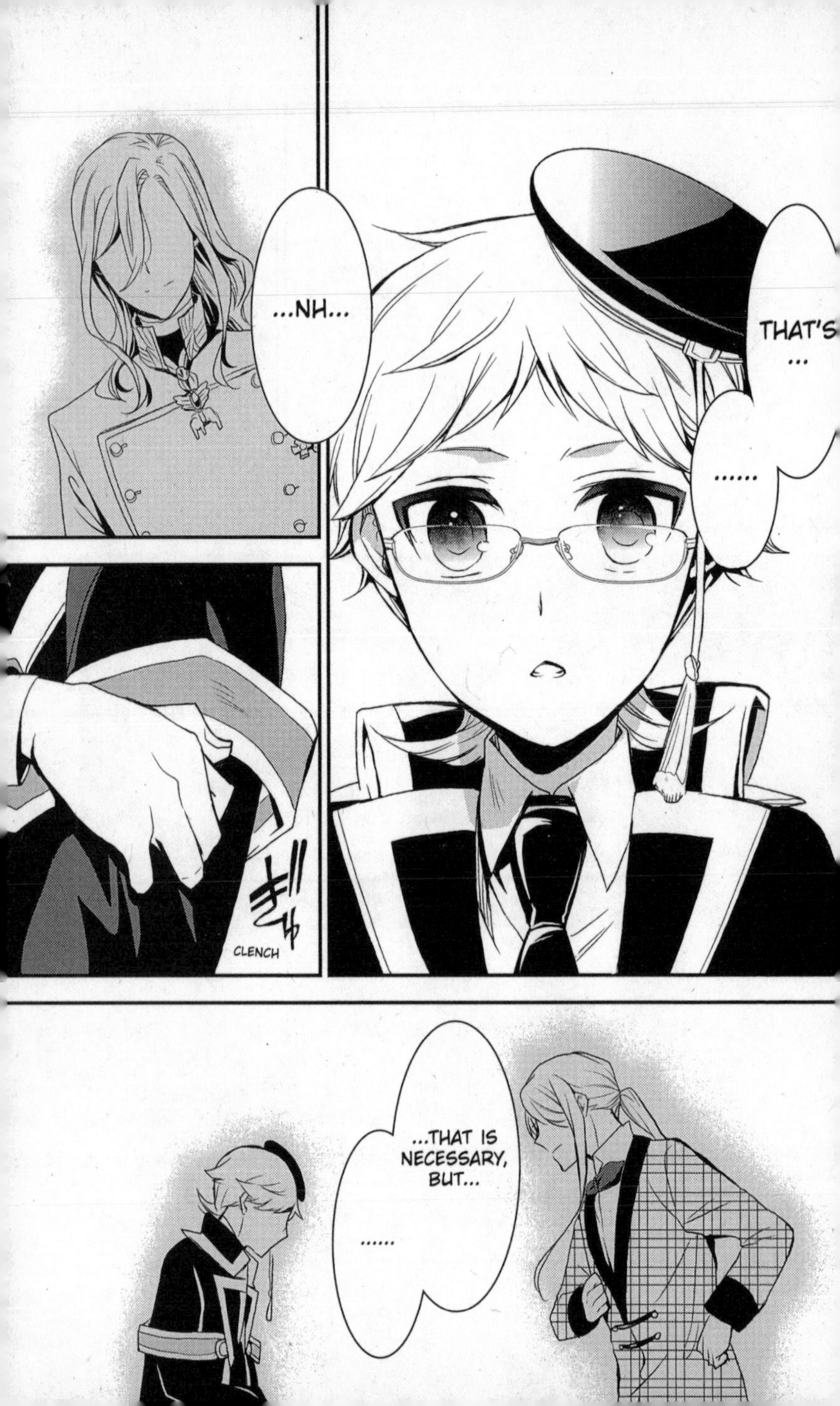
THAT'S ...
......
...NH...
CLENCH
...THAT IS NECESSARY, BUT...
......

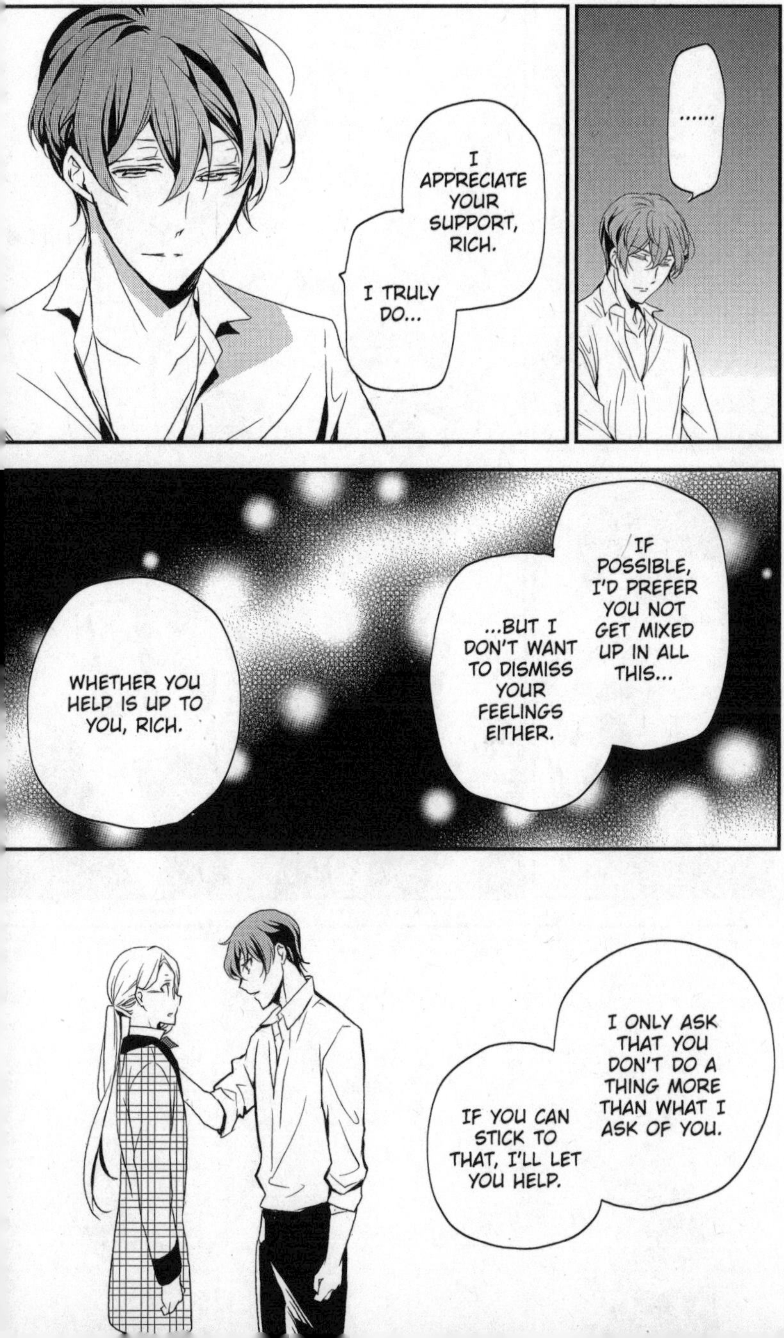
......
I APPRECIATE YOUR SUPPORT, RICH.
I TRULY DO...
IF POSSIBLE, I'D PREFER YOU NOT GET MIXED UP IN ALL THIS...
...BUT I DON'T WANT TO DISMISS YOUR FEELINGS EITHER.
WHETHER YOU HELP IS UP TO YOU, RICH.
I ONLY ASK THAT YOU DON'T DO A THING MORE THAN WHAT I ASK OF YOU.
IF YOU CAN STICK TO THAT, I'LL LET YOU HELP.

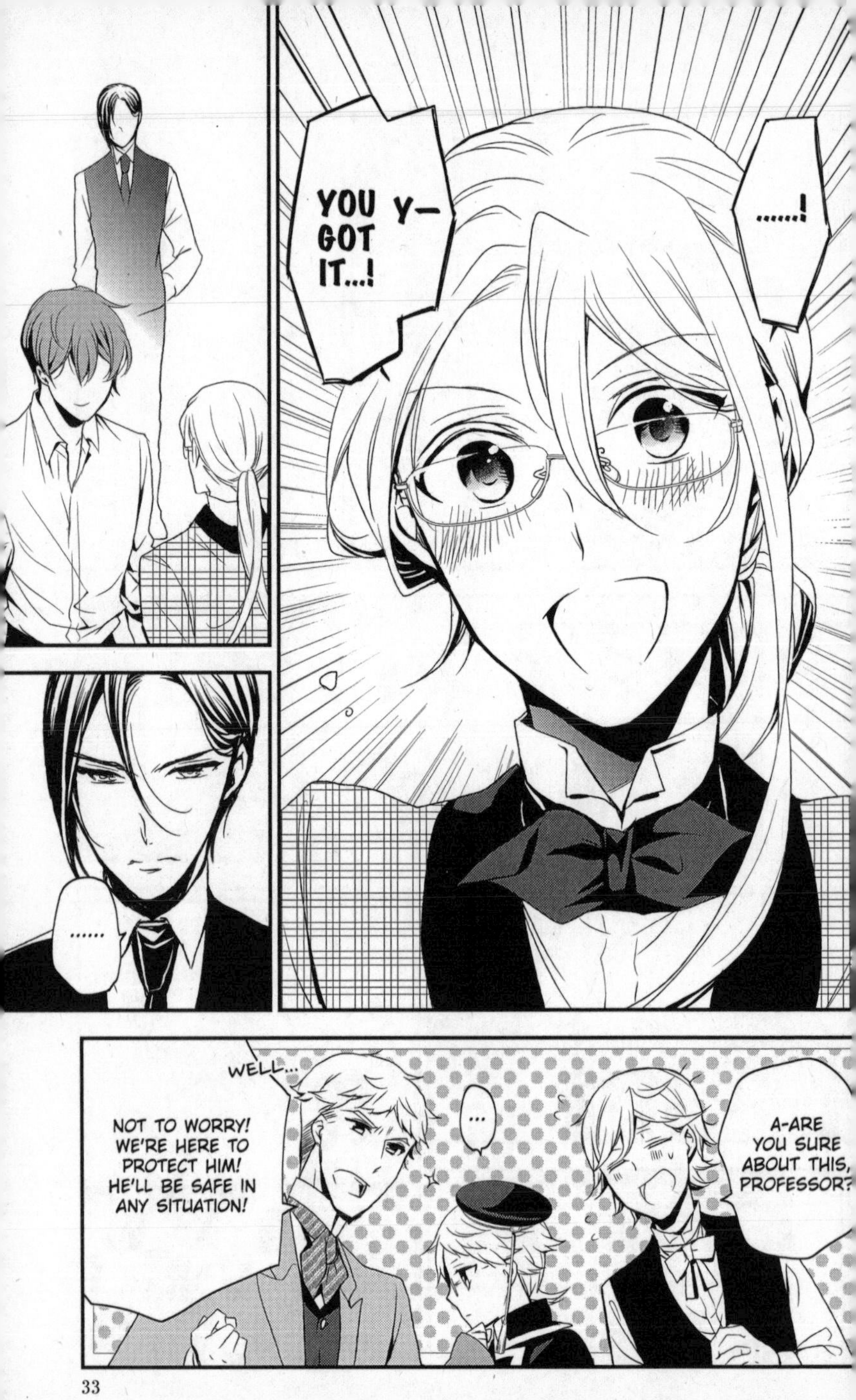
......!
YOU Y— GOT IT...!
......
A-ARE YOU SURE ABOUT THIS, PROFESSOR?
...
WELL...
NOT TO WORRY! WE'RE HERE TO PROTECT HIM! HE'LL BE SAFE IN ANY SITUATION!

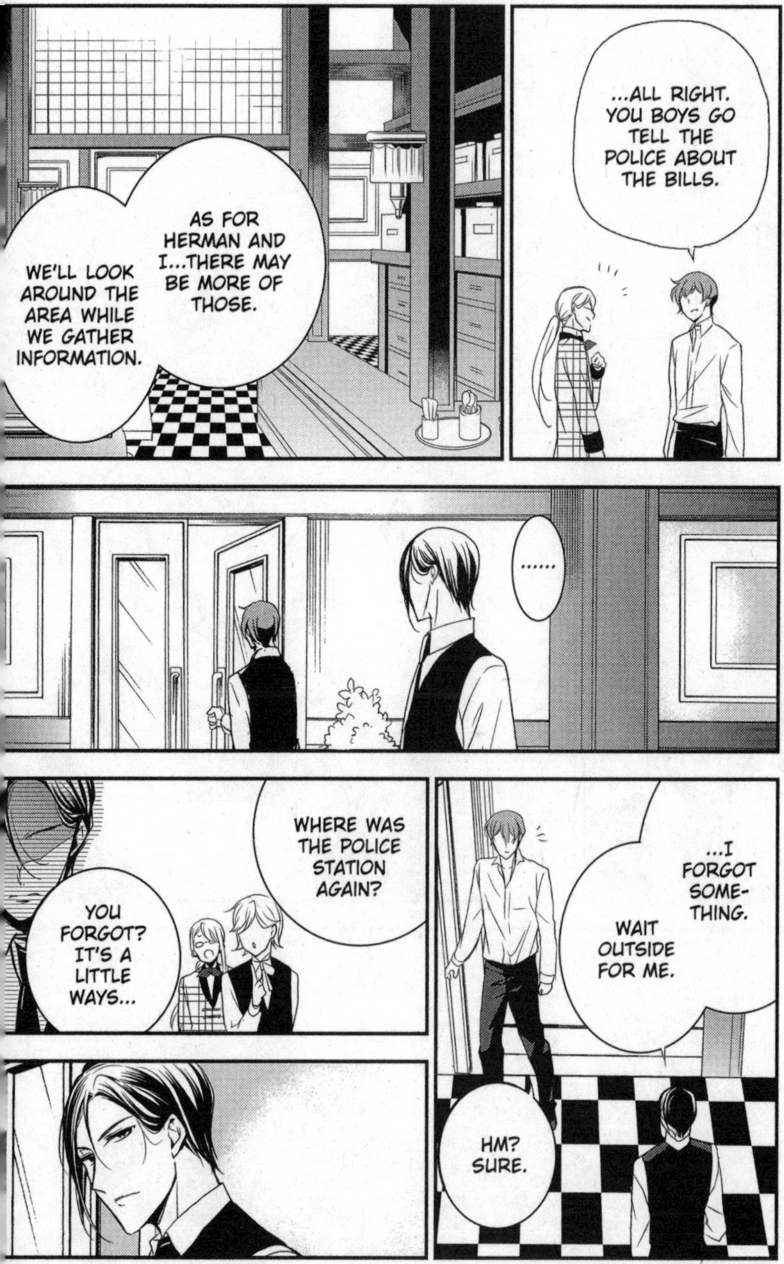
...ALL RIGHT. YOU BOYS GO TELL THE POLICE ABOUT THE BILLS.
AS FOR HERMAN AND I...THERE MAY BE MORE OF THOSE.
WE'LL LOOK AROUND THE AREA WHILE WE GATHER INFORMATION.
......
...I FORGOT SOME-THING.
WAIT OUTSIDE FOR ME.
HM? SURE.
WHERE WAS THE POLICE STATION AGAIN?
YOU FORGOT? IT'S A LITTLE WAYS...

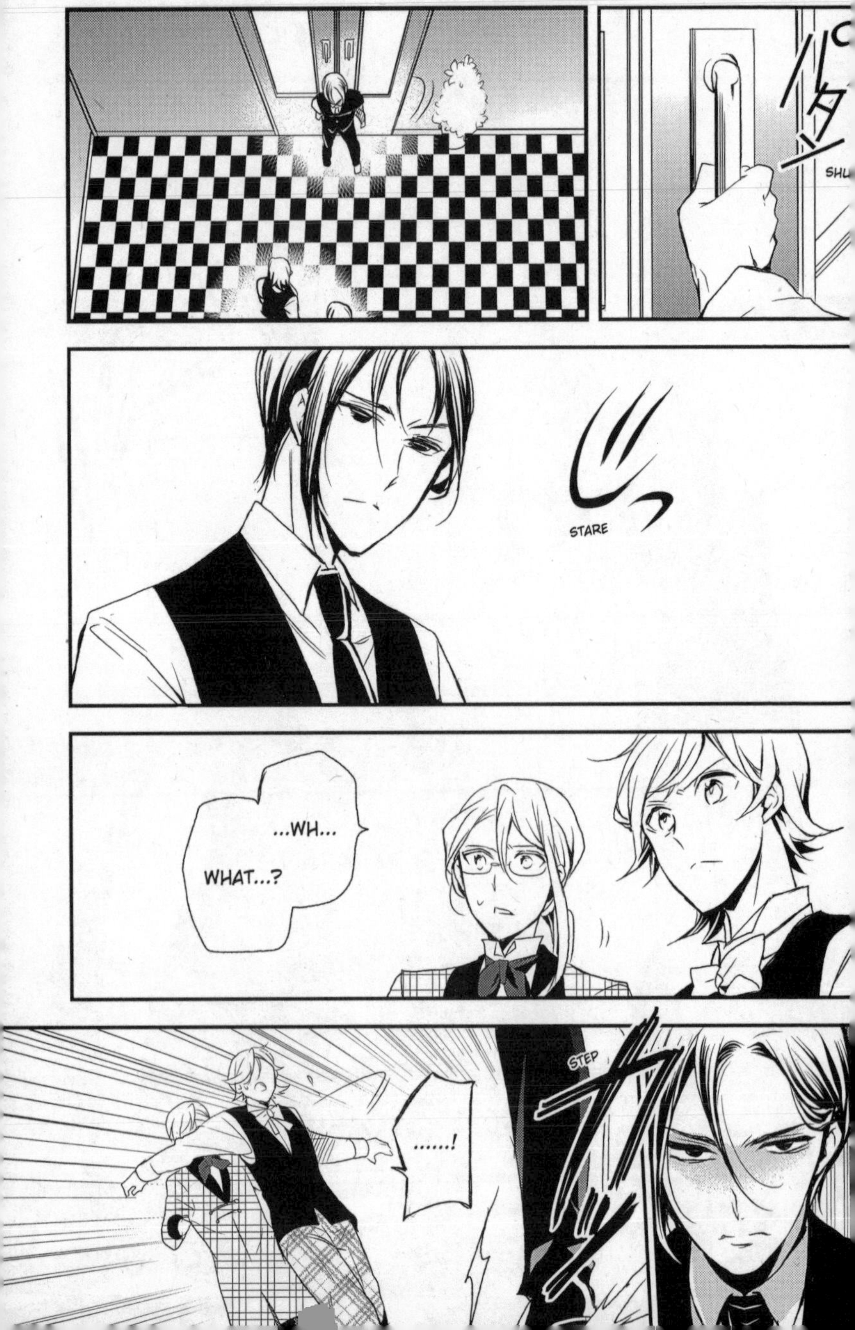
SHU
STARE
...WH...
WHAT...?
STEP
......!

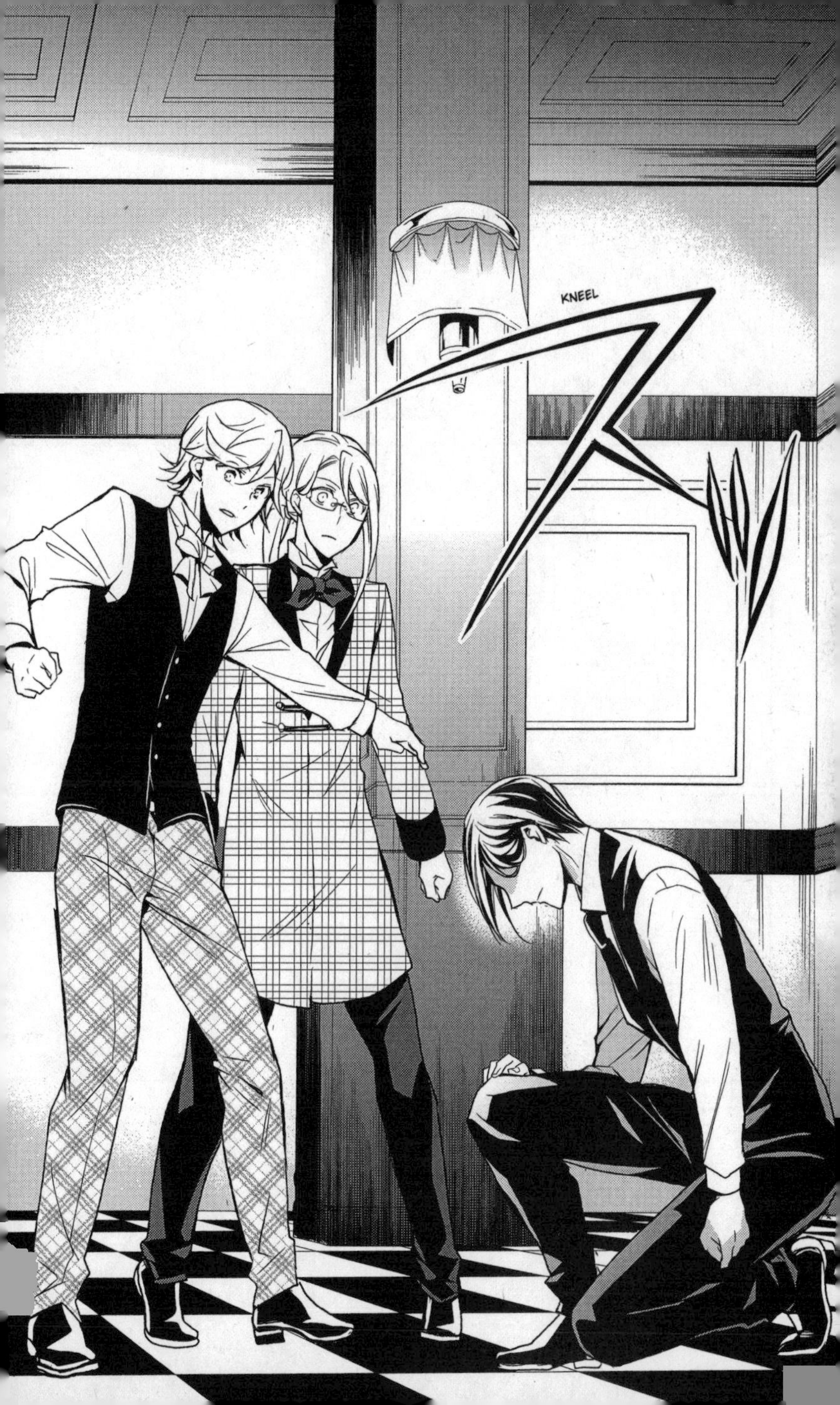
KNEEL

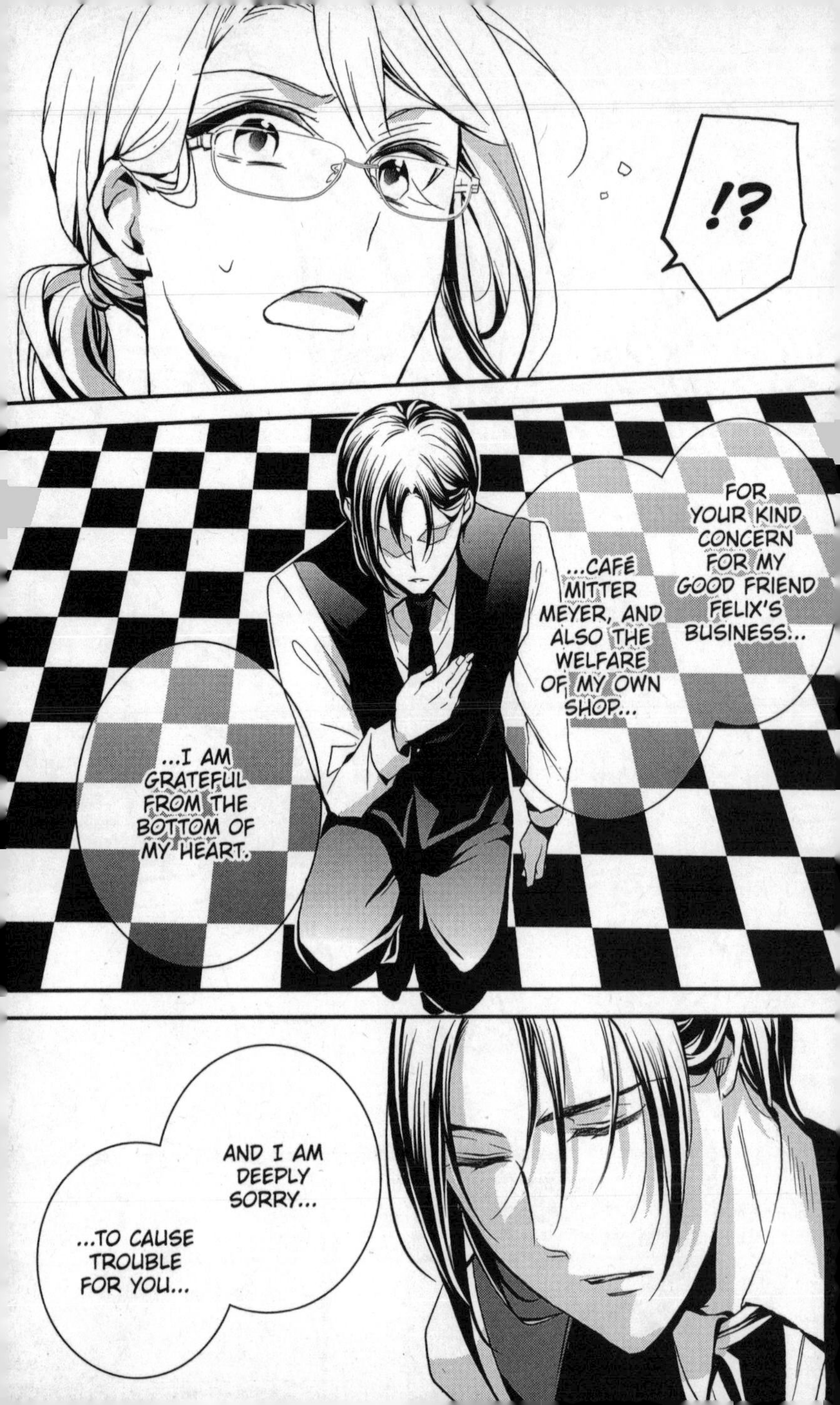
!?
FOR YOUR KIND CONCERN FOR MY GOOD FRIEND FELIX'S BUSINESS...
...CAFÉ MITTER MEYER, AND ALSO THE WELFARE OF MY OWN SHOP...
...I AM GRATEFUL FROM THE BOTTOM OF MY HEART.
AND I AM DEEPLY SORRY...
...TO CAUSE TROUBLE FOR YOU...

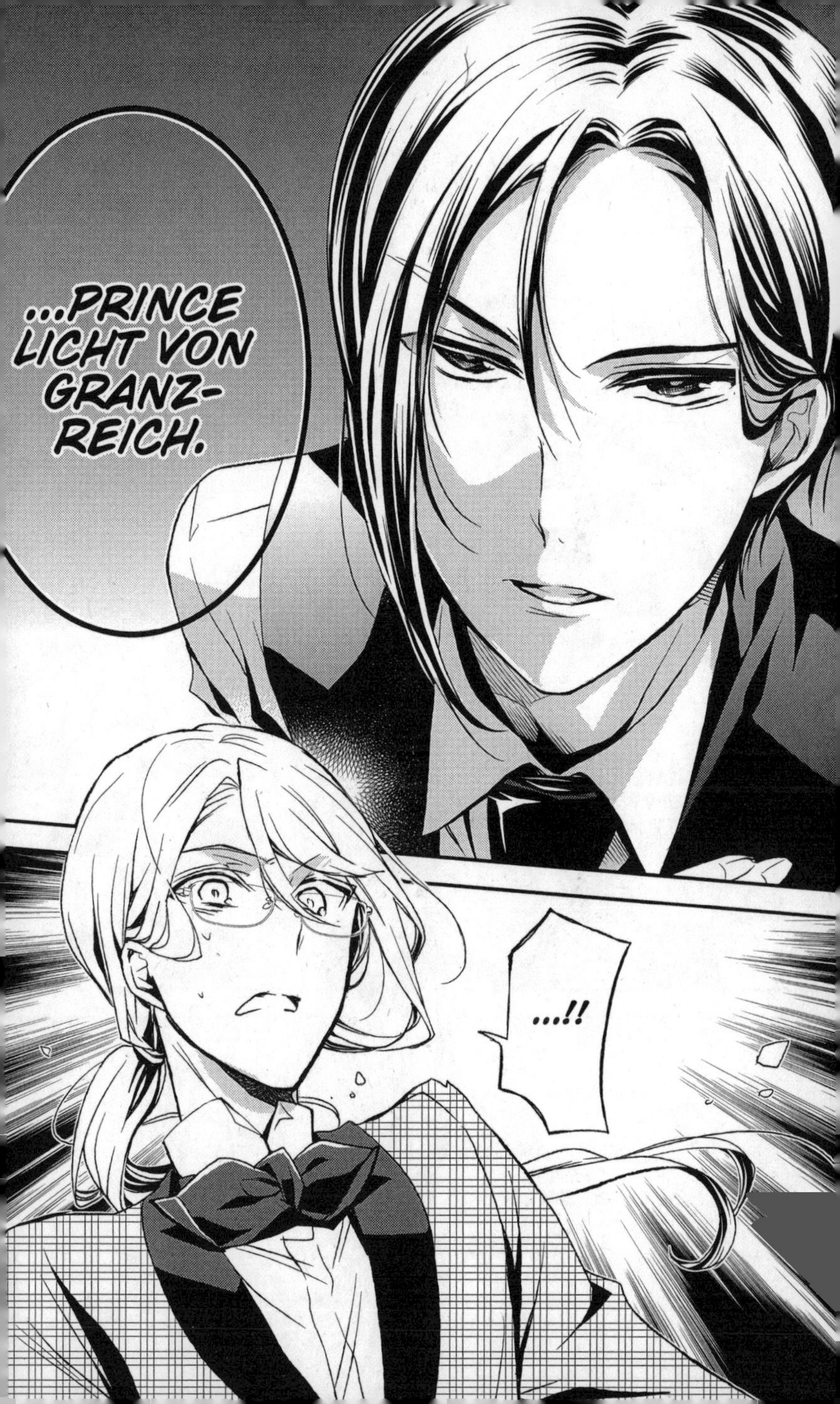
...PRINCE LICHT VON GRANZ-REICH.
...!!

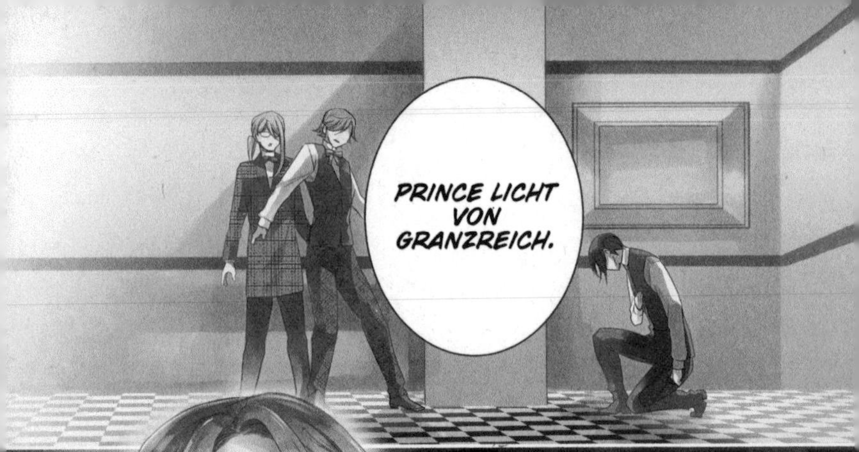
PRINCE LICHT VON GRANZREICH.

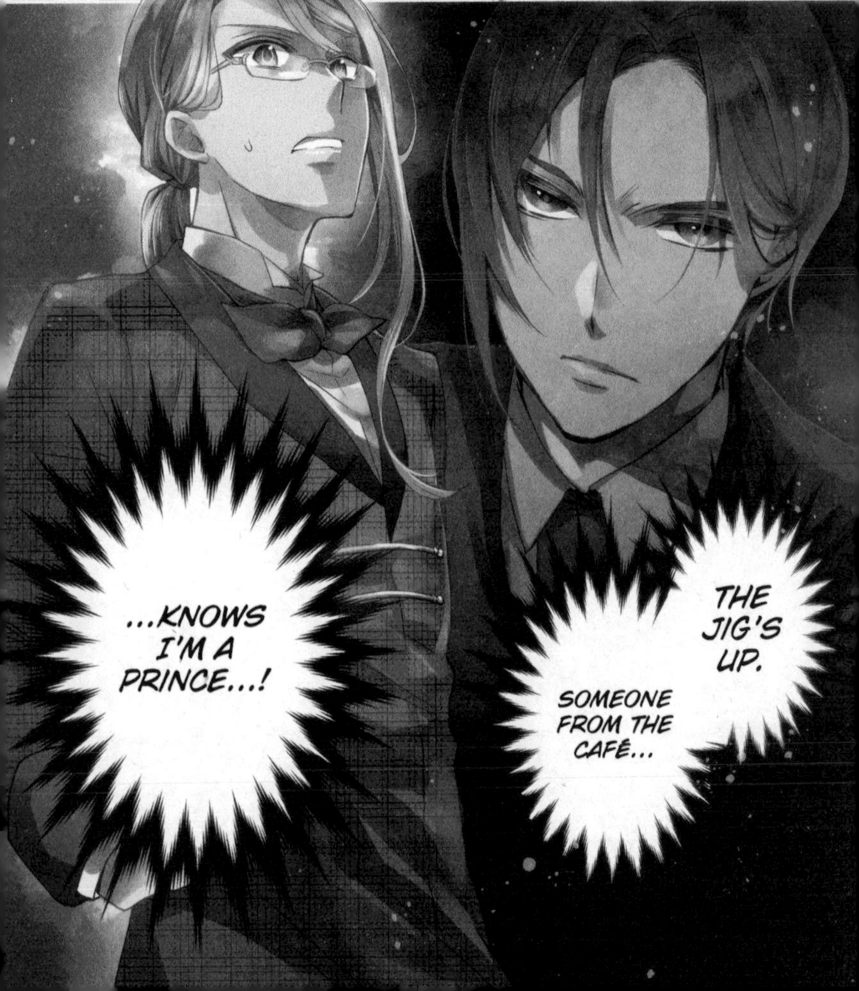
THE JIG'S UP.
SOMEONE FROM THE CAFÉ...
...KNOWS I'M A PRINCE...!

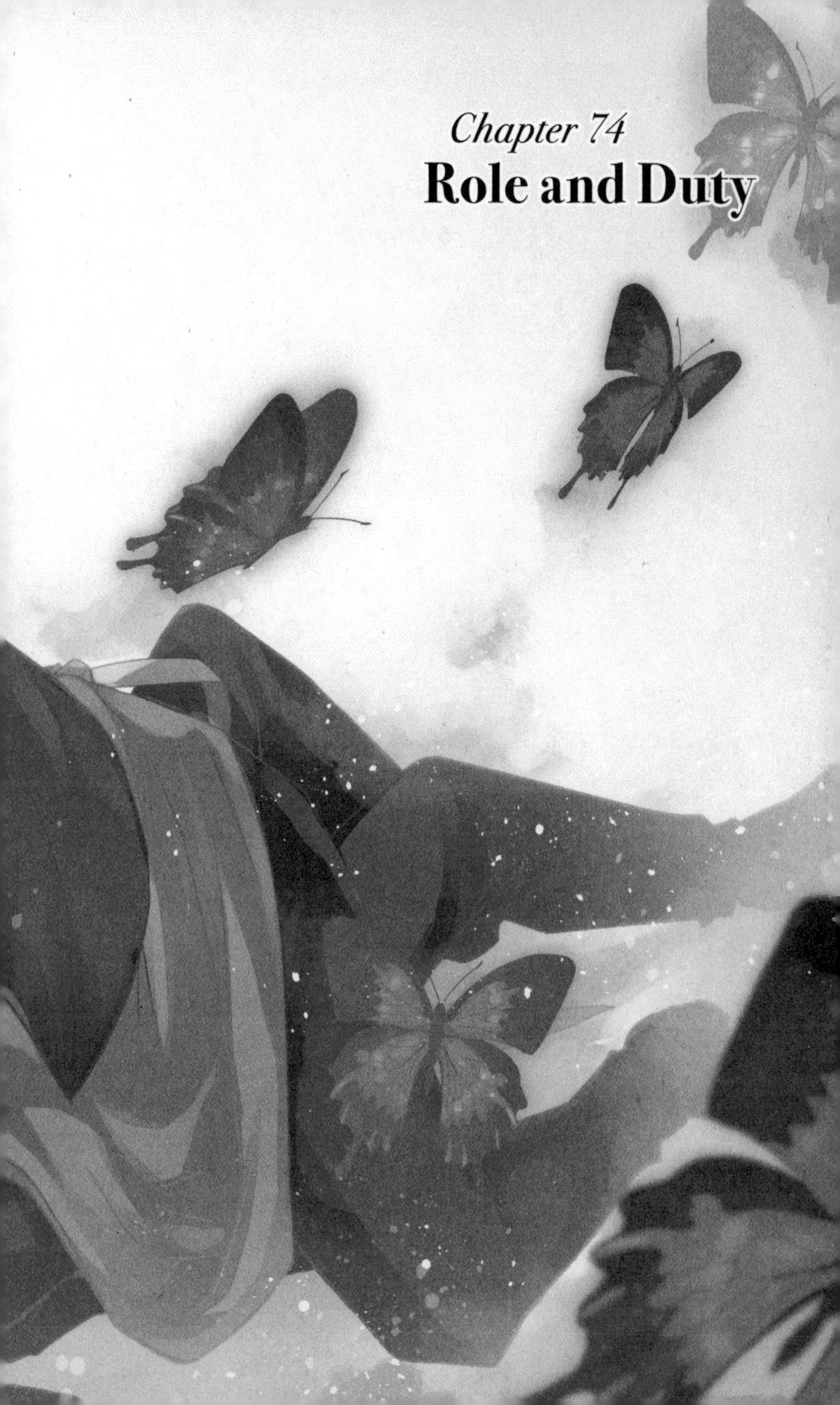
Chapter 74
Role and Duty

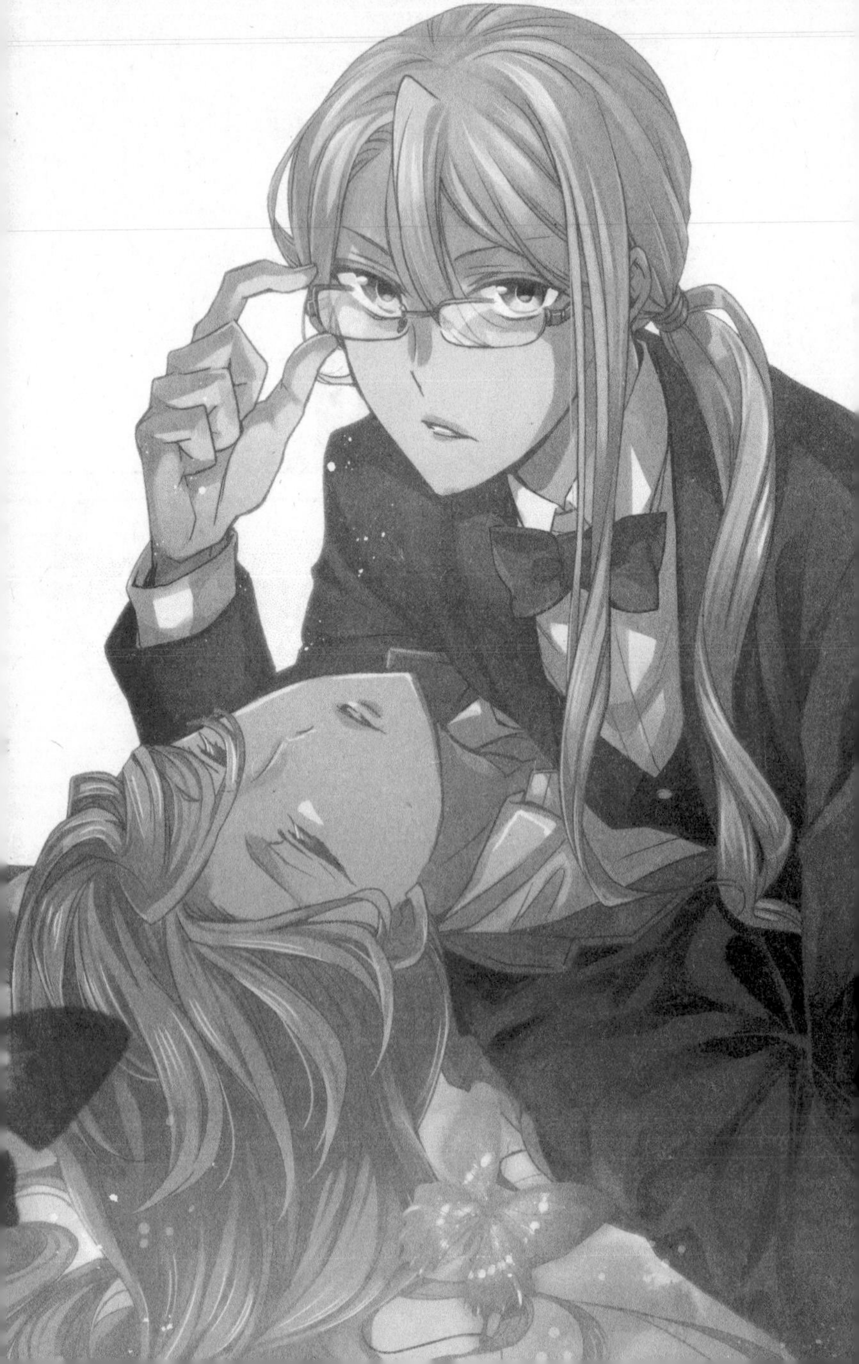

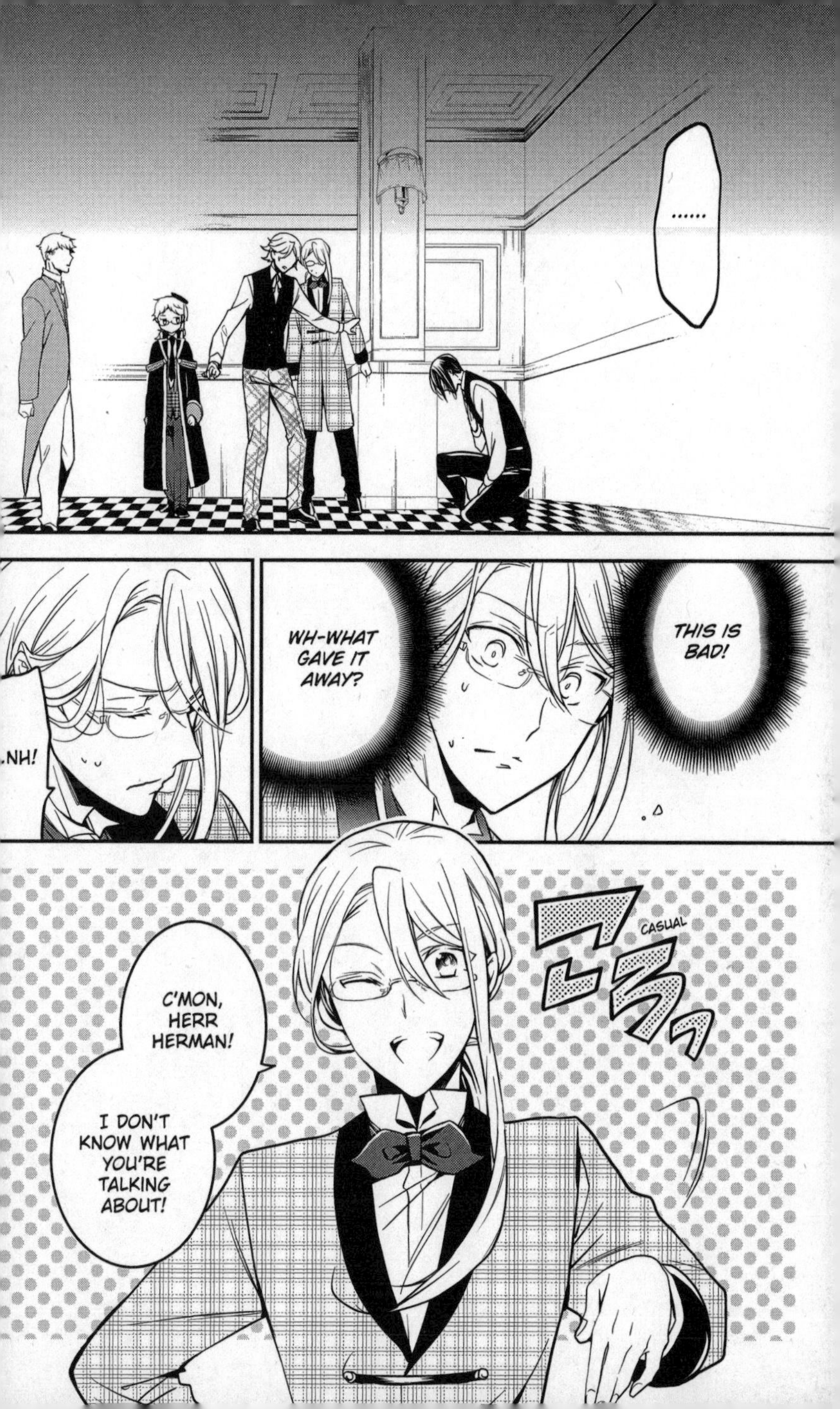
……
THIS IS BAD!
WH-WHAT GAVE IT AWAY?
.NH!
CASUAL
C'MON, HERR HERMAN!
I DON'T KNOW WHAT YOU'RE TALKING ABOUT!

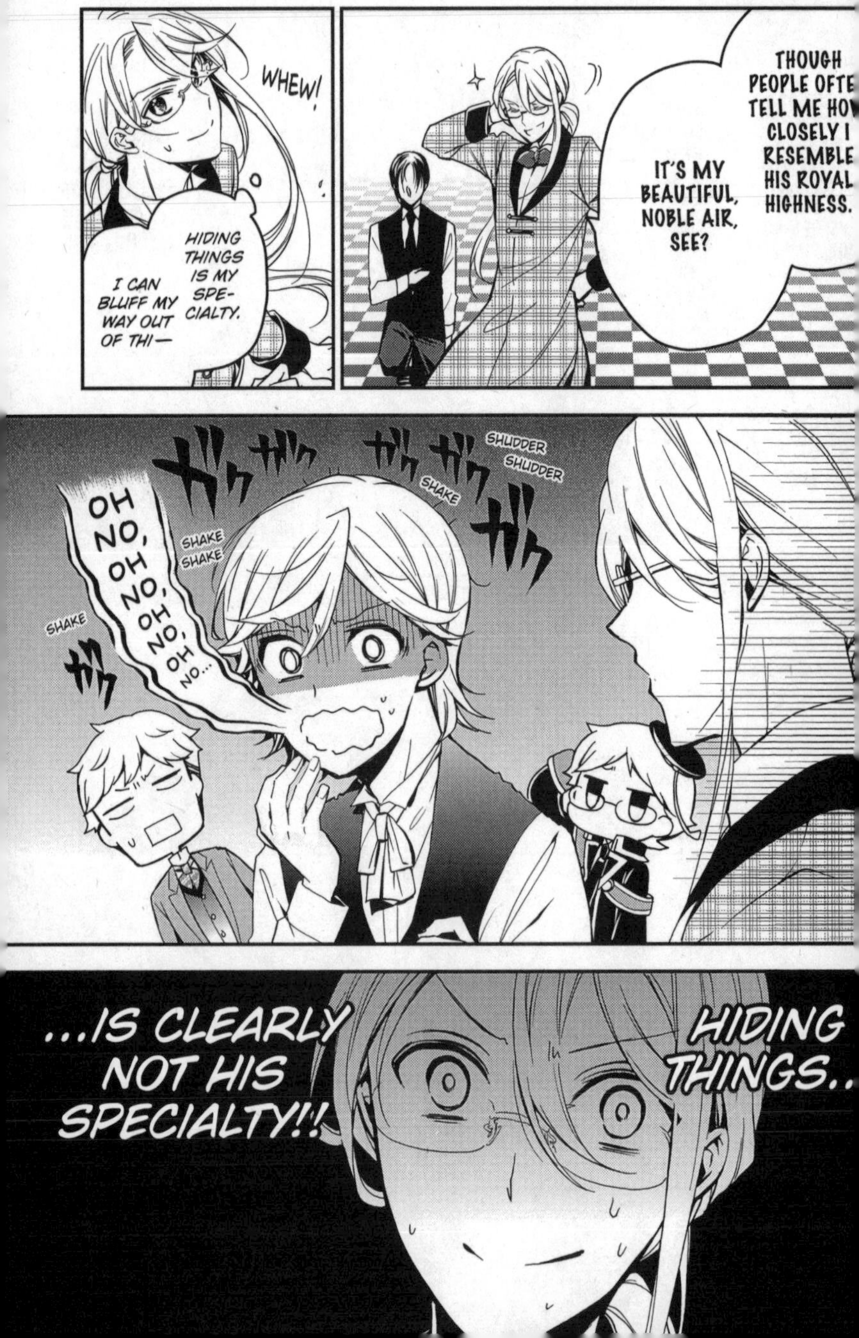
THOUGH PEOPLE OFTE TELL ME HO CLOSELY I RESEMBLE HIS ROYAL HIGHNESS.
IT'S MY BEAUTIFUL, NOBLE AIR, SEE?
WHEW!
HIDING THINGS IS MY SPE-CIALTY.
I CAN BLUFF MY WAY OUT OF THI—
SHUDDER SHUDDER
SHAKE
OH NO, OH NO, OH NO, OH NO...
SHAKE SHAKE
SHAKE
HIDING THINGS..
...IS CLEARLY NOT HIS SPECIALTY!!

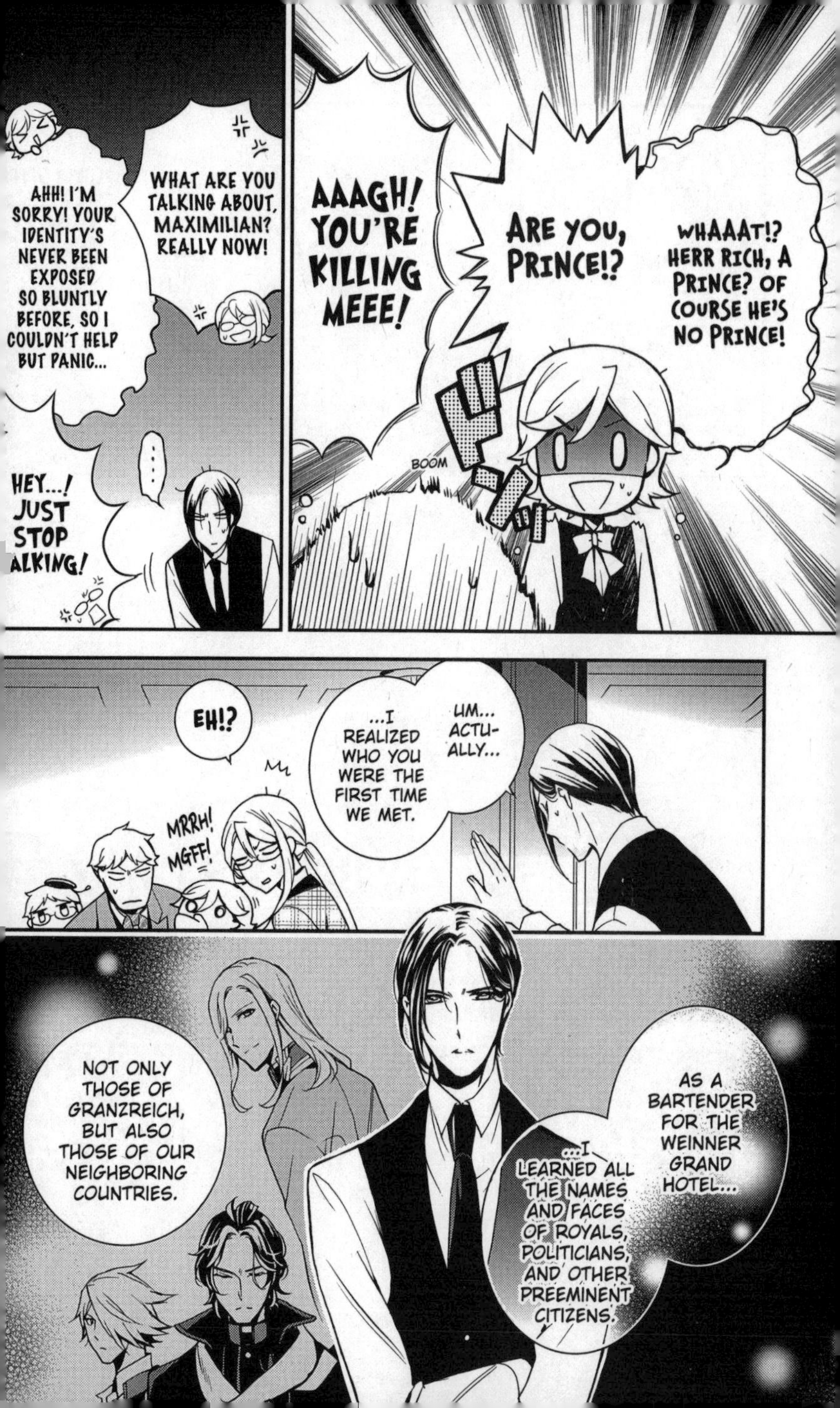
WHAAAT!? HERR RICH, A PRINCE? OF COURSE HE'S NO PRINCE!
ARE YOU, PRINCE!?
AAAGH! YOU'RE KILLING MEEE!
BOOM
WHAT ARE YOU TALKING ABOUT, MAXIMILIAN? REALLY NOW!
AHH! I'M SORRY! YOUR IDENTITY'S NEVER BEEN EXPOSED SO BLUNTLY BEFORE, SO I COULDN'T HELP BUT PANIC...
...
HEY...! JUST STOP ALKING!
UM... ACTU-ALLY...
...I REALIZED WHO YOU WERE THE FIRST TIME WE MET.
EH!?
MRRH! MGFF!
AS A BARTENDER FOR THE WEINNER GRAND HOTEL...
...I LEARNED ALL THE NAMES AND FACES OF ROYALS, POLITICIANS, AND OTHER PREEMINENT CITIZENS.
NOT ONLY THOSE OF GRANZREICH, BUT ALSO THOSE OF OUR NEIGHBORING COUNTRIES.

I'VE LEFT THAT JOB NOW, BUT I WAS WORKING A A PRO FO YEARS...
I WOULD NEVER MISTAKE A VIP'S FACE.
...THOUGH I ADMIT I WAS QUITE SHOCKED.
......
...S...
...SORRY. FOR HIDING IT...
IT SEEMS THAT HE...THAT FELIX DOESN'T KNOW, DOES HE?
ARE YOU GOING TO TELL HIM?

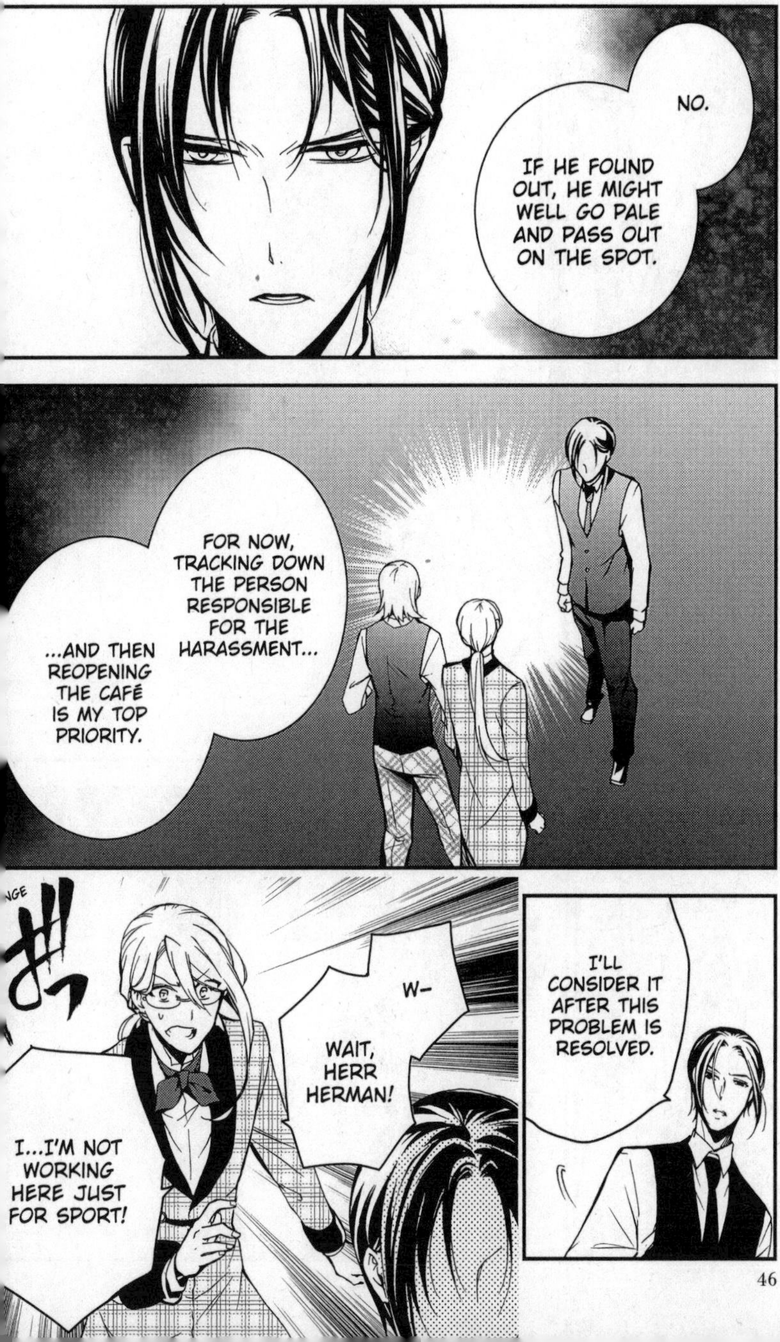
NO.
IF HE FOUND OUT, HE MIGHT WELL GO PALE AND PASS OUT ON THE SPOT.
FOR NOW, TRACKING DOWN THE PERSON RESPONSIBLE FOR THE HARASSMENT...
...AND THEN REOPENING THE CAFÉ IS MY TOP PRIORITY.
I'LL CONSIDER IT AFTER THIS PROBLEM IS RESOLVED.
W-
WAIT, HERR HERMAN!
I...I'M NOT WORKING HERE JUST FOR SPORT!

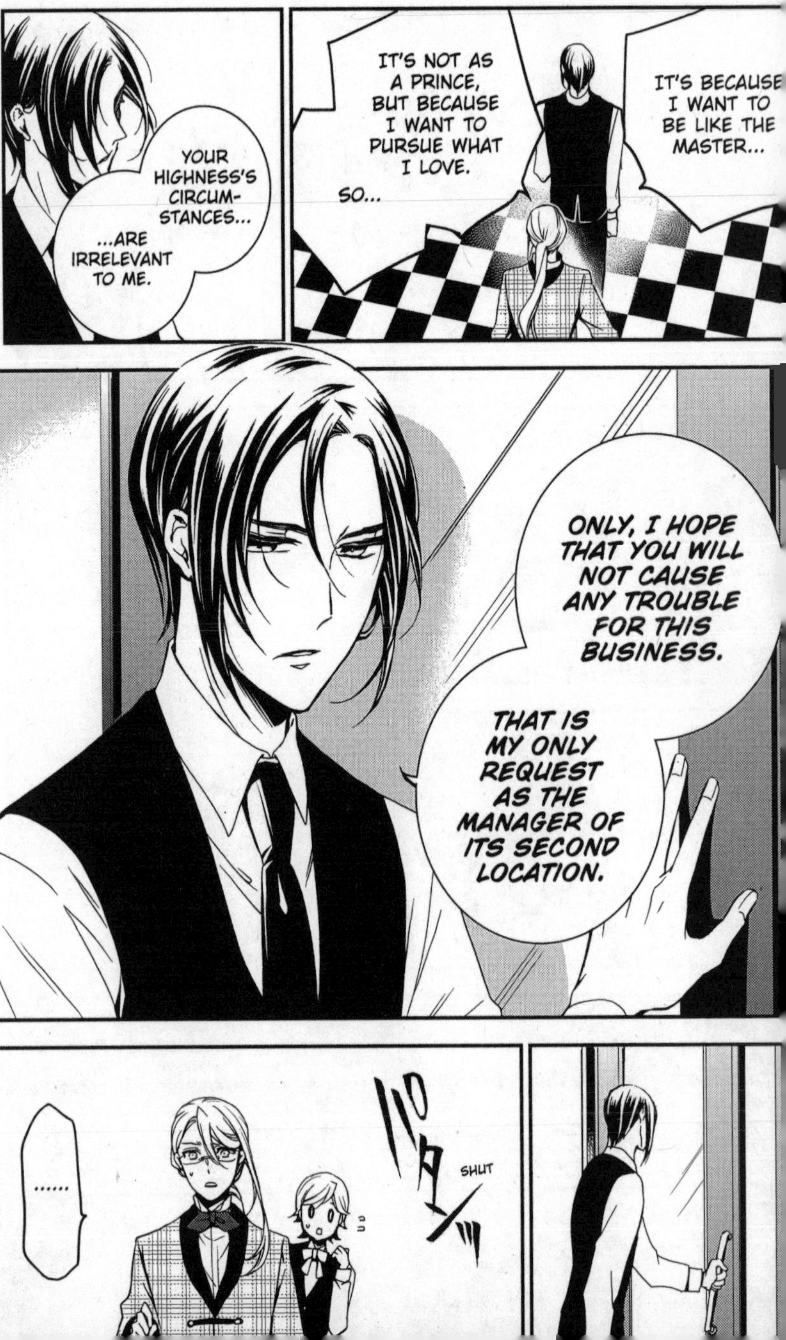
IT'S BECAUSE I WANT TO BE LIKE THE MASTER...
IT'S NOT AS A PRINCE, BUT BECAUSE I WANT TO PURSUE WHAT I LOVE.
SO...
YOUR HIGHNESS'S CIRCUM-STANCES...
...ARE IRRELEVANT TO ME.
ONLY, I HOPE THAT YOU WILL NOT CAUSE ANY TROUBLE FOR THIS BUSINESS.
THAT IS MY ONLY REQUEST AS THE MANAGER OF ITS SECOND LOCATION.
SHUT
......

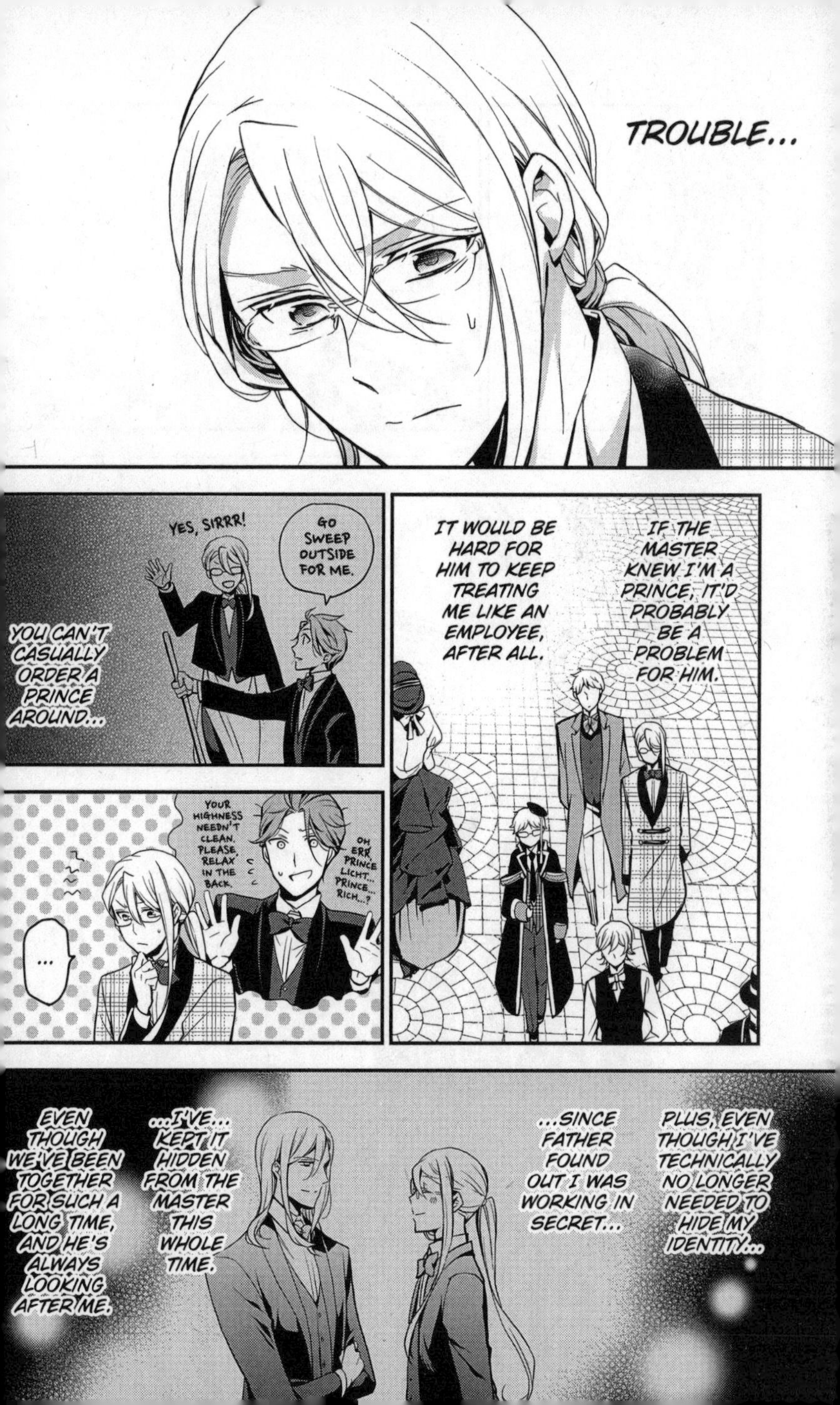
TROUBLE...
IF THE MASTER KNEW I'M A PRINCE, IT'D PROBABLY BE A PROBLEM FOR HIM.
IT WOULD BE HARD FOR HIM TO KEEP TREATING ME LIKE AN EMPLOYEE, AFTER ALL.
GO SWEEP OUTSIDE FOR ME.
YES, SIRRR!
YOU CAN'T CASUALLY ORDER A PRINCE AROUND...
OH ERR, PRINCE LICHT... PRINCE RICH...?
YOUR HIGHNESS NEEDN'T CLEAN. PLEASE, RELAX IN THE BACK.
...
PLUS, EVEN THOUGH I'VE TECHNICALLY NO LONGER NEEDED TO HIDE MY IDENTITY...
...SINCE FATHER FOUND OUT I WAS WORKING IN SECRET...
...I'VE... KEPT IT HIDDEN FROM THE MASTER THIS WHOLE TIME.
EVEN THOUGH WE'VE BEEN TOGETHER FOR SUCH A LONG TIME, AND HE'S ALWAYS LOOKING AFTER ME.

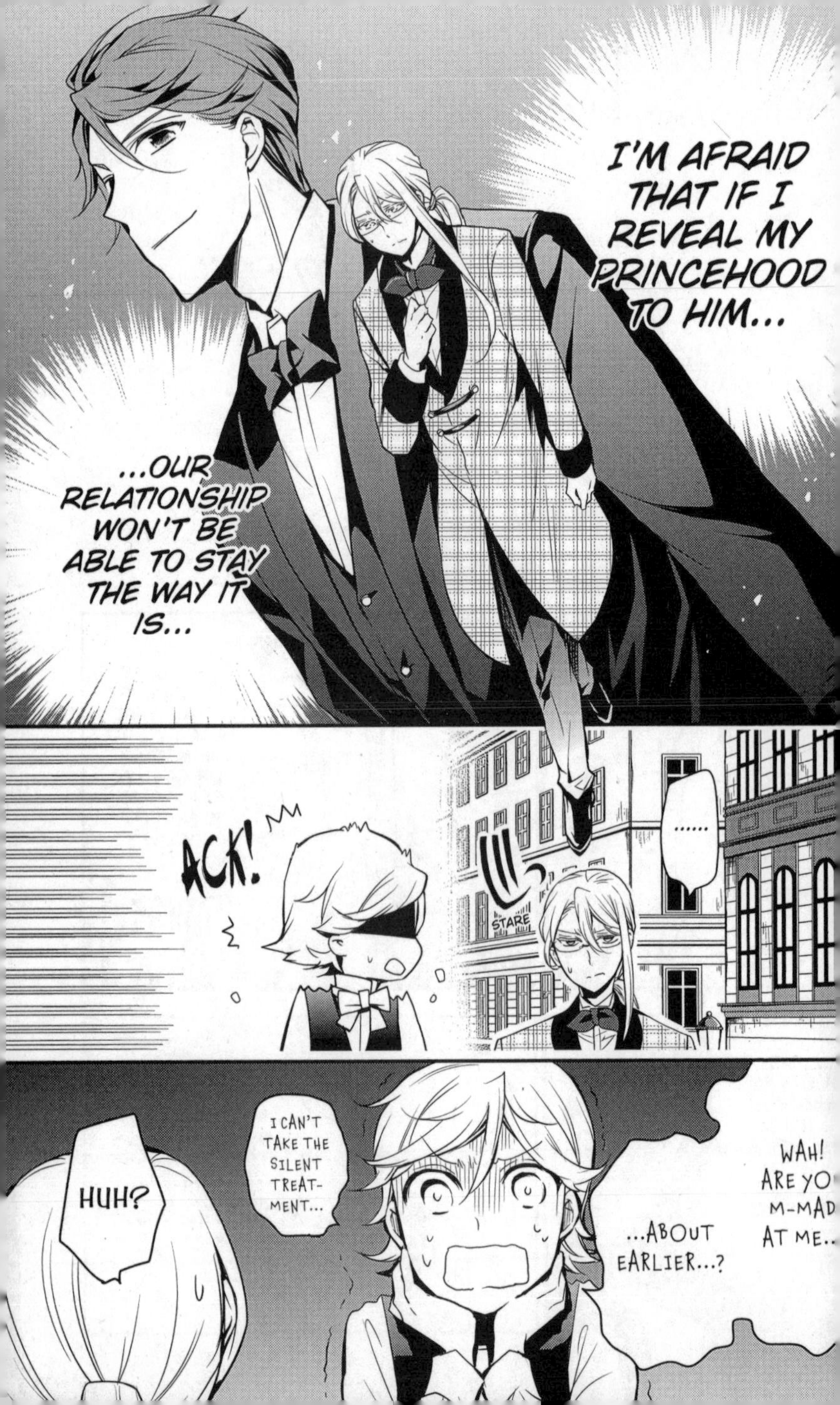
I'M AFRAID THAT IF I REVEAL MY PRINCEHOOD TO HIM...
...OUR RELATIONSHIP WON'T BE ABLE TO STAY THE WAY IT IS...
......
STARE
ACK!
WAH! ARE YO M-MAD AT ME..
...ABOUT EARLIER...?
I CAN'T TAKE THE SILENT TREAT-MENT...
HUH?

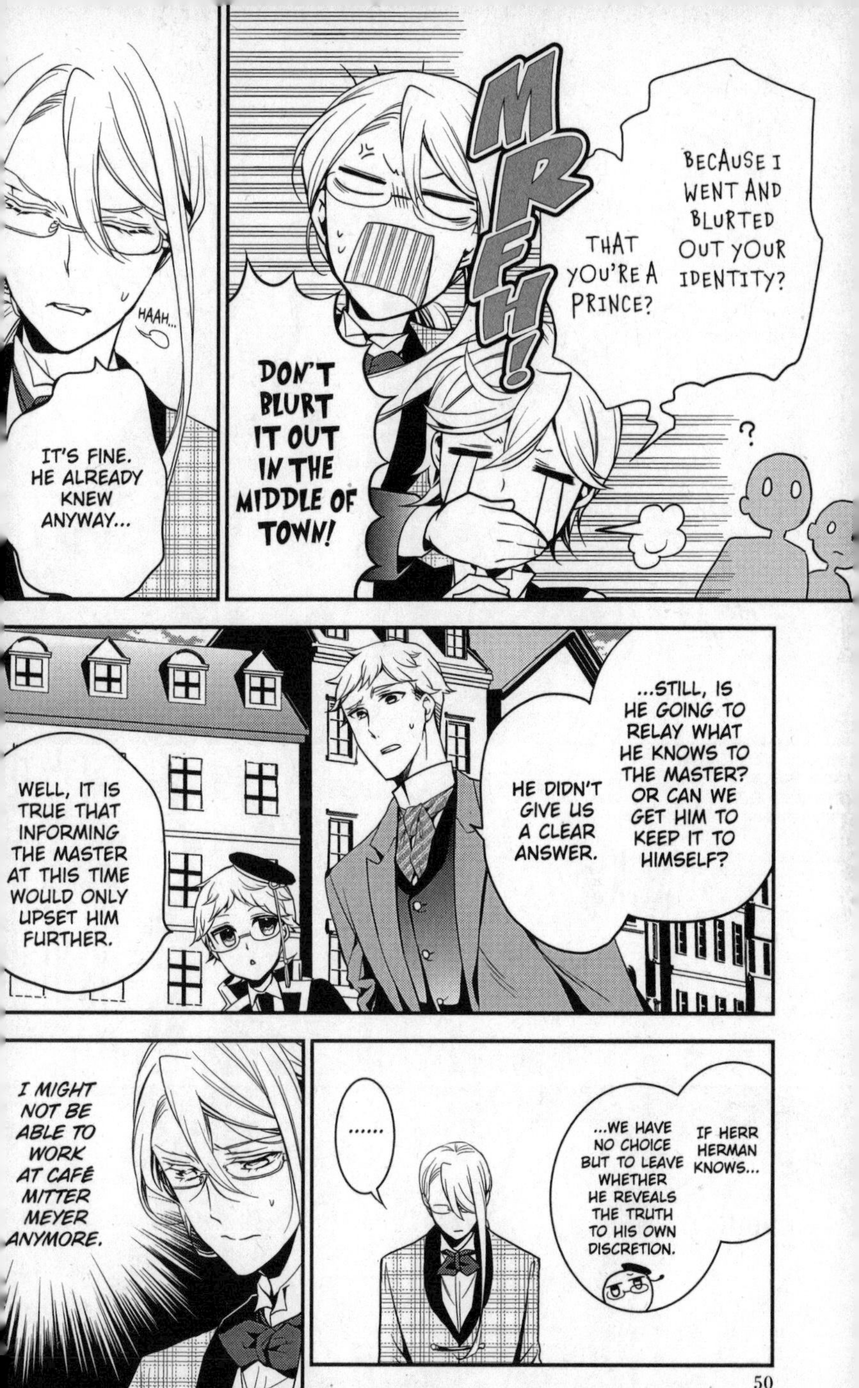
BECAUSE I WENT AND BLURTED OUT YOUR IDENTITY?
THAT YOU'RE A PRINCE?
MRFH!
DON'T BLURT IT OUT IN THE MIDDLE OF TOWN!
?
HAAH...
IT'S FINE. HE ALREADY KNEW ANYWAY...
...STILL, IS HE GOING TO RELAY WHAT HE KNOWS TO THE MASTER? OR CAN WE GET HIM TO KEEP IT TO HIMSELF?
HE DIDN'T GIVE US A CLEAR ANSWER.
WELL, IT IS TRUE THAT INFORMING THE MASTER AT THIS TIME WOULD ONLY UPSET HIM FURTHER.
IF HERR HERMAN KNOWS...
...WE HAVE NO CHOICE BUT TO LEAVE WHETHER HE REVEALS THE TRUTH TO HIS OWN DISCRETION.
......
I MIGHT NOT BE ABLE TO WORK AT CAFÉ MITTER MEYER ANYMORE.

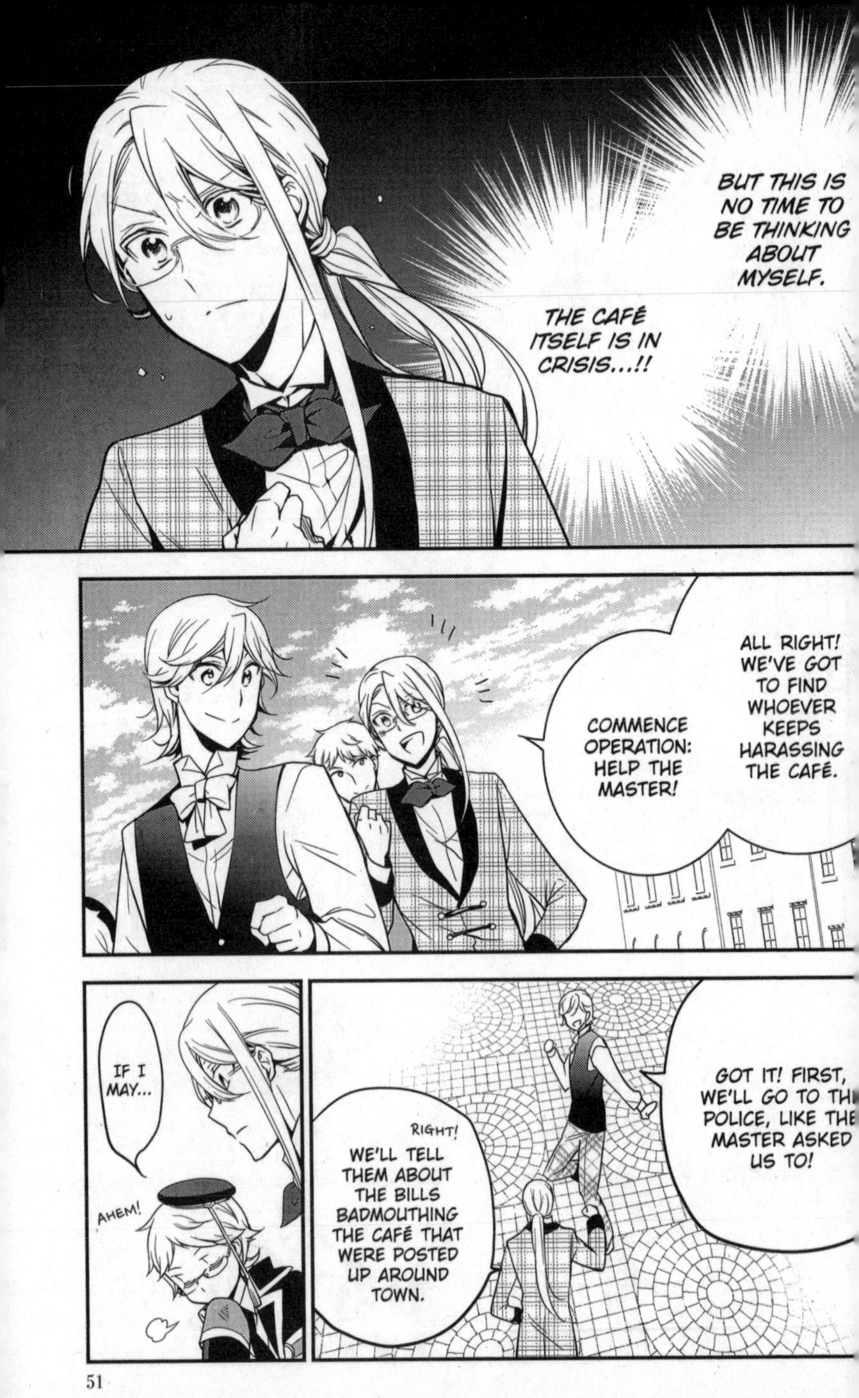
BUT THIS IS NO TIME TO BE THINKING ABOUT MYSELF.
THE CAFÉ ITSELF IS IN CRISIS...!!
ALL RIGHT! WE'VE GOT TO FIND WHOEVER KEEPS HARASSING THE CAFÉ.
COMMENCE OPERATION: HELP THE MASTER!
GOT IT! FIRST, WE'LL GO TO TH POLICE, LIKE THE MASTER ASKED US TO!
RIGHT!
WE'LL TELL THEM ABOUT THE BILLS BADMOUTHING THE CAFÉ THAT WERE POSTED UP AROUND TOWN.
IF I MAY...
AHEM!

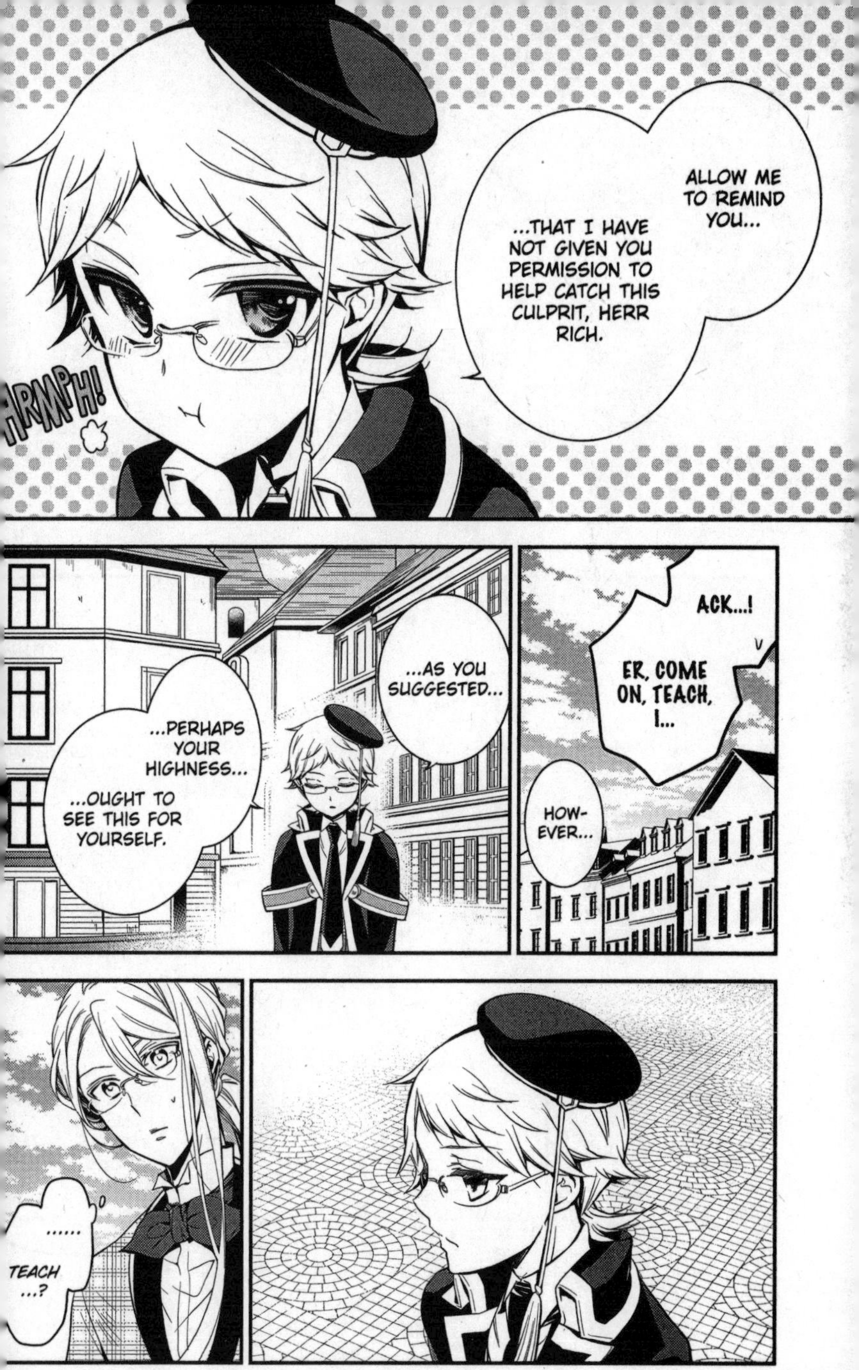
ALLOW ME TO REMIND YOU...
...THAT I HAVE NOT GIVEN YOU PERMISSION TO HELP CATCH THIS CULPRIT, HERR RICH.
HRMPH!
ACK...!
ER, COME ON, TEACH, I...
HOW-EVER...
...AS YOU SUGGESTED...
...PERHAPS YOUR HIGHNESS...
...OUGHT TO SEE THIS FOR YOURSELF.
......
TEACH ...?

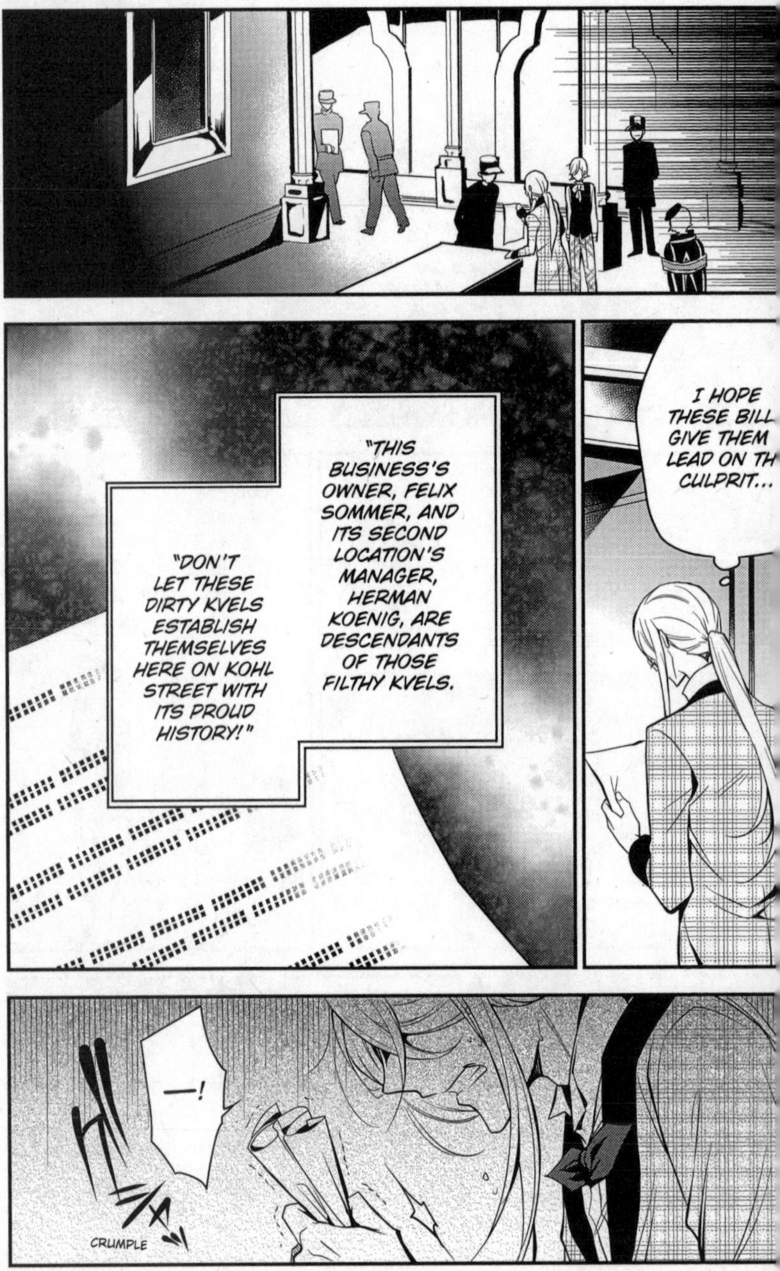
I HOPE THESE BILL GIVE THEM LEAD ON TH CULPRIT...
"THIS BUSINESS'S OWNER, FELIX SOMMER, AND ITS SECOND LOCATION'S MANAGER, HERMAN KOENIG, ARE DESCENDANTS OF THOSE FILTHY KVELS.
"DON'T LET THESE DIRTY KVELS ESTABLISH THEMSELVES HERE ON KOHL STREET WITH ITS PROUD HISTORY!"
—!
CRUMPLE

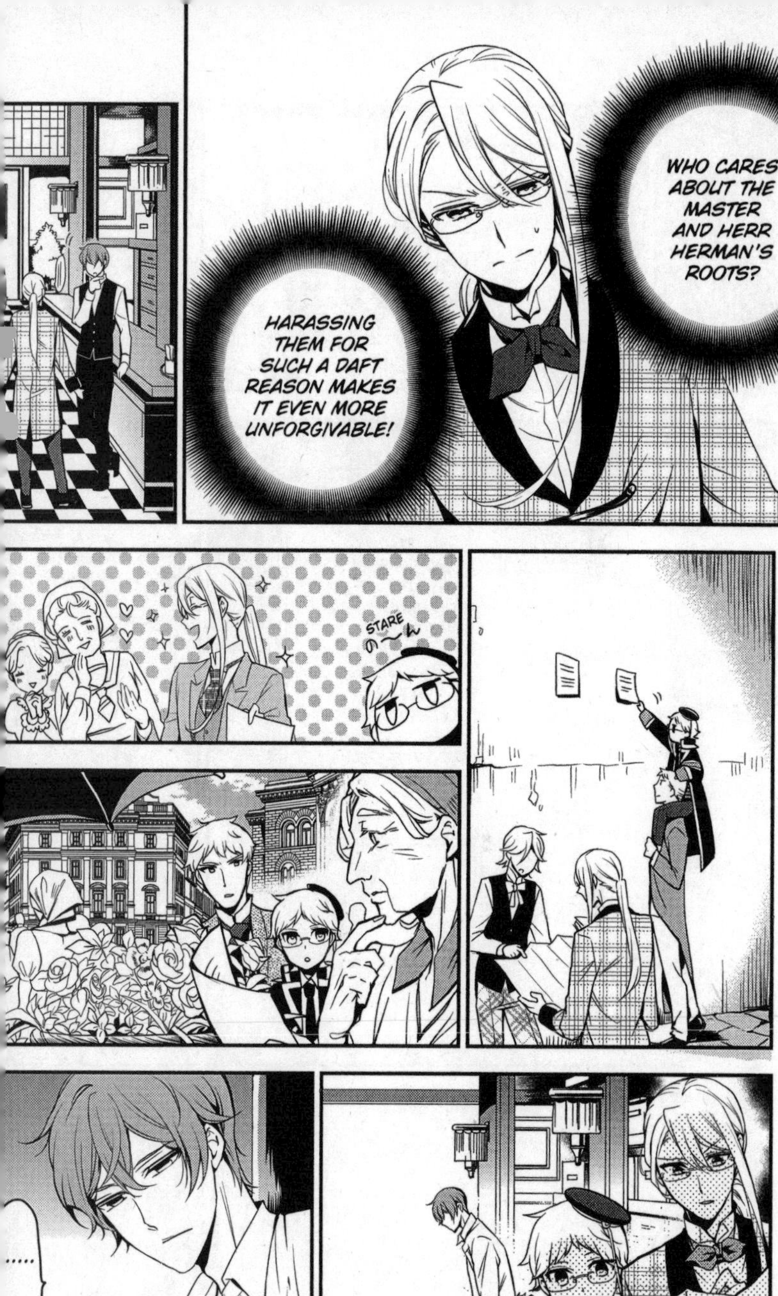
WHO CARES ABOUT THE MASTER AND HERR HERMAN'S ROOTS?
HARASSING THEM FOR SUCH A DAFT REASON MAKES IT EVEN MORE UNFORGIVABLE!
STARE
の〜ん
......

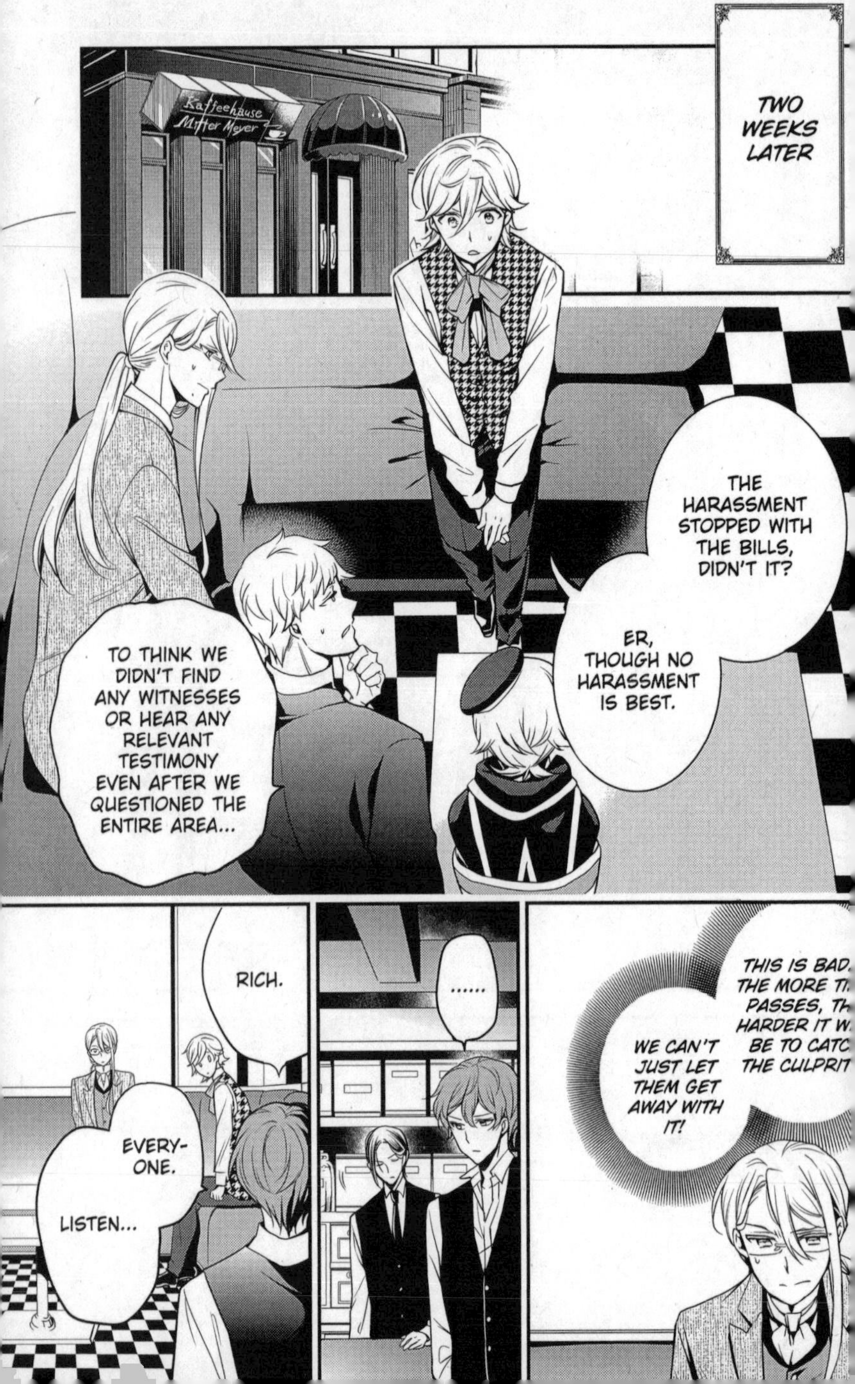
TWO WEEKS LATER
Kaffeehause Mitter Meyer
THE HARASSMENT STOPPED WITH THE BILLS, DIDN'T IT?
ER, THOUGH NO HARASSMENT IS BEST.
TO THINK WE DIDN'T FIND ANY WITNESSES OR HEAR ANY RELEVANT TESTIMONY EVEN AFTER WE QUESTIONED THE ENTIRE AREA...
THIS IS BAD. THE MORE TI PASSES, TH HARDER IT W BE TO CATC THE CULPRIT
WE CAN'T JUST LET THEM GET AWAY WITH IT!
....
RICH.
EVERY-ONE.
LISTEN...

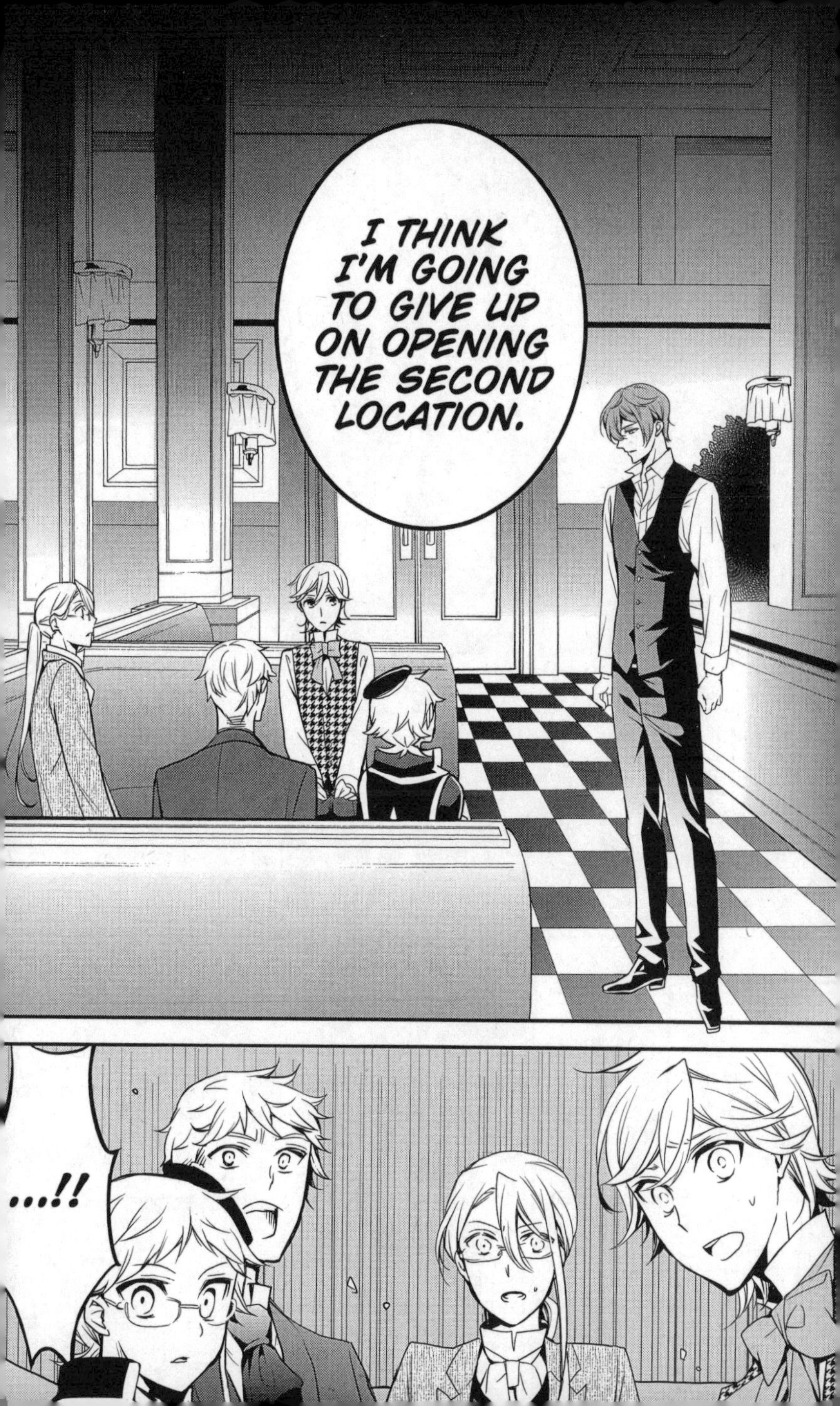
I THINK I'M GOING TO GIVE UP ON OPENING THE SECOND LOCATION.
...!!

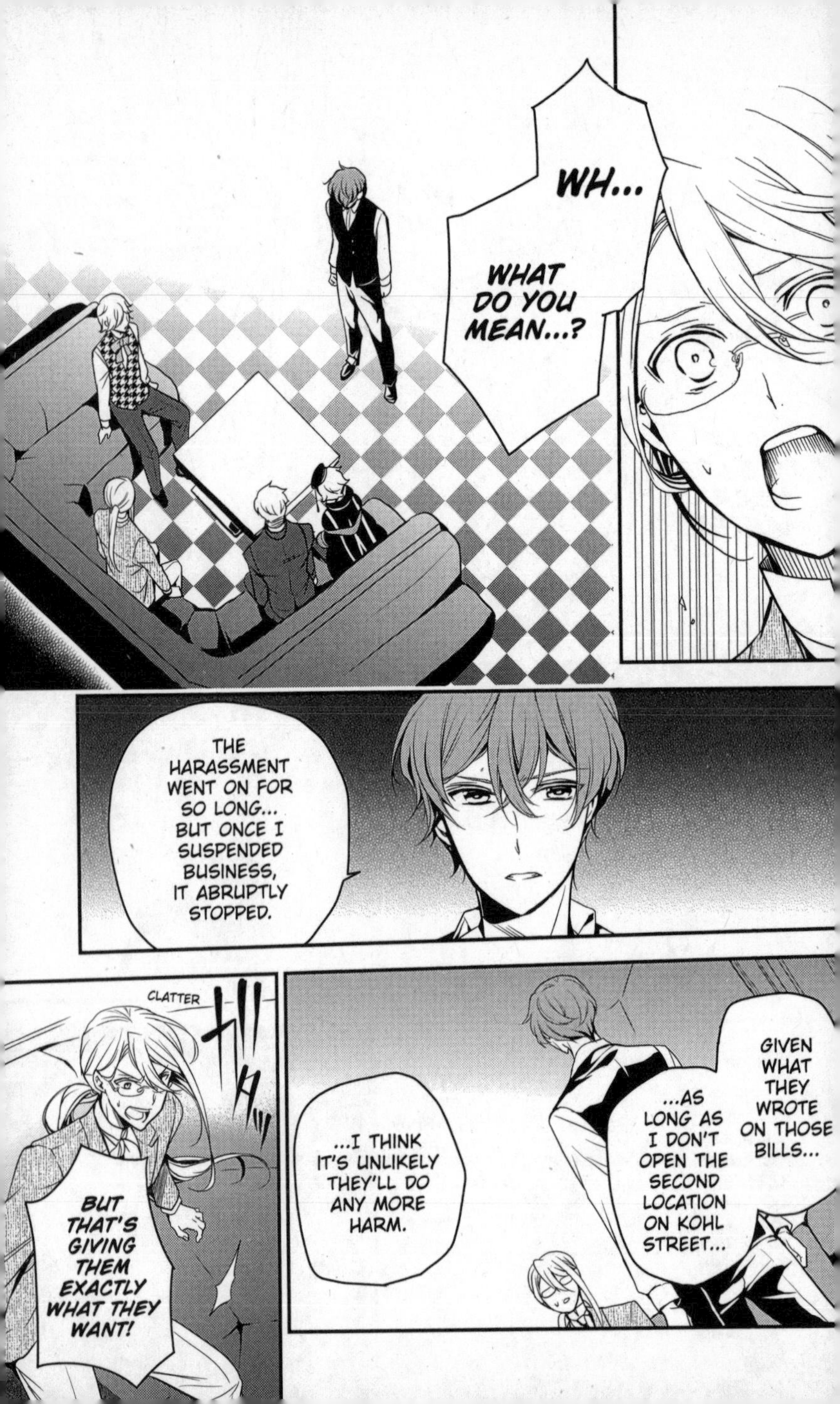
WH...
WHAT DO YOU MEAN...?
THE HARASSMENT WENT ON FOR SO LONG... BUT ONCE I SUSPENDED BUSINESS, IT ABRUPTLY STOPPED.
GIVEN WHAT THEY WROTE ON THOSE BILLS...
...AS LONG AS I DON'T OPEN THE SECOND LOCATION ON KOHL STREET...
...I THINK IT'S UNLIKELY THEY'LL DO ANY MORE HARM.
CLATTER
BUT THAT'S GIVING THEM EXACTLY WHAT THEY WANT!

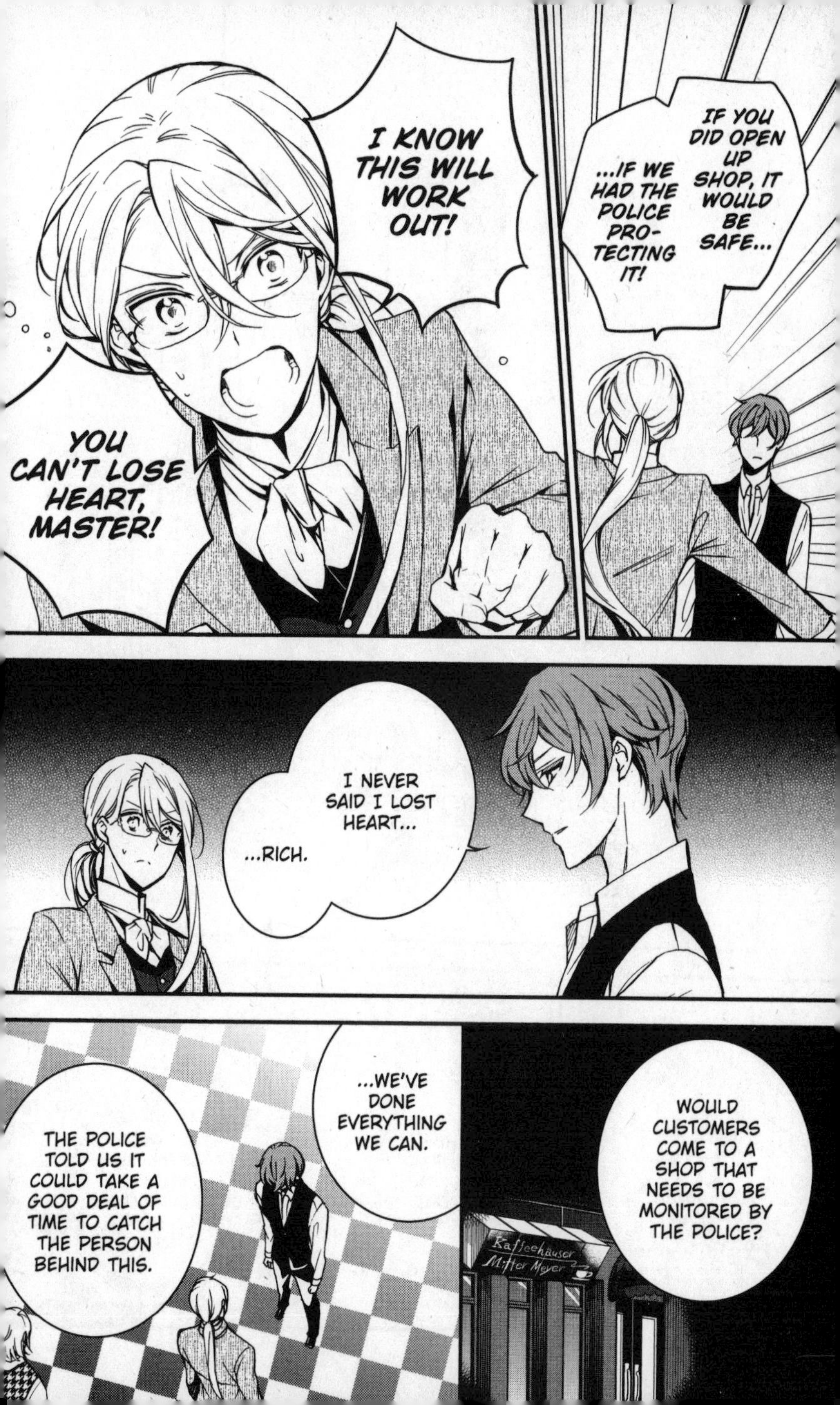
IF YOU DID OPEN UP SHOP, IT WOULD BE SAFE...
...IF WE HAD THE POLICE PROTECTING IT!
I KNOW THIS WILL WORK OUT!
YOU CAN'T LOSE HEART, MASTER!
I NEVER SAID I LOST HEART...
...RICH.
WOULD CUSTOMERS COME TO A SHOP THAT NEEDS TO BE MONITORED BY THE POLICE?
Kaffeehäuser
...WE'VE DONE EVERYTHING WE CAN.
THE POLICE TOLD US IT COULD TAKE A GOOD DEAL OF TIME TO CATCH THE PERSON BEHIND THIS.

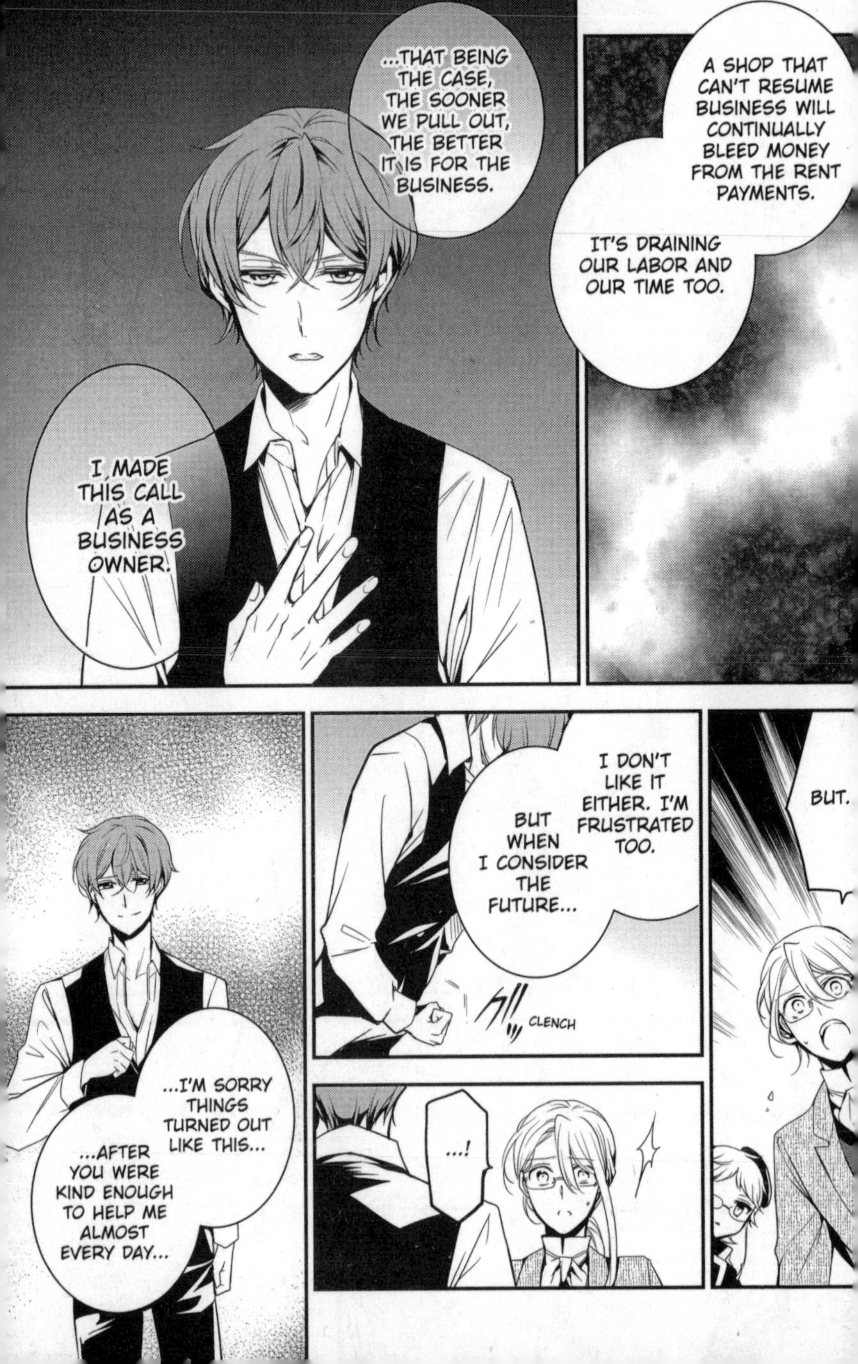
A SHOP THAT CAN'T RESUME BUSINESS WILL CONTINUALLY BLEED MONEY FROM THE RENT PAYMENTS.
IT'S DRAINING OUR LABOR AND OUR TIME TOO.
...THAT BEING THE CASE, THE SOONER WE PULL OUT, THE BETTER IT IS FOR THE BUSINESS.
I MADE THIS CALL AS A BUSINESS OWNER.
BUT.
I DON'T LIKE IT EITHER. I'M FRUSTRATED TOO.
BUT WHEN I CONSIDER THE FUTURE...
CLENCH
...!
...I'M SORRY THINGS TURNED OUT LIKE THIS...
...AFTER YOU WERE KIND ENOUGH TO HELP ME ALMOST EVERY DAY...

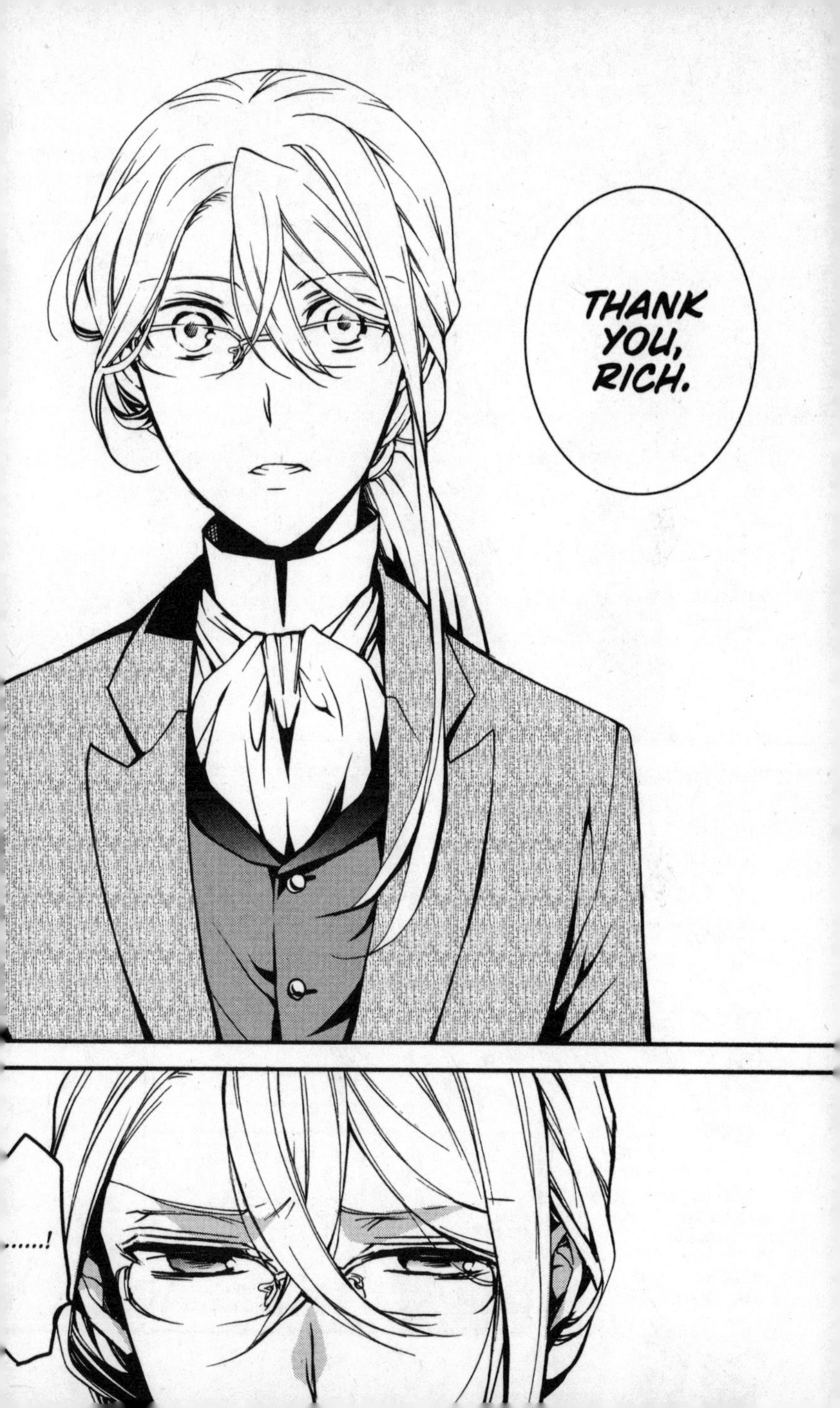
THANK YOU, RICH.
......!

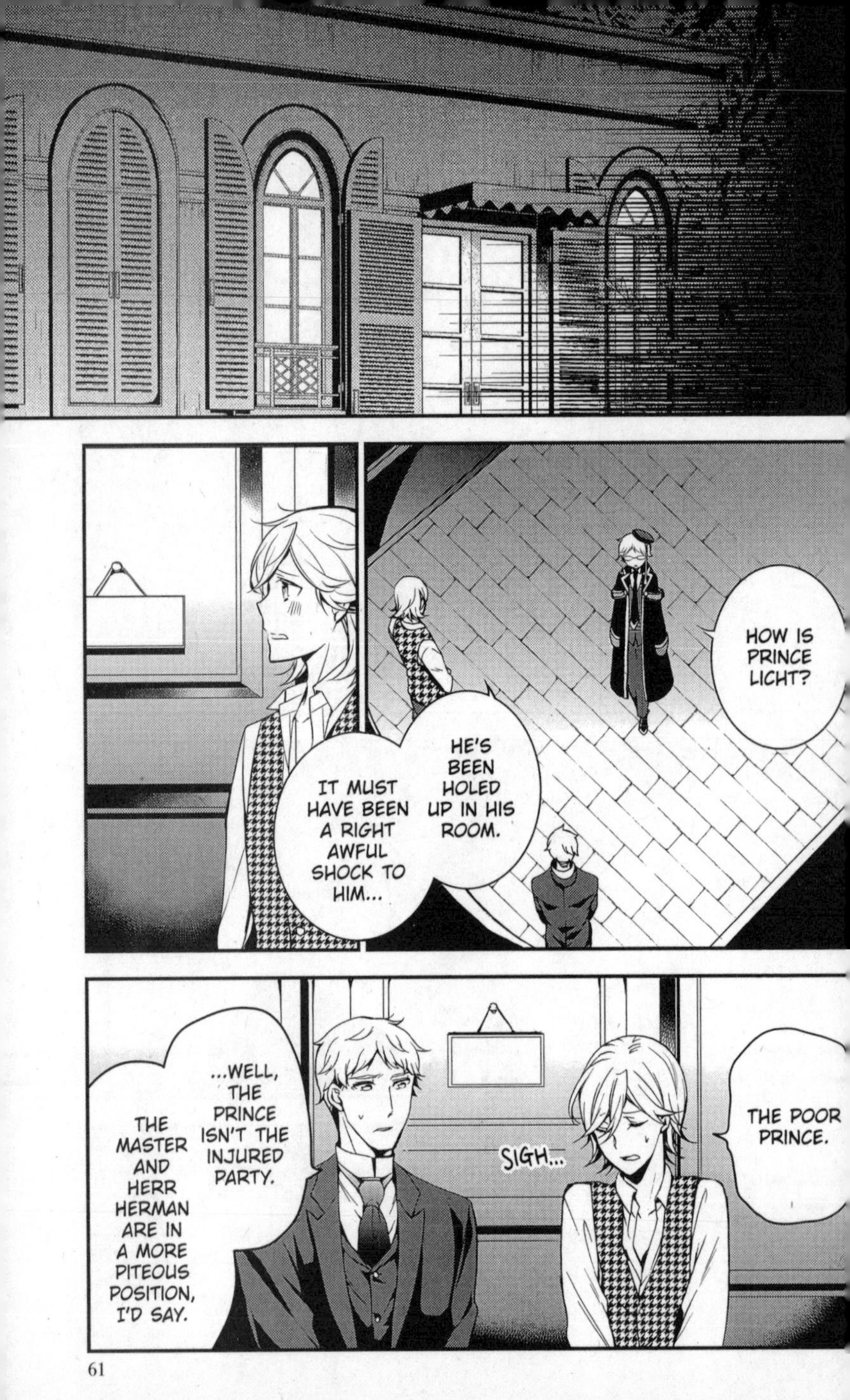
HOW IS PRINCE LICHT?
HE'S BEEN HOLED UP IN HIS ROOM.
IT MUST HAVE BEEN A RIGHT AWFUL SHOCK TO HIM...
THE POOR PRINCE.
SIGH...
...WELL, THE PRINCE ISN'T THE INJURED PARTY.
THE MASTER AND HERR HERMAN ARE IN A MORE PITEOUS POSITION, I'D SAY.

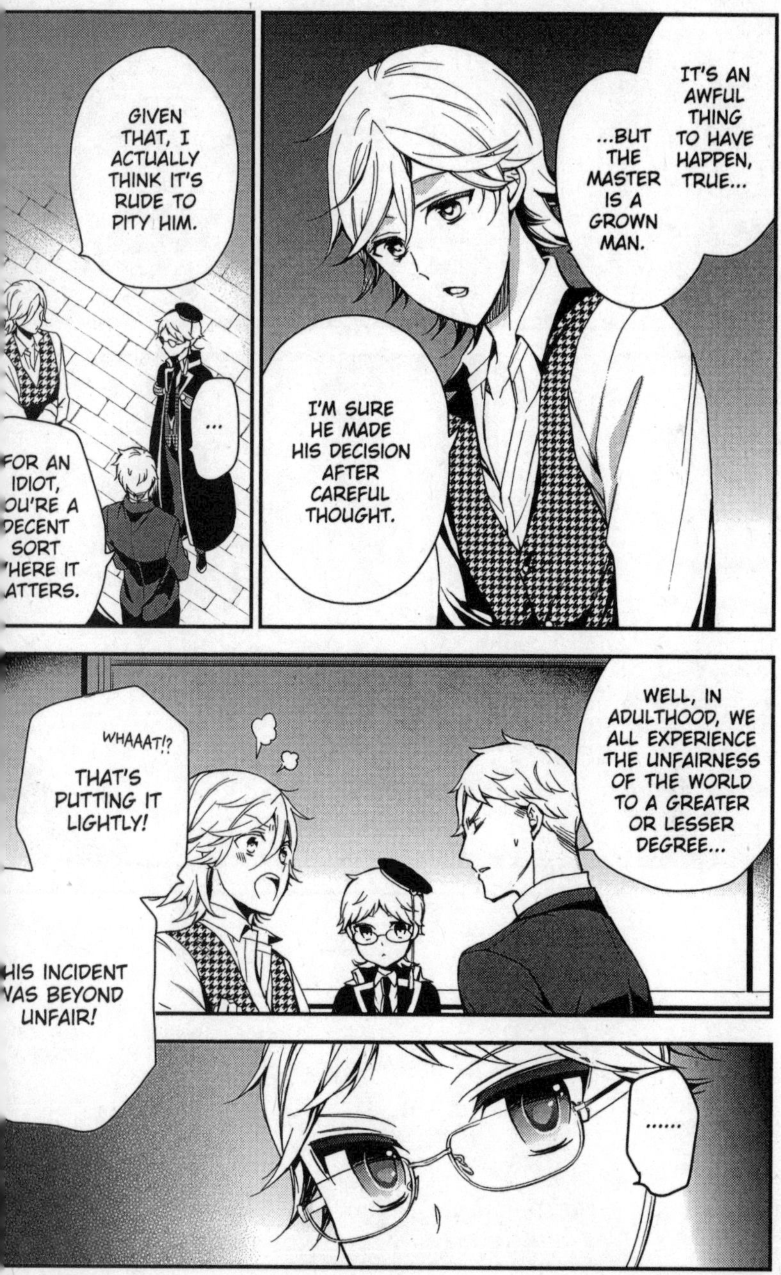
IT'S AN AWFUL THING TO HAVE HAPPEN, TRUE...
...BUT THE MASTER IS A GROWN MAN.
I'M SURE HE MADE HIS DECISION AFTER CAREFUL THOUGHT.
GIVEN THAT, I ACTUALLY THINK IT'S RUDE TO PITY HIM.
...
FOR AN IDIOT, OU'RE A DECENT SORT HERE IT ATTERS.
WELL, IN ADULTHOOD, WE ALL EXPERIENCE THE UNFAIRNESS OF THE WORLD TO A GREATER OR LESSER DEGREE...
WHAAAT!?
THAT'S PUTTING IT LIGHTLY!
HIS INCIDENT VAS BEYOND UNFAIR!
......

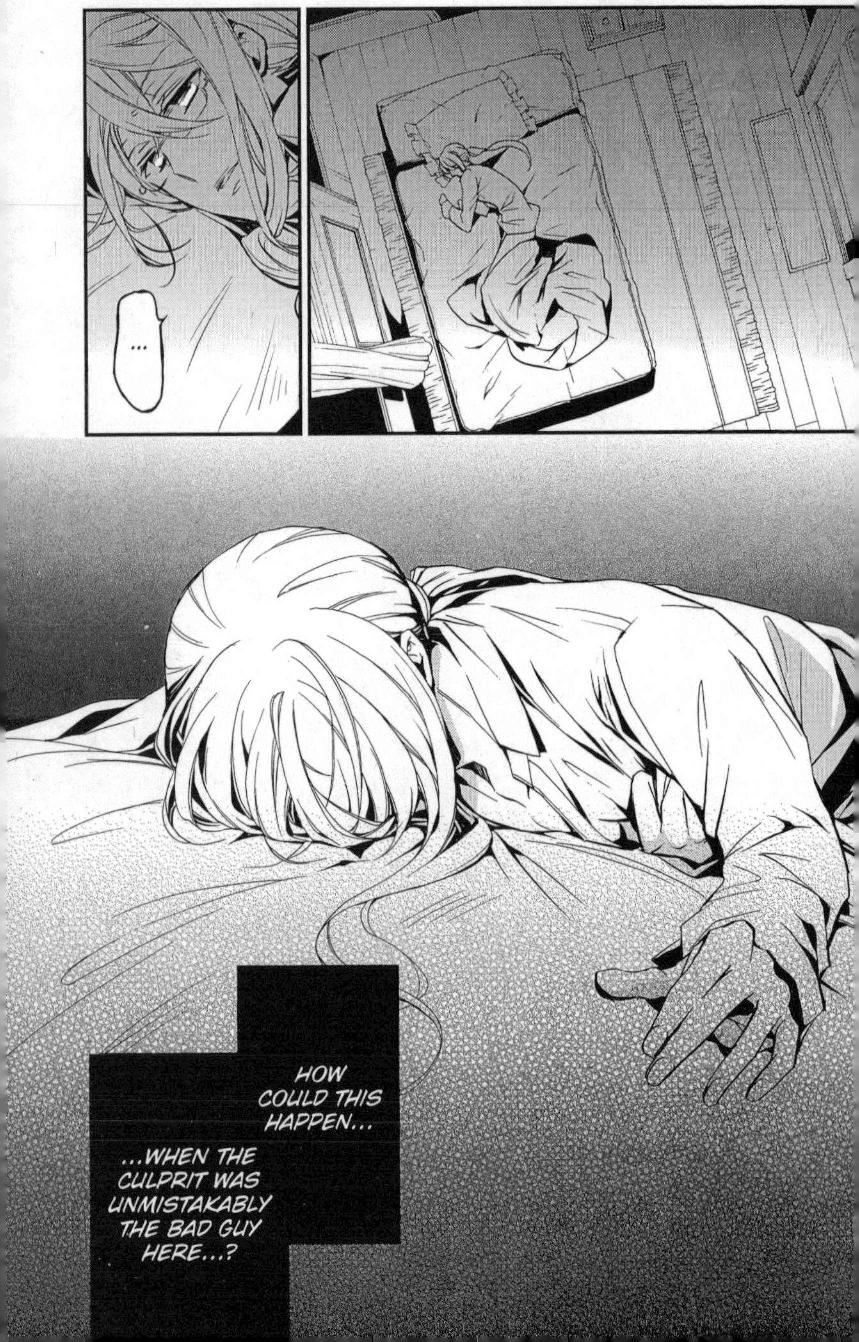
...
HOW COULD THIS HAPPEN...
...WHEN THE CULPRIT WAS UNMISTAKABLY THE BAD GUY HERE...?

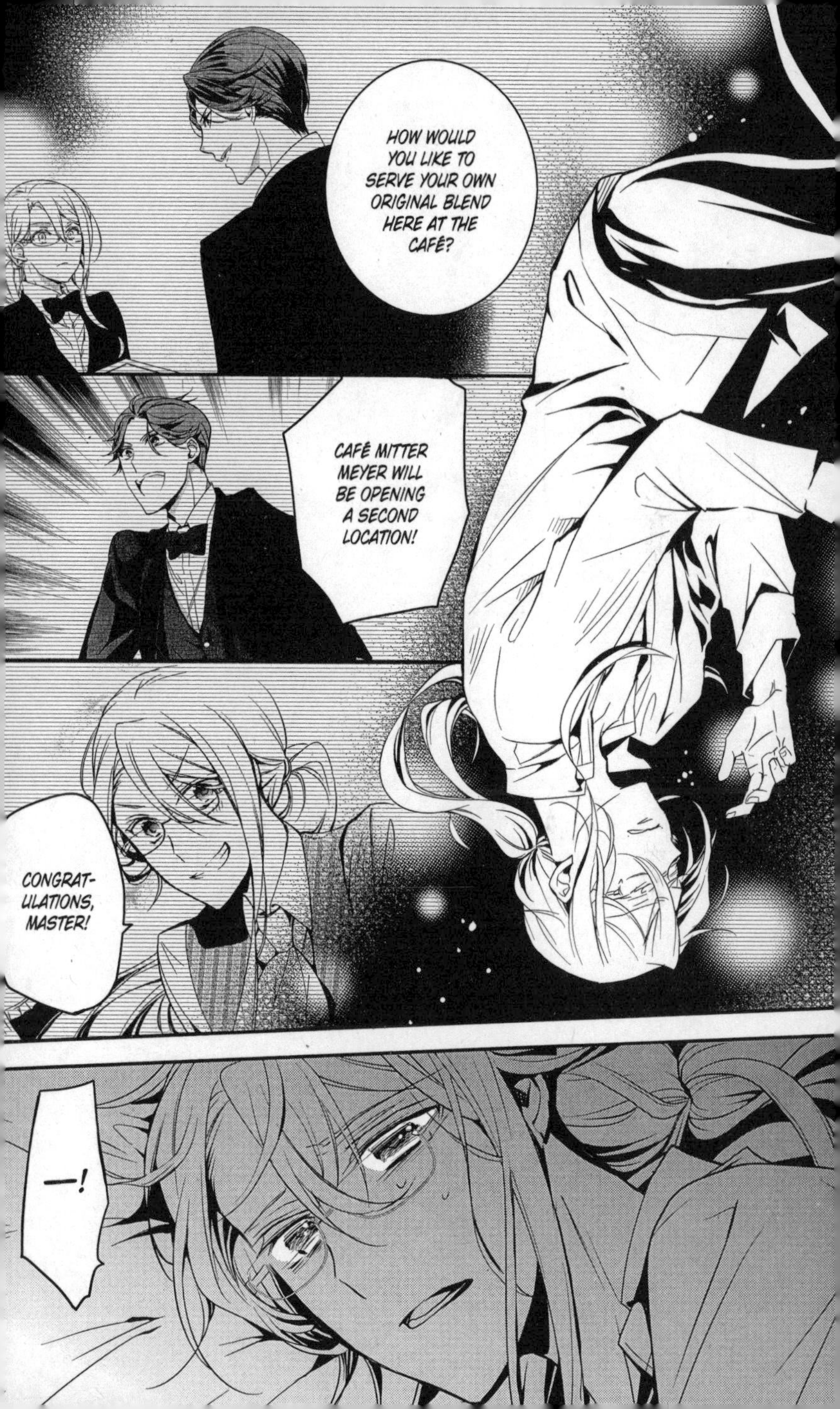
HOW WOULD YOU LIKE TO SERVE YOUR OWN ORIGINAL BLEND HERE AT THE CAFÉ?
CAFÉ MITTER MEYER WILL BE OPENING A SECOND LOCATION!
CONGRAT-ULATIONS, MASTER!
—!

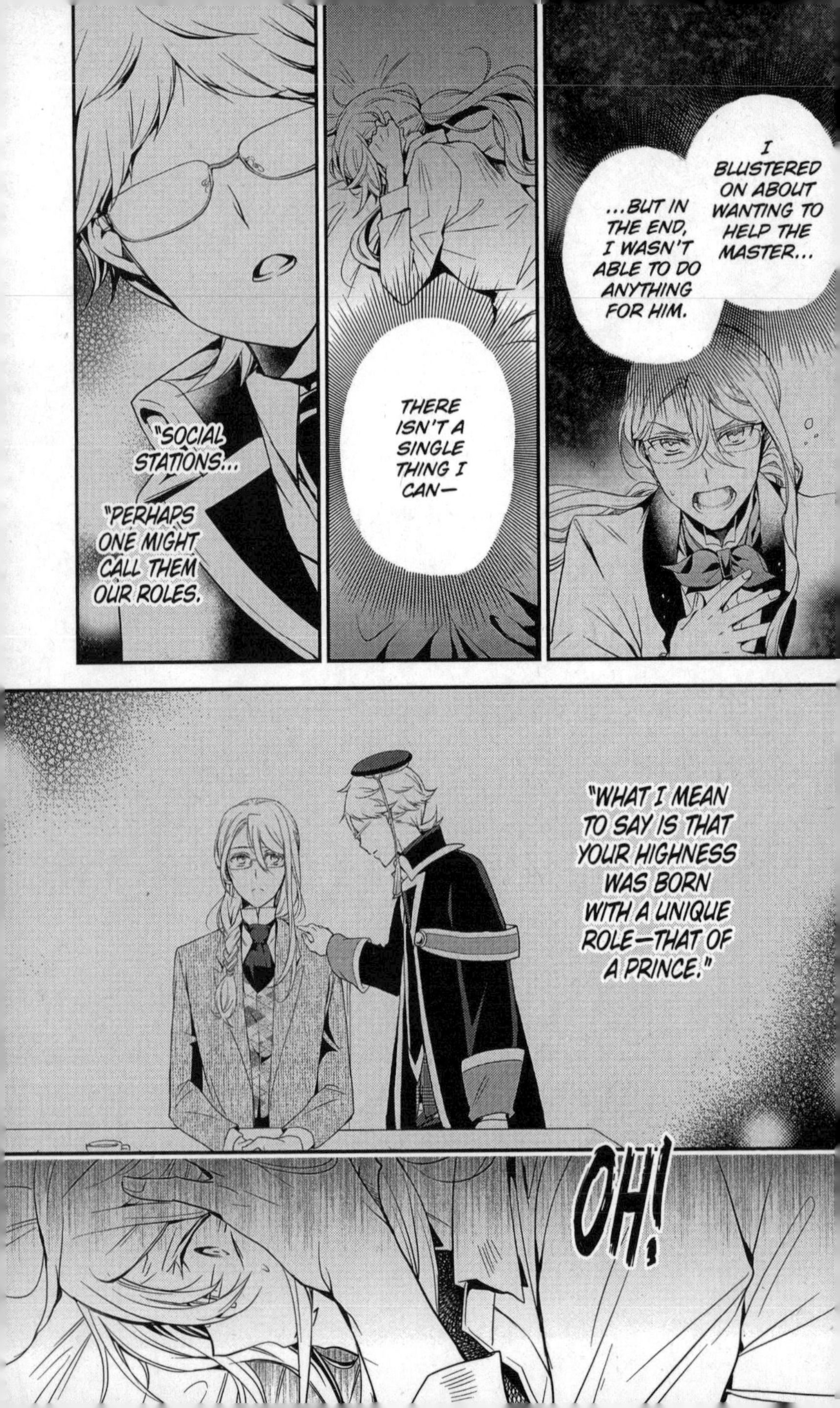
I BLUSTERED ON ABOUT WANTING TO HELP THE MASTER...
...BUT IN THE END, I WASN'T ABLE TO DO ANYTHING FOR HIM.
THERE ISN'T A SINGLE THING I CAN—
"SOCIAL STATIONS...
"PERHAPS ONE MIGHT CALL THEM OUR ROLES.
"WHAT I MEAN TO SAY IS THAT YOUR HIGHNESS WAS BORN WITH A UNIQUE ROLE—THAT OF A PRINCE."
OH!

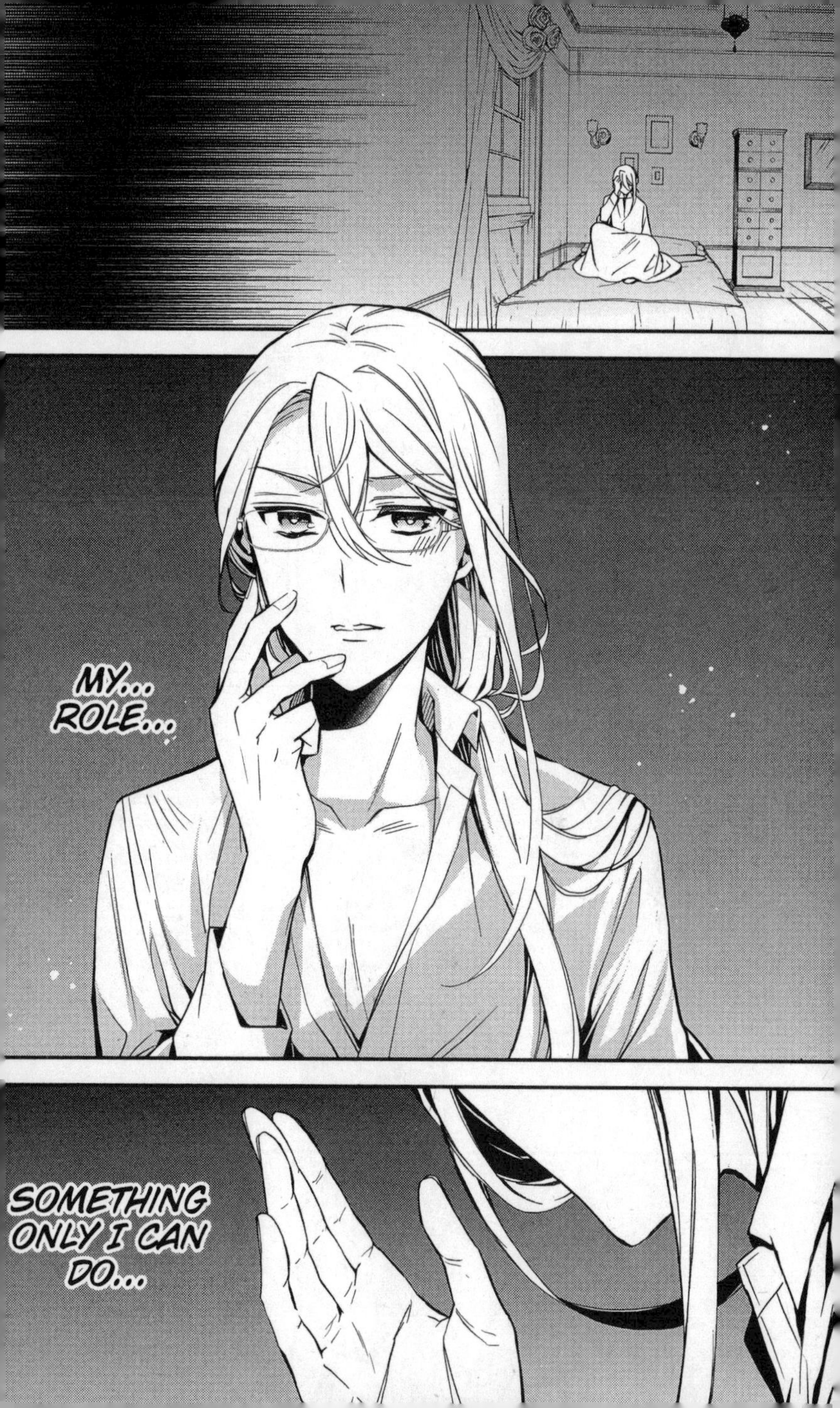
MY... ROLE...
SOMETHING ONLY I CAN DO...

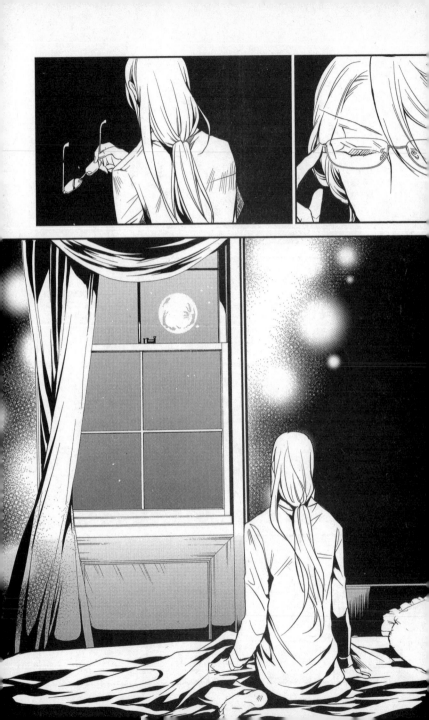

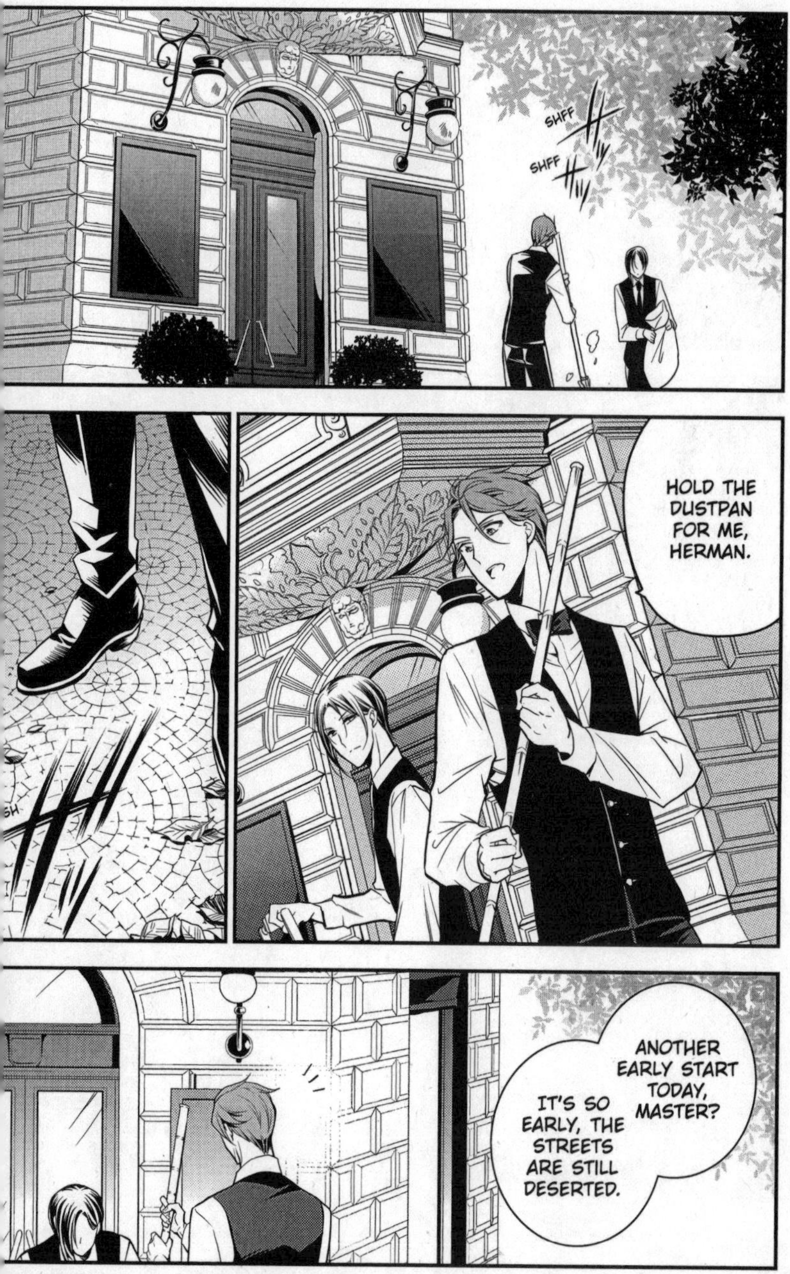
SHFF
SHFF
HOLD THE DUSTPAN FOR ME, HERMAN.
ANOTHER EARLY START TODAY, MASTER?
IT'S SO EARLY, THE STREETS ARE STILL DESERTED.

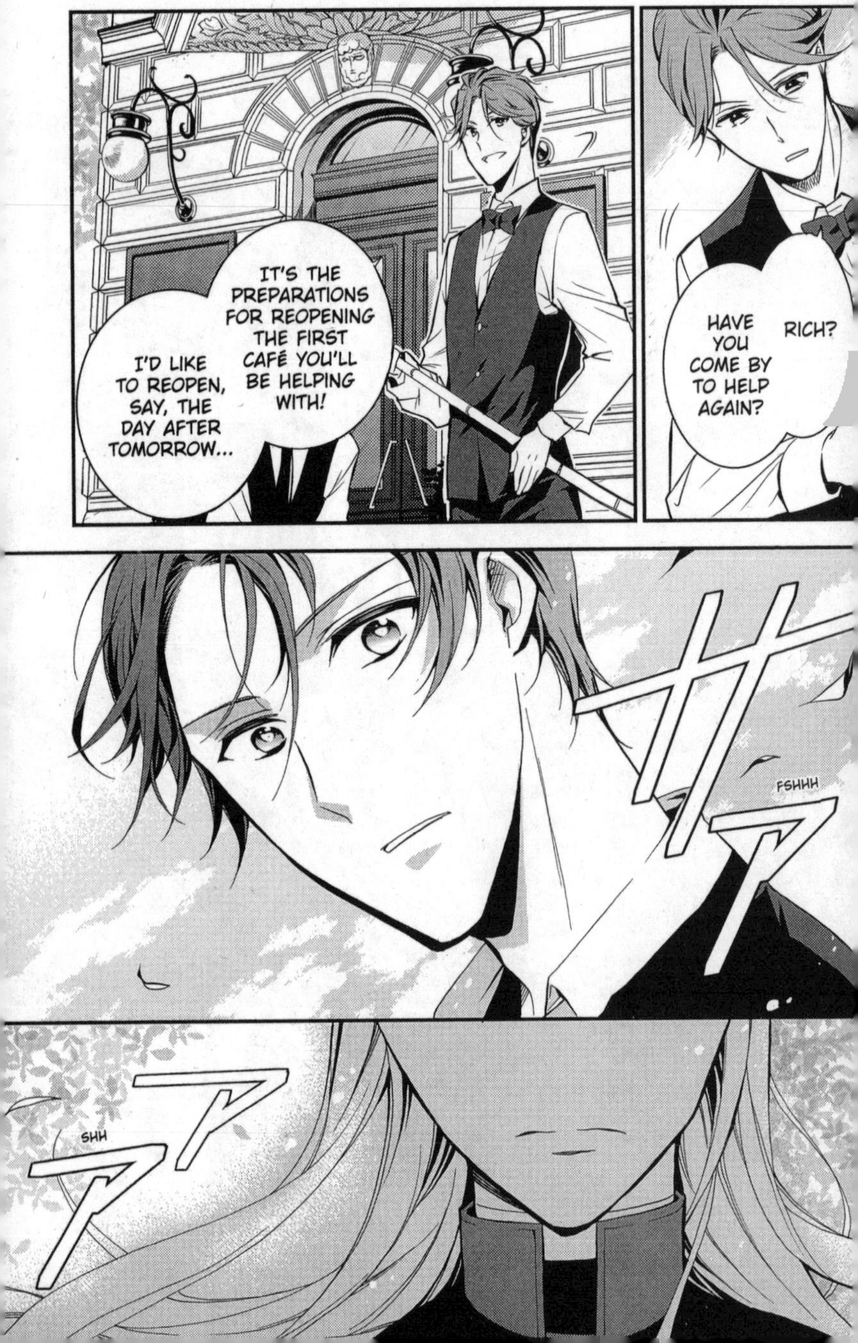
RICH?
HAVE YOU COME BY TO HELP AGAIN?
IT'S THE PREPARATIONS FOR REOPENING THE FIRST CAFÉ YOU'LL BE HELPING WITH!
I'D LIKE TO REOPEN, SAY, THE DAY AFTER TOMORROW...
FSHHH
SHH

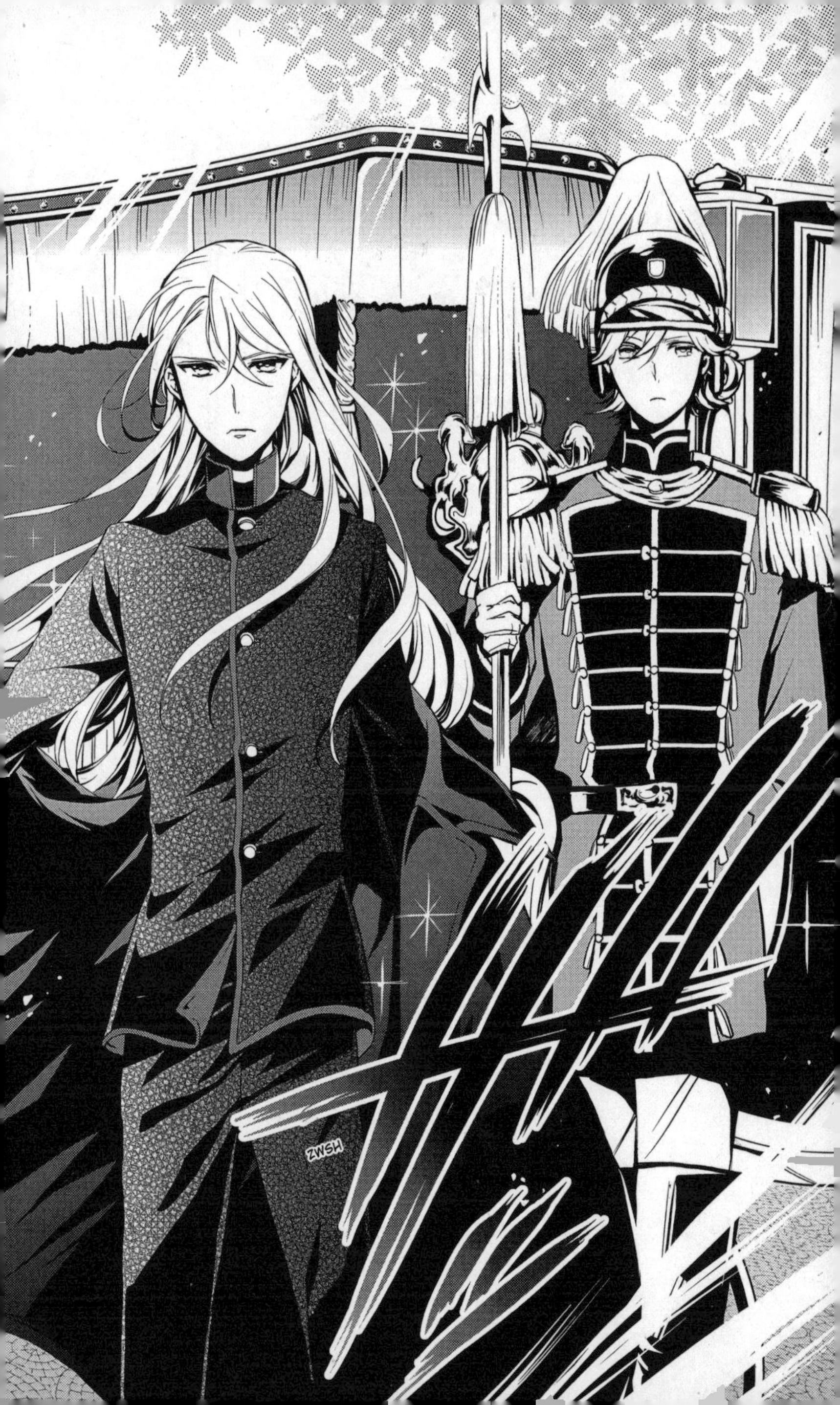
ZWSH

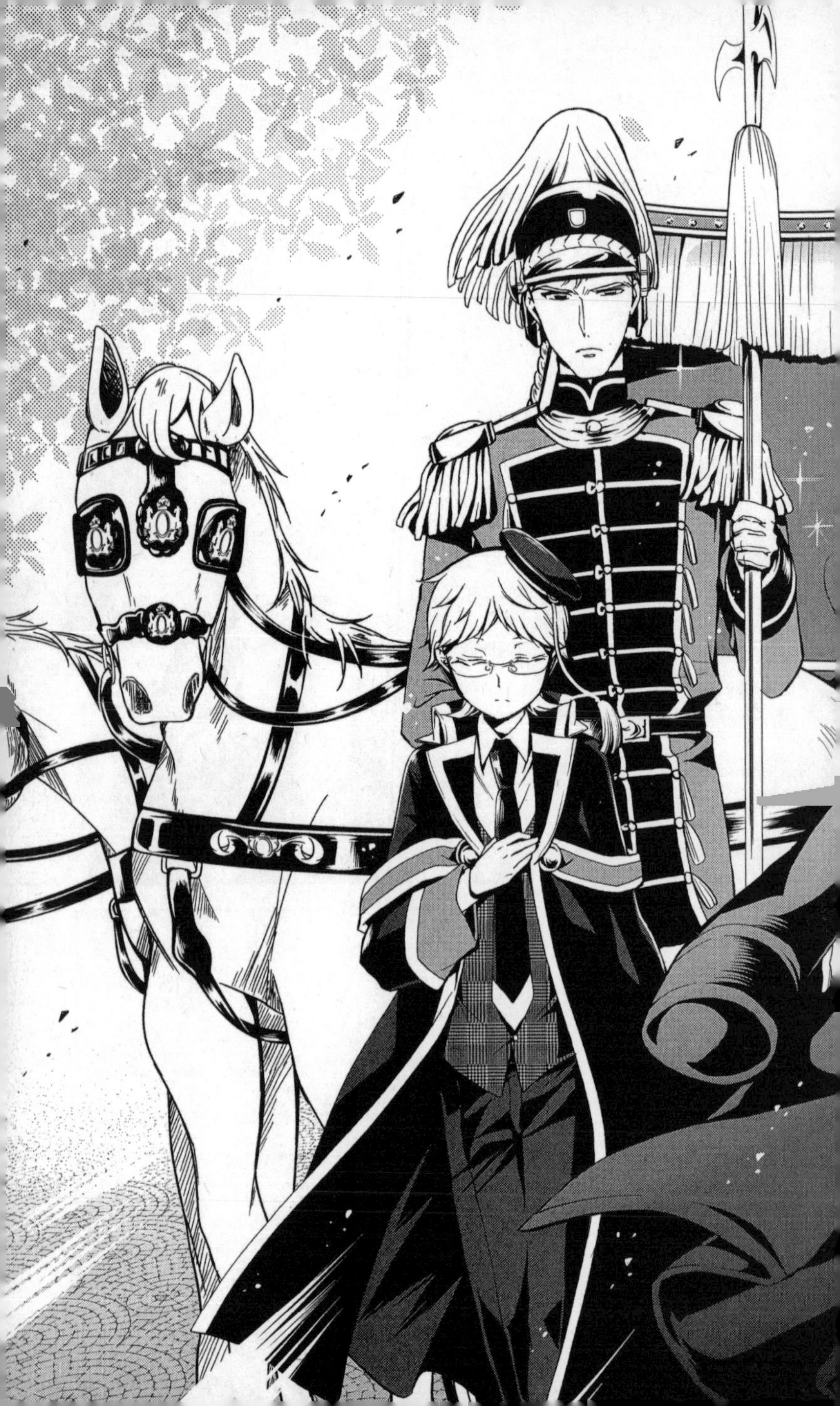

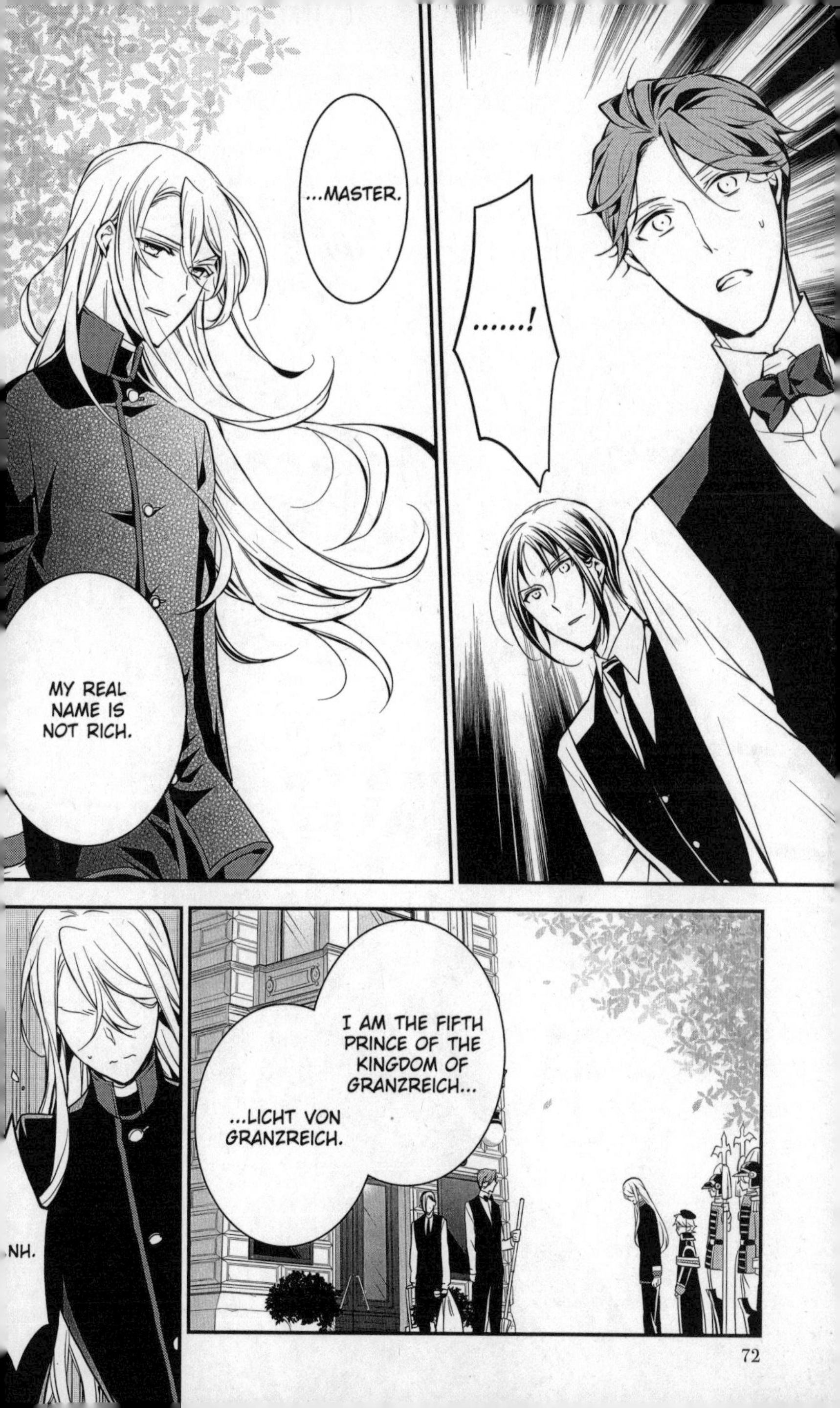
......!
...MASTER.
MY REAL NAME IS NOT RICH.
I AM THE FIFTH PRINCE OF THE KINGDOM OF GRANZREICH...
...LICHT VON GRANZREICH.
NH.

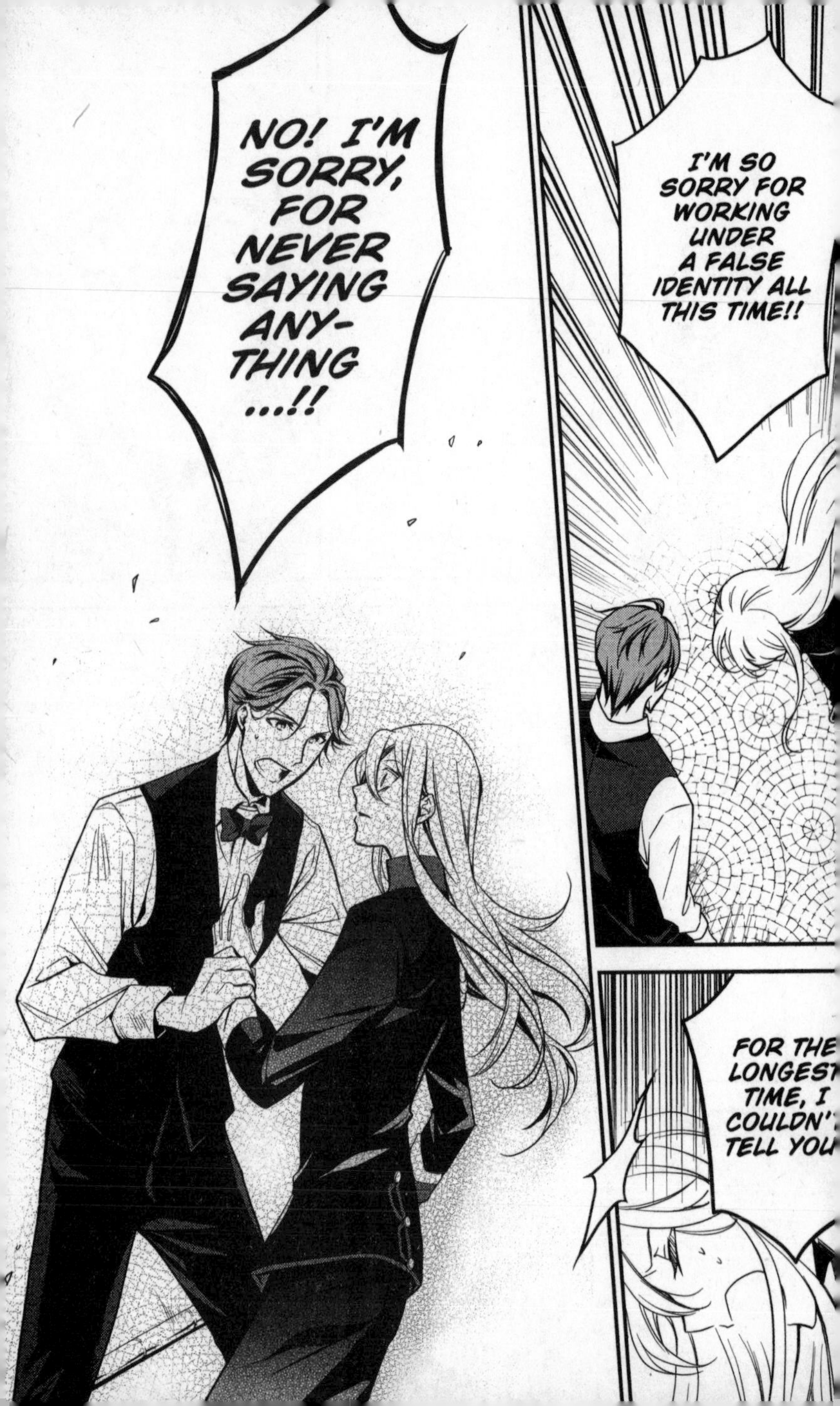
I'M SO SORRY FOR WORKING UNDER A FALSE IDENTITY ALL THIS TIME!!
FOR THE LONGES TIME, I COULDN' TELL YOU
NO! I'M SORRY, FOR NEVER SAYING ANY-THING ...!!

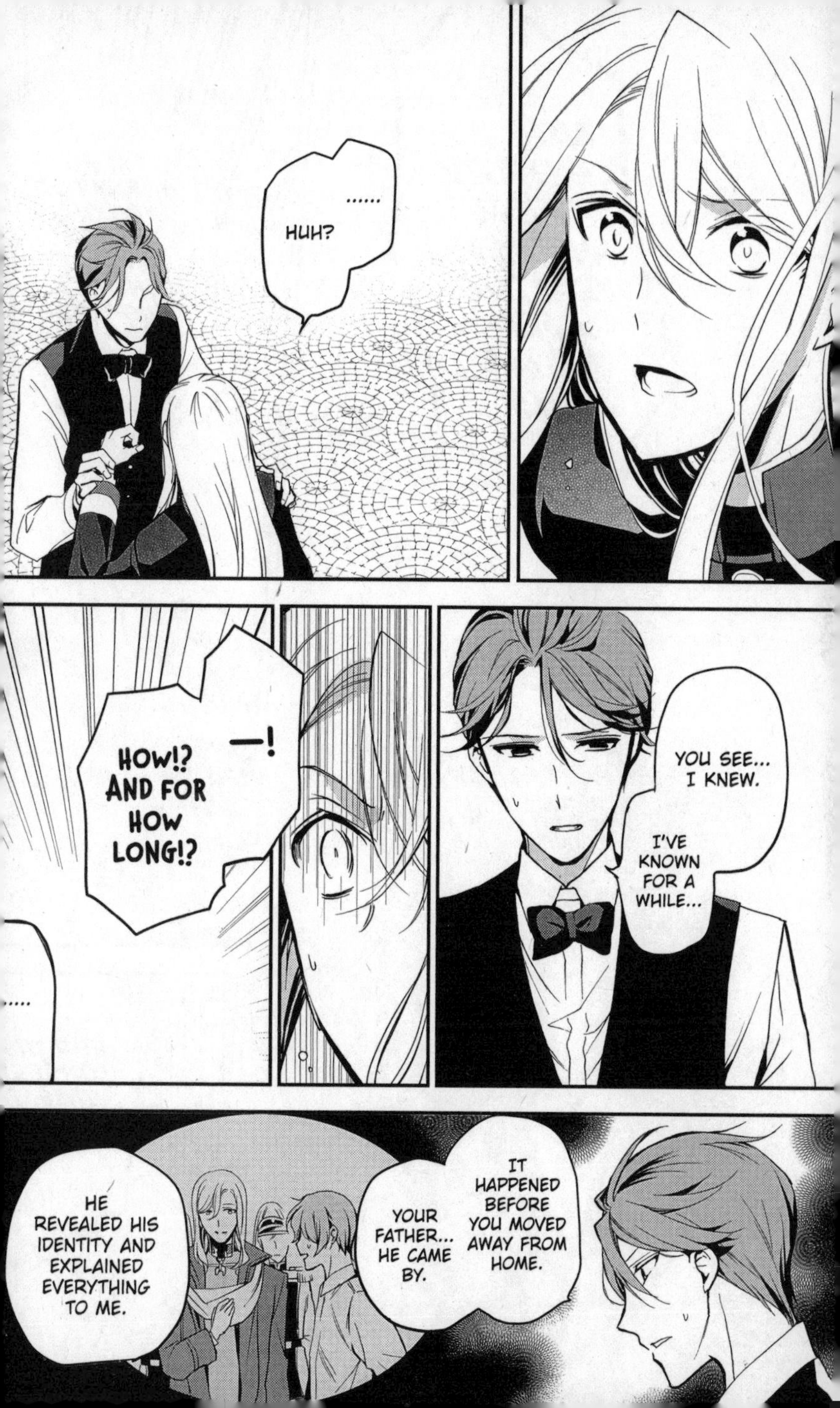
......
HUH?
YOU SEE... I KNEW.
I'VE KNOWN FOR A WHILE...
—!
HOW!? AND FOR HOW LONG!?
.....
IT HAPPENED BEFORE YOU MOVED AWAY FROM HOME.
YOUR FATHER... HE CAME BY.
HE REVEALED HIS IDENTITY AND EXPLAINED EVERYTHING TO ME.

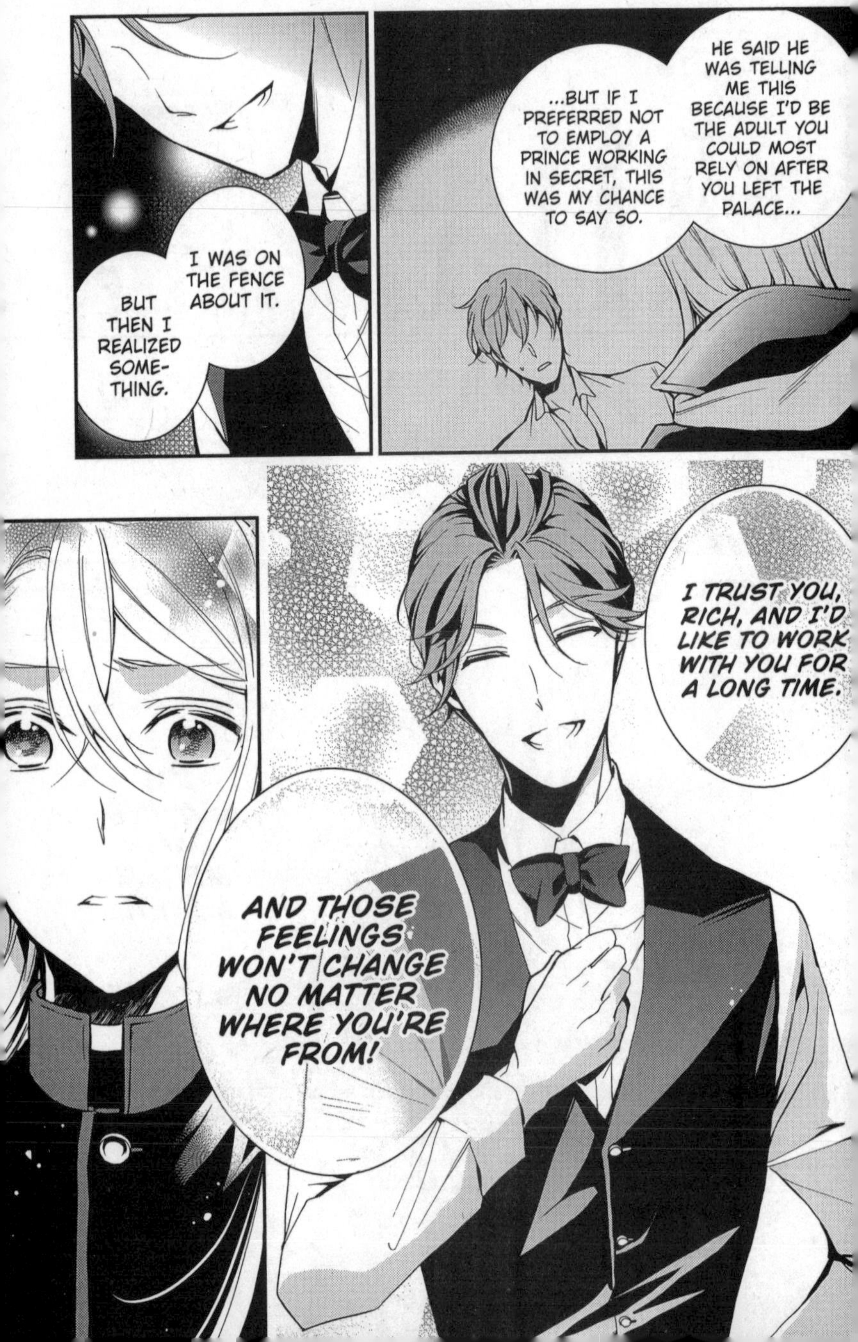
HE SAID HE WAS TELLING ME THIS BECAUSE I'D BE THE ADULT YOU COULD MOST RELY ON AFTER YOU LEFT THE PALACE...
...BUT IF I PREFERRED NOT TO EMPLOY A PRINCE WORKING IN SECRET, THIS WAS MY CHANCE TO SAY SO.
I WAS ON THE FENCE ABOUT IT.
BUT THEN I REALIZED SOME-THING.
I TRUST YOU, RICH, AND I'D LIKE TO WORK WITH YOU FOR A LONG TIME.
AND THOSE FEELINGS WON'T CHANGE NO MATTER WHERE YOU'RE FROM!

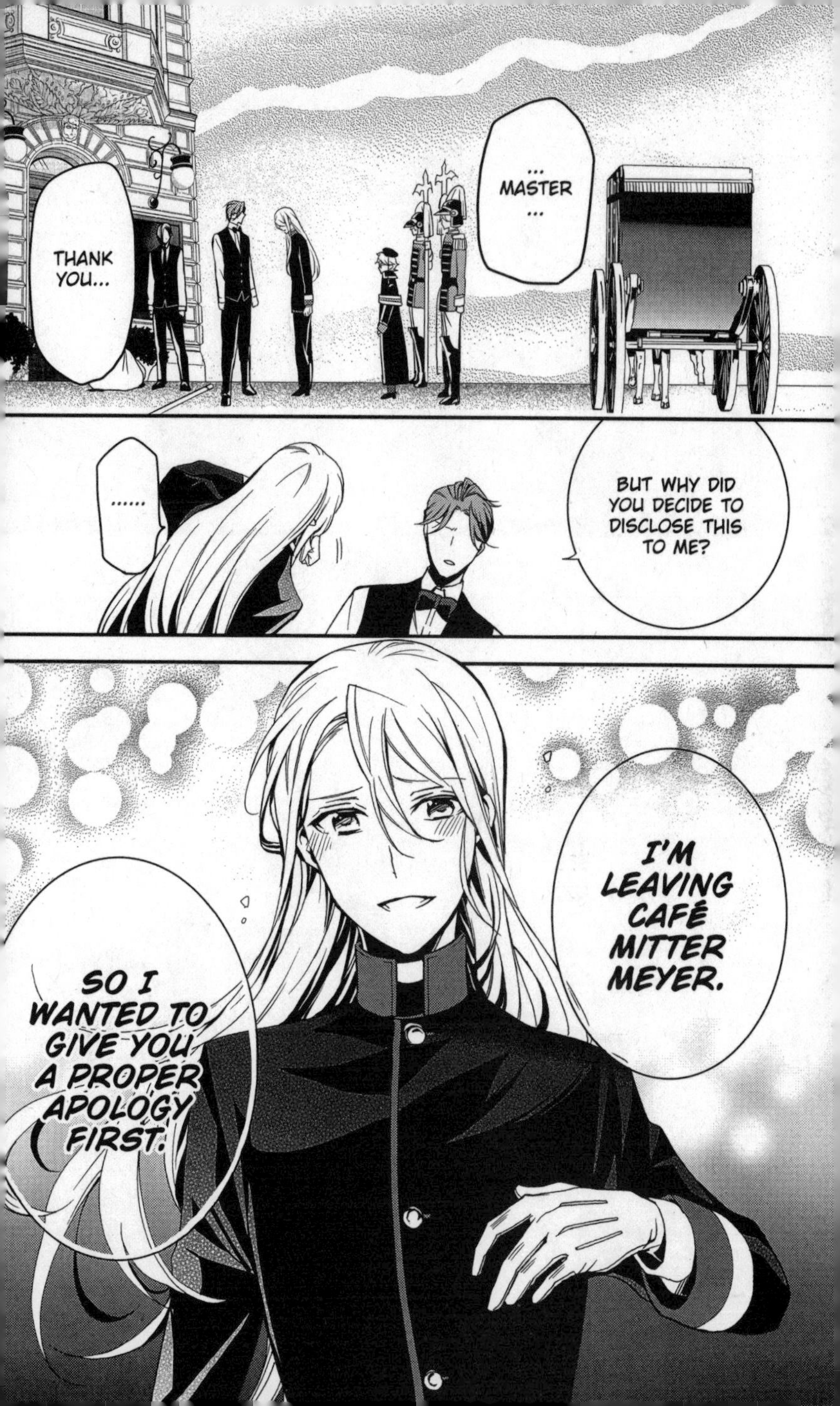
... MASTER ...
THANK YOU...
BUT WHY DID YOU DECIDE TO DISCLOSE THIS TO ME?
......
I'M LEAVING CAFÉ MITTER MEYER.
SO I WANTED TO GIVE YOU A PROPER APOLOGY FIRST.

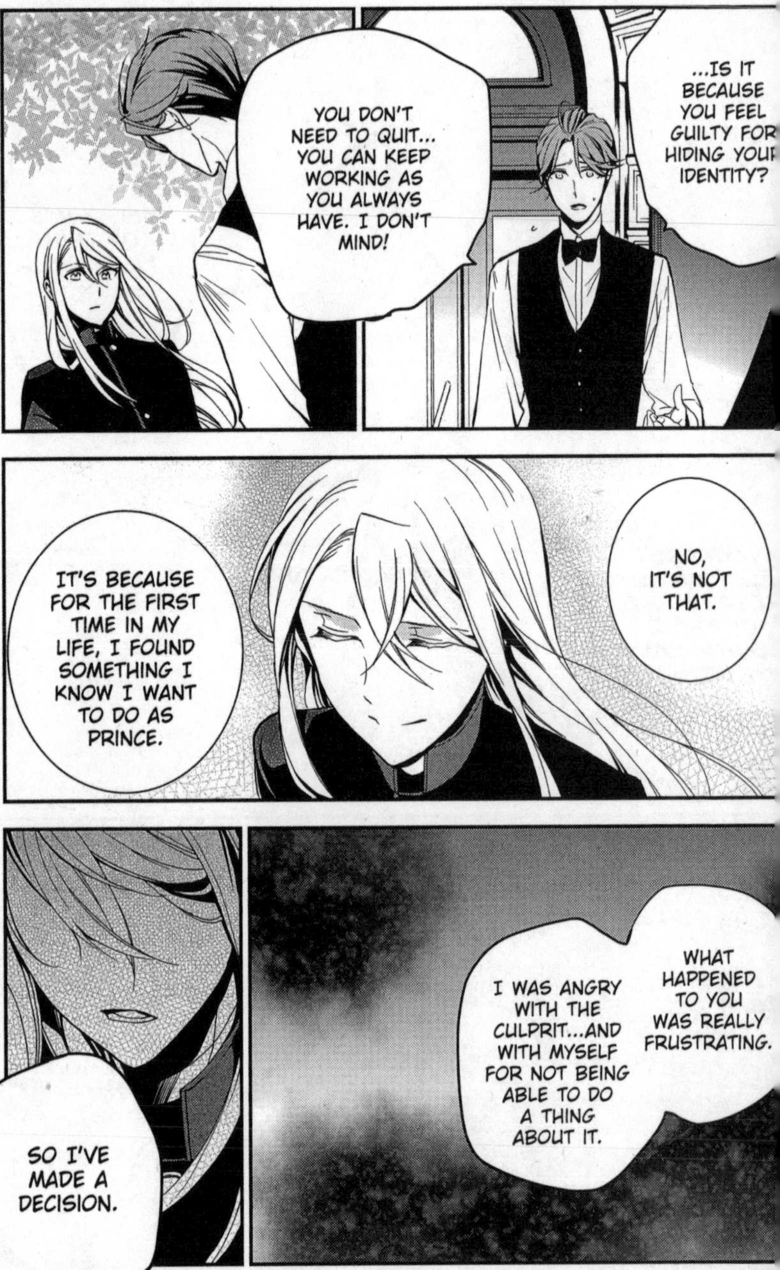
...IS IT BECAUSE YOU FEEL GUILTY FOR HIDING YOUR IDENTITY?
YOU DON'T NEED TO QUIT... YOU CAN KEEP WORKING AS YOU ALWAYS HAVE. I DON'T MIND!
NO, IT'S NOT THAT.
IT'S BECAUSE FOR THE FIRST TIME IN MY LIFE, I FOUND SOMETHING I KNOW I WANT TO DO AS PRINCE.
WHAT HAPPENED TO YOU WAS REALLY FRUSTRATING.
I WAS ANGRY WITH THE CULPRIT...AND WITH MYSELF FOR NOT BEING ABLE TO DO A THING ABOUT IT.
SO I'VE MADE A DECISION.

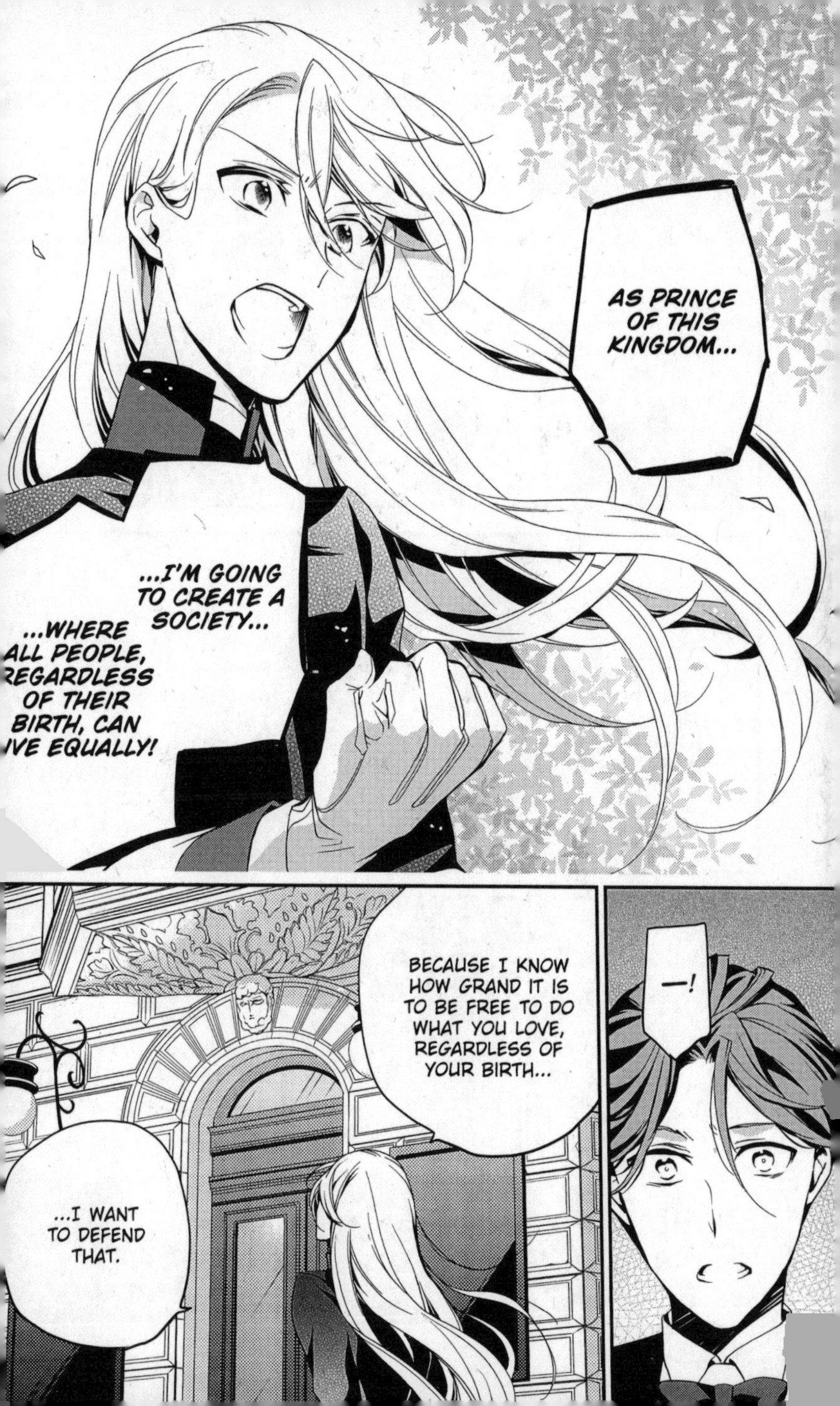
AS PRINCE OF THIS KINGDOM...
...I'M GOING TO CREATE A SOCIETY...
...WHERE ALL PEOPLE, EGARDLESS OF THEIR BIRTH, CAN IVE EQUALLY!
—!
BECAUSE I KNOW HOW GRAND IT IS TO BE FREE TO DO WHAT YOU LOVE, REGARDLESS OF YOUR BIRTH...
...I WANT TO DEFEND THAT.

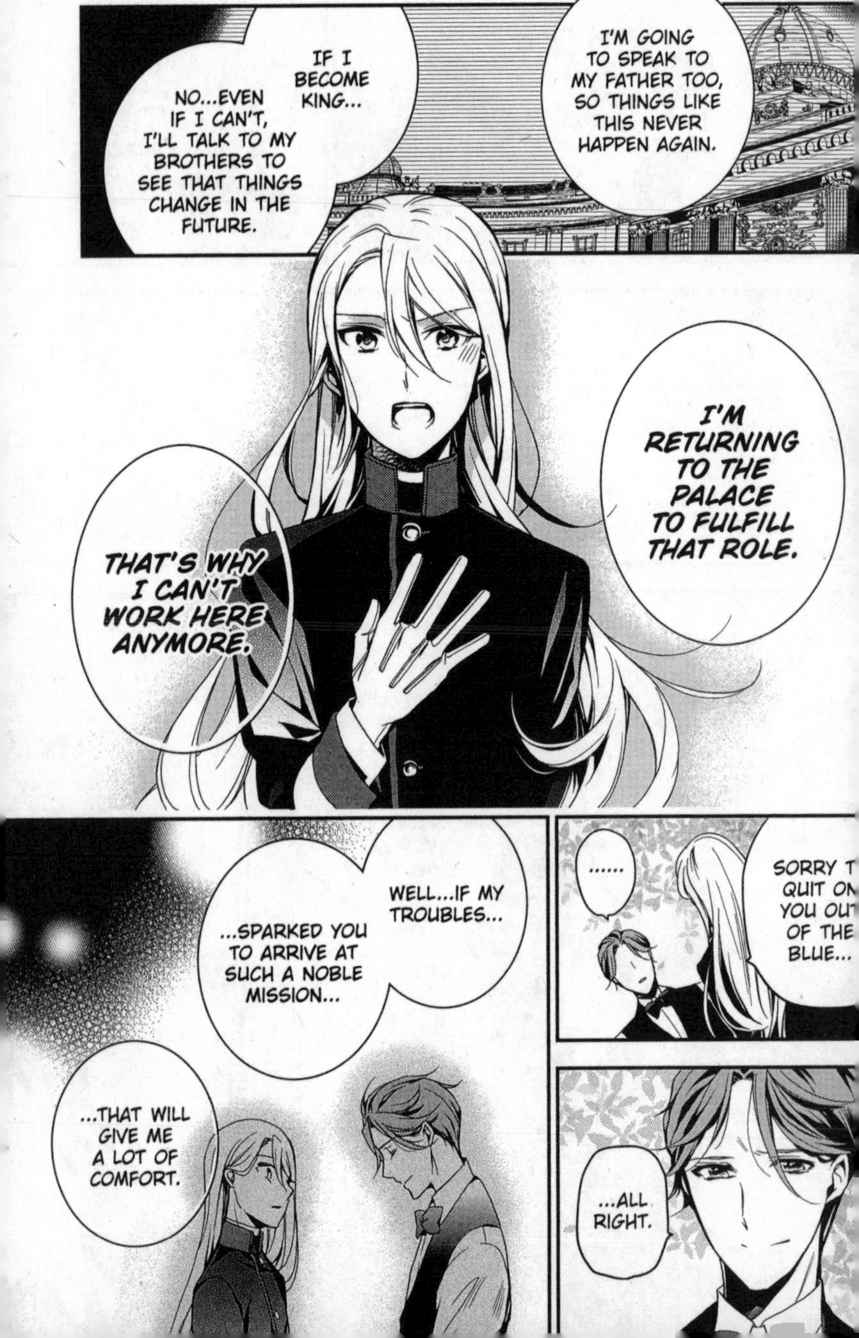
I'M GOING TO SPEAK TO MY FATHER TOO, SO THINGS LIKE THIS NEVER HAPPEN AGAIN.
IF I BECOME KING...
NO...EVEN IF I CAN'T, I'LL TALK TO MY BROTHERS TO SEE THAT THINGS CHANGE IN THE FUTURE.
I'M RETURNING TO THE PALACE TO FULFILL THAT ROLE.
THAT'S WHY I CAN'T WORK HERE ANYMORE.
SORRY T QUIT ON YOU OUT OF THE BLUE...
......
...ALL RIGHT.
WELL...IF MY TROUBLES...
...SPARKED YOU TO ARRIVE AT SUCH A NOBLE MISSION...
...THAT WILL GIVE ME A LOT OF COMFORT.

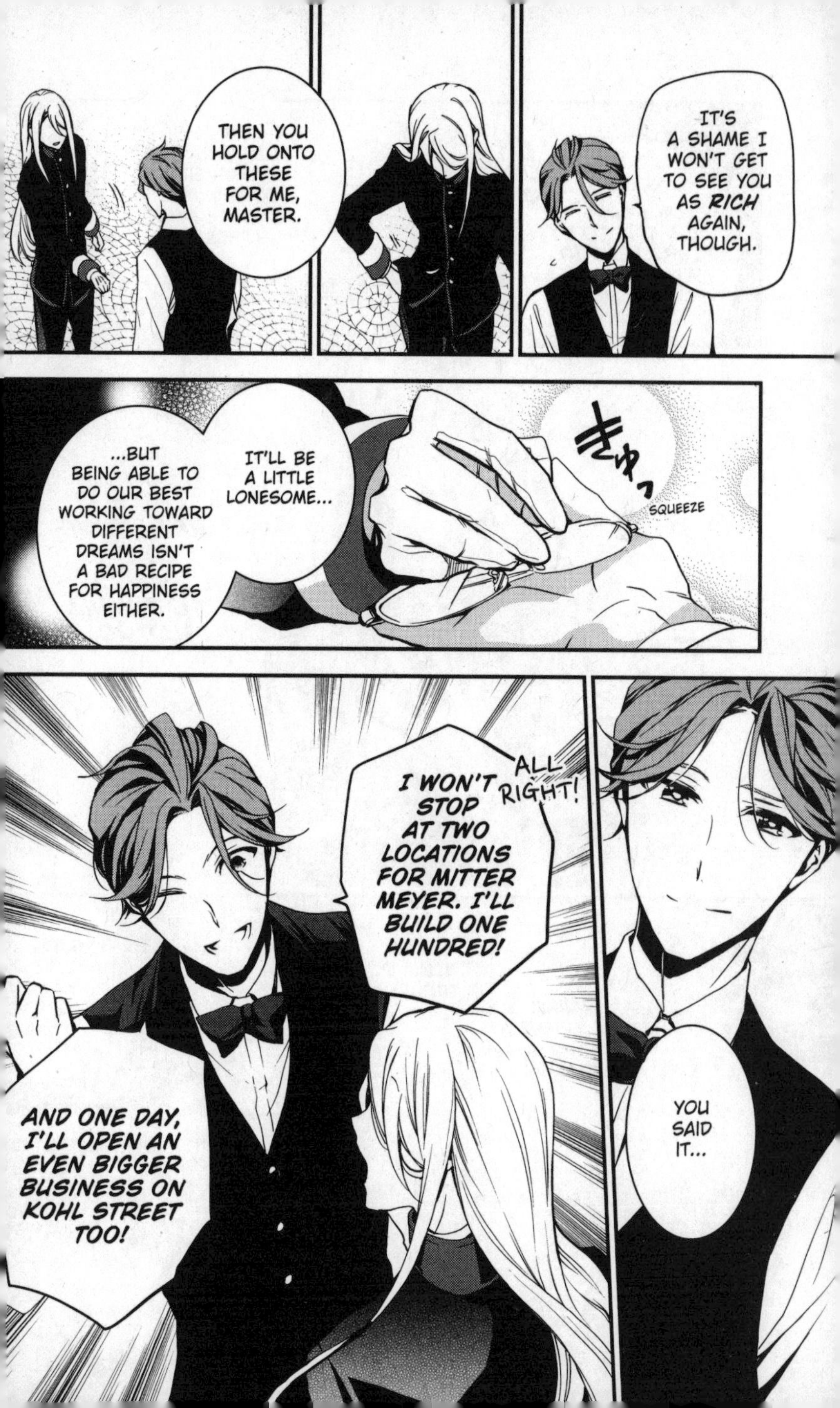
IT'S A SHAME I WON'T GET TO SEE YOU AS RICH AGAIN, THOUGH.
THEN YOU HOLD ONTO THESE FOR ME, MASTER.
きゅっ
SQUEEZE
IT'LL BE A LITTLE LONESOME...
...BUT BEING ABLE TO DO OUR BEST WORKING TOWARD DIFFERENT DREAMS ISN'T A BAD RECIPE FOR HAPPINESS EITHER.
YOU SAID IT...
ALL RIGHT!
I WON'T STOP AT TWO LOCATIONS FOR MITTER MEYER. I'LL BUILD ONE HUNDRED!
AND ONE DAY, I'LL OPEN AN EVEN BIGGER BUSINESS ON KOHL STREET TOO!

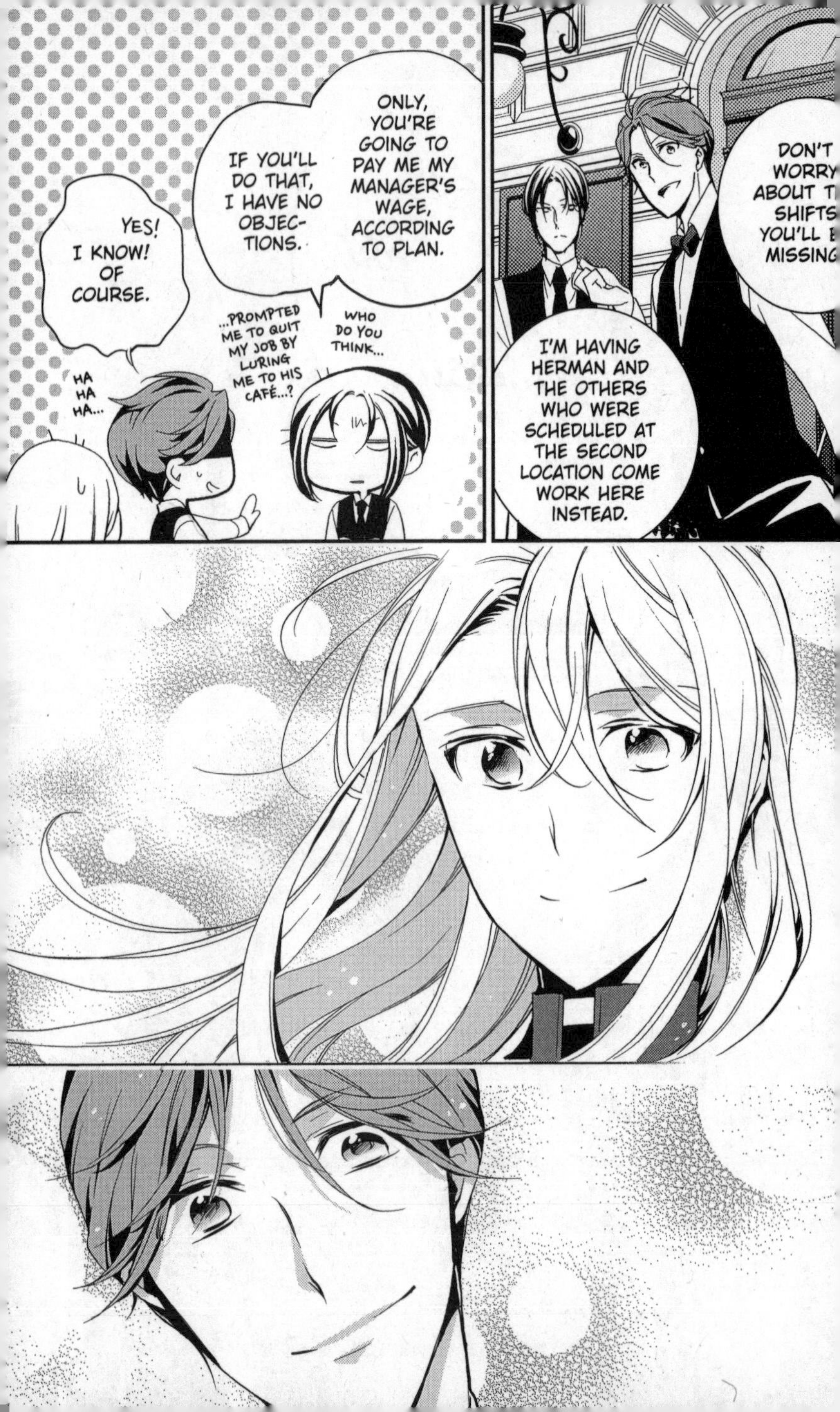

DON'T WORRY ABOUT T SHIFTS YOU'LL B MISSING
I'M HAVING HERMAN AND THE OTHERS WHO WERE SCHEDULED AT THE SECOND LOCATION COME WORK HERE INSTEAD.
ONLY, YOU'RE GOING TO PAY ME MY MANAGER'S WAGE, ACCORDING TO PLAN.
IF YOU'LL DO THAT, I HAVE NO OBJECTIONS.
WHO DO YOU THINK...
...PROMPTED ME TO QUIT MY JOB BY LURING ME TO HIS CAFÉ...?
YES! I KNOW! OF COURSE.
HA HA HA...

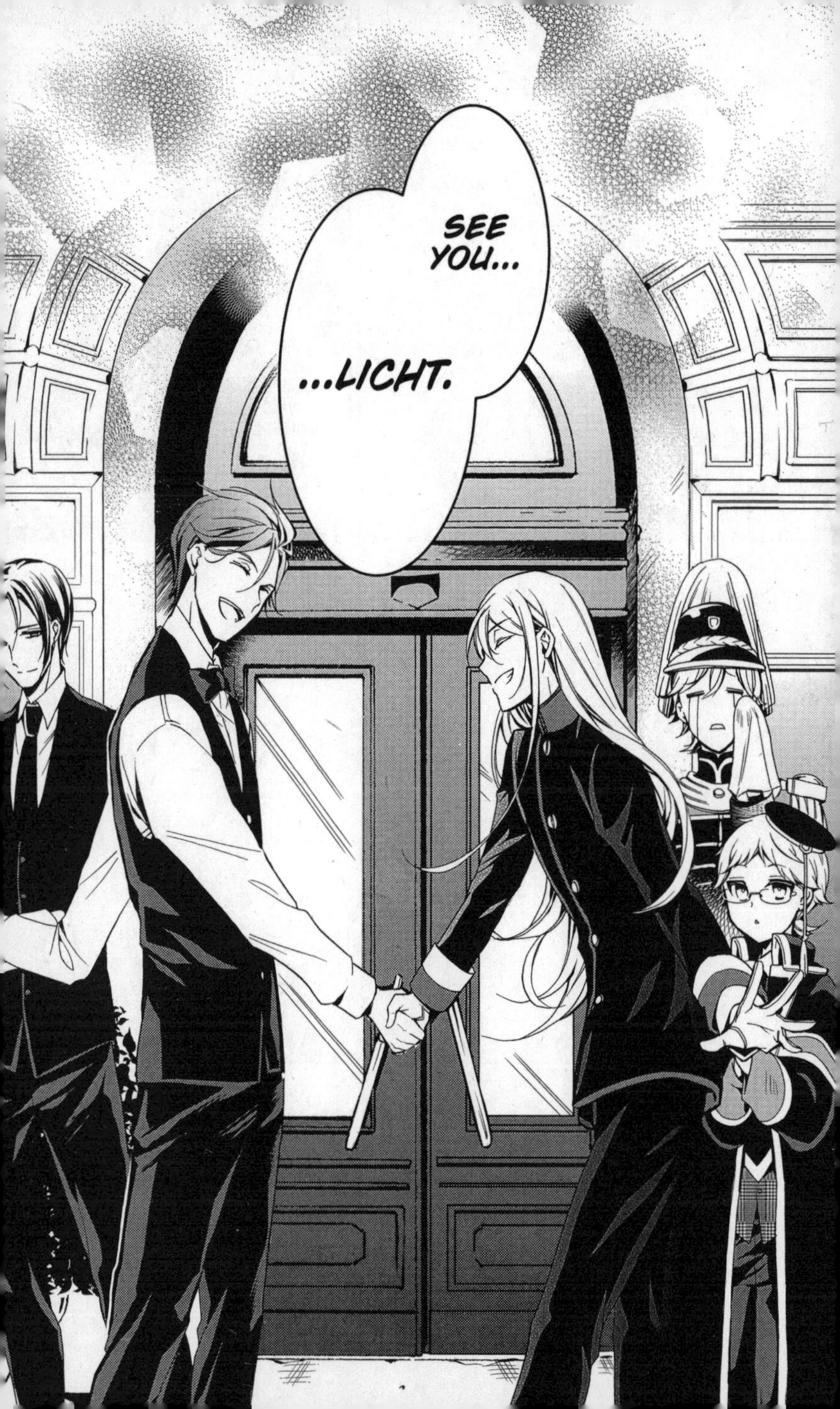
SEE YOU...
...LICHT.

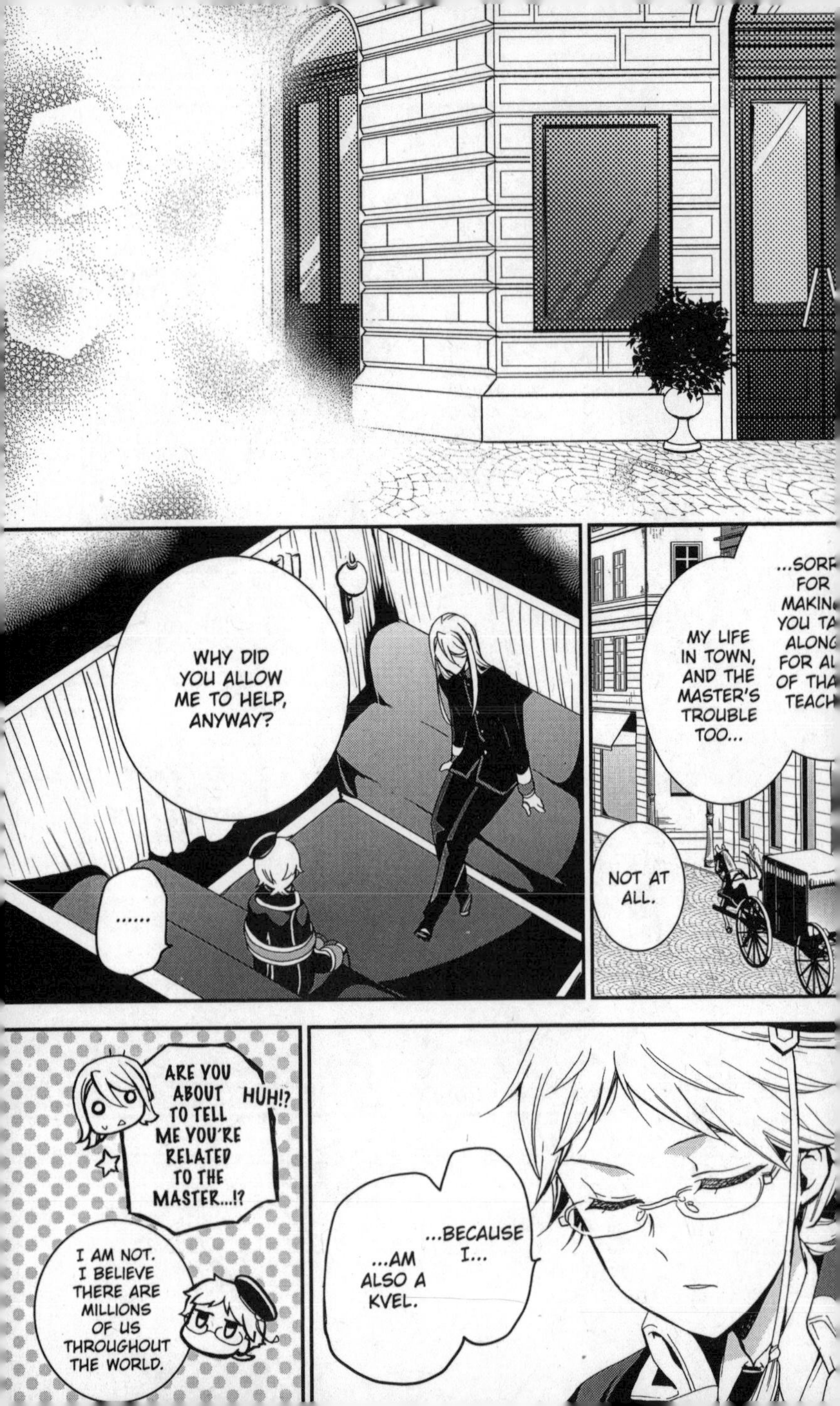
...SORR FOR MAKIN YOU TA ALONG FOR AL OF THA TEACH
MY LIFE IN TOWN, AND THE MASTER'S TROUBLE TOO...
NOT AT ALL.
WHY DID YOU ALLOW ME TO HELP, ANYWAY?
......
...BECAUSE I...
...AM ALSO A KVEL.
HUH!?
ARE YOU ABOUT TO TELL ME YOU'RE RELATED TO THE MASTER...!?
I AM NOT. I BELIEVE THERE ARE MILLIONS OF US THROUGHOUT THE WORLD.

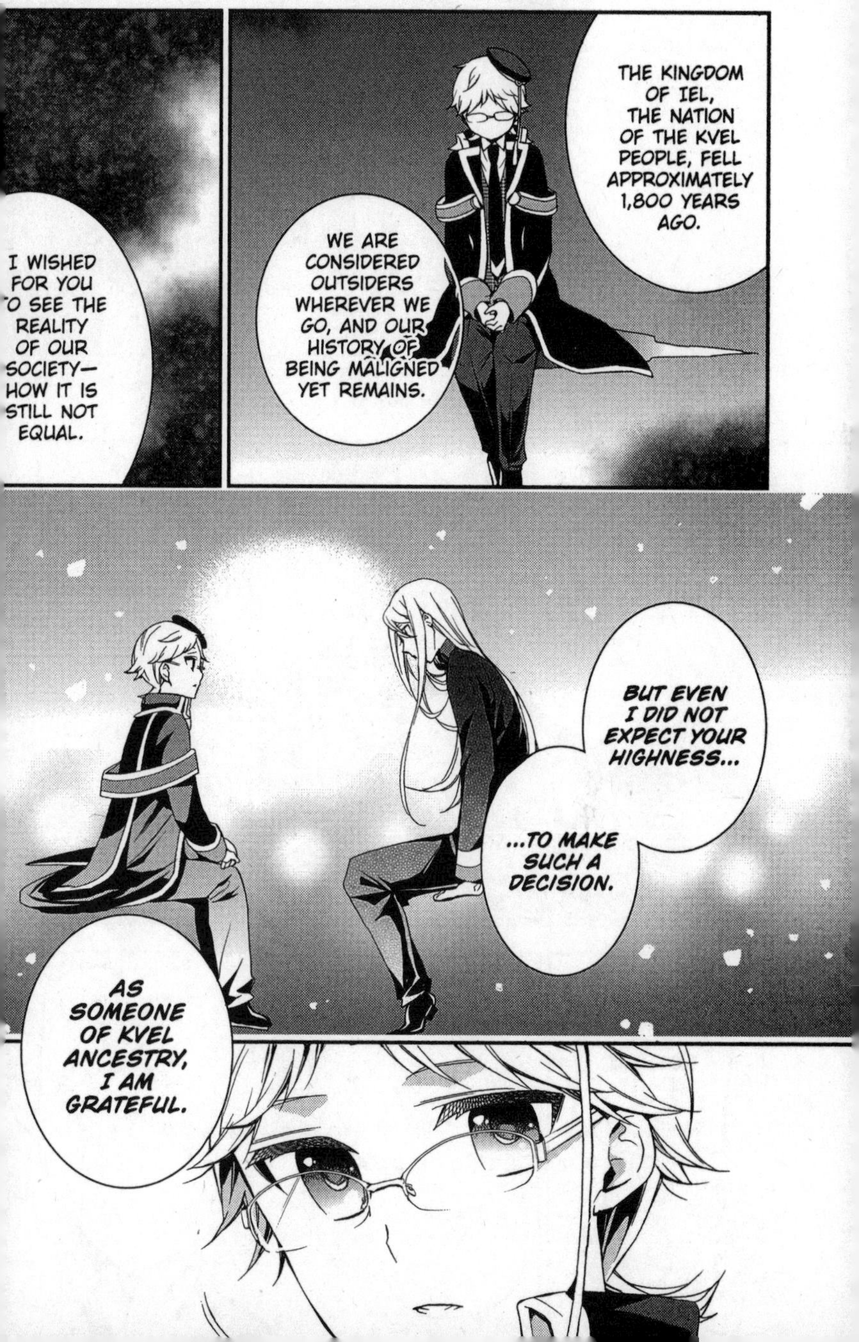
THE KINGDOM OF IEL, THE NATION OF THE KVEL PEOPLE, FELL APPROXIMATELY 1,800 YEARS AGO.
WE ARE CONSIDERED OUTSIDERS WHEREVER WE GO, AND OUR HISTORY OF BEING MALIGNED YET REMAINS.
I WISHED FOR YOU TO SEE THE REALITY OF OUR SOCIETY—HOW IT IS STILL NOT EQUAL.
BUT EVEN I DID NOT EXPECT YOUR HIGHNESS...
...TO MAKE SUCH A DECISION.
AS SOMEONE OF KVEL ANCESTRY, I AM GRATEFUL.

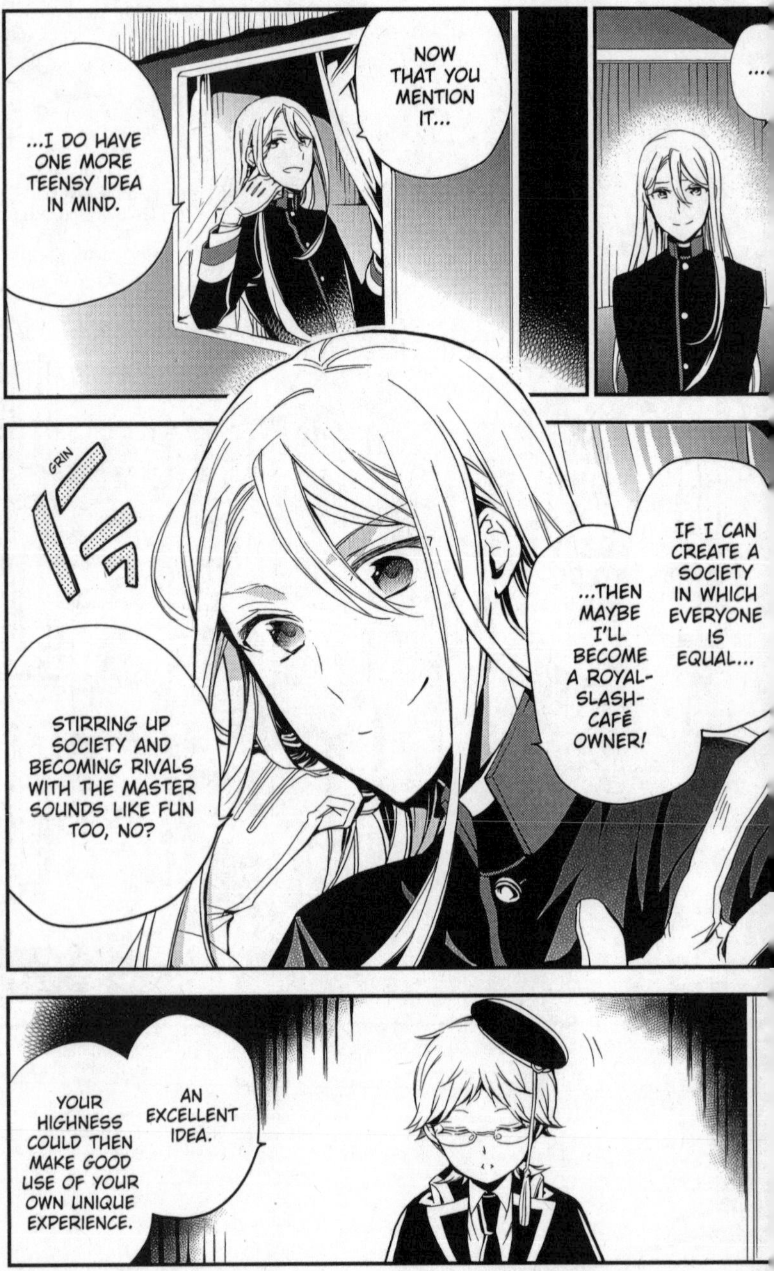
....
NOW THAT YOU MENTION IT...
...I DO HAVE ONE MORE TEENSY IDEA IN MIND.
IF I CAN CREATE A SOCIETY IN WHICH EVERYONE IS EQUAL...
...THEN MAYBE I'LL BECOME A ROYAL-SLASH-CAFÉ OWNER!
GRIN
STIRRING UP SOCIETY AND BECOMING RIVALS WITH THE MASTER SOUNDS LIKE FUN TOO, NO?
AN EXCELLENT IDEA.
YOUR HIGHNESS COULD THEN MAKE GOOD USE OF YOUR OWN UNIQUE EXPERIENCE.

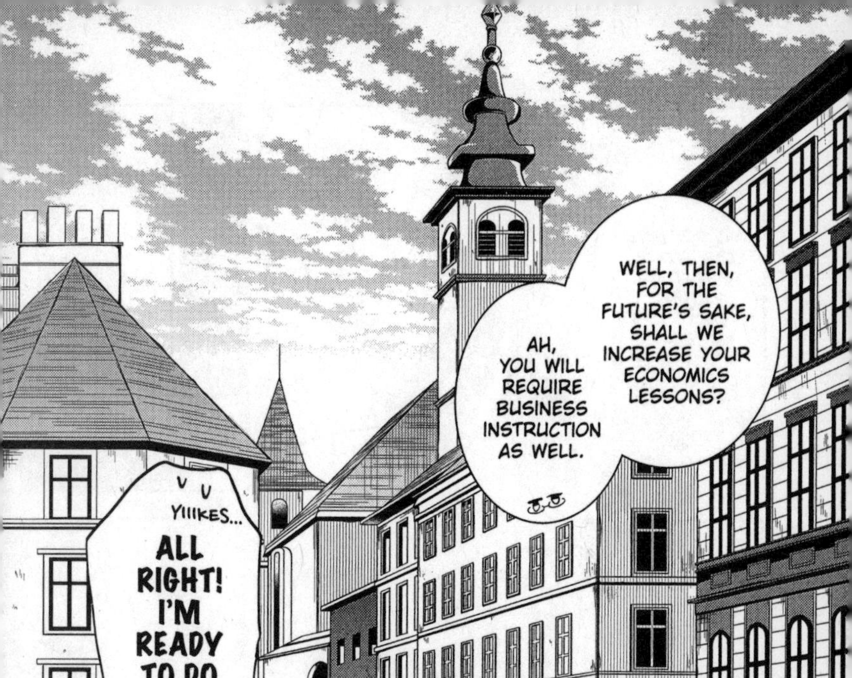
WELL, THEN, FOR THE FUTURE'S SAKE, SHALL WE INCREASE YOUR ECONOMICS LESSONS?
AH, YOU WILL REQUIRE BUSINESS INSTRUCTION AS WELL.
YIIIKES...
ALL RIGHT! I'M READY TO DO THIS!

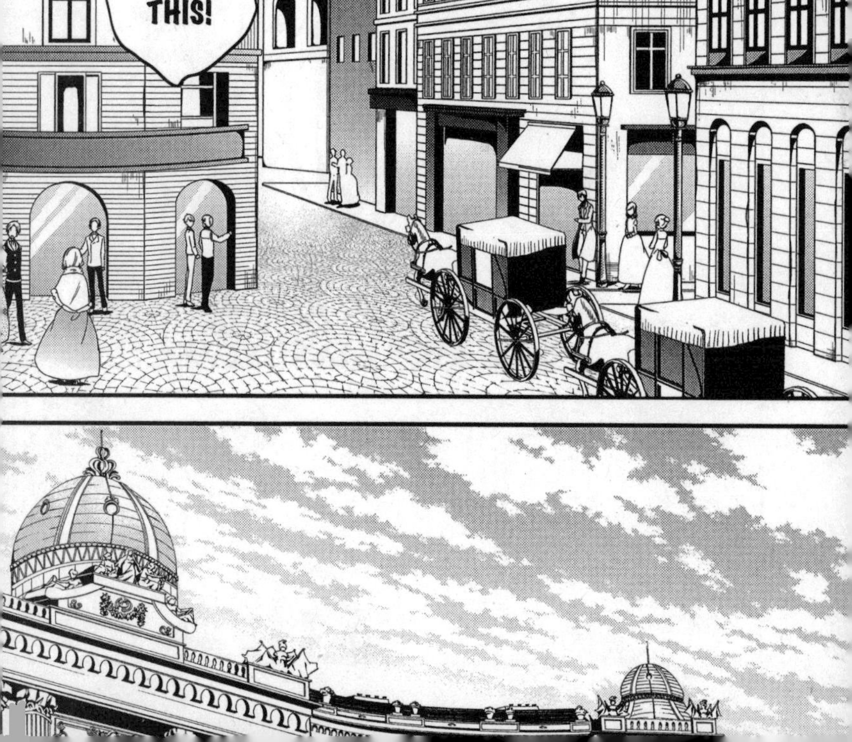

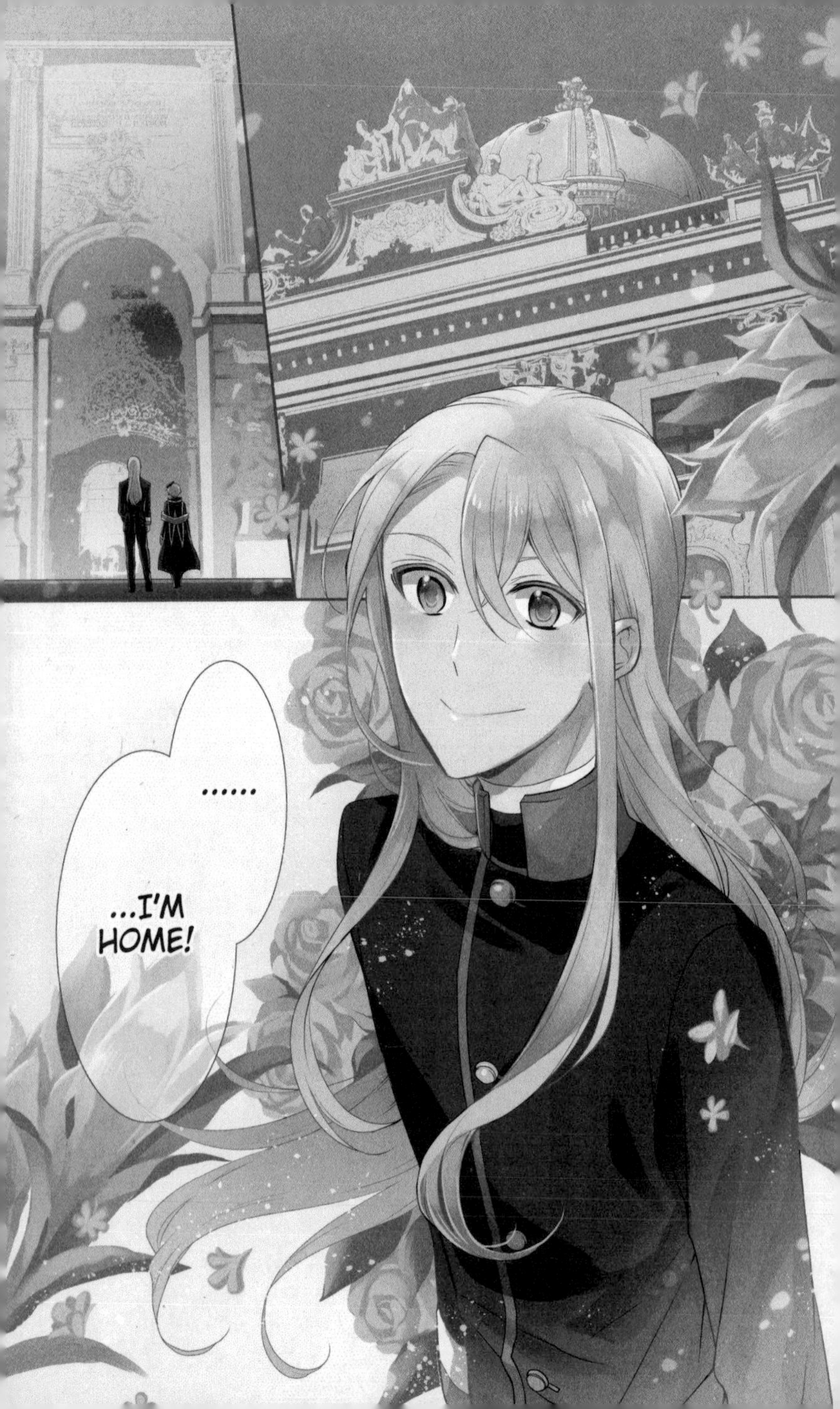

......
...I'M HOME!

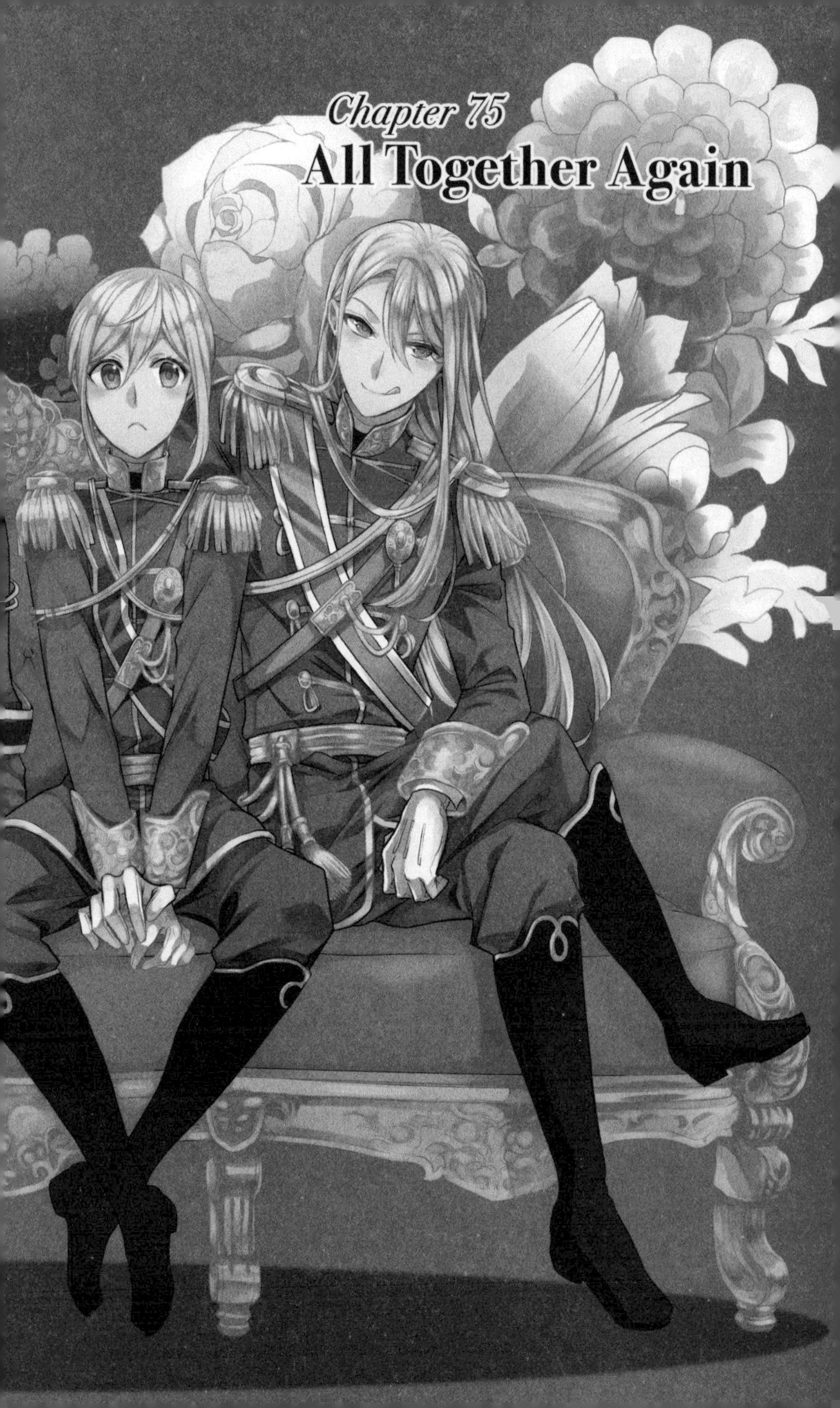
Chapter 75
All Together Again

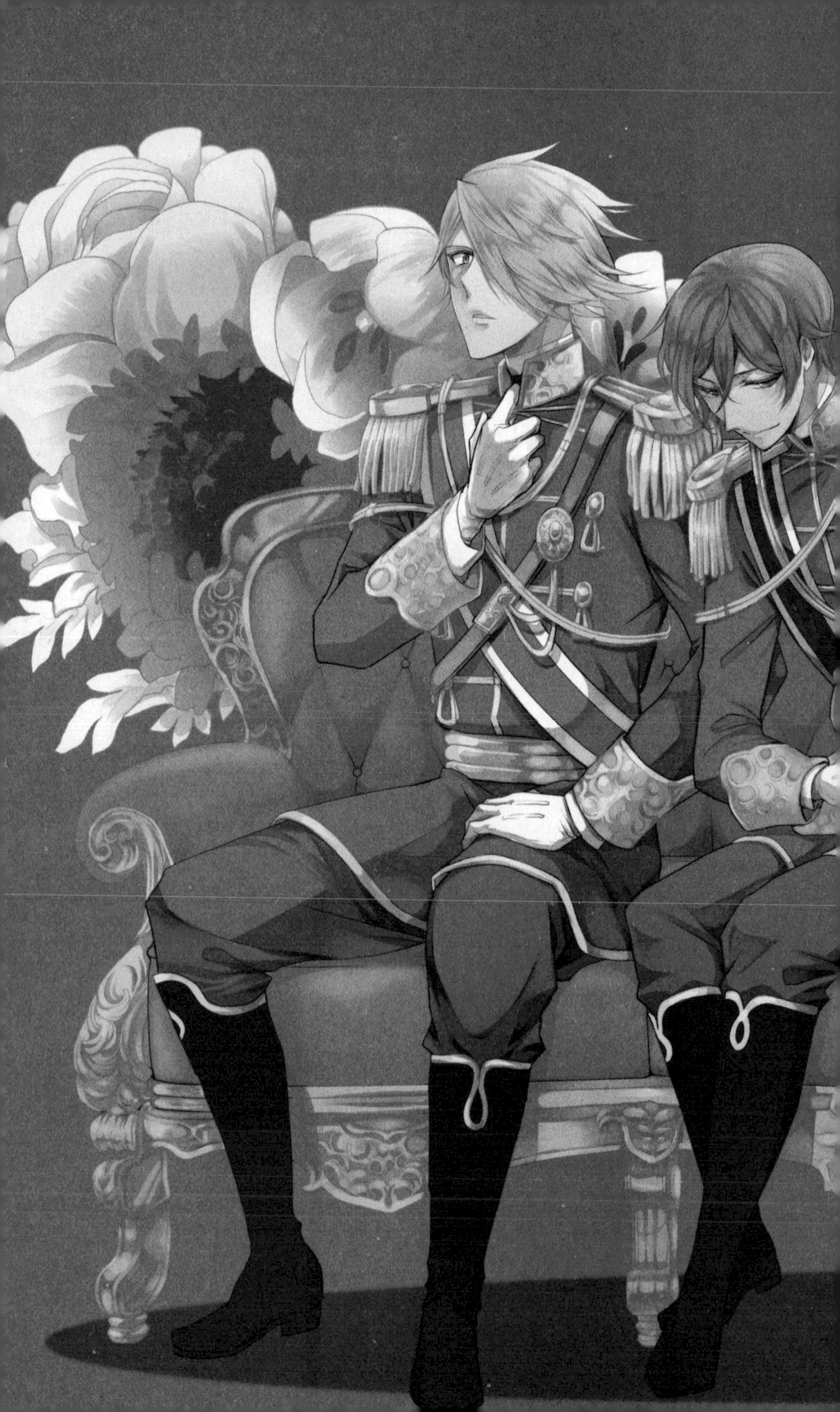

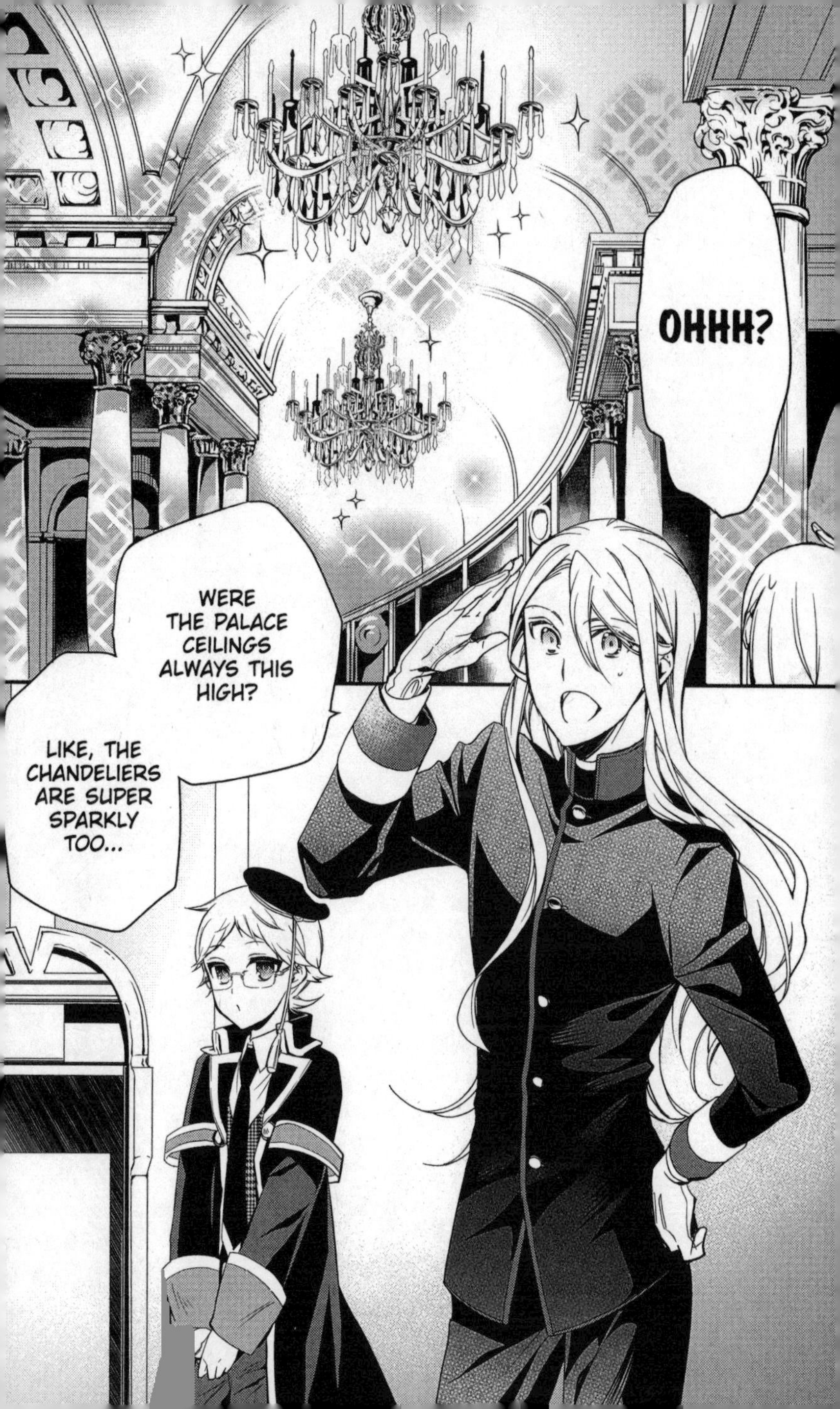
OHHH?
WERE THE PALACE CEILINGS ALWAYS THIS HIGH?
LIKE, THE CHANDELIERS ARE SUPER SPARKLY TOO...

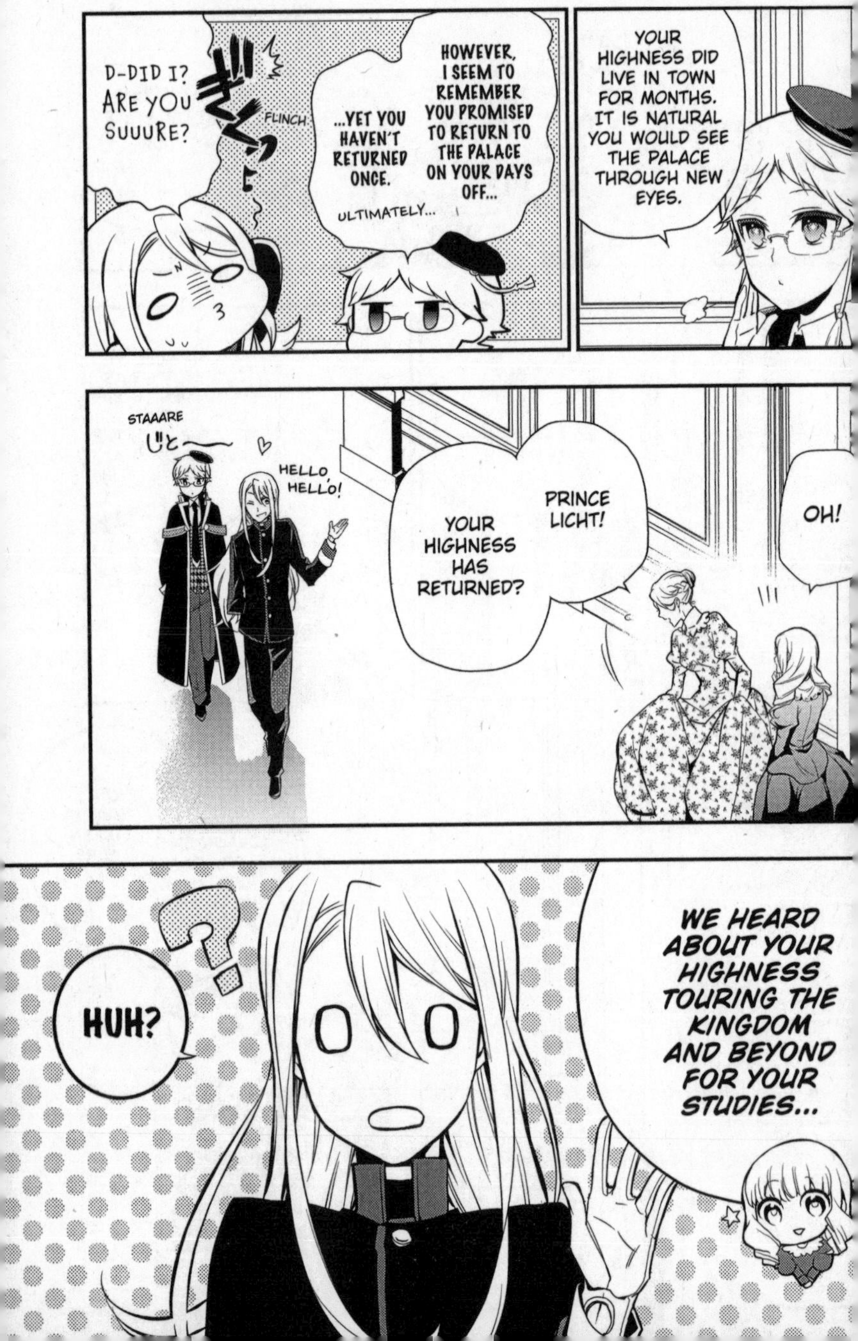
YOUR HIGHNESS DID LIVE IN TOWN FOR MONTHS. IT IS NATURAL YOU WOULD SEE THE PALACE THROUGH NEW EYES.
ULTIMATELY...
HOWEVER, I SEEM TO REMEMBER YOU PROMISED TO RETURN TO THE PALACE ON YOUR DAYS OFF...
...YET YOU HAVEN'T RETURNED ONCE.
FLINCH
D-DID I? ARE YOU SUUURE?
OH!
PRINCE LICHT!
YOUR HIGHNESS HAS RETURNED?
HELLO, HELLO!
STAAARE
じとー
WE HEARD ABOUT YOUR HIGHNESS TOURING THE KINGDOM AND BEYOND FOR YOUR STUDIES...
HUH?

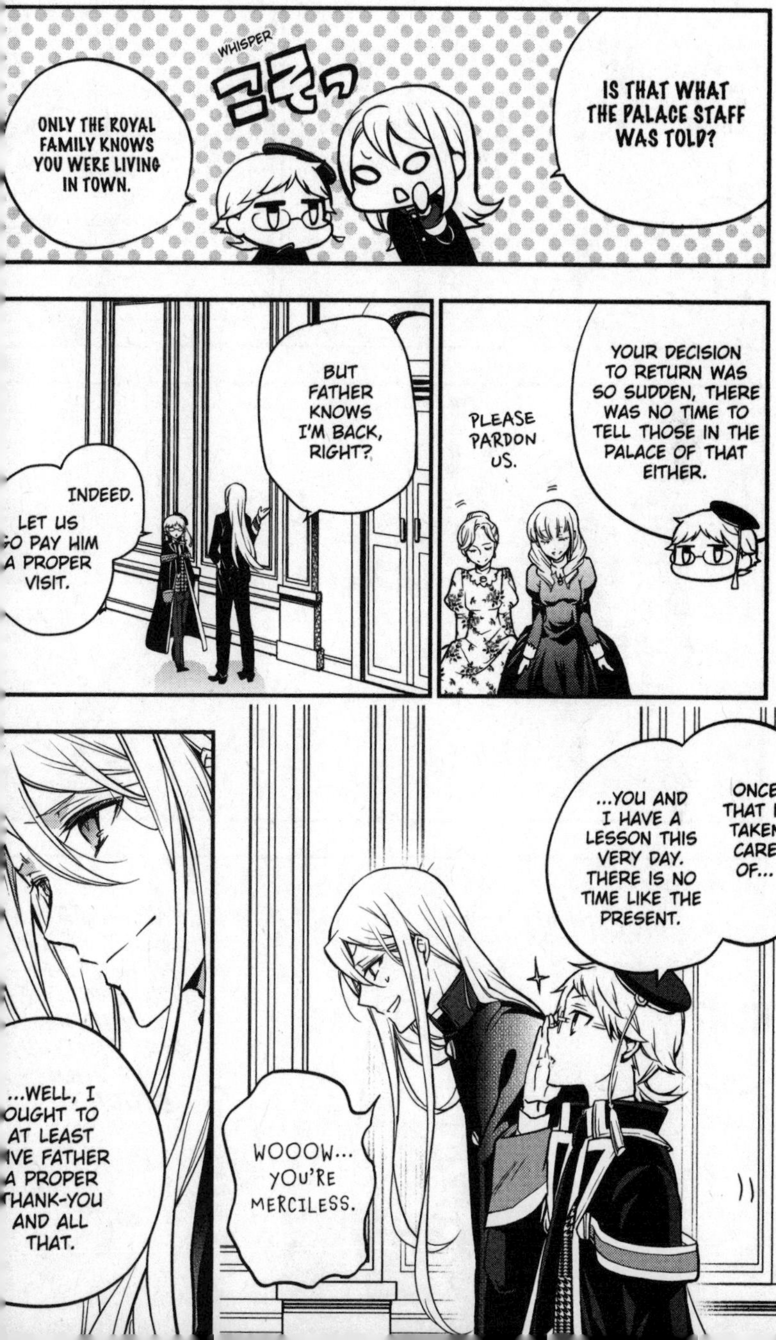
IS THAT WHAT THE PALACE STAFF WAS TOLD?
WHISPER
ONLY THE ROYAL FAMILY KNOWS YOU WERE LIVING IN TOWN.
YOUR DECISION TO RETURN WAS SO SUDDEN, THERE WAS NO TIME TO TELL THOSE IN THE PALACE OF THAT EITHER.
PLEASE PARDON US.
BUT FATHER KNOWS I'M BACK, RIGHT?
INDEED. LET US O PAY HIM A PROPER VISIT.
ONCE THAT IS TAKEN CARE OF...
...YOU AND I HAVE A LESSON THIS VERY DAY. THERE IS NO TIME LIKE THE PRESENT.
WOOOW... YOU'RE MERCILESS.
...WELL, I OUGHT TO AT LEAST IVE FATHER A PROPER HANK-YOU AND ALL THAT.

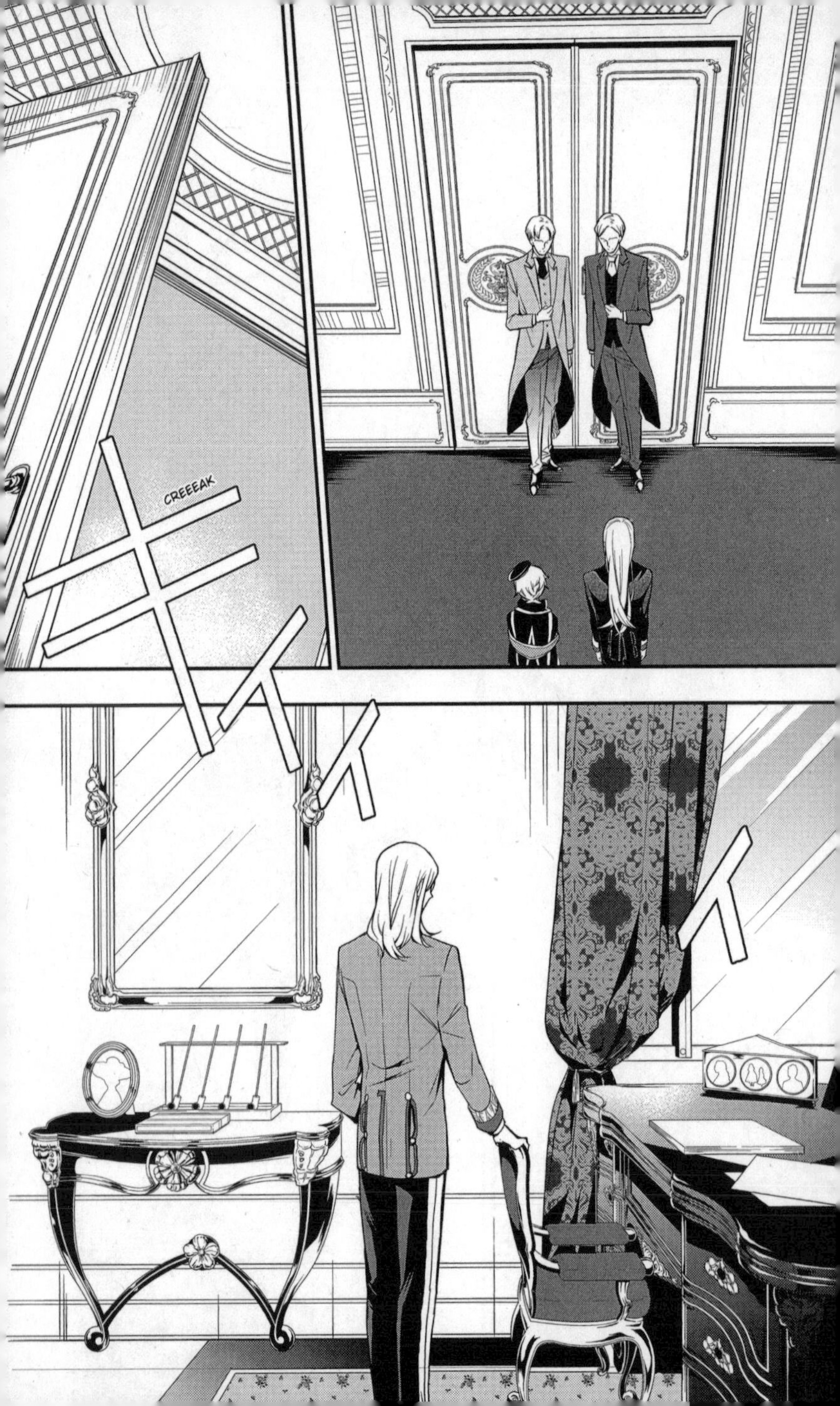
CREEEAK

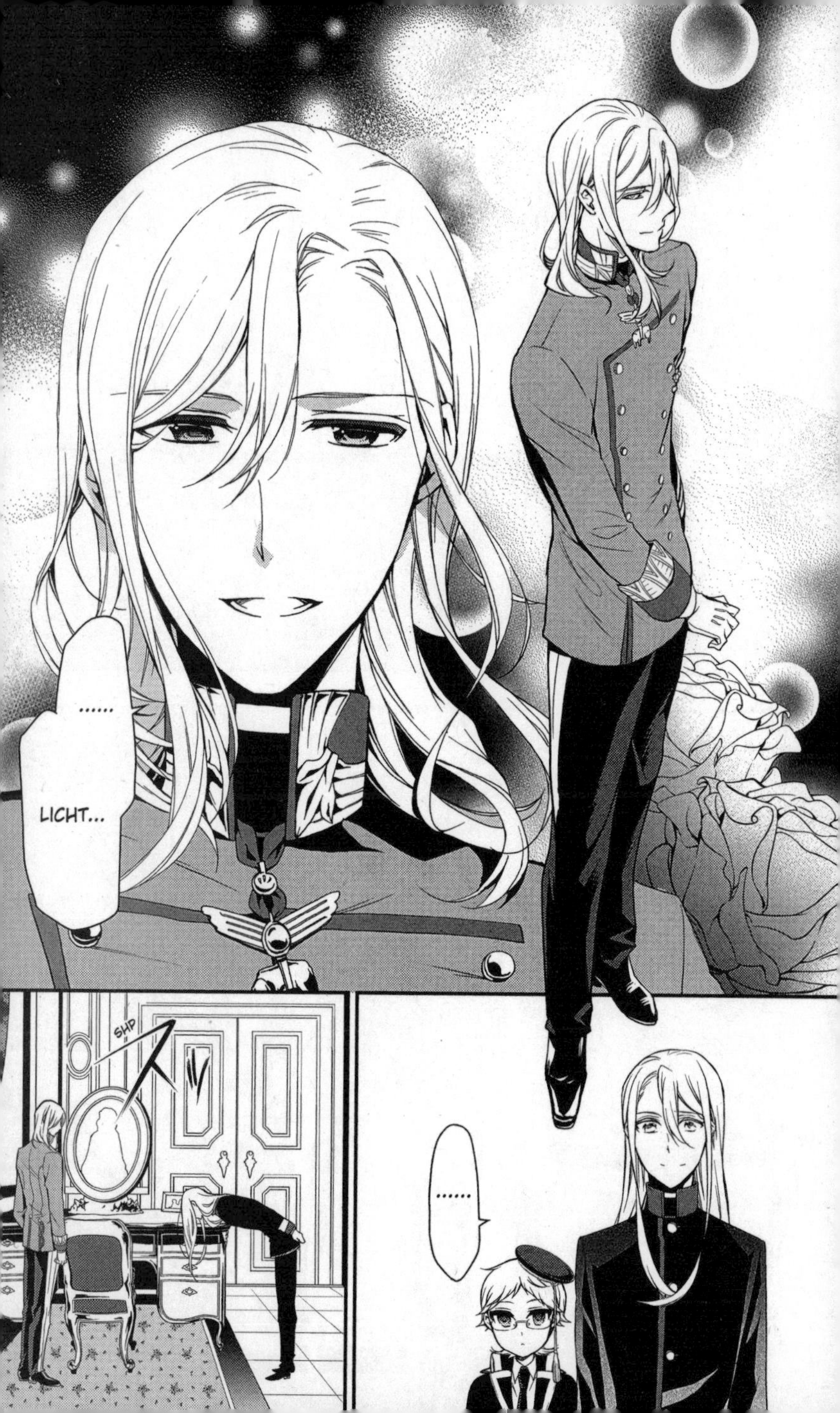
......
LICHT...
......
SHP

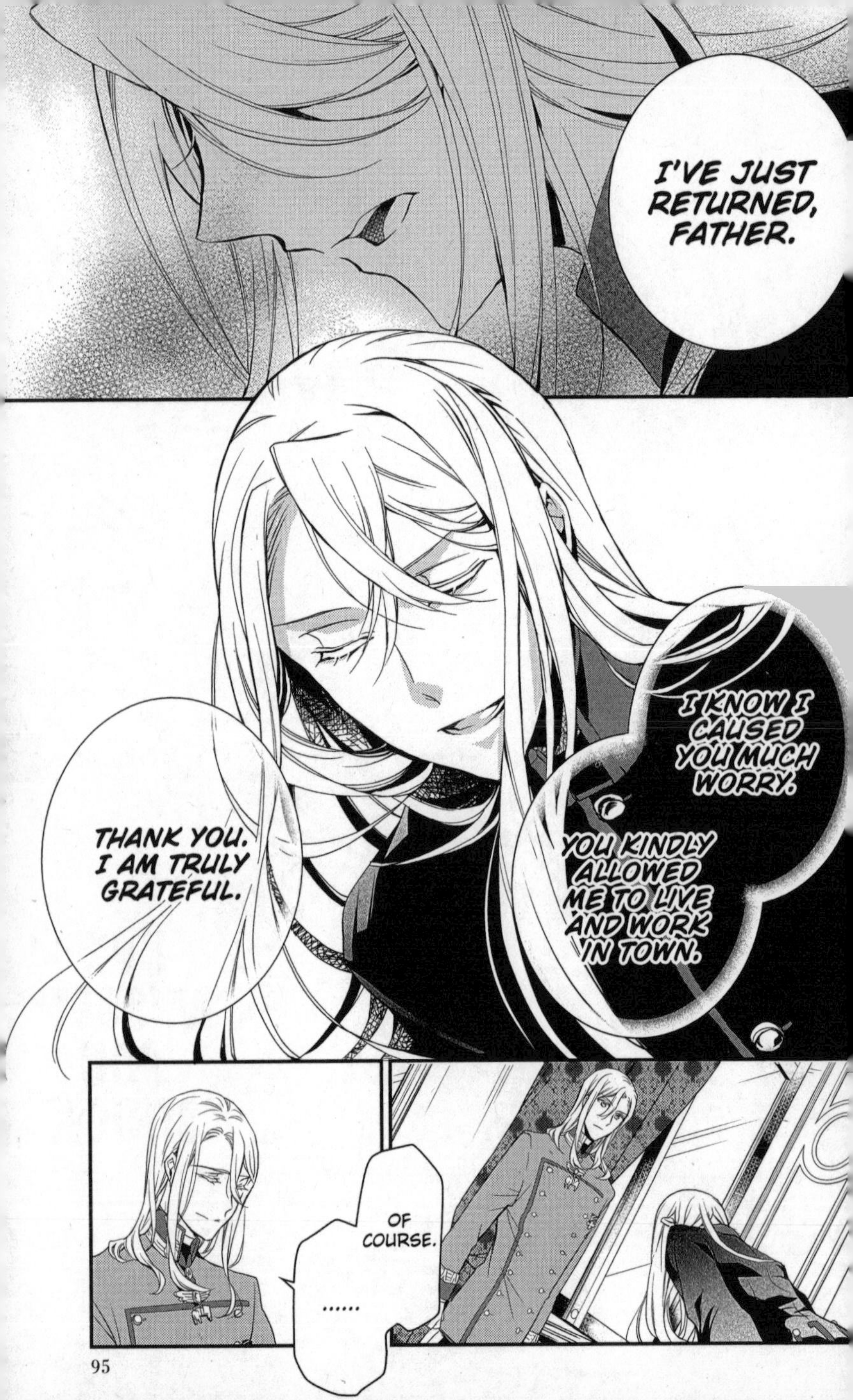
I'VE JUST RETURNED, FATHER.
I KNOW I CAUSED YOU MUCH WORRY.
YOU KINDLY ALLOWED ME TO LIVE AND WORK IN TOWN.
THANK YOU. I AM TRULY GRATEFUL.
OF COURSE.
......

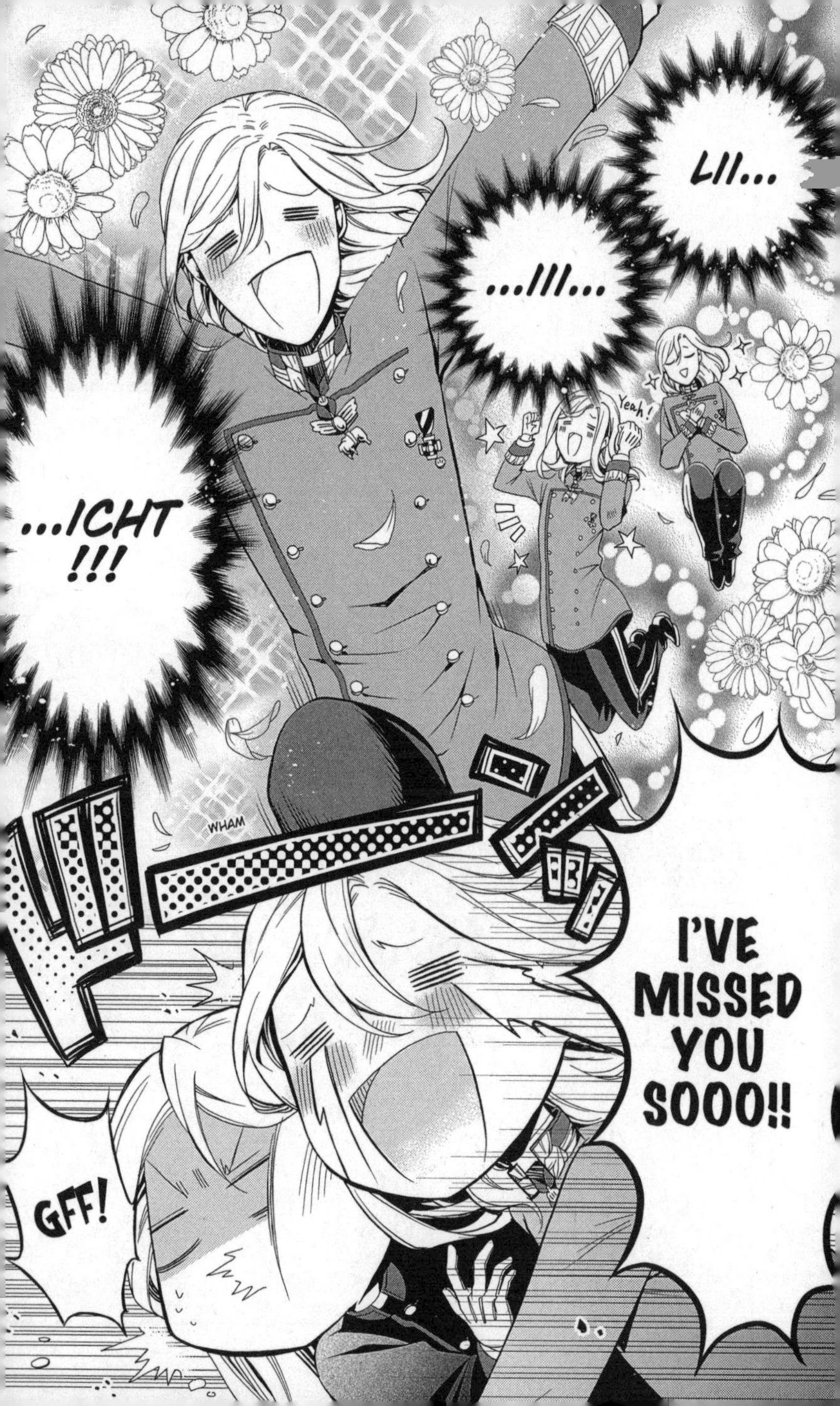
LII...
...III...
Yeah!
...ICHT !!!
I'VE MISSED YOU SOOO!!
WHAM
GFF!

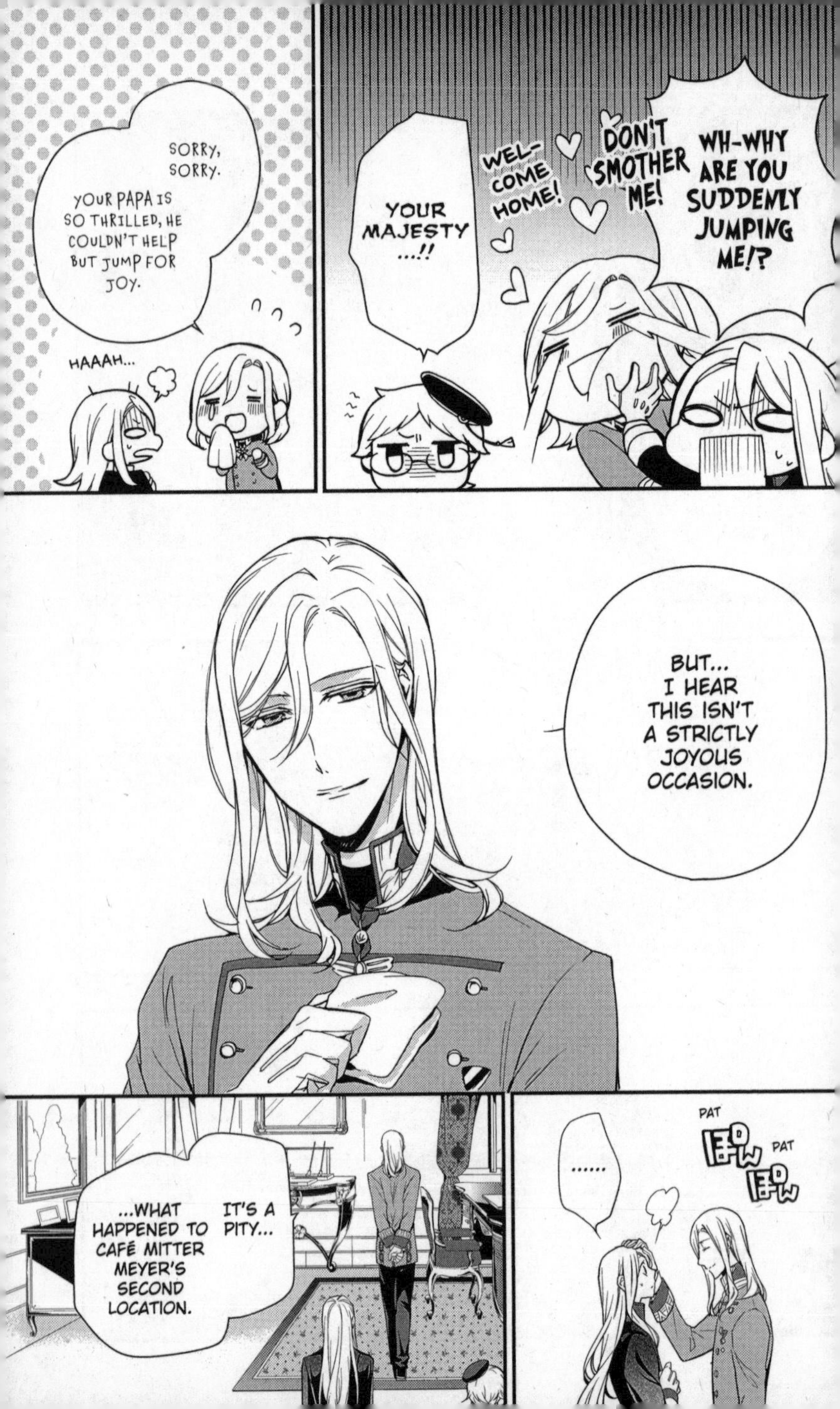
WH-WHY ARE YOU SUDDENLY JUMPING ME!?
DON'T SMOTHER ME!
WEL-COME HOME!
YOUR MAJESTY ...!!
SORRY, SORRY.
YOUR PAPA IS SO THRILLED, HE COULDN'T HELP BUT JUMP FOR JOY.
HAAAH...
BUT... I HEAR THIS ISN'T A STRICTLY JOYOUS OCCASION.
PAT
PAT
......
IT'S A PITY...
...WHAT HAPPENED TO CAFÉ MITTER MEYER'S SECOND LOCATION.

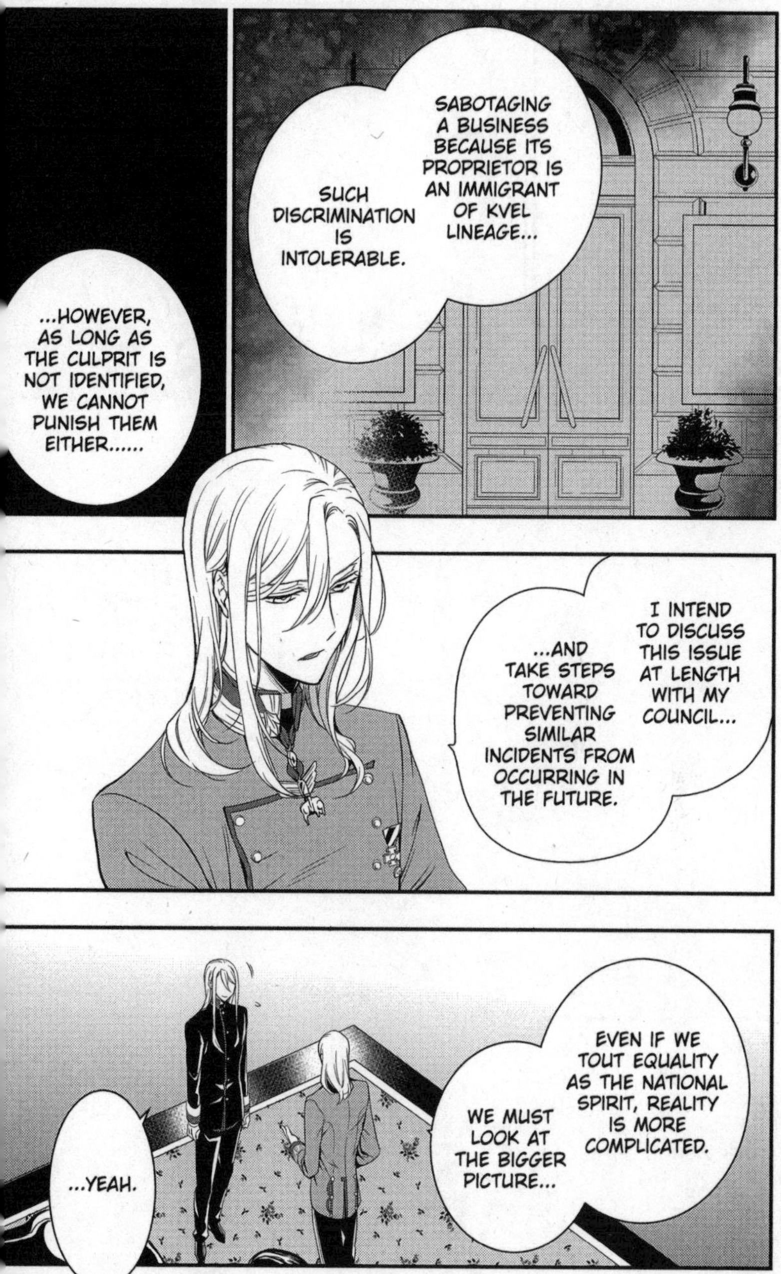
SABOTAGING A BUSINESS BECAUSE ITS PROPRIETOR IS AN IMMIGRANT OF KVEL LINEAGE...
SUCH DISCRIMINATION IS INTOLERABLE.
...HOWEVER, AS LONG AS THE CULPRIT IS NOT IDENTIFIED, WE CANNOT PUNISH THEM EITHER......
I INTEND TO DISCUSS THIS ISSUE AT LENGTH WITH MY COUNCIL...
...AND TAKE STEPS TOWARD PREVENTING SIMILAR INCIDENTS FROM OCCURRING IN THE FUTURE.
EVEN IF WE TOUT EQUALITY AS THE NATIONAL SPIRIT, REALITY IS MORE COMPLICATED.
WE MUST LOOK AT THE BIGGER PICTURE...
...YEAH.

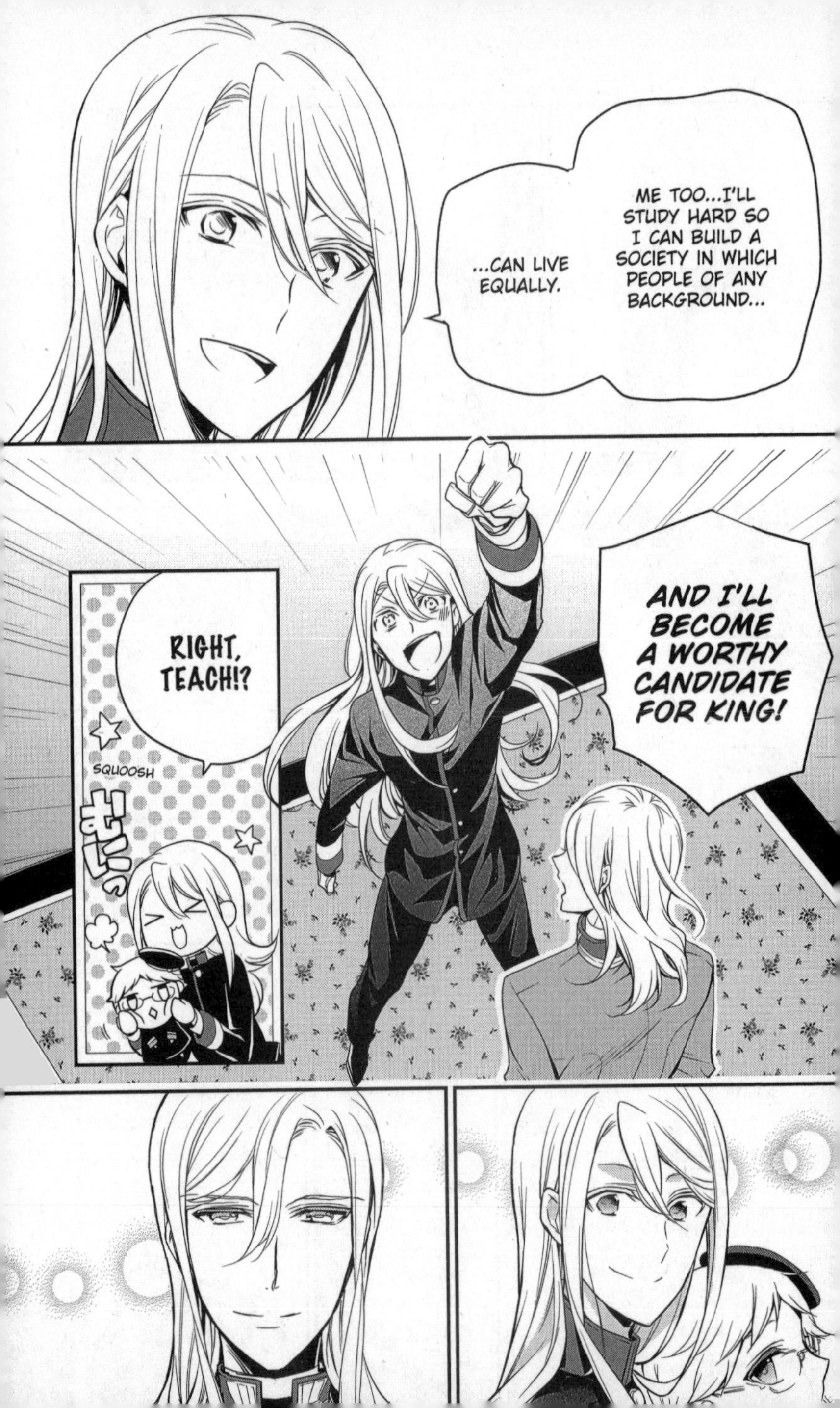
ME TOO...I'LL STUDY HARD SO I CAN BUILD A SOCIETY IN WHICH PEOPLE OF ANY BACKGROUND...
...CAN LIVE EQUALLY.
AND I'LL BECOME A WORTHY CANDIDATE FOR KING!
RIGHT, TEACH!?
SQUOOSH

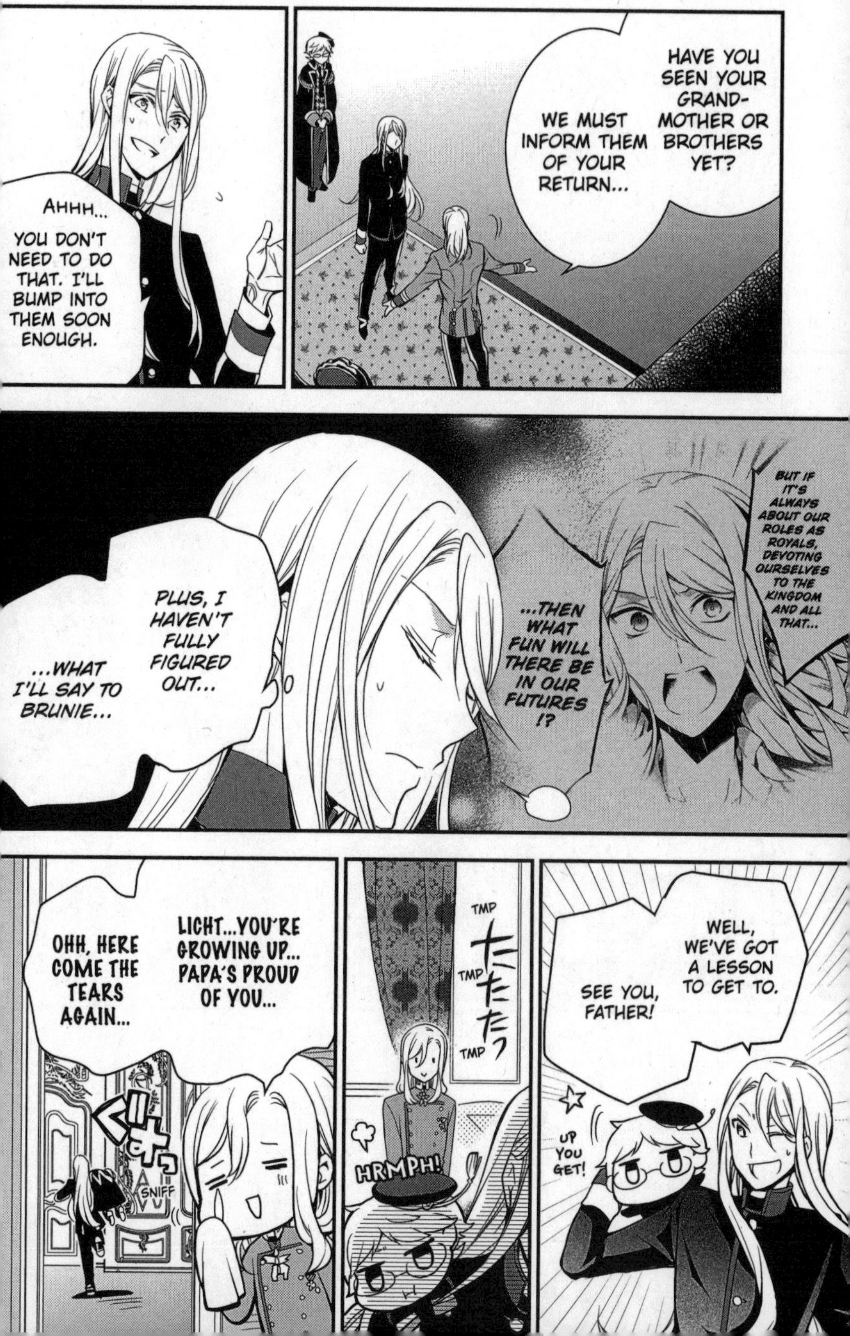
HAVE YOU SEEN YOUR GRANDMOTHER OR BROTHERS YET?
WE MUST INFORM THEM OF YOUR RETURN...
AHHH...
YOU DON'T NEED TO DO THAT. I'LL BUMP INTO THEM SOON ENOUGH.
BUT IF IT'S ALWAYS ABOUT OUR ROLES AS ROYALS, DEVOTING OURSELVES TO THE KINGDOM AND ALL THAT...
...THEN WHAT FUN WILL THERE BE IN OUR FUTURES!?
PLUS, I HAVEN'T FULLY FIGURED OUT...
...WHAT I'LL SAY TO BRUNIE...
WELL, WE'VE GOT A LESSON TO GET TO.
SEE YOU, FATHER!
UP YOU GET!
TMP
TMP
TMP
HRMPH!
LICHT...YOU'RE GROWING UP... PAPA'S PROUD OF YOU...
OHH, HERE COME THE TEARS AGAIN...
SNIFF

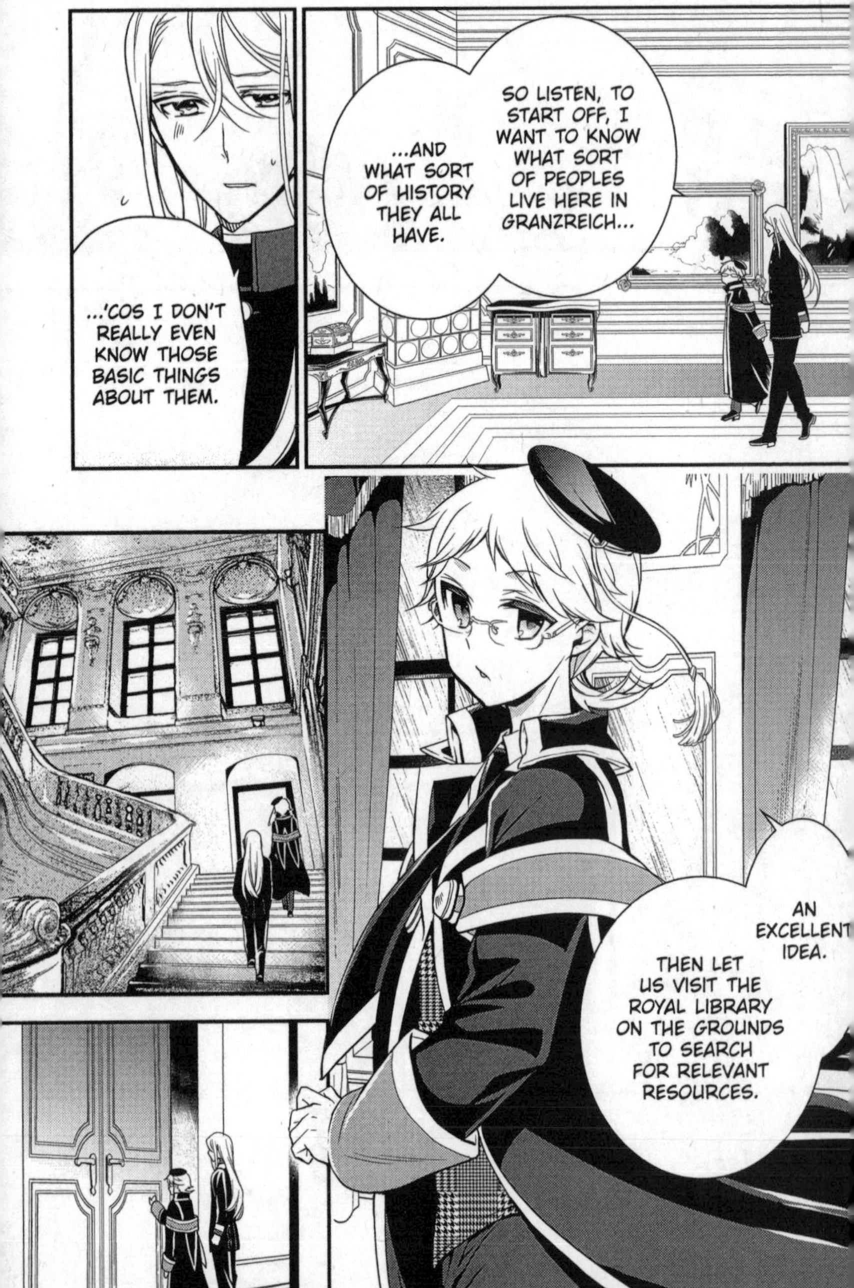
SO LISTEN, TO START OFF, I WANT TO KNOW WHAT SORT OF PEOPLES LIVE HERE IN GRANZREICH...
...AND WHAT SORT OF HISTORY THEY ALL HAVE.
...'COS I DON'T REALLY EVEN KNOW THOSE BASIC THINGS ABOUT THEM.
AN EXCELLENT IDEA.
THEN LET US VISIT THE ROYAL LIBRARY ON THE GROUNDS TO SEARCH FOR RELEVANT RESOURCES.

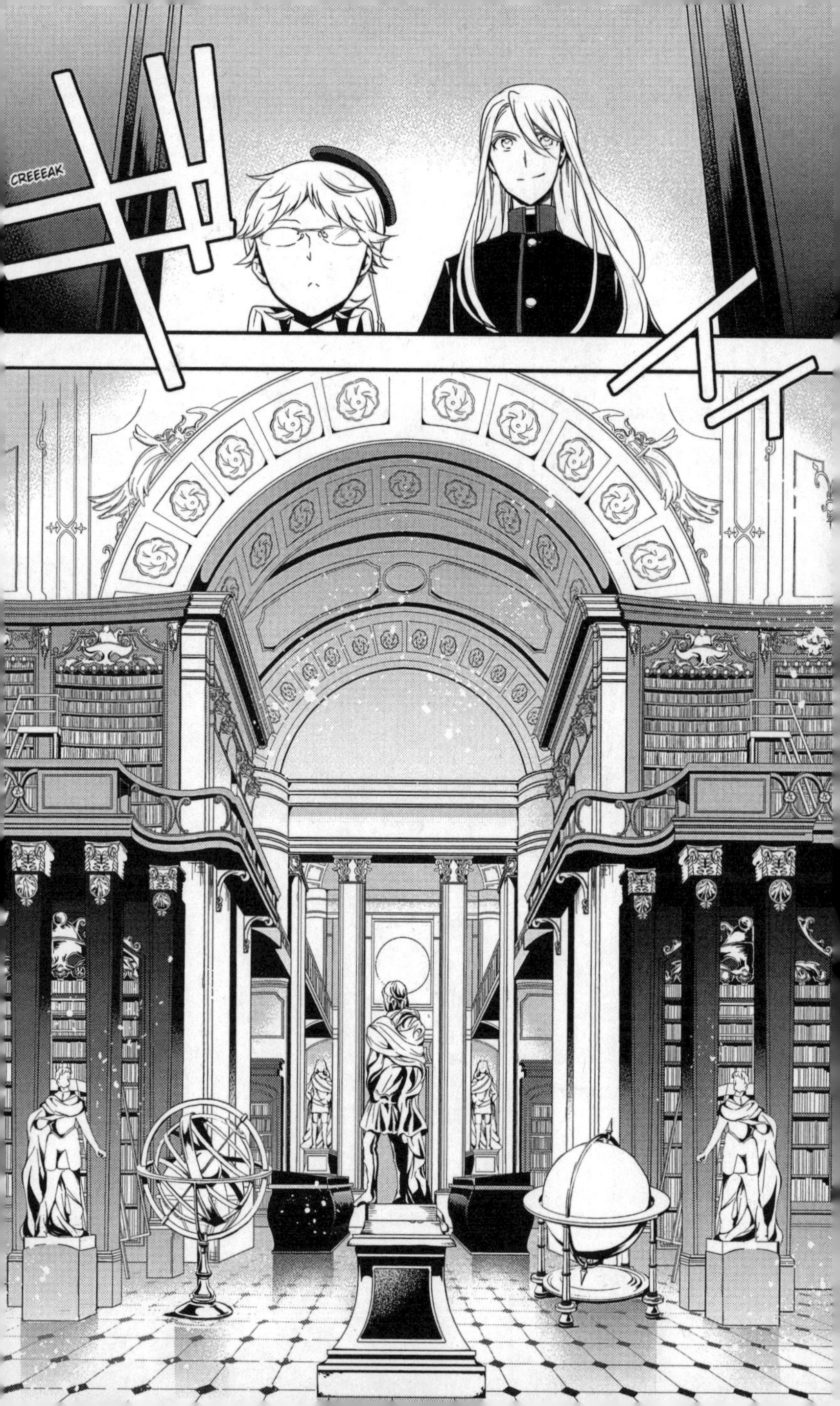
CREEEAK

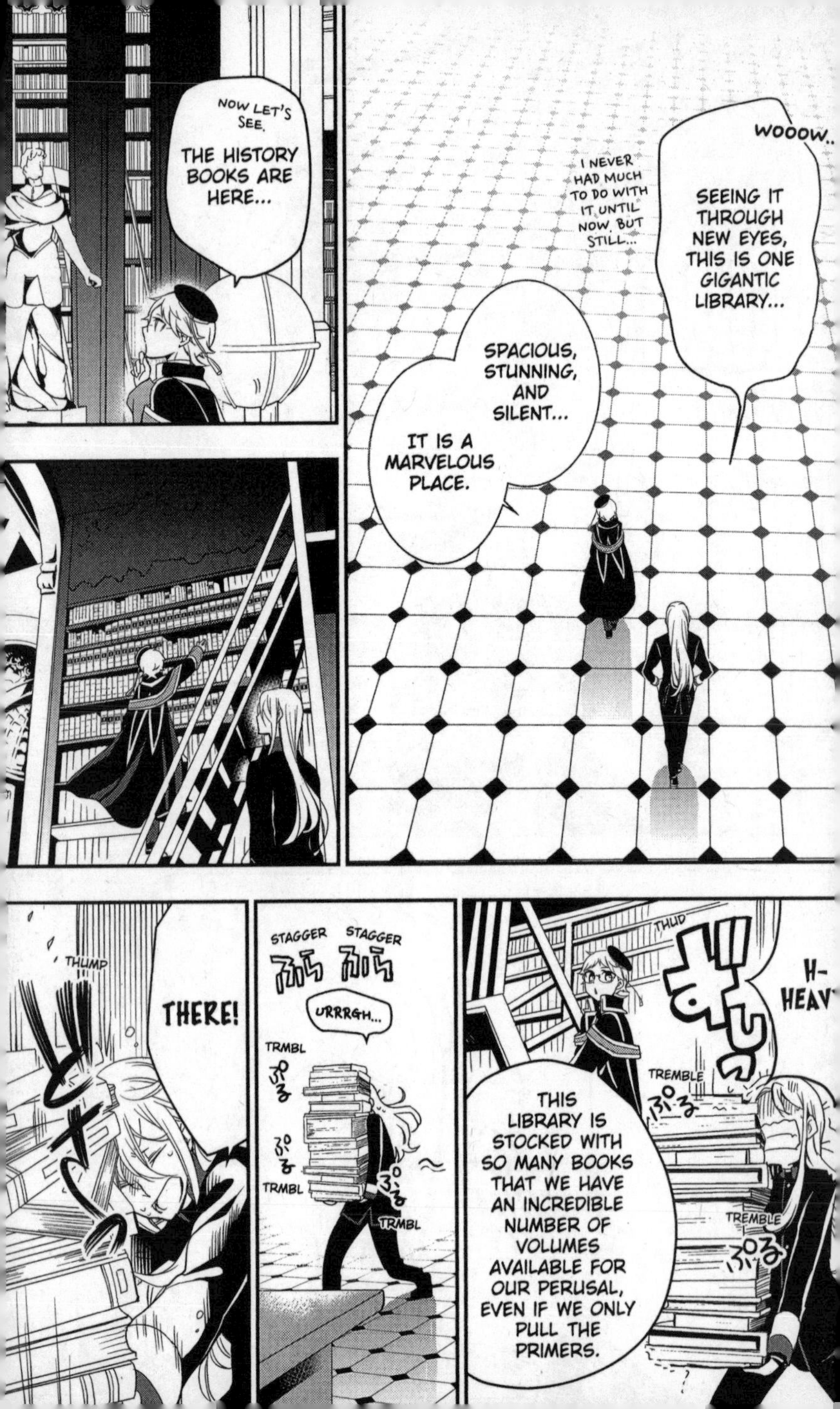
WOOOW..
SEEING IT THROUGH NEW EYES, THIS IS ONE GIGANTIC LIBRARY...
I NEVER HAD MUCH TO DO WITH IT UNTIL NOW, BUT STILL...
SPACIOUS, STUNNING, AND SILENT...
IT IS A MARVELOUS PLACE.
NOW LET'S SEE.
THE HISTORY BOOKS ARE HERE...
H-HEAV
THUD
TREMBLE
THIS LIBRARY IS STOCKED WITH SO MANY BOOKS THAT WE HAVE AN INCREDIBLE NUMBER OF VOLUMES AVAILABLE FOR OUR PERUSAL, EVEN IF WE ONLY PULL THE PRIMERS.
TREMBLE
STAGGER STAGGER
ふら ふら
URRRGH...
TRMBL
TRMBL
TRMBL
THERE!
THUMP

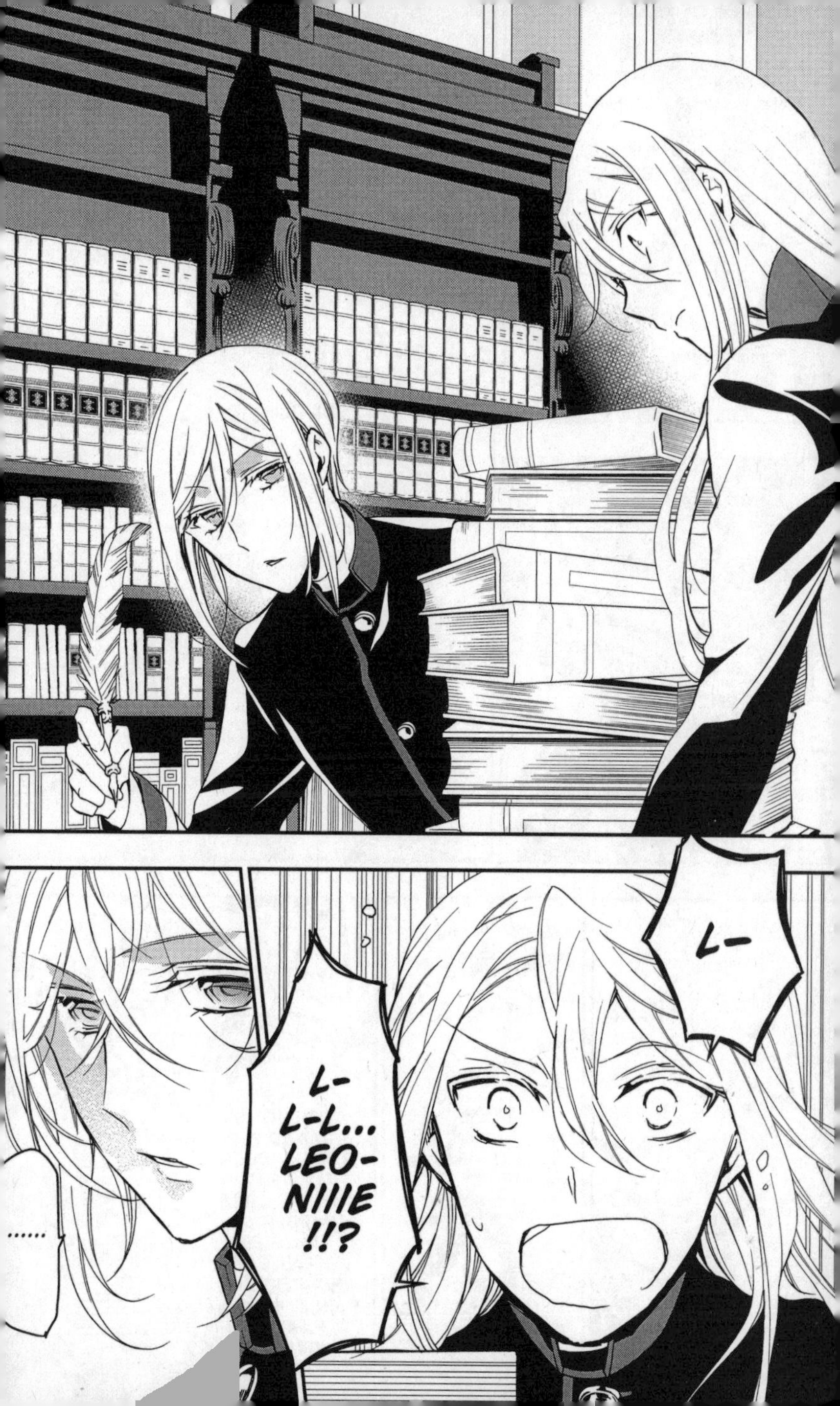
L—
L-L-L... LEO-NIIIE!!?
......

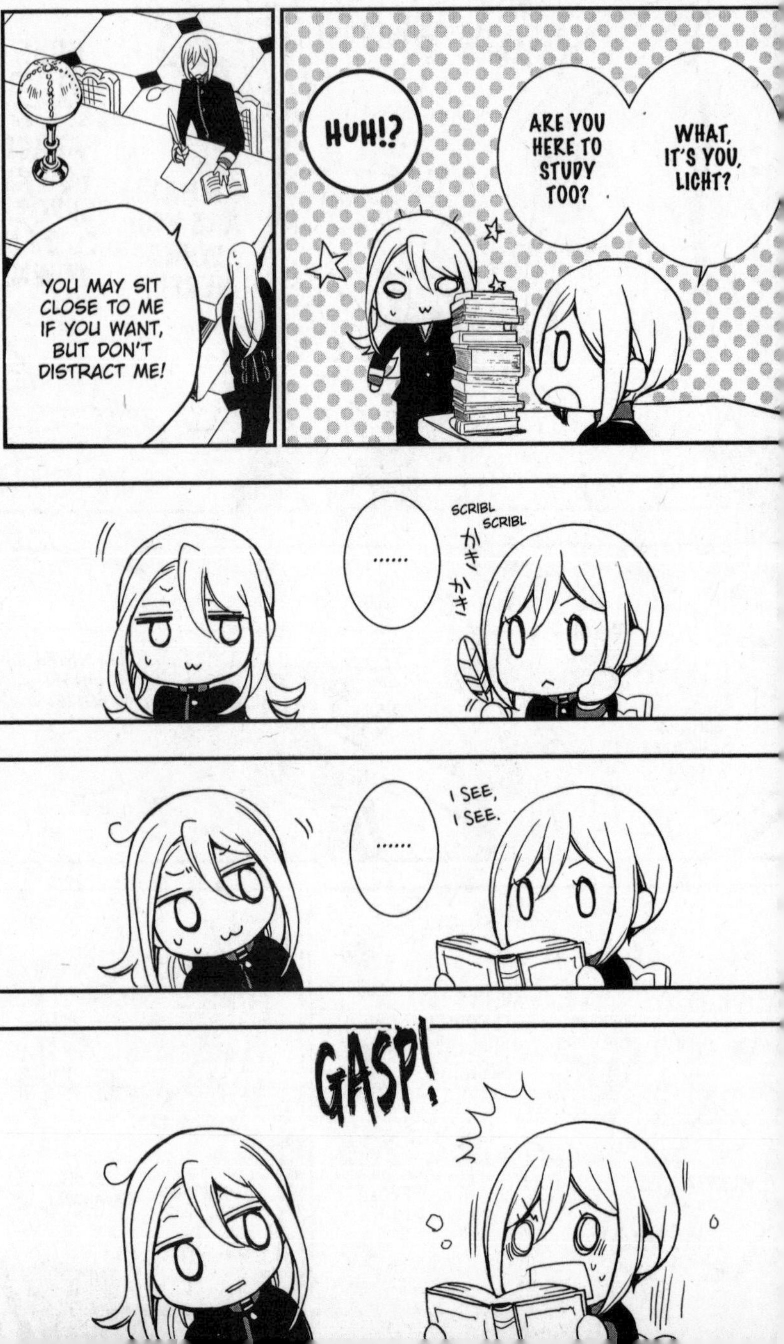
WHAT, IT'S YOU, LICHT?
ARE YOU HERE TO STUDY TOO?
HUH!?
YOU MAY SIT CLOSE TO ME IF YOU WANT, BUT DON'T DISTRACT ME!
SCRIBL SCRIBL
かき かき
......
I SEE, I SEE.
......
GASP!

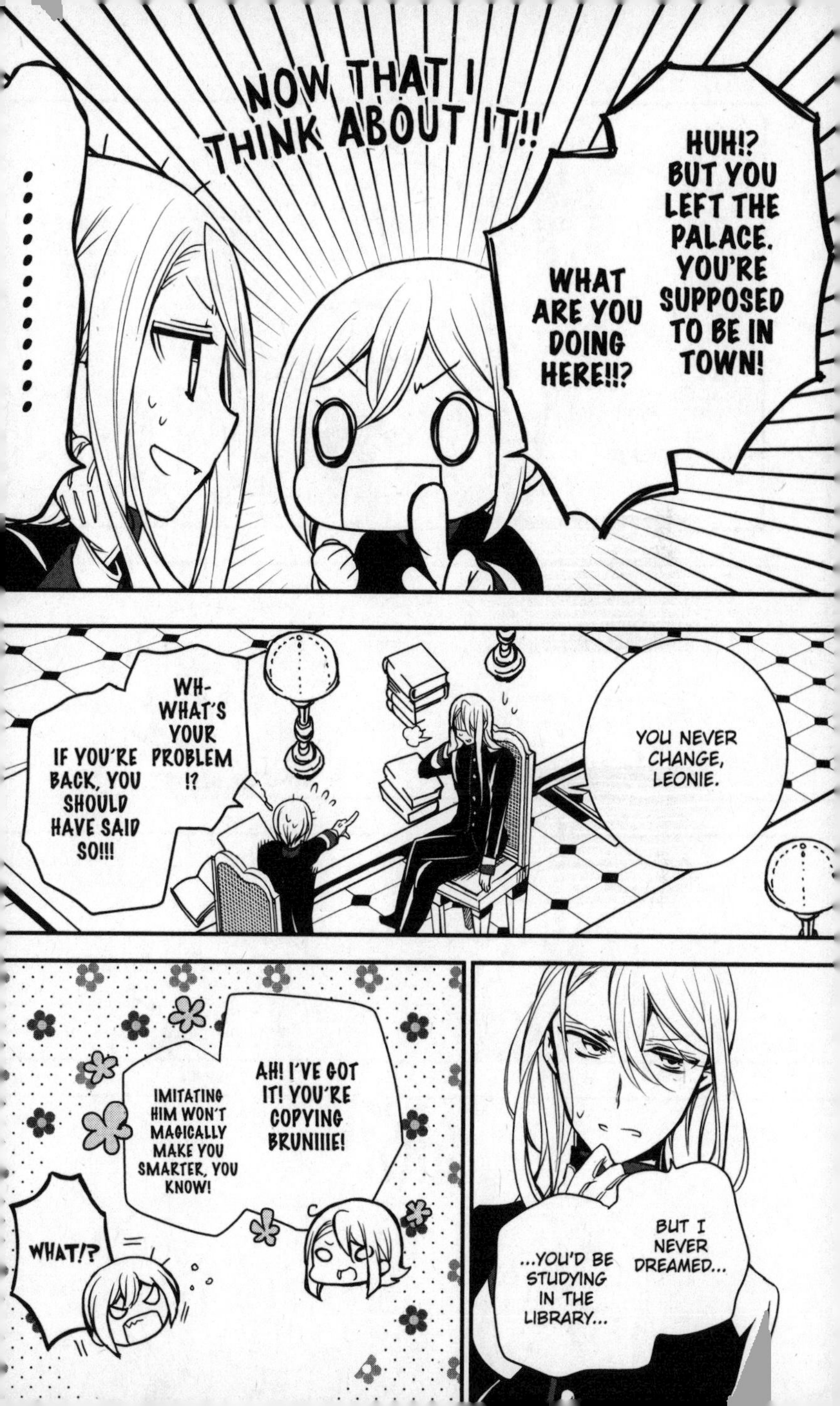
HUH!? BUT YOU LEFT THE PALACE. YOU'RE SUPPOSED TO BE IN TOWN!
WHAT ARE YOU DOING HERE!!?
NOW THAT I THINK ABOUT IT!!
....
YOU NEVER CHANGE, LEONIE.
WH-WHAT'S YOUR PROBLEM!?
IF YOU'RE BACK, YOU SHOULD HAVE SAID SO!!!
BUT I NEVER DREAMED...
...YOU'D BE STUDYING IN THE LIBRARY...
AH! I'VE GOT IT! YOU'RE COPYING BRUNIIIE!
IMITATING HIM WON'T MAGICALLY MAKE YOU SMARTER, YOU KNOW!
WHAT!?

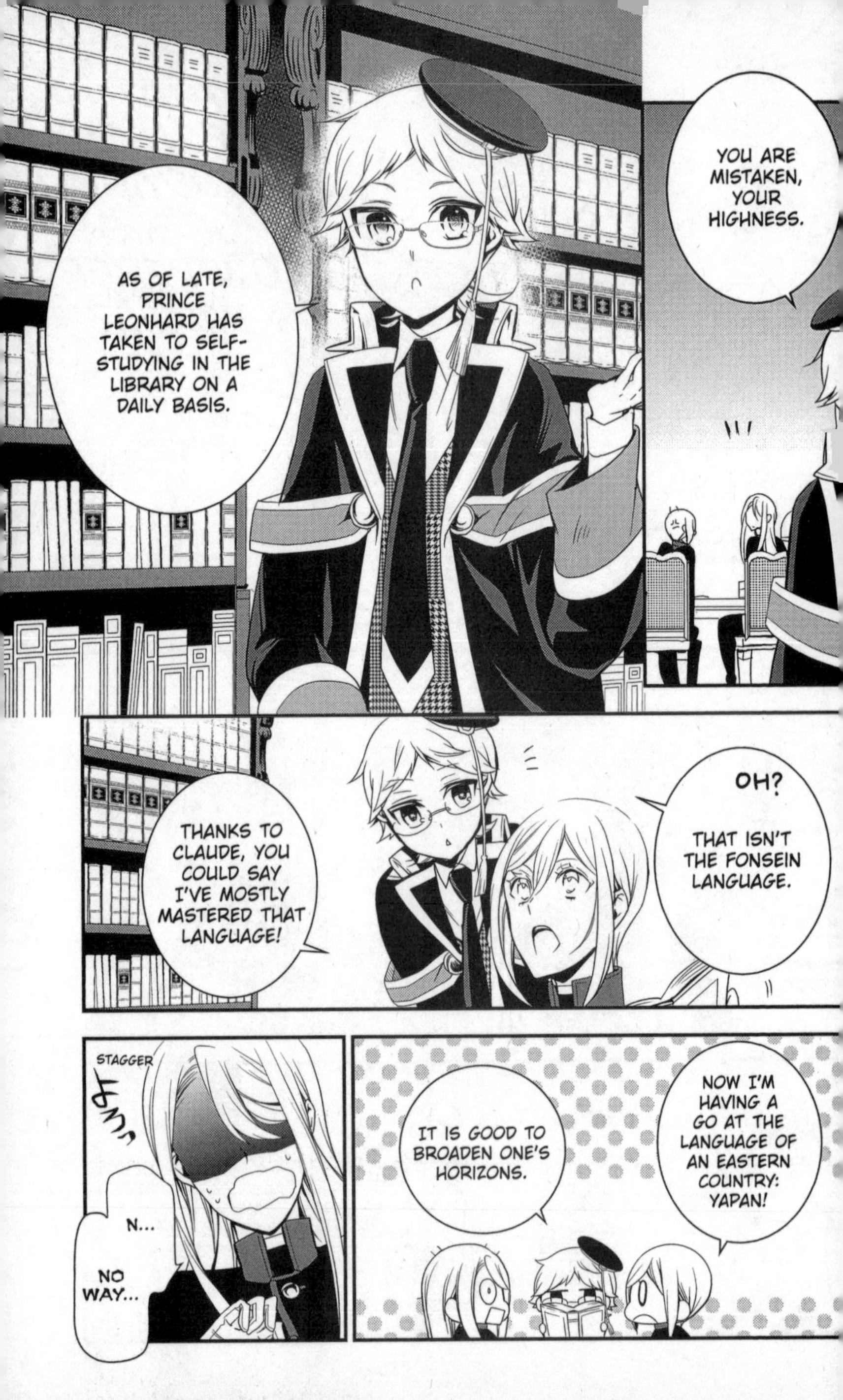
YOU ARE MISTAKEN, YOUR HIGHNESS.
AS OF LATE, PRINCE LEONHARD HAS TAKEN TO SELF-STUDYING IN THE LIBRARY ON A DAILY BASIS.
OH?
THAT ISN'T THE FONSEIN LANGUAGE.
THANKS TO CLAUDE, YOU COULD SAY I'VE MOSTLY MASTERED THAT LANGUAGE!
NOW I'M HAVING A GO AT THE LANGUAGE OF AN EASTERN COUNTRY: YAPAN!
IT IS GOOD TO BROADEN ONE'S HORIZONS.
STAGGER
N...
NO WAY...

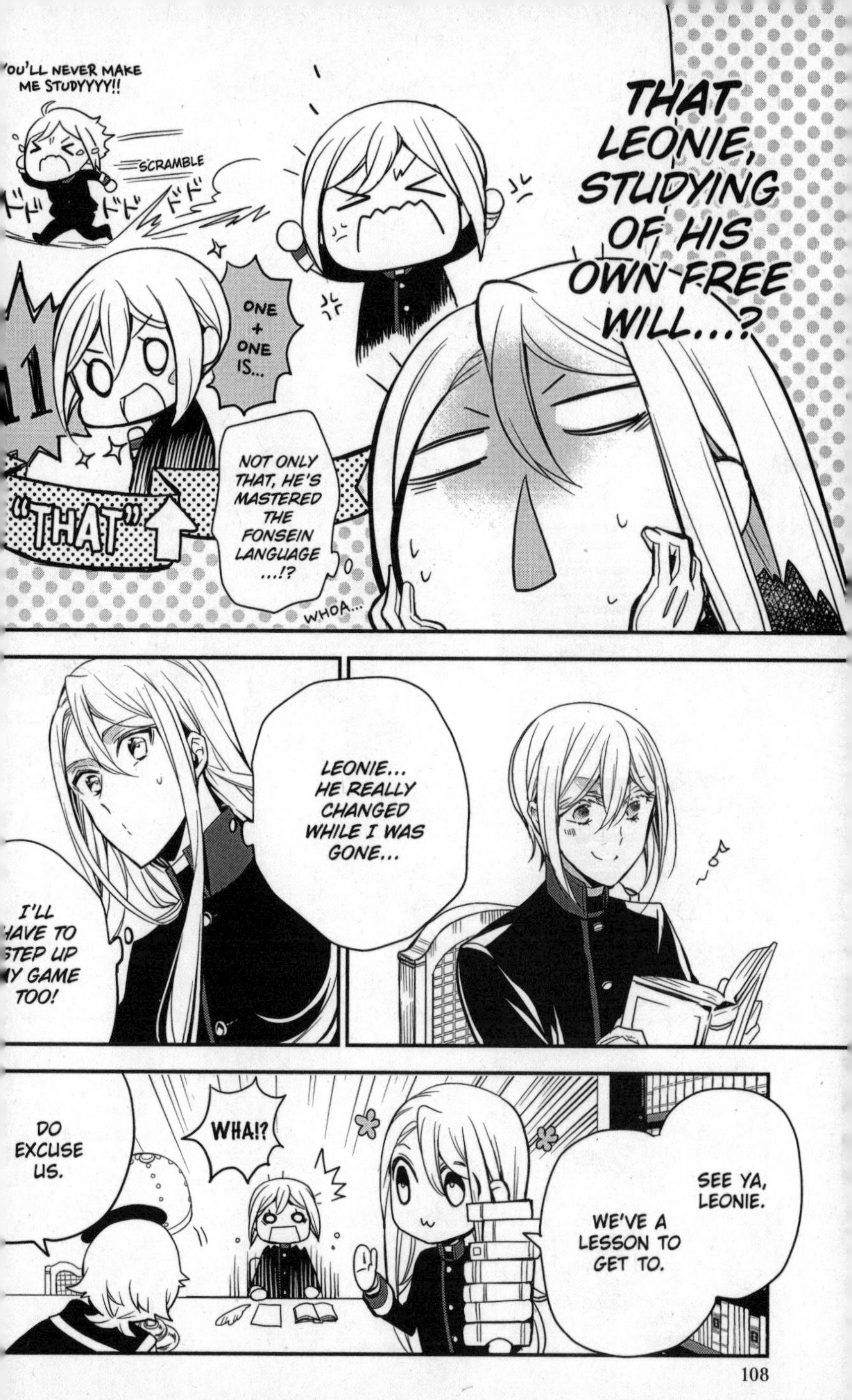
THAT LEONIE, STUDYING OF HIS OWN FREE WILL...?
NOT ONLY THAT, HE'S MASTERED THE FONSEIN LANGUAGE ...!?
WHOA...
ONE + ONE IS...
11
"THAT"
YOU'LL NEVER MAKE ME STUDYYYY!!
SCRAMBLE
ドドドドドド
LEONIE... HE REALLY CHANGED WHILE I WAS GONE...
I'LL HAVE TO STEP UP MY GAME TOO!
SEE YA, LEONIE.
WE'VE A LESSON TO GET TO.
WHA!?
DO EXCUSE US.

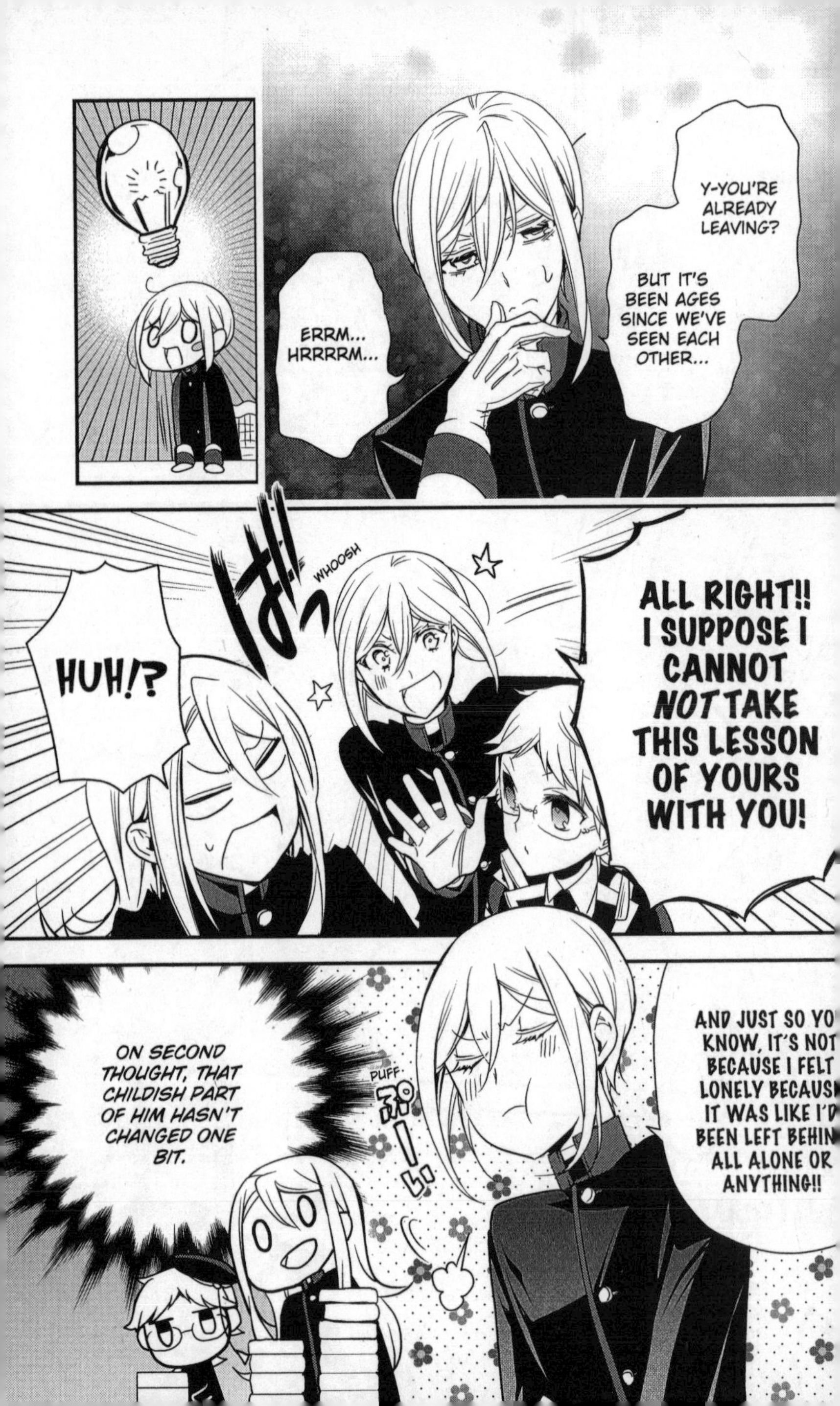
Y-YOU'RE ALREADY LEAVING?
BUT IT'S BEEN AGES SINCE WE'VE SEEN EACH OTHER...
ERRM... HRRRRM...
ALL RIGHT!! I SUPPOSE I CANNOT *NOT* TAKE THIS LESSON OF YOURS WITH YOU!
WHOOSH
HUH!?
AND JUST SO YO KNOW, IT'S NOT BECAUSE I FELT LONELY BECAUS IT WAS LIKE I'D BEEN LEFT BEHIN ALL ALONE OR ANYTHING!!
PUFF
ON SECOND THOUGHT, THAT CHILDISH PART OF HIM HASN'T CHANGED ONE BIT.

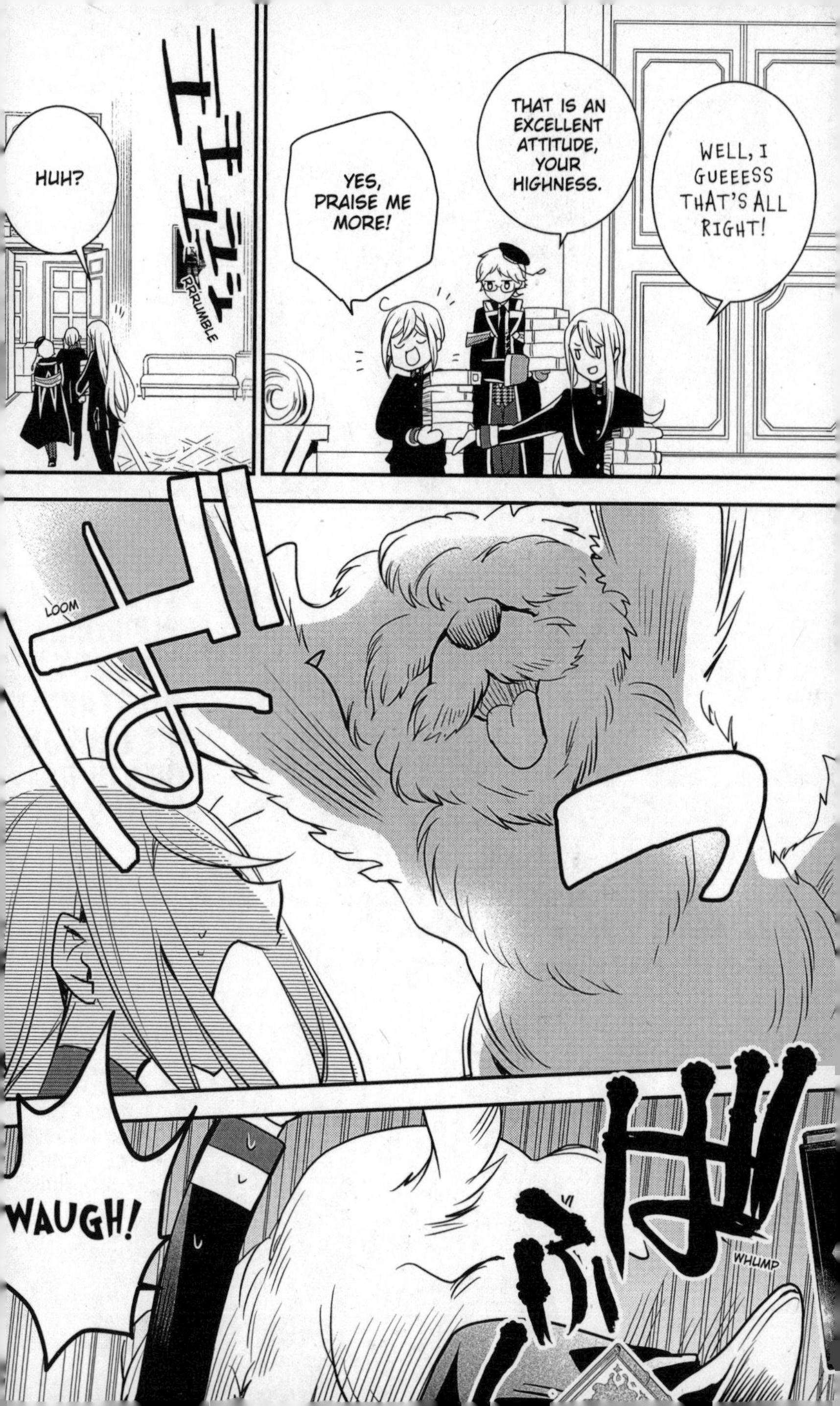
WELL, I GUEEESS THAT'S ALL RIGHT!
THAT IS AN EXCELLENT ATTITUDE, YOUR HIGHNESS.
YES, PRAISE ME MORE!
RRRUMBLE
HUH?
LOOM
WHUMP
WAUGH!

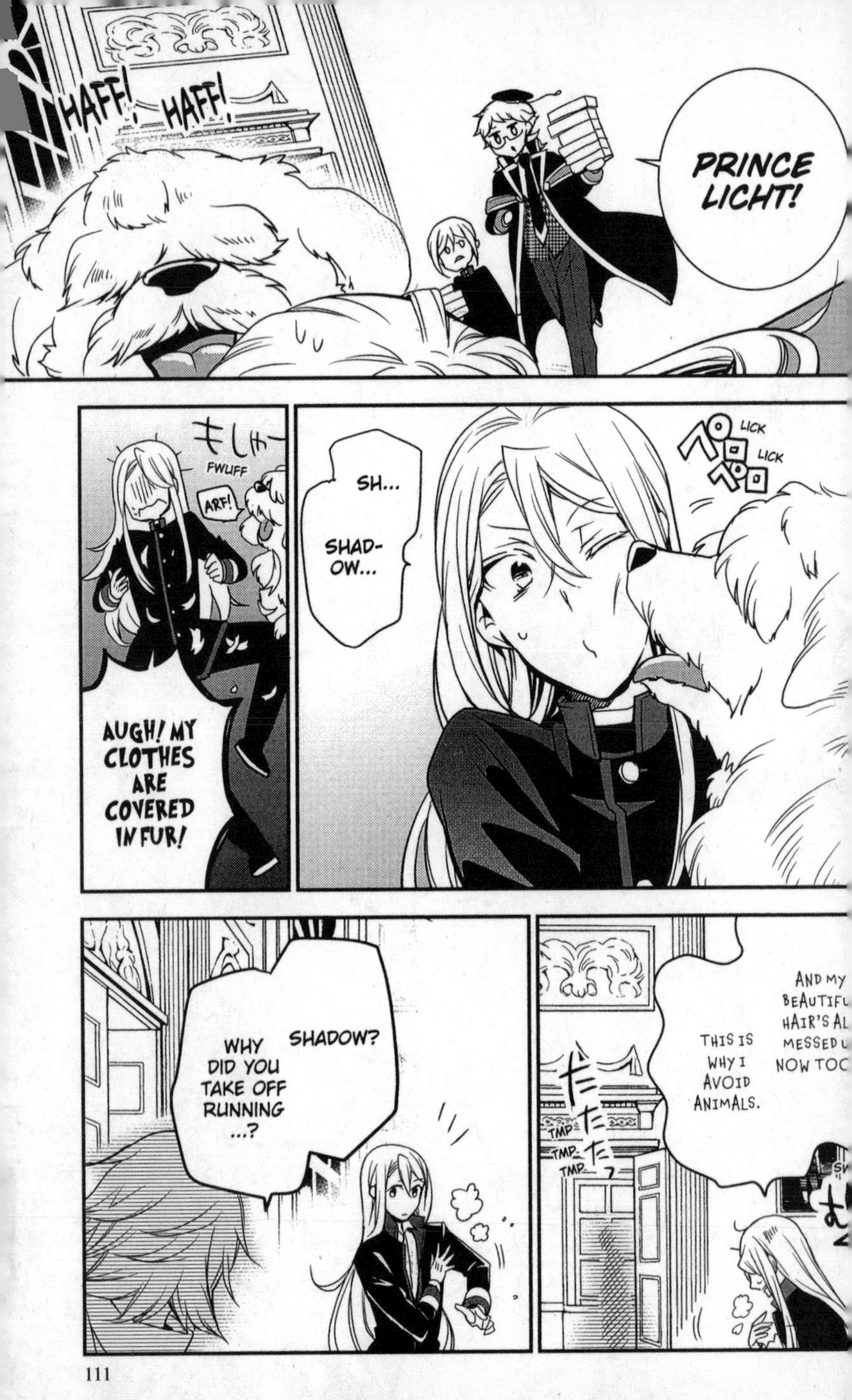

PRINCE LICHT!
HAFF! HAFF!
LICK LICK
SH... SHADOW...
FWUFF
ARF!
AUGH! MY CLOTHES ARE COVERED IN FUR!
AND MY BEAUTIFU HAIR'S AL MESSED U NOW TOO
THIS IS WHY I AVOID ANIMALS.
TMP TMP TMP
SHADOW?
WHY DID YOU TAKE OFF RUNNING ...?

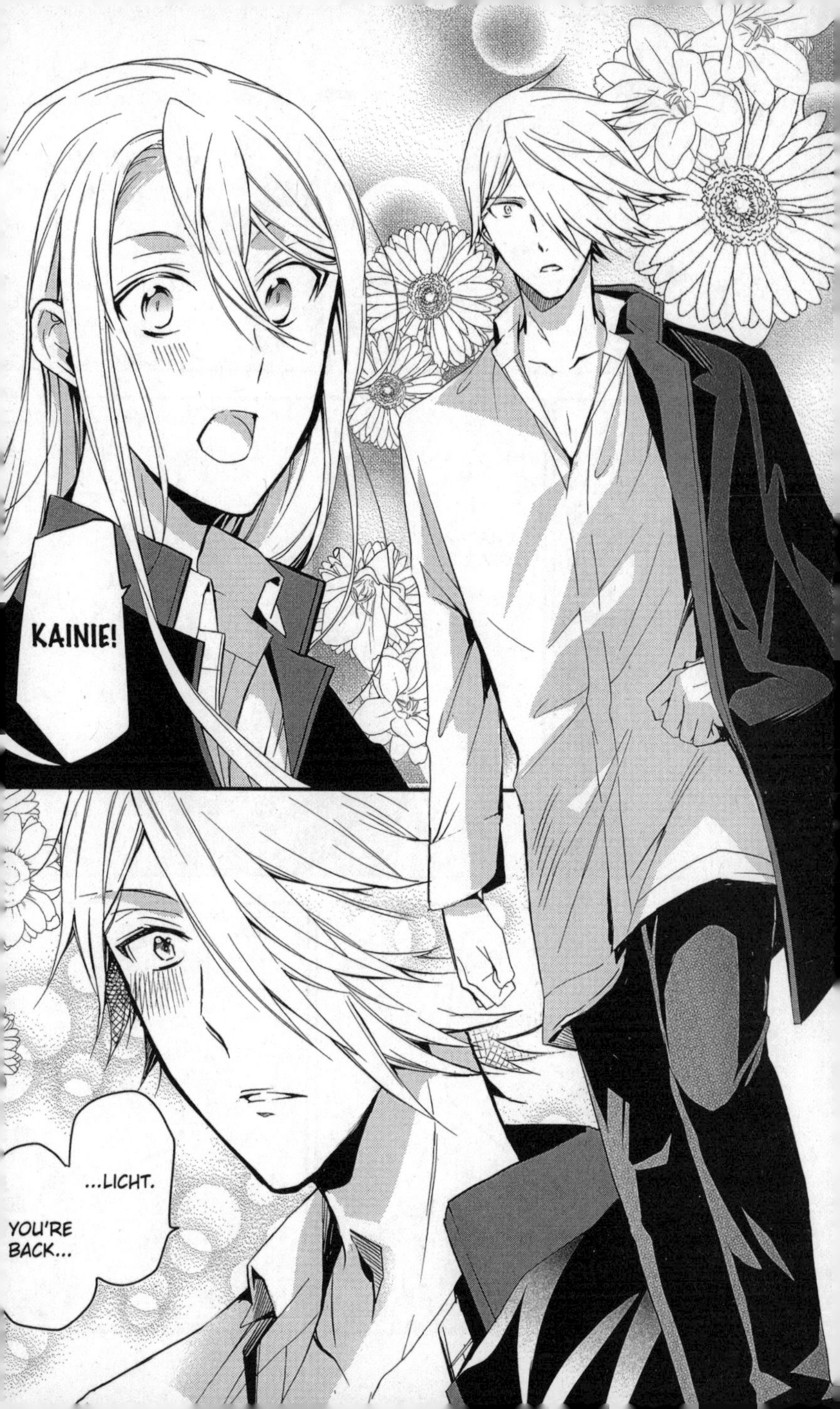
KAINIE!
...LICHT.
YOU'RE BACK...

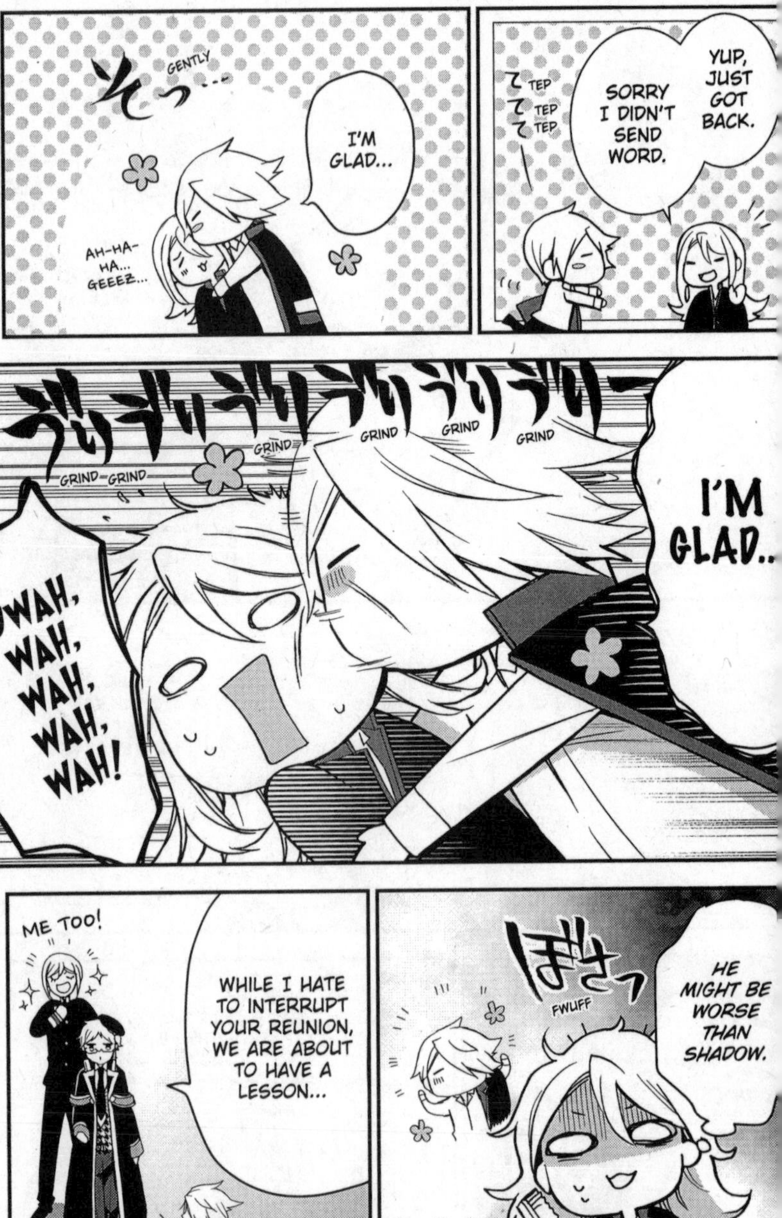
YUP, JUST GOT BACK.
SORRY I DIDN'T SEND WORD.
てててー
TEP TEP TEP
そっ…
GENTLY
I'M GLAD...
AH-HA-HA... GEEEZ...
I'M GLAD..
GRIND GRIND GRIND GRIND GRIND GRIND
UWAH, WAH, WAH, WAH, WAH!
HE MIGHT BE WORSE THAN SHADOW.
ぼさっ
FWUFF
WHILE I HATE TO INTERRUPT YOUR REUNION, WE ARE ABOUT TO HAVE A LESSON...
ME TOO!

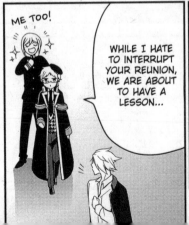

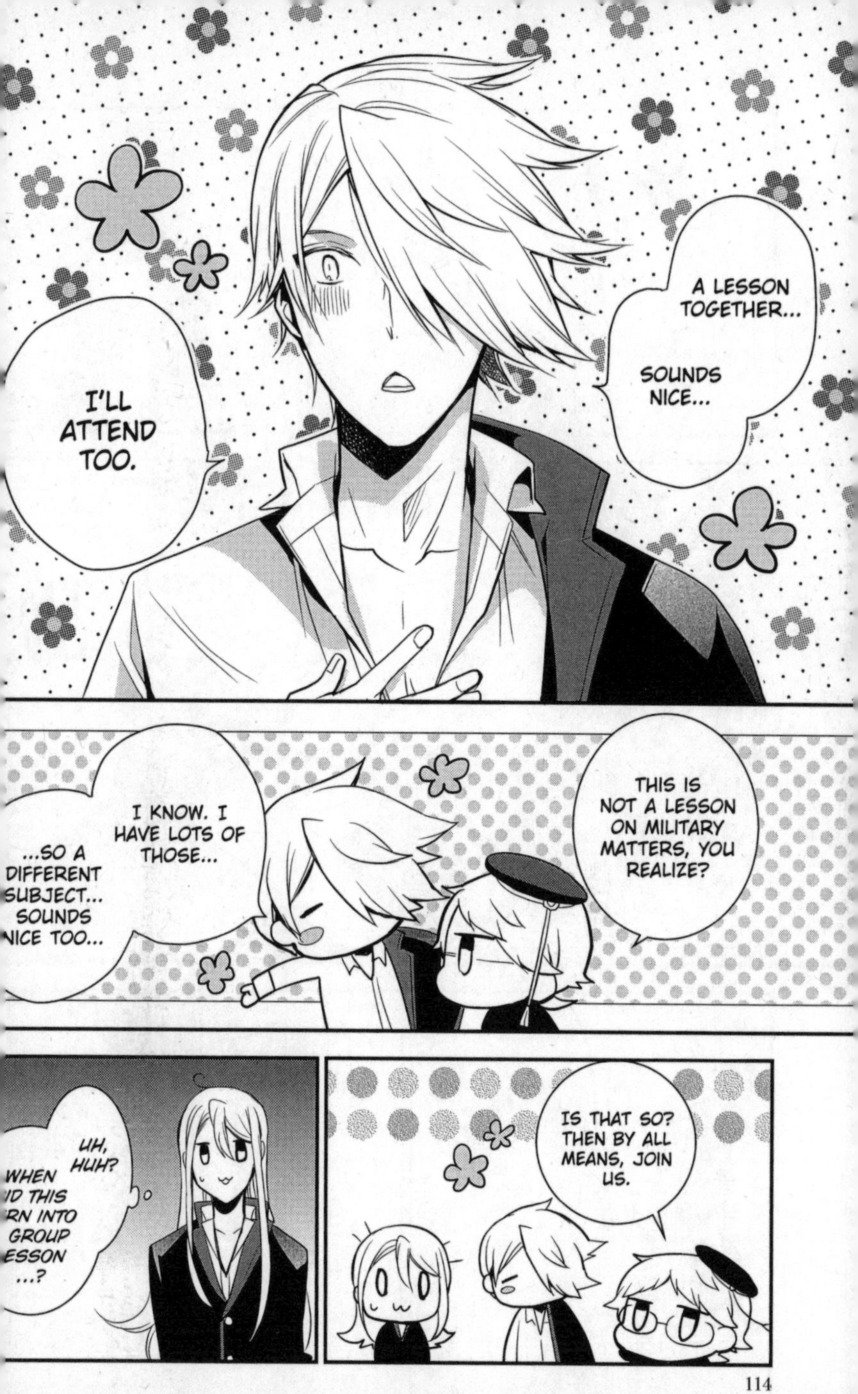
A LESSON TOGETHER... SOUNDS NICE...
I'LL ATTEND TOO.
THIS IS NOT A LESSON ON MILITARY MATTERS, YOU REALIZE?
I KNOW. I HAVE LOTS OF THOSE...
...SO A DIFFERENT SUBJECT... SOUNDS NICE TOO...
IS THAT SO? THEN BY ALL MEANS, JOIN US.
UH, HUH?
WHEN ID THIS RN INTO GROUP ESSON ...?

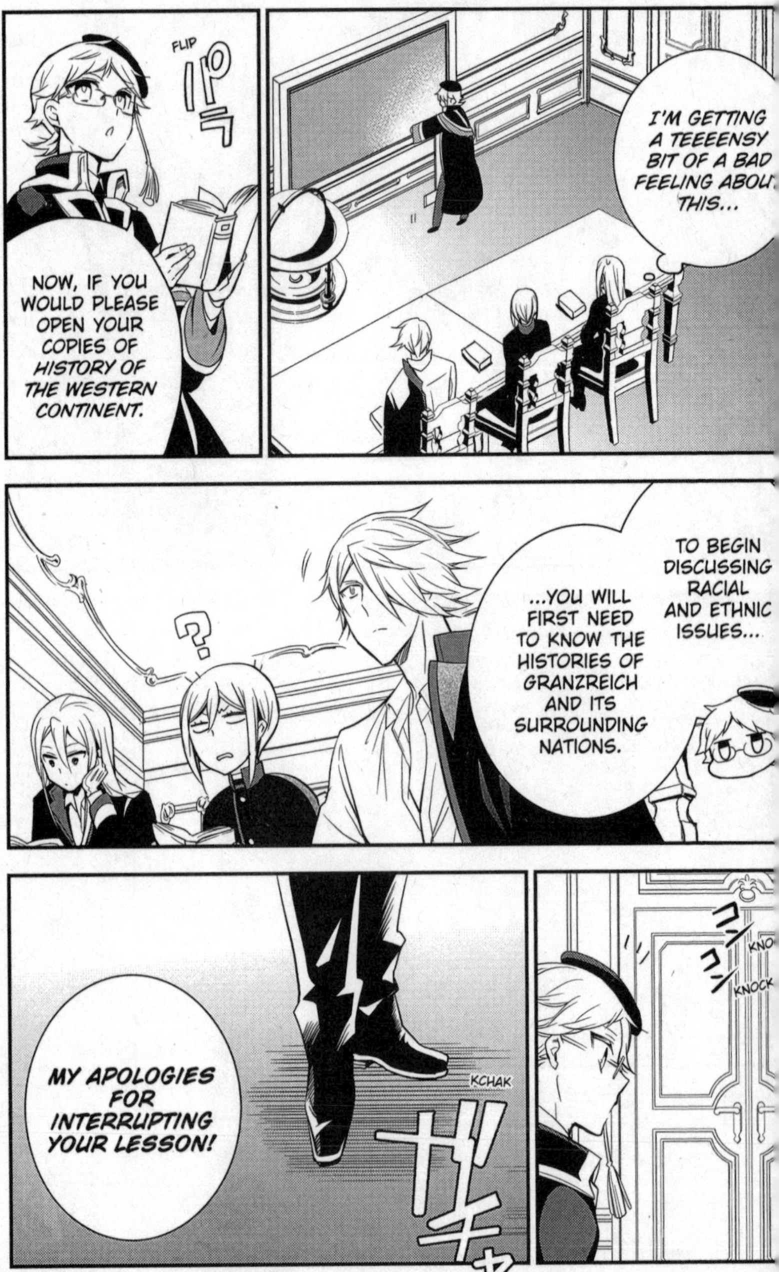
I'M GETTING A TEEEENSY BIT OF A BAD FEELING ABOUT THIS...
FLIP
NOW, IF YOU WOULD PLEASE OPEN YOUR COPIES OF *HISTORY OF THE WESTERN CONTINENT.*
TO BEGIN DISCUSSING RACIAL AND ETHNIC ISSUES...
...YOU WILL FIRST NEED TO KNOW THE HISTORIES OF GRANZREICH AND ITS SURROUNDING NATIONS.
KNOCK
KCHAK
MY APOLOGIES FOR INTERRUPTING YOUR LESSON!

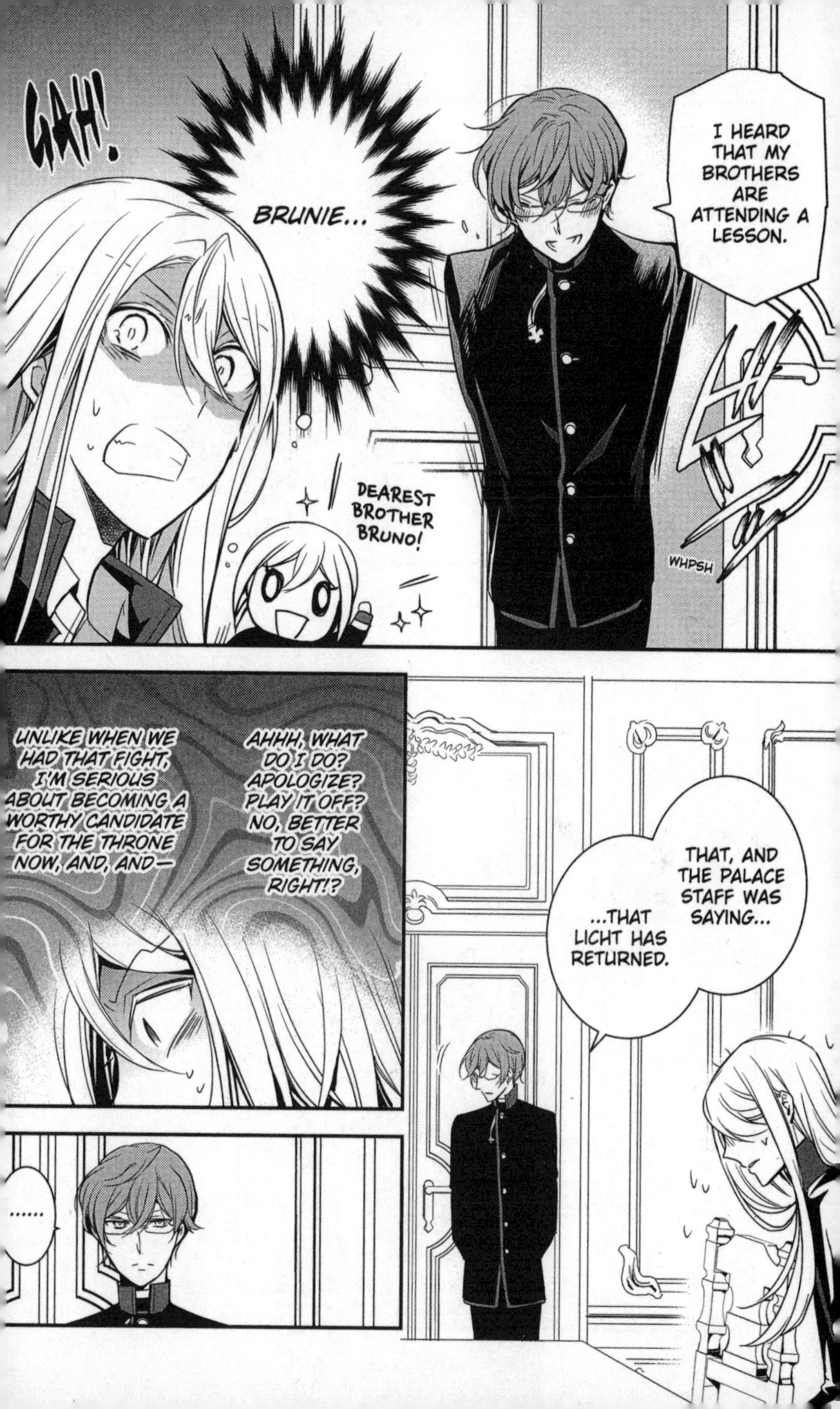
I HEARD THAT MY BROTHERS ARE ATTENDING A LESSON.
WHPSH
BRUNIE...
GAH!
DEAREST BROTHER BRUNO!
THAT, AND THE PALACE STAFF WAS SAYING...
...THAT LICHT HAS RETURNED.
AHHH, WHAT DO I DO? APOLOGIZE? PLAY IT OFF? NO, BETTER TO SAY SOMETHING, RIGHT!?
UNLIKE WHEN WE HAD THAT FIGHT, I'M SERIOUS ABOUT BECOMING A WORTHY CANDIDATE FOR THE THRONE NOW, AND, AND—
......

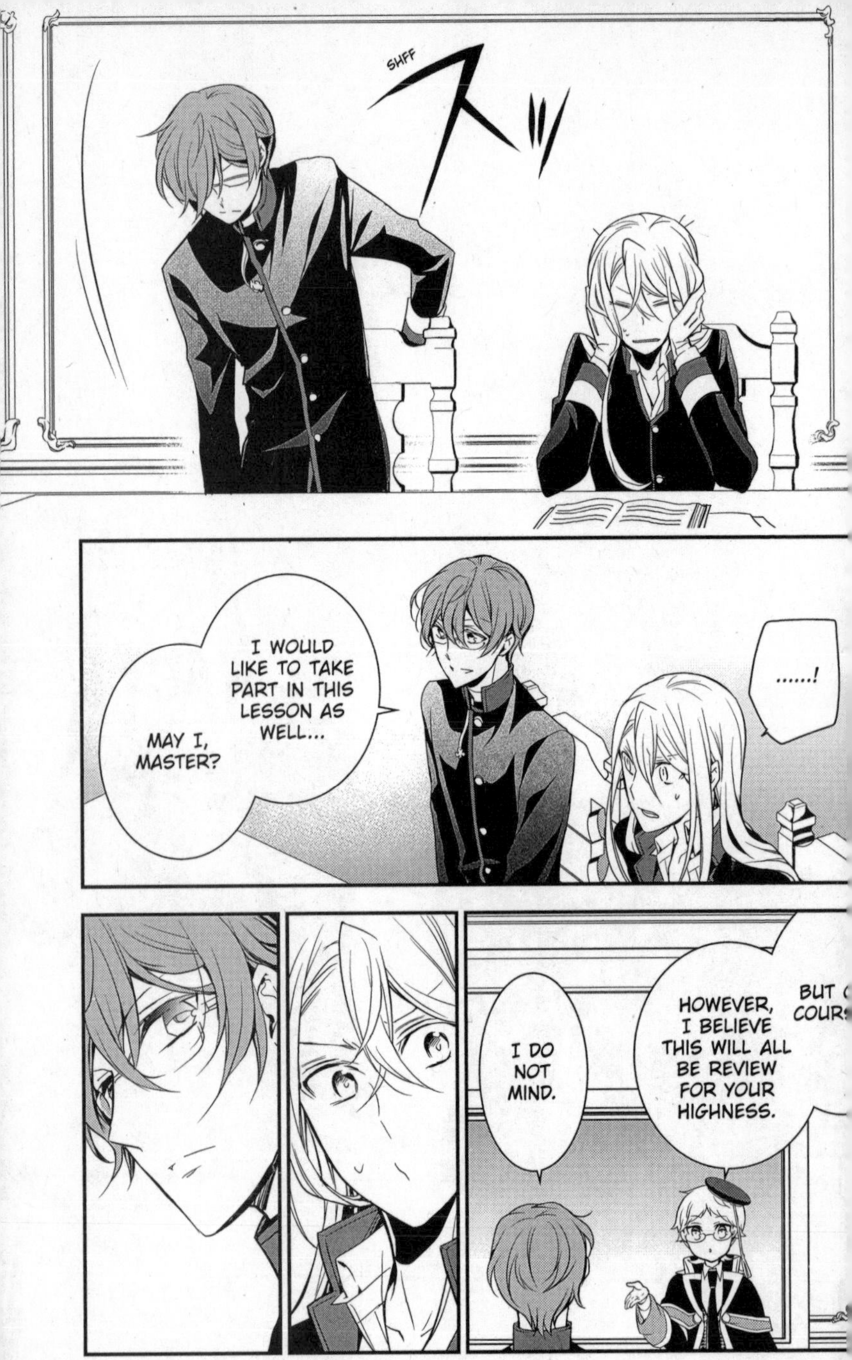
SHFF
I WOULD LIKE TO TAKE PART IN THIS LESSON AS WELL...
MAY I, MASTER?
......!
BUT COUR
HOWEVER, I BELIEVE THIS WILL ALL BE REVIEW FOR YOUR HIGHNESS.
I DO NOT MIND.

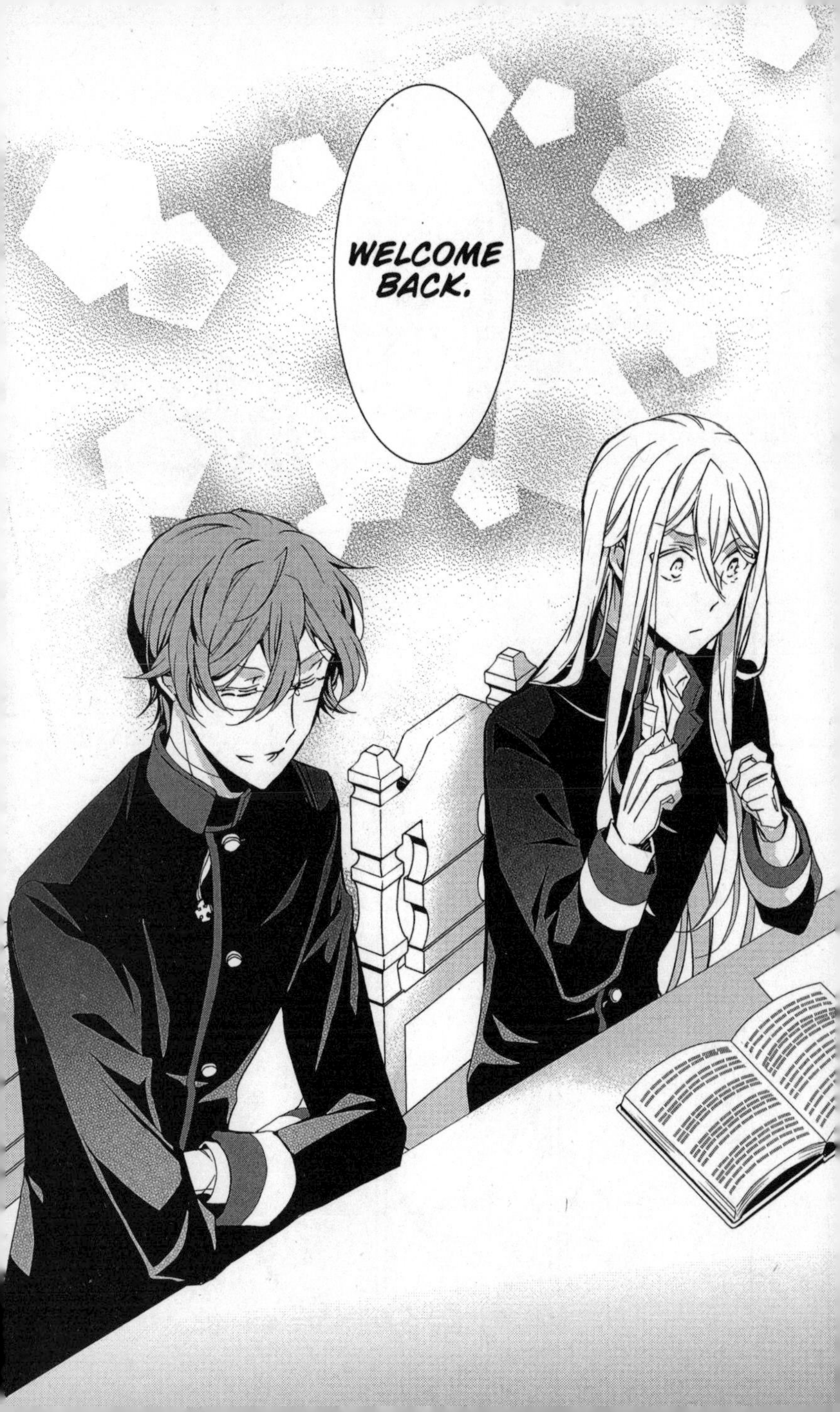
WELCOME BACK.

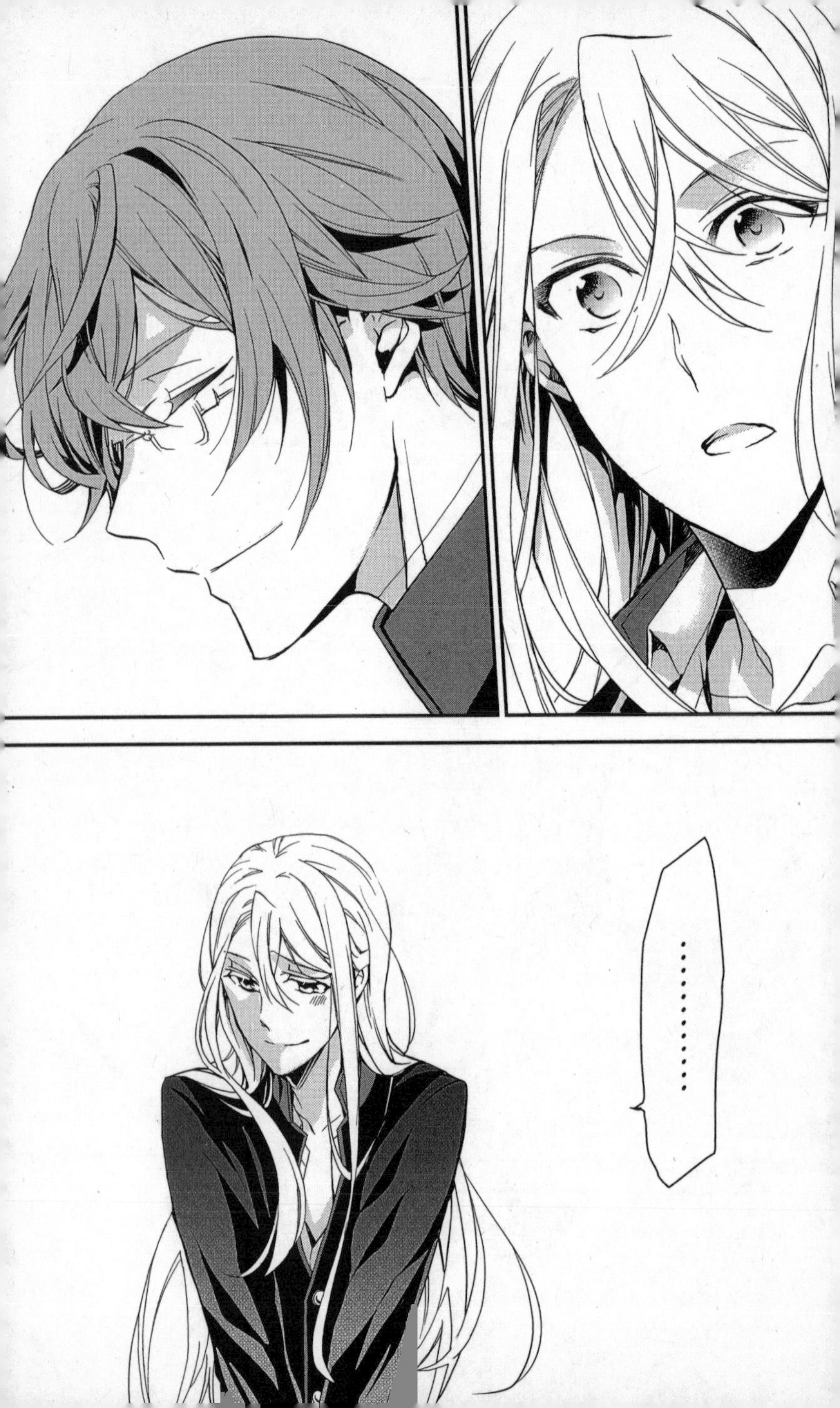
......

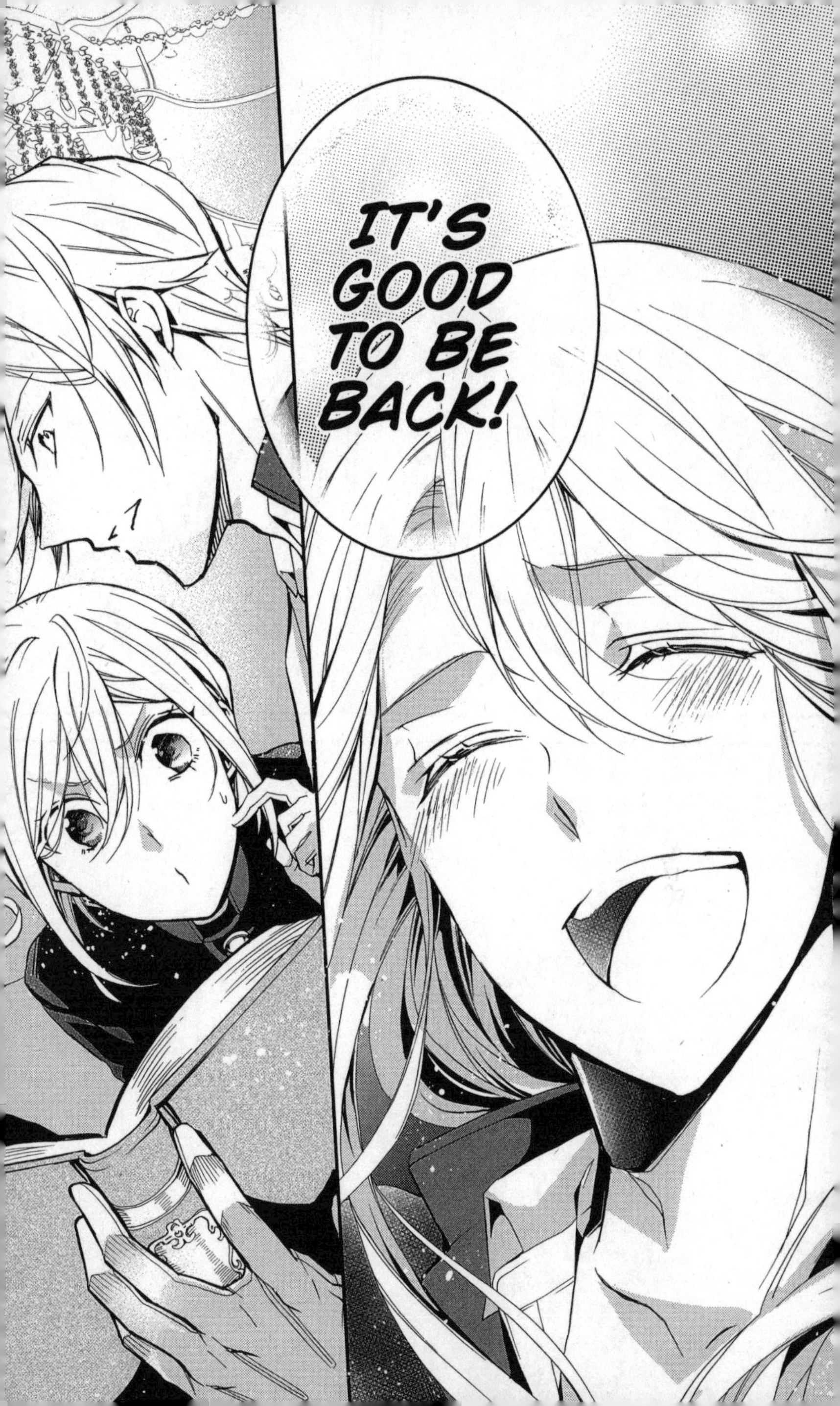
IT'S GOOD TO BE BACK!

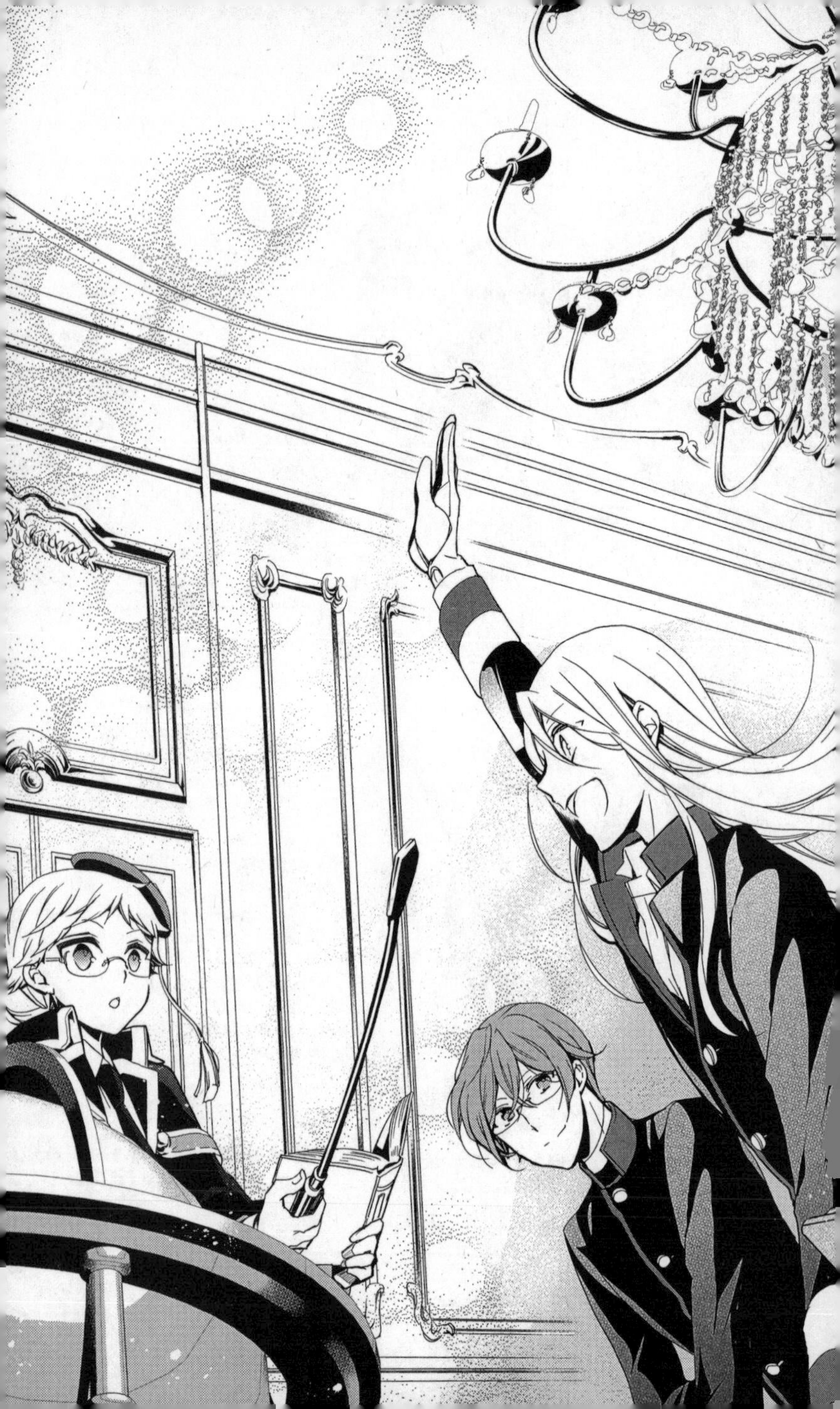

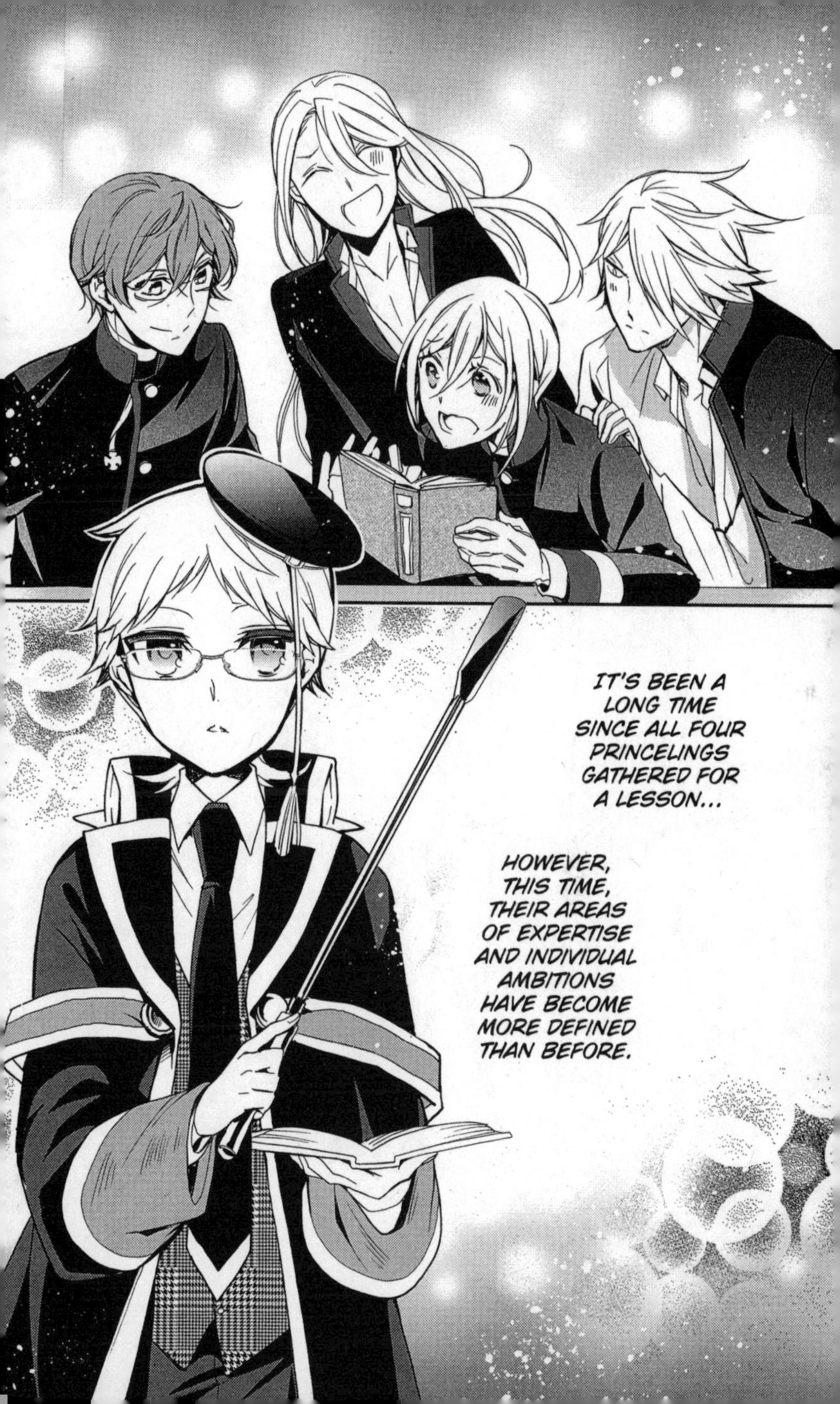
IT'S BEEN A LONG TIME SINCE ALL FOUR PRINCELINGS GATHERED FOR A LESSON...
HOWEVER, THIS TIME, THEIR AREAS OF EXPERTISE AND INDIVIDUAL AMBITIONS HAVE BECOME MORE DEFINED THAN BEFORE.

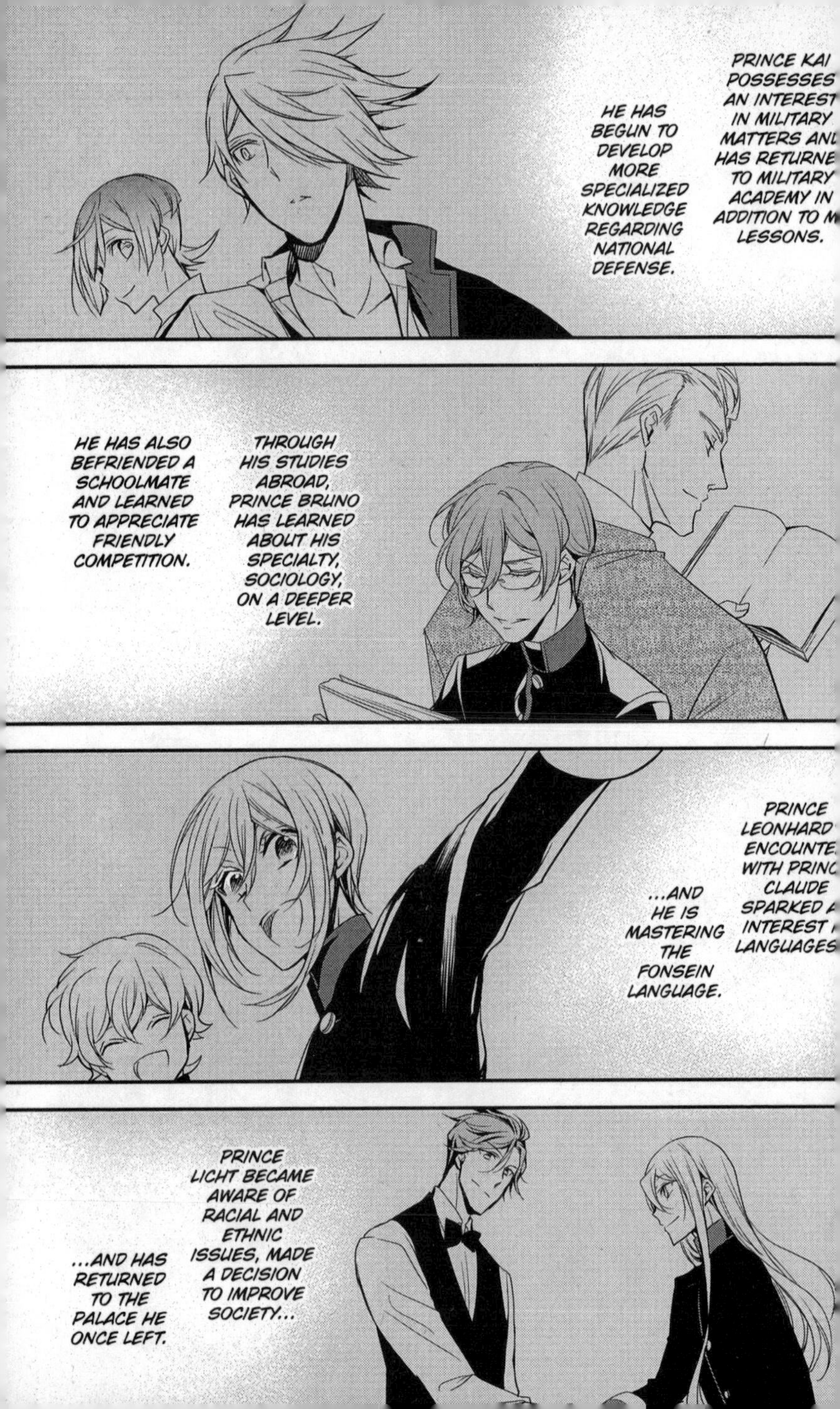
PRINCE KAI POSSESSES AN INTEREST IN MILITARY MATTERS AN HAS RETURNE TO MILITARY ACADEMY IN ADDITION TO M LESSONS.
HE HAS BEGUN TO DEVELOP MORE SPECIALIZED KNOWLEDGE REGARDING NATIONAL DEFENSE.
THROUGH HIS STUDIES ABROAD, PRINCE BRUNO HAS LEARNED ABOUT HIS SPECIALTY, SOCIOLOGY, ON A DEEPER LEVEL.
HE HAS ALSO BEFRIENDED A SCHOOLMATE AND LEARNED TO APPRECIATE FRIENDLY COMPETITION.
PRINCE LEONHARD ENCOUNTE WITH PRINC CLAUDE SPARKED A INTEREST LANGUAGES
...AND HE IS MASTERING THE FONSEIN LANGUAGE.
PRINCE LICHT BECAME AWARE OF RACIAL AND ETHNIC ISSUES, MADE A DECISION TO IMPROVE SOCIETY...
...AND HAS RETURNED TO THE PALACE HE ONCE LEFT.

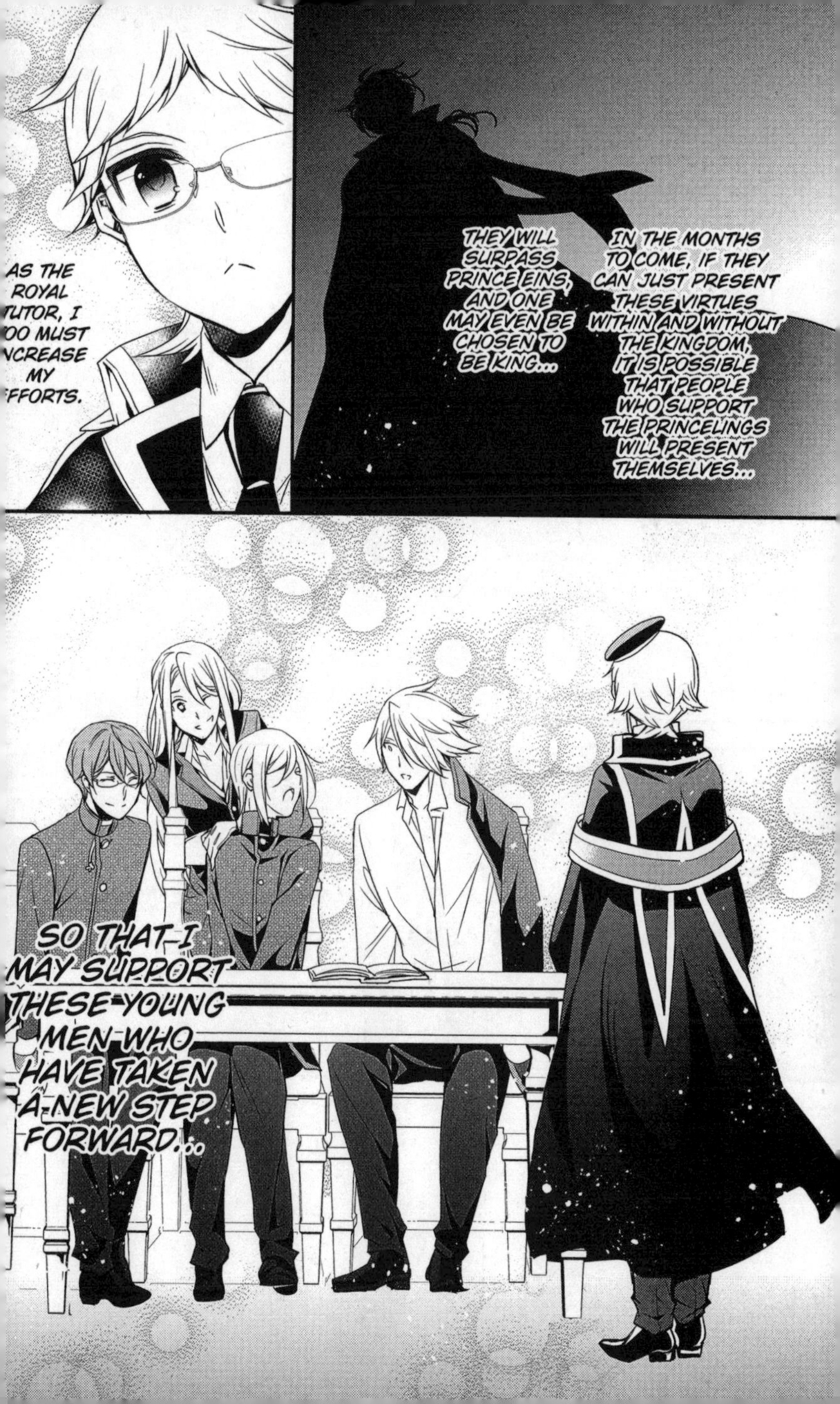
IN THE MONTHS TO COME, IF THEY CAN JUST PRESENT THESE VIRTUES WITHIN AND WITHOUT THE KINGDOM, IT IS POSSIBLE THAT PEOPLE WHO SUPPORT THE PRINCELINGS WILL PRESENT THEMSELVES...
THEY WILL SURPASS PRINCE EINS, AND ONE MAY EVEN BE CHOSEN TO BE KING...
AS THE ROYAL TUTOR, I OO MUST NCREASE MY FFORTS.
SO THAT I MAY SUPPORT THESE YOUNG MEN WHO HAVE TAKEN A NEW STEP FORWARD...

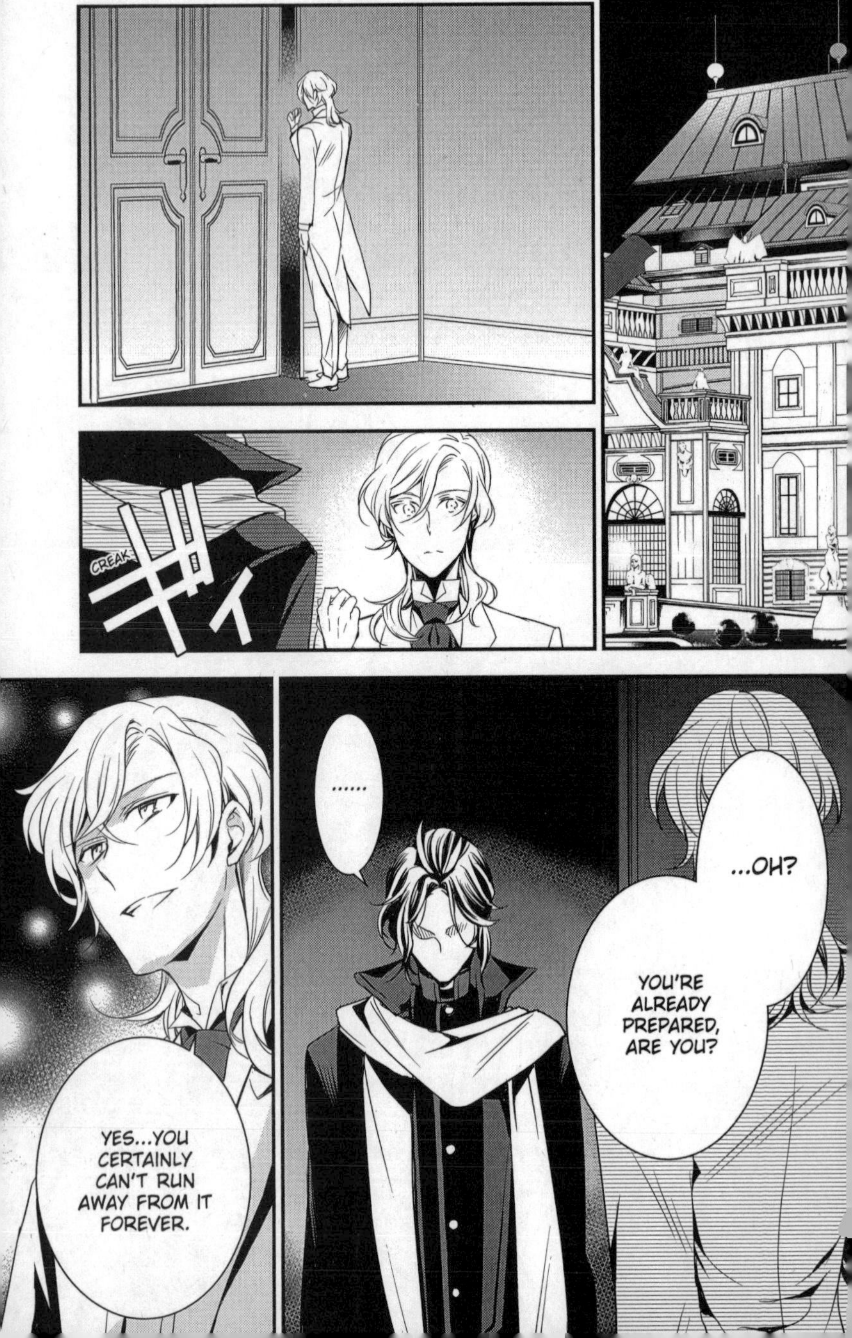
CREAK
ギィ
...OH?
YOU'RE ALREADY PREPARED, ARE YOU?
......
YES...YOU CERTAINLY CAN'T RUN AWAY FROM IT FOREVER.

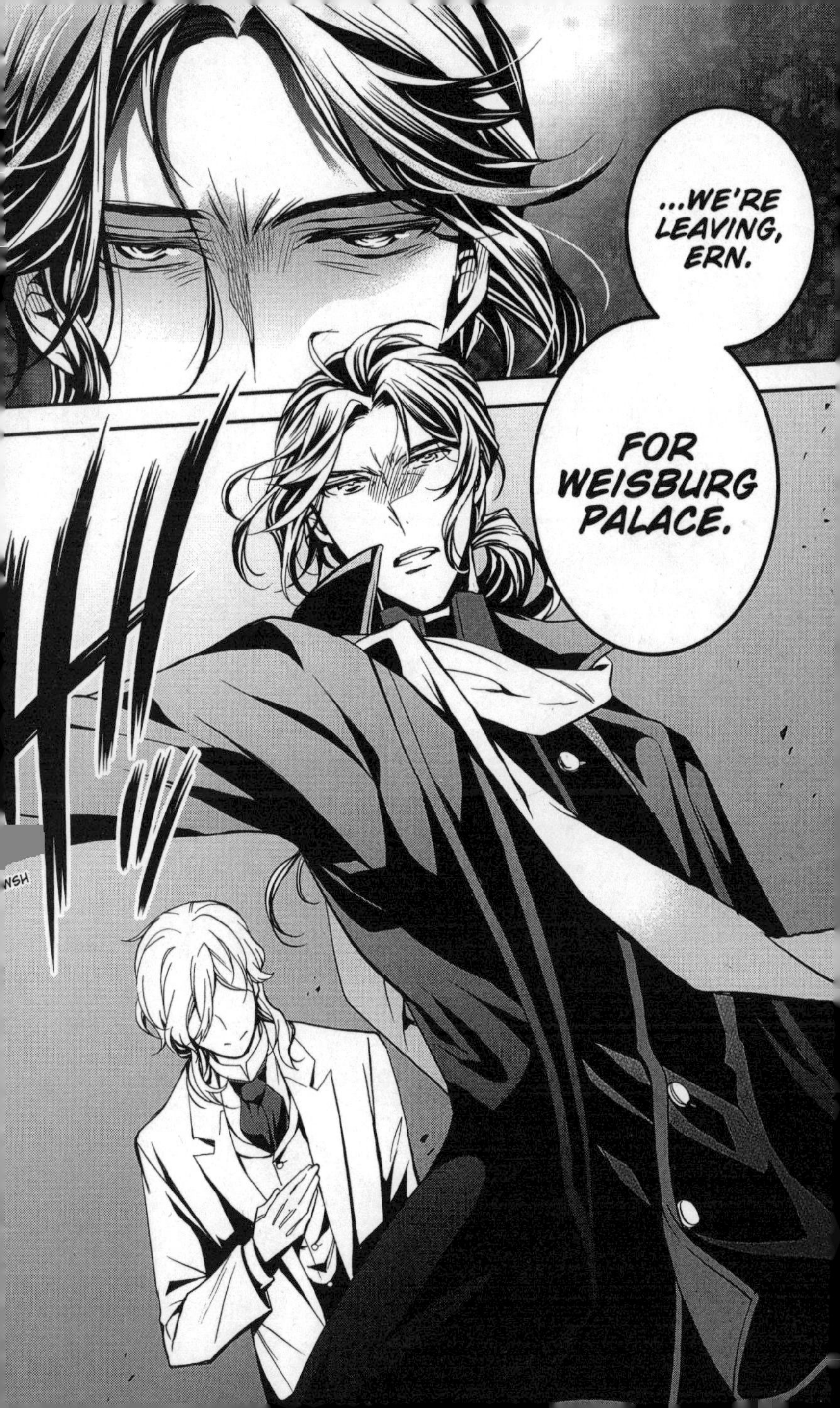
...WE'RE LEAVING, ERN.
FOR WEISBURG PALACE.
WSH

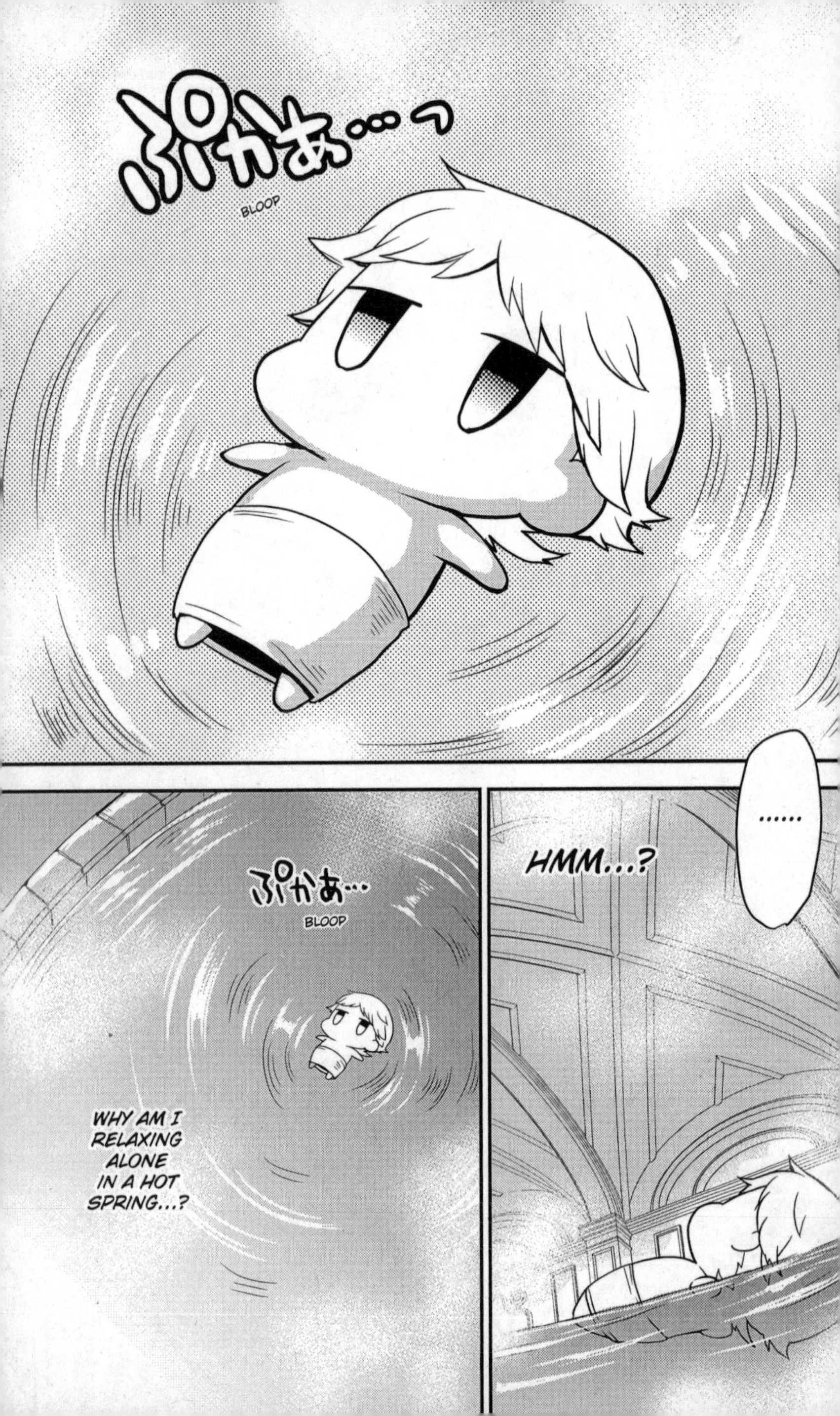
ぷかあ…っ
BLOOP
……
HMM…?
ぷかあ…
BLOOP
WHY AM I RELAXING ALONE IN A HOT SPRING…?

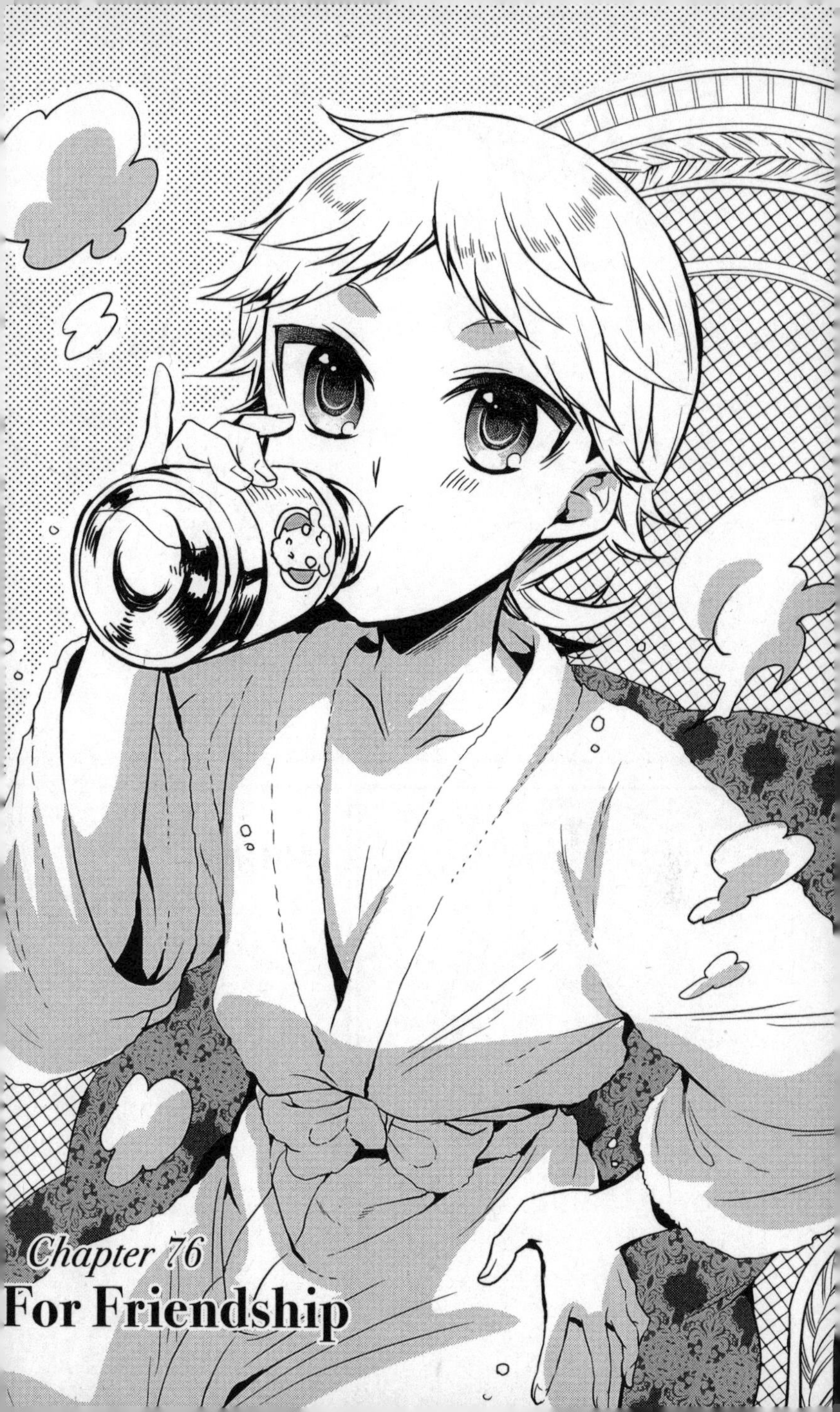
Chapter 76
For Friendship

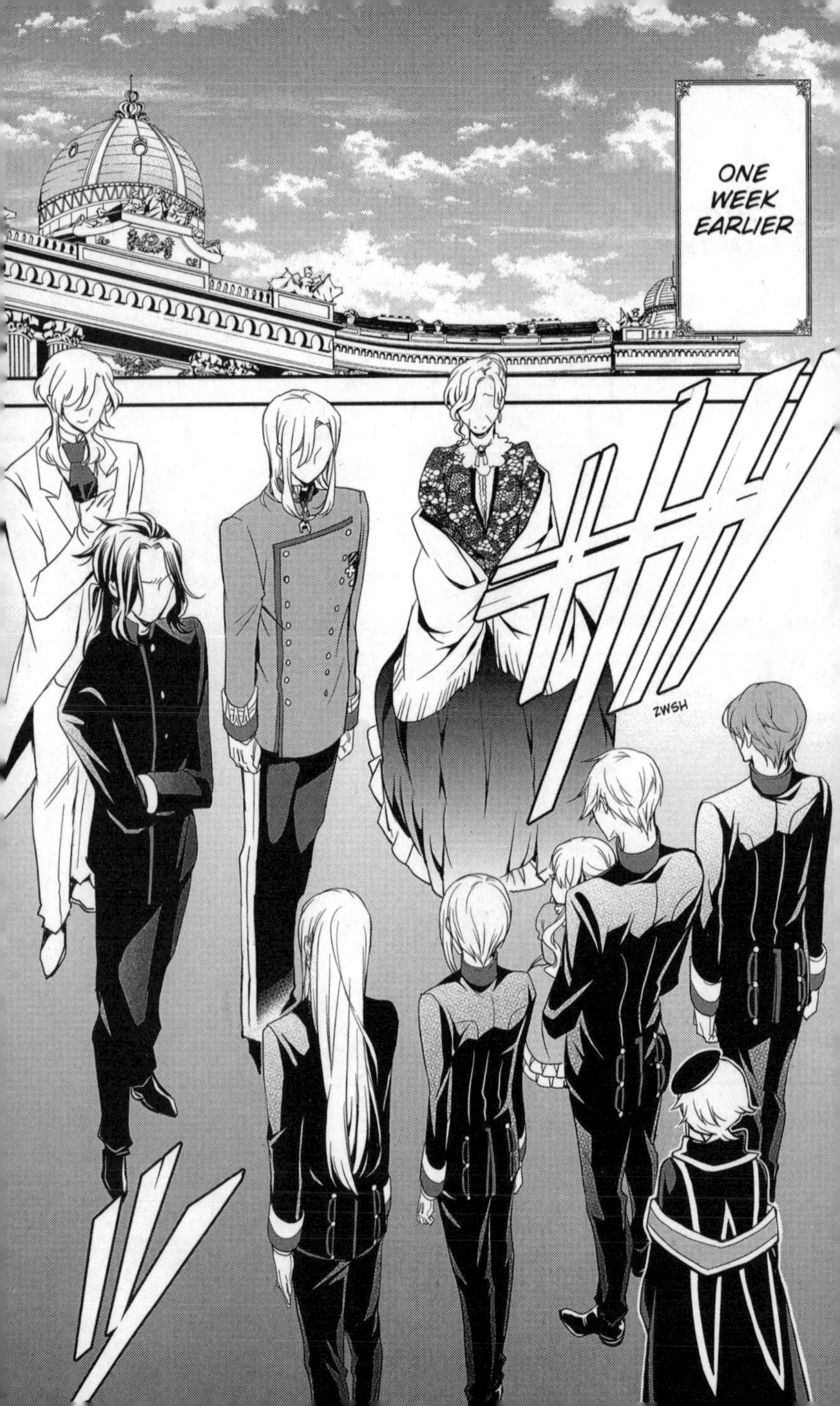
ONE WEEK EARLIER
ZWSH

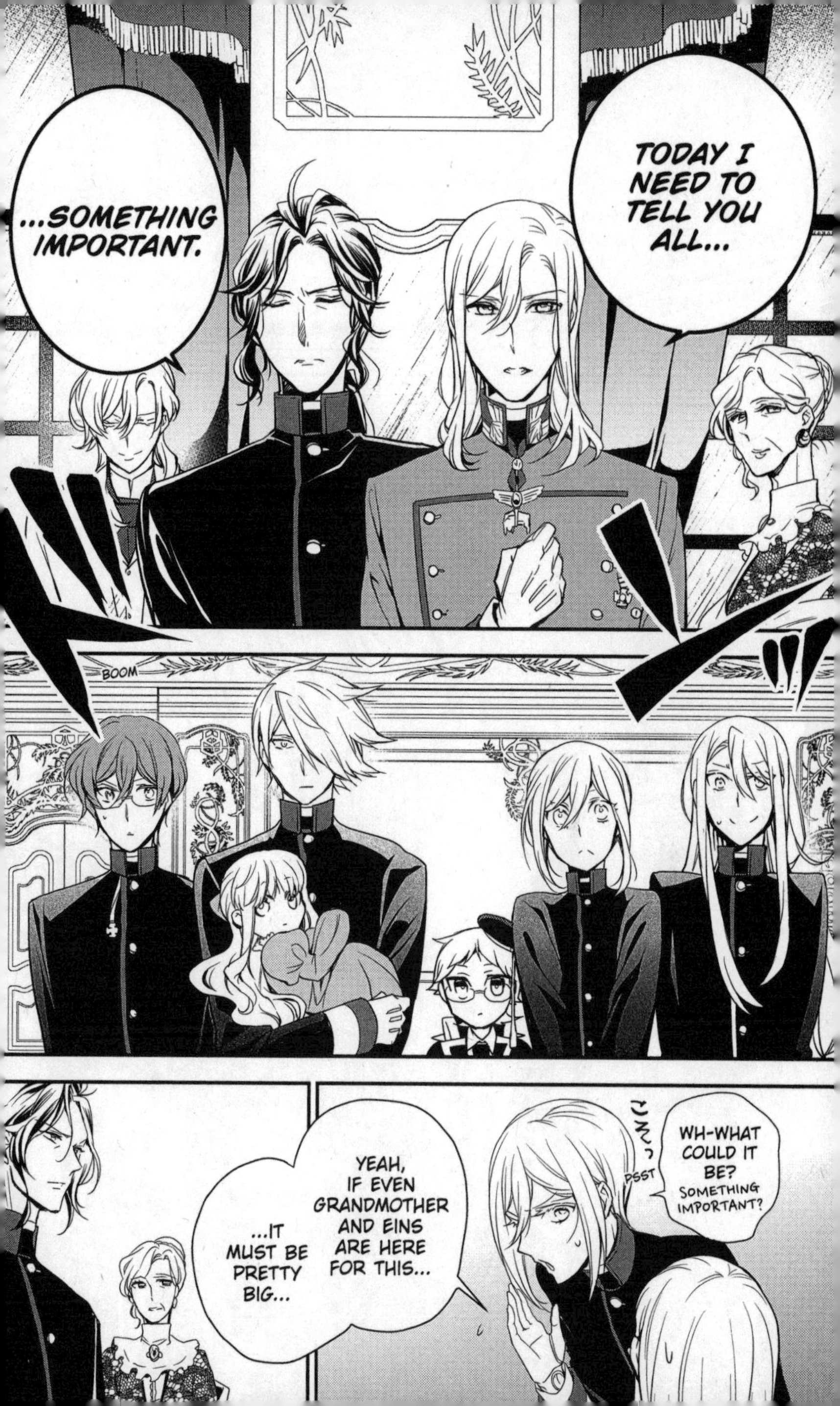
TODAY I NEED TO TELL YOU ALL...
...SOMETHING IMPORTANT.
BOOM
こそっ
PSST
WH-WHAT COULD IT BE? SOMETHING IMPORTANT?
YEAH, IF EVEN GRANDMOTHER AND EINS ARE HERE FOR THIS...
...IT MUST BE PRETTY BIG...

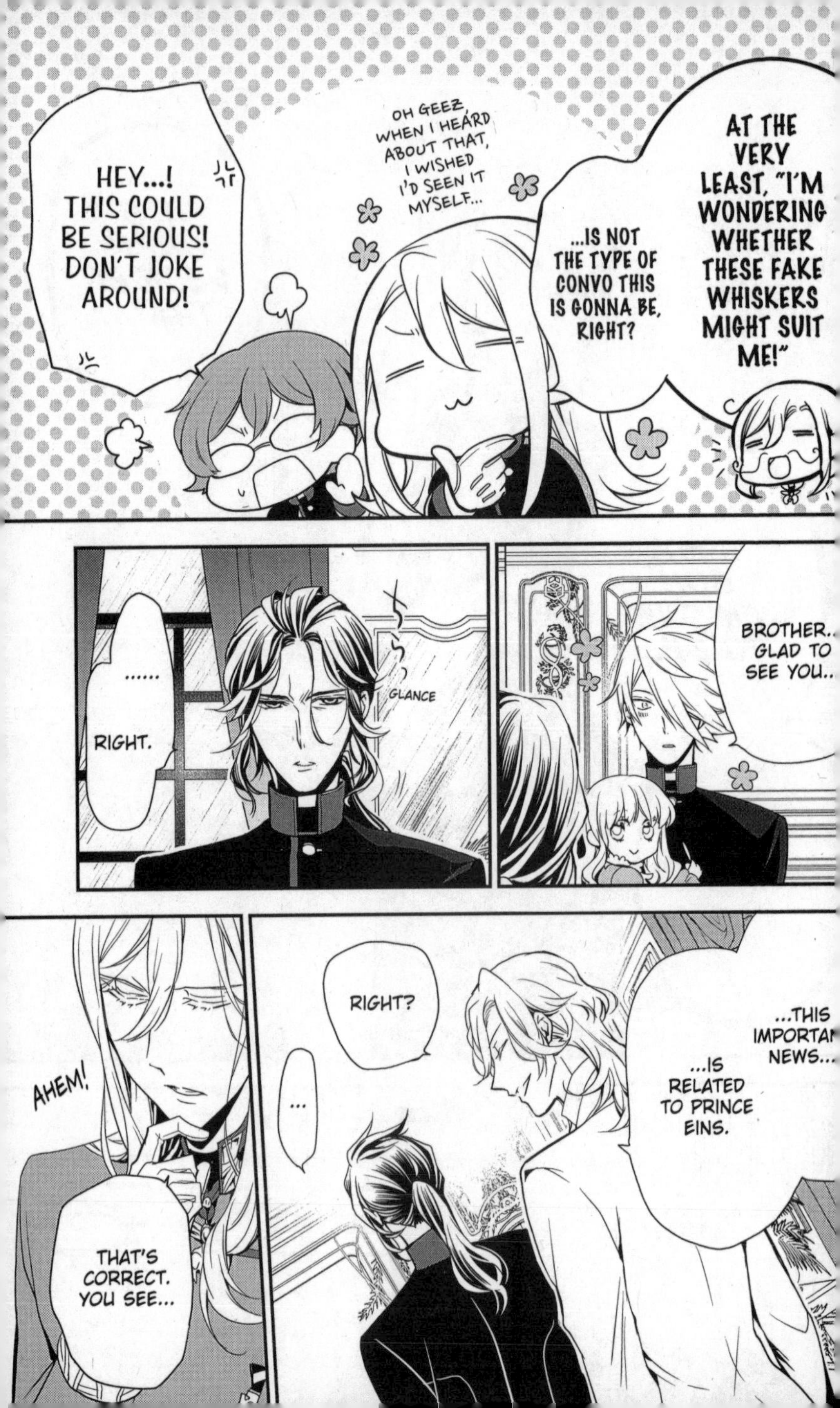
AT THE VERY LEAST, "I'M WONDERING WHETHER THESE FAKE WHISKERS MIGHT SUIT ME!"
...IS NOT THE TYPE OF CONVO THIS IS GONNA BE, RIGHT?
OH GEEZ, WHEN I HEARD ABOUT THAT, I WISHED I'D SEEN IT MYSELF...
HEY...! THIS COULD BE SERIOUS! DON'T JOKE AROUND!
BROTHER.. GLAD TO SEE YOU...
GLANCE
...... RIGHT.
...THIS IMPORTAN NEWS...
...IS RELATED TO PRINCE EINS.
RIGHT?
...
AHEM!
THAT'S CORRECT. YOU SEE...

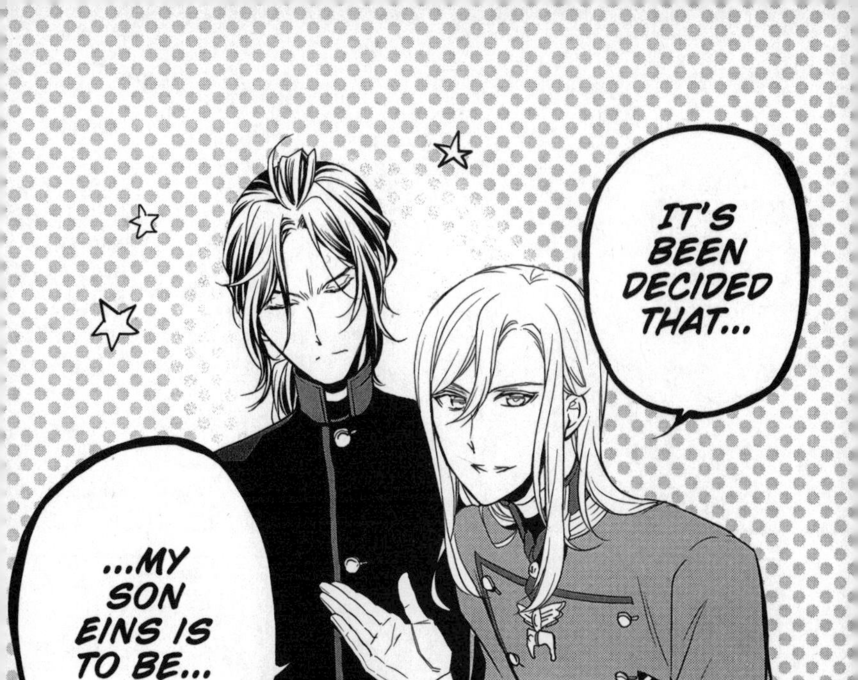
IT'S BEEN DECIDED THAT...
...MY SON EINS IS TO BE...
...MARRIED!
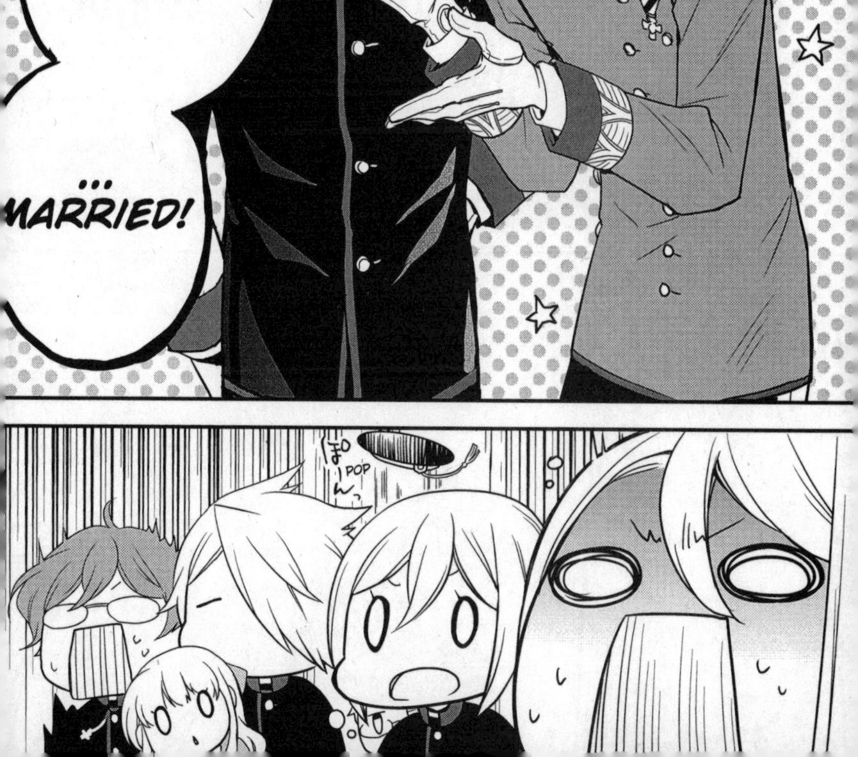
POP

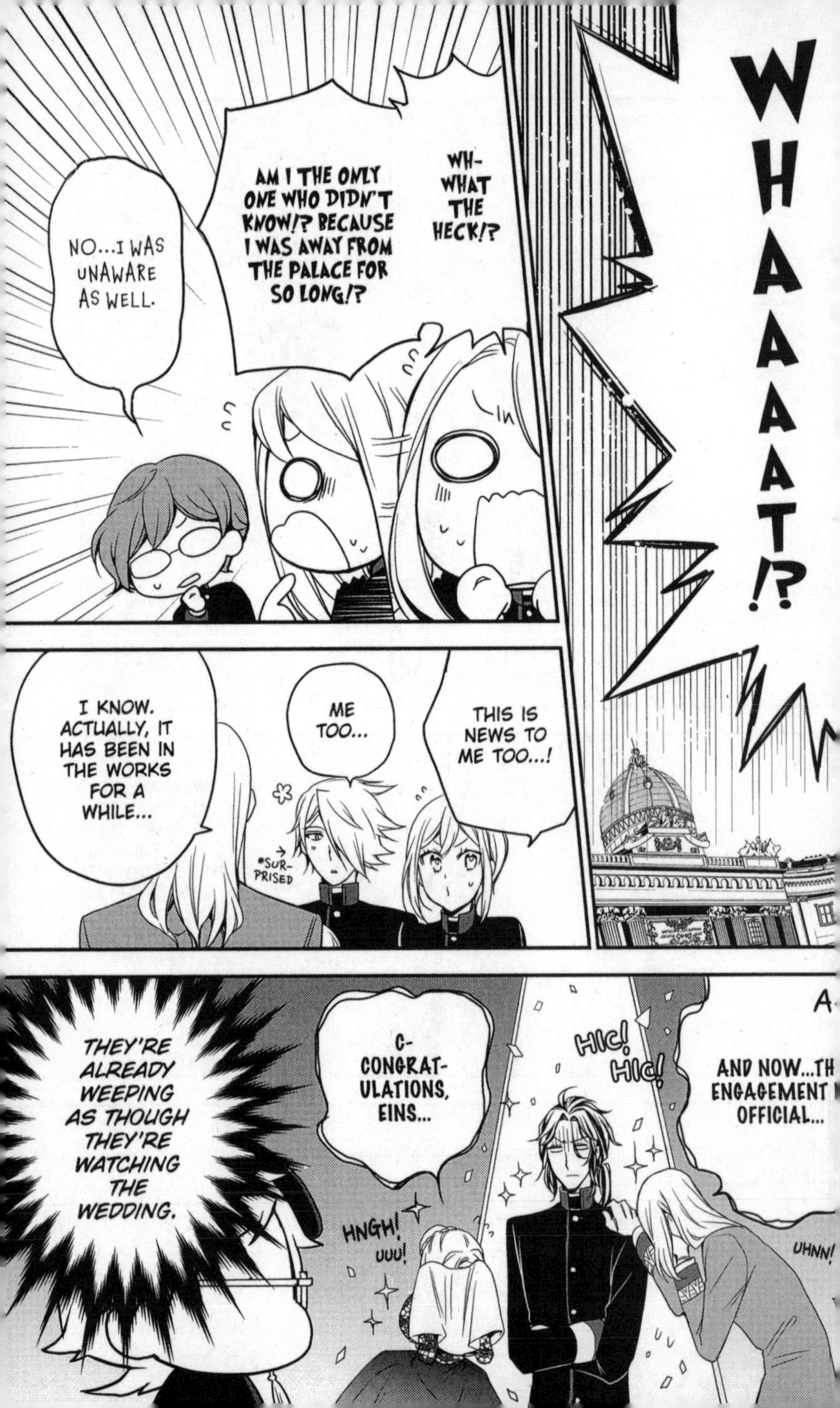
WHAAAAT!?
WH-WHAT THE HECK!?
AM I THE ONLY ONE WHO DIDN'T KNOW!? BECAUSE I WAS AWAY FROM THE PALACE FOR SO LONG!?
NO...I WAS UNAWARE AS WELL.
THIS IS NEWS TO ME TOO...!
ME TOO...
*SURPRISED
I KNOW. ACTUALLY, IT HAS BEEN IN THE WORKS FOR A WHILE...
A
AND NOW...TH ENGAGEMENT OFFICIAL...
HIC! HIC!
UHNN!
C-CONGRATULATIONS, EINS...
HNGH! UUU!
THEY'RE ALREADY WEEPING AS THOUGH THEY'RE WATCHING THE WEDDING.

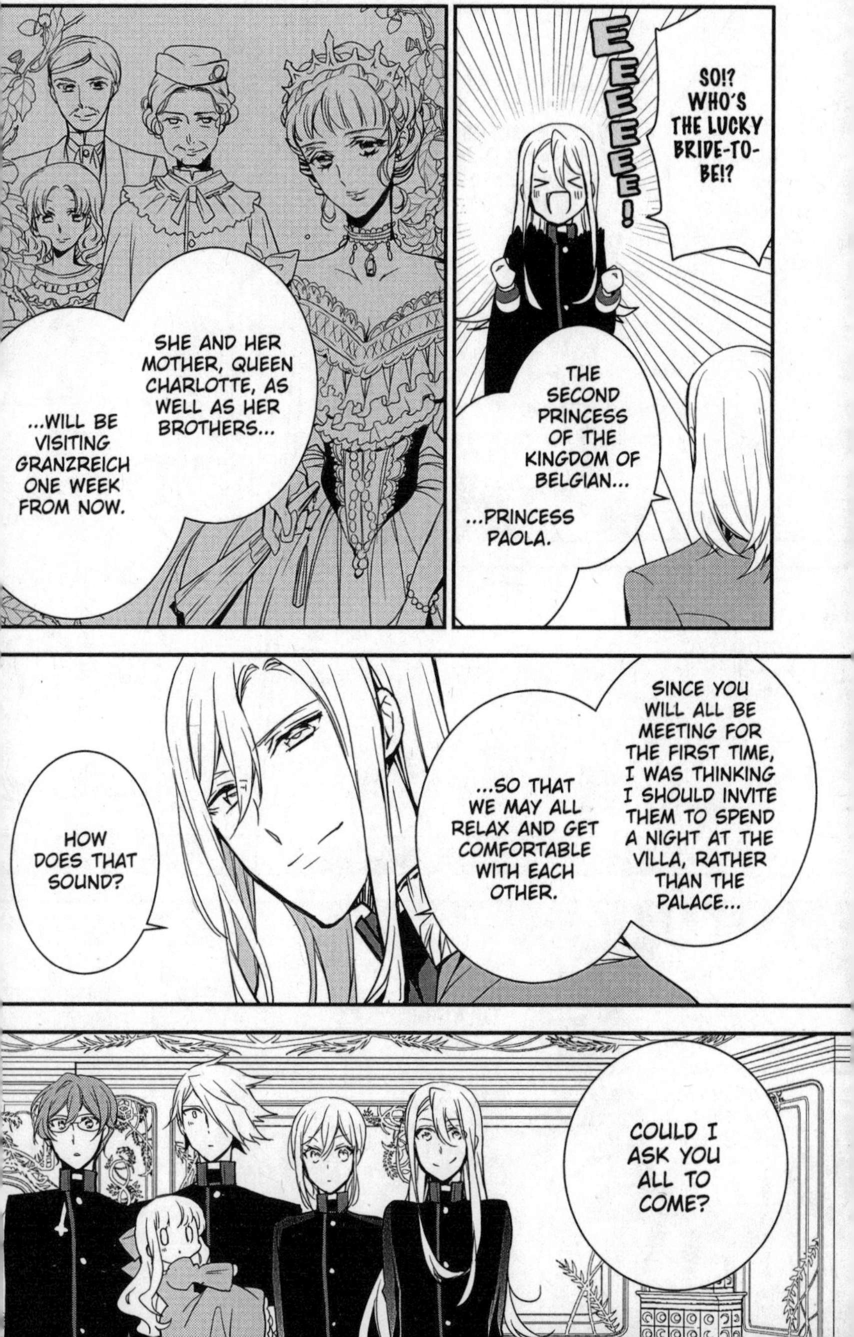
SO!? WHO'S THE LUCKY BRIDE-TO-BE!?
EEEEEE!
THE SECOND PRINCESS OF THE KINGDOM OF BELGIAN... ...PRINCESS PAOLA.
SHE AND HER MOTHER, QUEEN CHARLOTTE, AS WELL AS HER BROTHERS...
...WILL BE VISITING GRANZREICH ONE WEEK FROM NOW.
SINCE YOU WILL ALL BE MEETING FOR THE FIRST TIME, I WAS THINKING I SHOULD INVITE THEM TO SPEND A NIGHT AT THE VILLA, RATHER THAN THE PALACE...
...SO THAT WE MAY ALL RELAX AND GET COMFORTABLE WITH EACH OTHER.
HOW DOES THAT SOUND?
COULD I ASK YOU ALL TO COME?

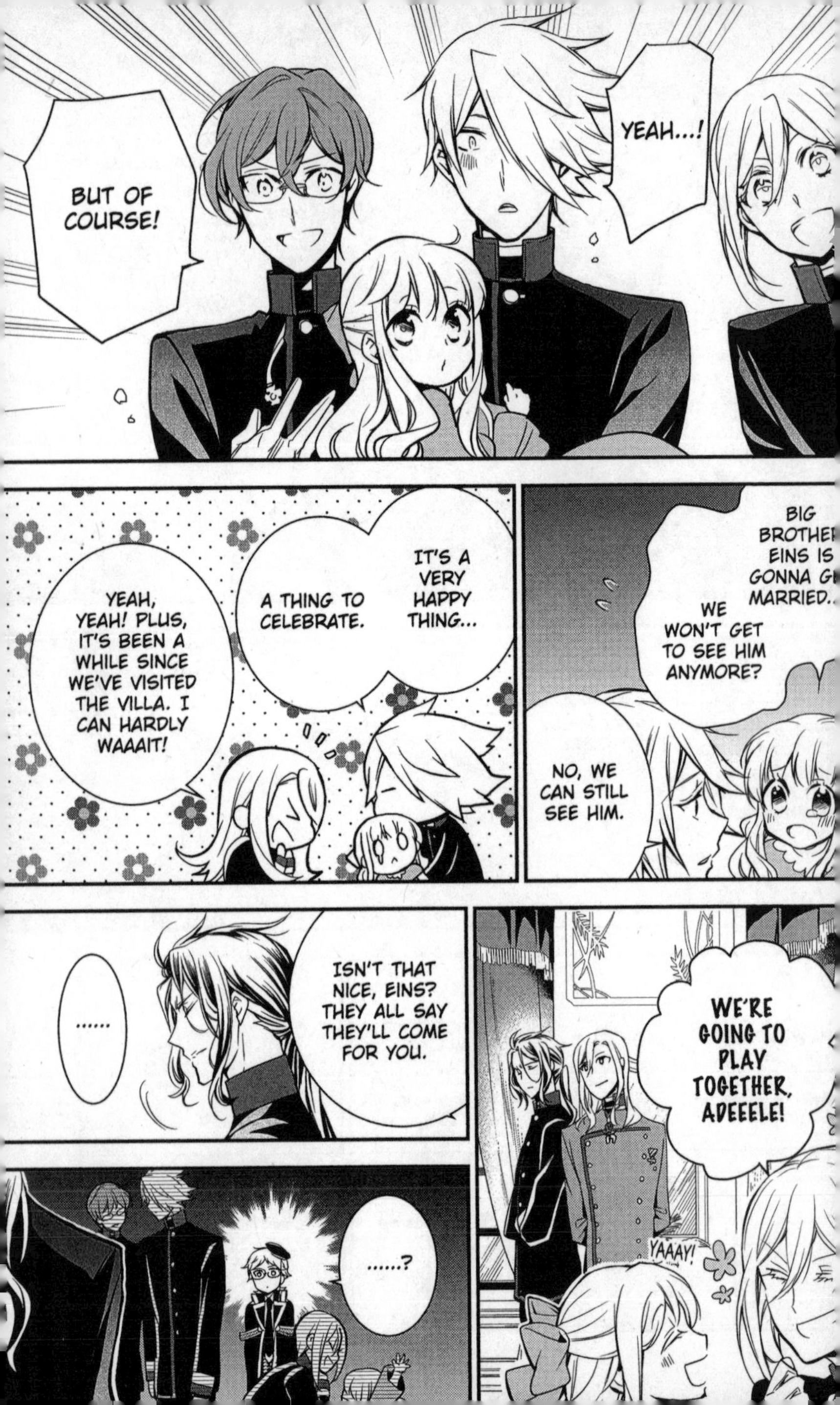
YEAH...!
BUT OF COURSE!
BIG BROTHE EINS IS GONNA G MARRIED...
WE WON'T GET TO SEE HIM ANYMORE?
NO, WE CAN STILL SEE HIM.
IT'S A VERY HAPPY THING...
A THING TO CELEBRATE.
YEAH, YEAH! PLUS, IT'S BEEN A WHILE SINCE WE'VE VISITED THE VILLA. I CAN HARDLY WAAAIT!
WE'RE GOING TO PLAY TOGETHER, ADEEELE!
YAAAY!
ISN'T THAT NICE, EINS? THEY ALL SAY THEY'LL COME FOR YOU.
......
......?

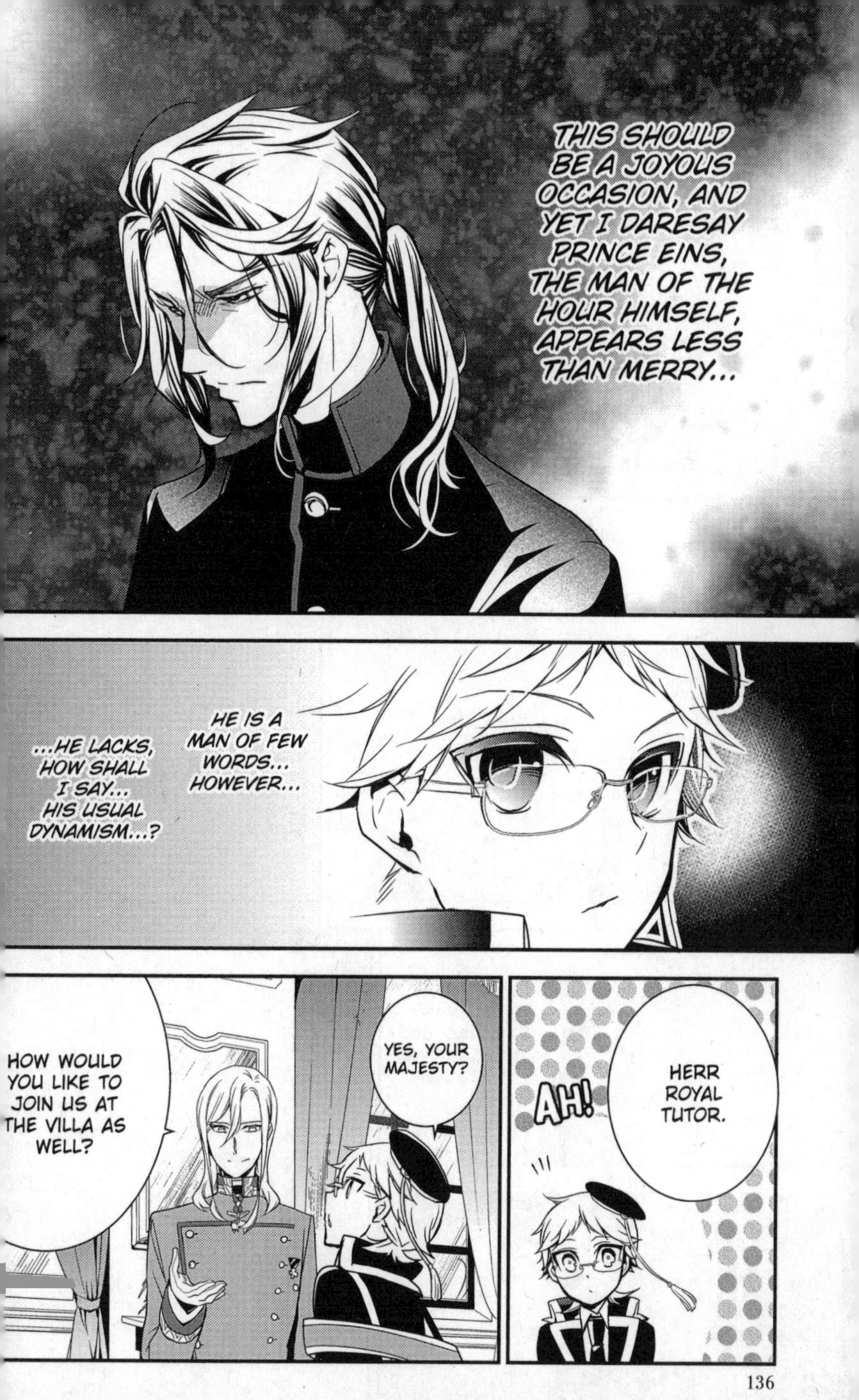
THIS SHOULD BE A JOYOUS OCCASION, AND YET I DARESAY PRINCE EINS, THE MAN OF THE HOUR HIMSELF, APPEARS LESS THAN MERRY...
HE IS A MAN OF FEW WORDS... HOWEVER...
...HE LACKS, HOW SHALL I SAY... HIS USUAL DYNAMISM...?
HERR ROYAL TUTOR.
AH!
YES, YOUR MAJESTY?
HOW WOULD YOU LIKE TO JOIN US AT THE VILLA AS WELL?

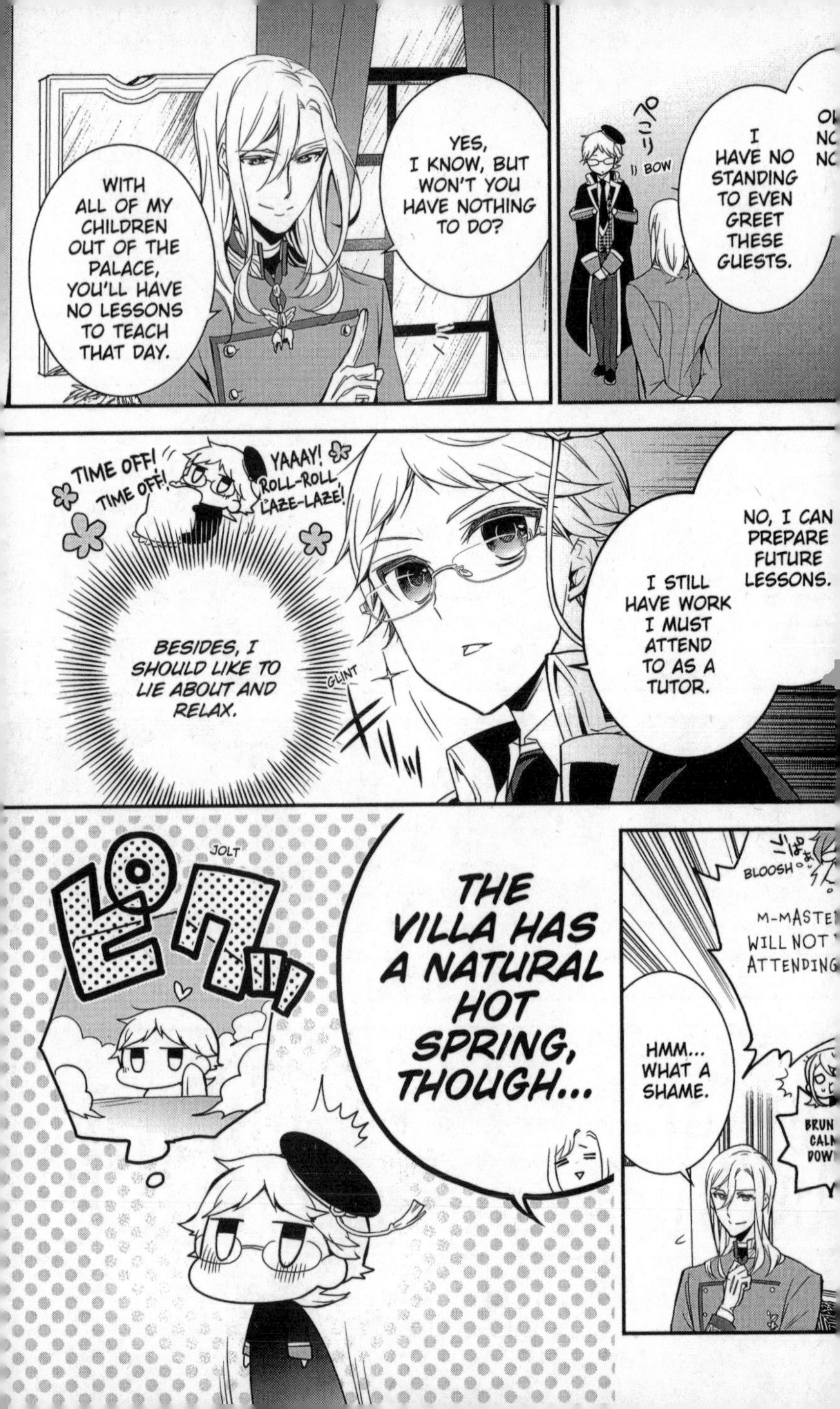
BOW
I HAVE NO STANDING TO EVEN GREET THESE GUESTS.
YES, I KNOW, BUT WON'T YOU HAVE NOTHING TO DO?
WITH ALL OF MY CHILDREN OUT OF THE PALACE, YOU'LL HAVE NO LESSONS TO TEACH THAT DAY.
NO, I CAN PREPARE FUTURE LESSONS.
I STILL HAVE WORK I MUST ATTEND TO AS A TUTOR.
GLINT
BESIDES, I SHOULD LIKE TO LIE ABOUT AND RELAX.
YAAAY! ROLL-ROLL LAZE-LAZE!
TIME OFF! TIME OFF!
BLOOSH
HMM... WHAT A SHAME.
THE VILLA HAS A NATURAL HOT SPRING, THOUGH...
JOLT

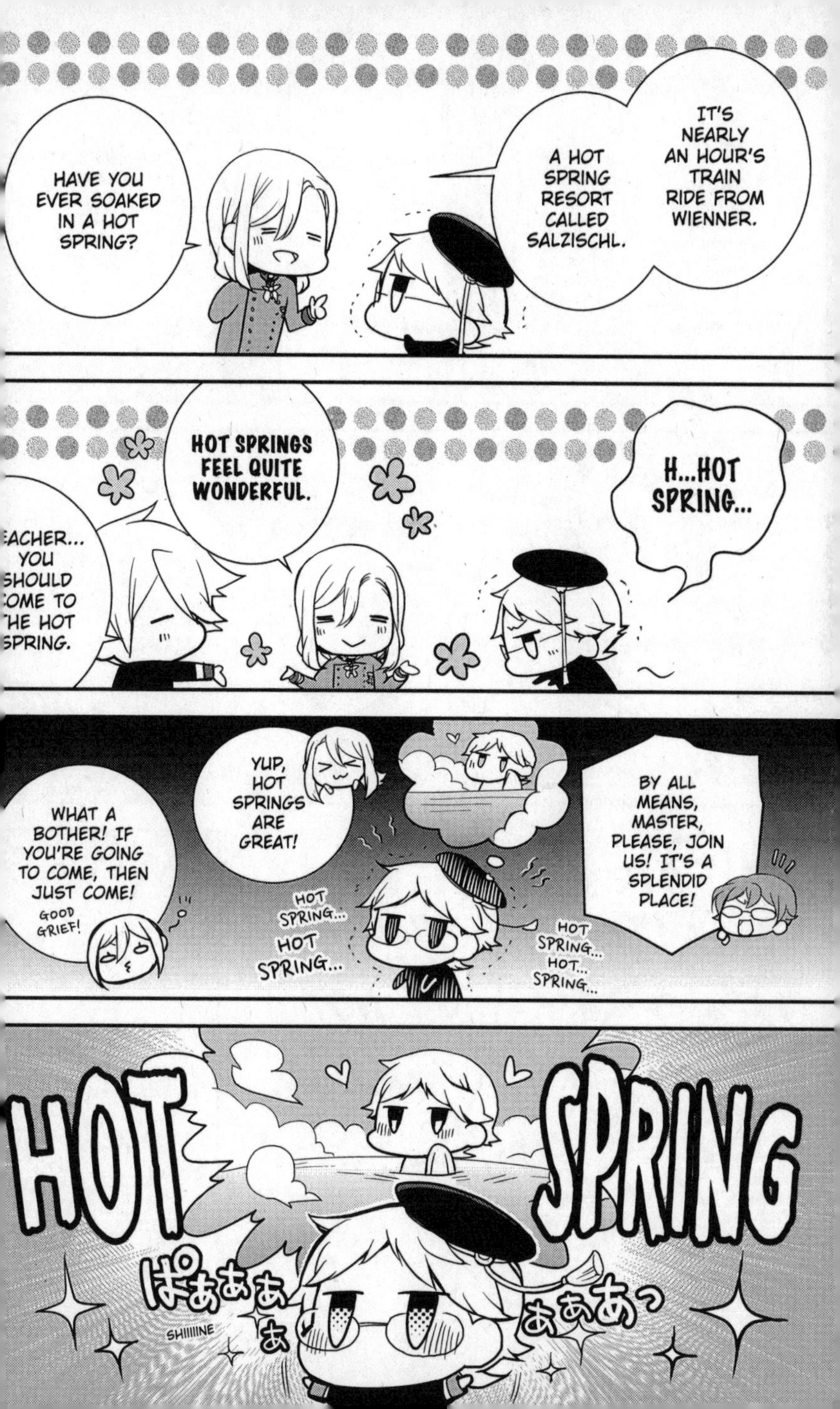

IT'S NEARLY AN HOUR'S TRAIN RIDE FROM WIENNER.
A HOT SPRING RESORT CALLED SALZISCHL.
HAVE YOU EVER SOAKED IN A HOT SPRING?
H...HOT SPRING...
HOT SPRINGS FEEL QUITE WONDERFUL.
EACHER... YOU SHOULD COME TO THE HOT SPRING.
BY ALL MEANS, MASTER, PLEASE, JOIN US! IT'S A SPLENDID PLACE!
HOT SPRING... HOT... SPRING...
YUP, HOT SPRINGS ARE GREAT!
HOT SPRING... HOT SPRING...
WHAT A BOTHER! IF YOU'RE GOING TO COME, THEN JUST COME!
GOOD GRIEF!
HOT SPRING
ぱあああああああっ
SHIIIIINE

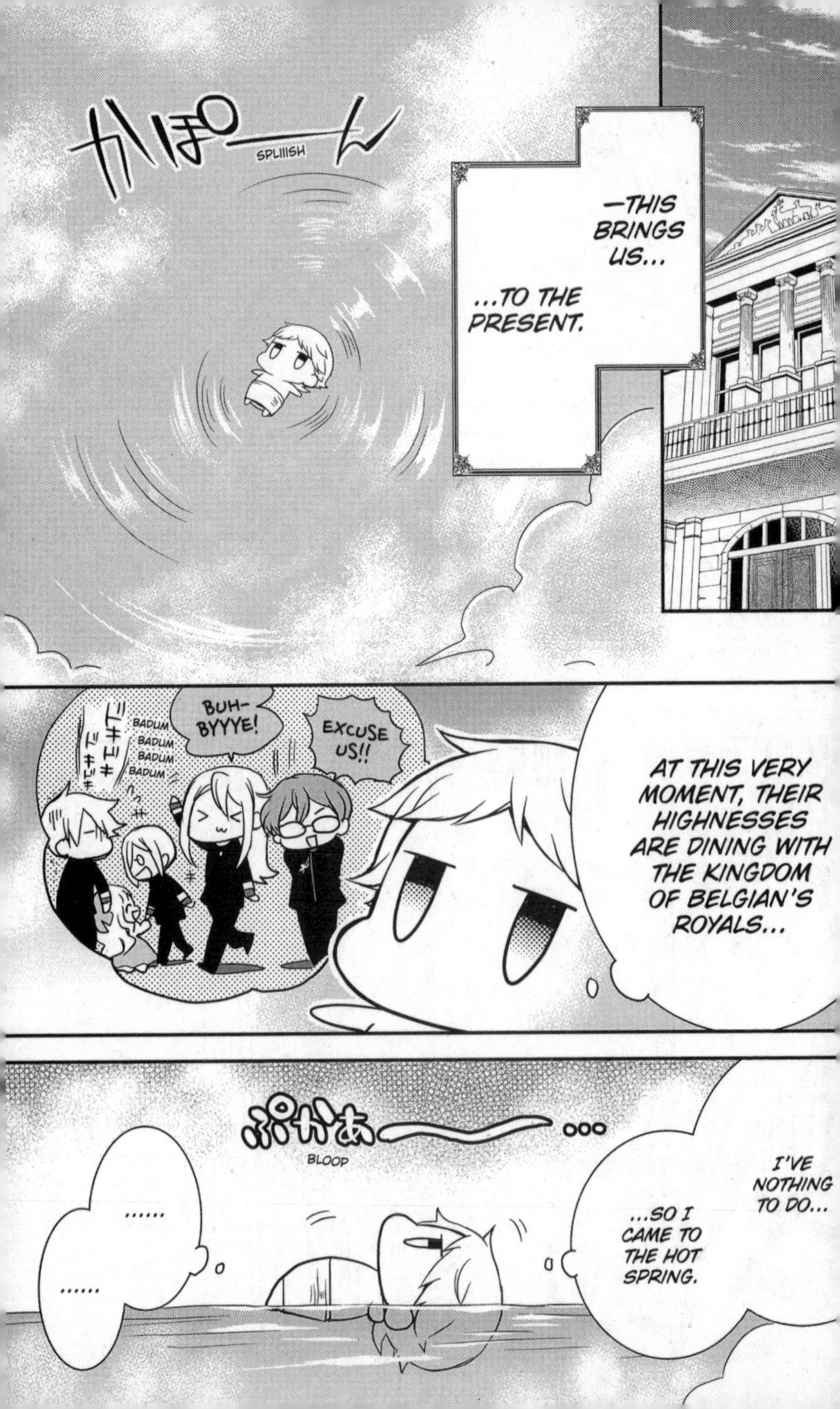
—THIS BRINGS US...
...TO THE PRESENT.
かぽーん
SPLIIISH
AT THIS VERY MOMENT, THEIR HIGHNESSES ARE DINING WITH THE KINGDOM OF BELGIAN'S ROYALS...
EXCUSE US!!
BUH-BYYYE!
ドキドキドキドキ
BADUM BADUM BADUM BADUM
I'VE NOTHING TO DO...
...SO I CAME TO THE HOT SPRING.
ぷかあ
BLOOP
......
......

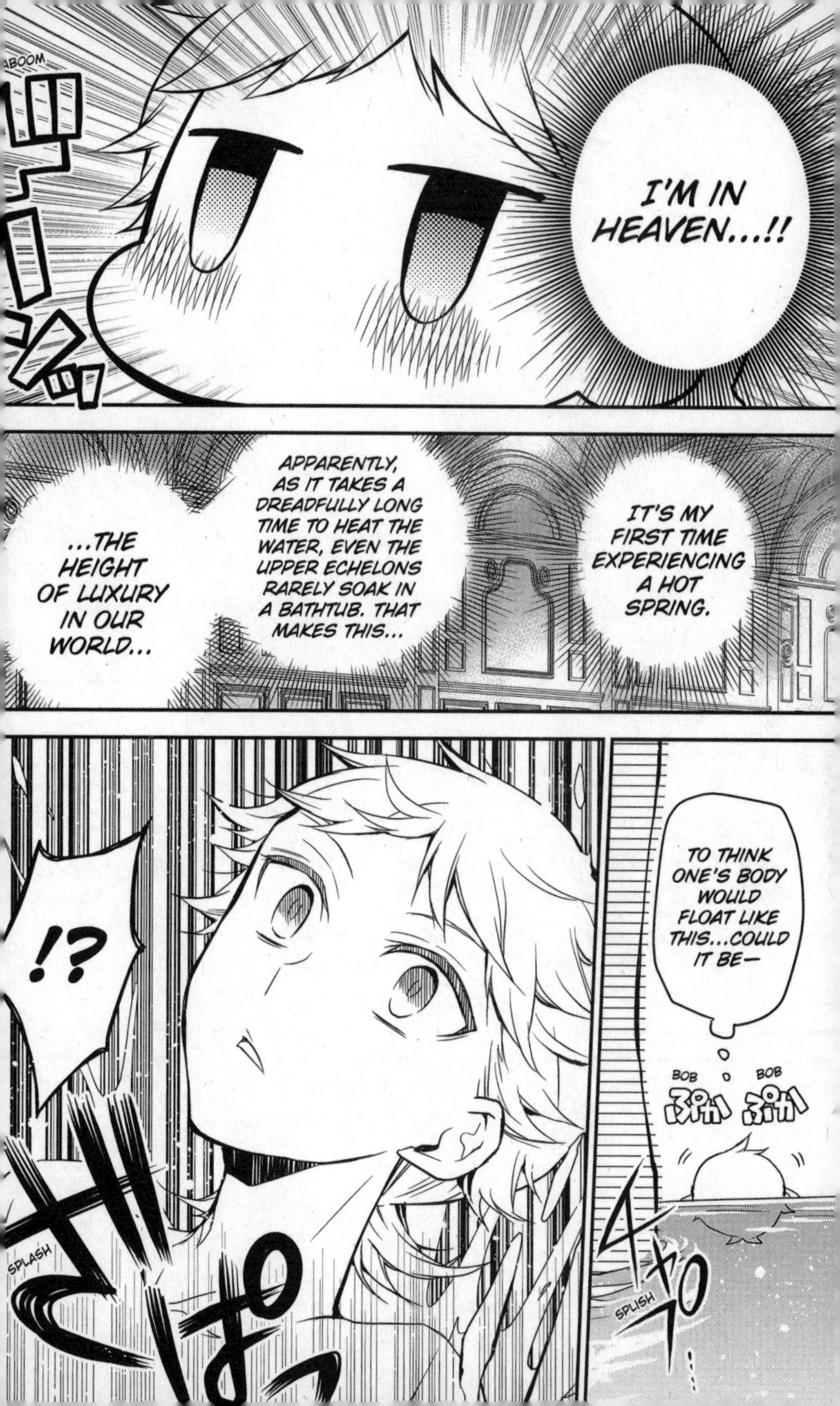
I'M IN HEAVEN...!!
KABOOM
IT'S MY FIRST TIME EXPERIENCING A HOT SPRING.
APPARENTLY, AS IT TAKES A DREADFULLY LONG TIME TO HEAT THE WATER, EVEN THE UPPER ECHELONS RARELY SOAK IN A BATHTUB. THAT MAKES THIS...
...THE HEIGHT OF LUXURY IN OUR WORLD...
TO THINK ONE'S BODY WOULD FLOAT LIKE THIS...COULD IT BE—
BOB
BOB
SPLISH
!?
SPLASH

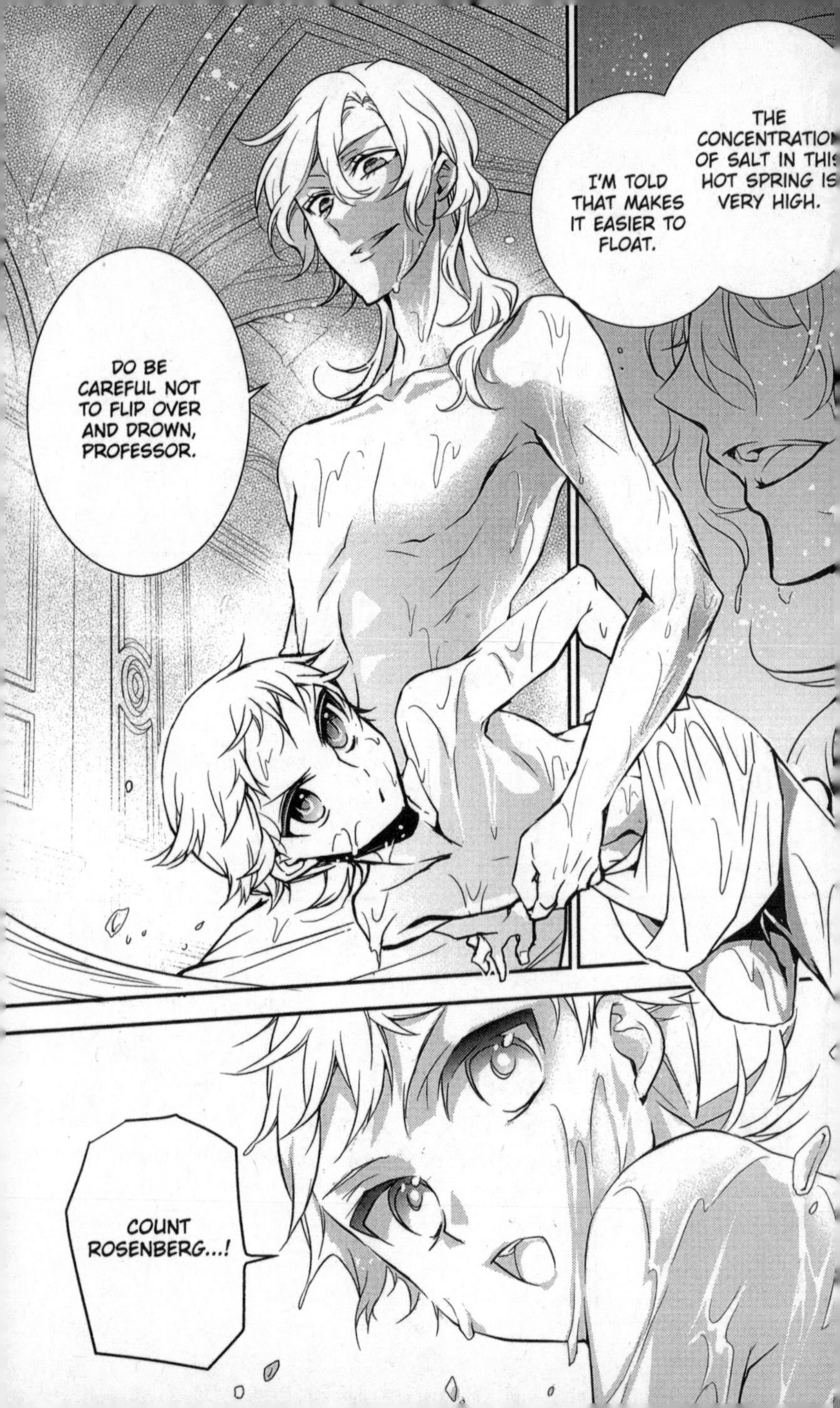
THE CONCENTRATION OF SALT IN THIS HOT SPRING IS VERY HIGH.
I'M TOLD THAT MAKES IT EASIER TO FLOAT.
DO BE CAREFUL NOT TO FLIP OVER AND DROWN, PROFESSOR.
COUNT ROSENBERG...!

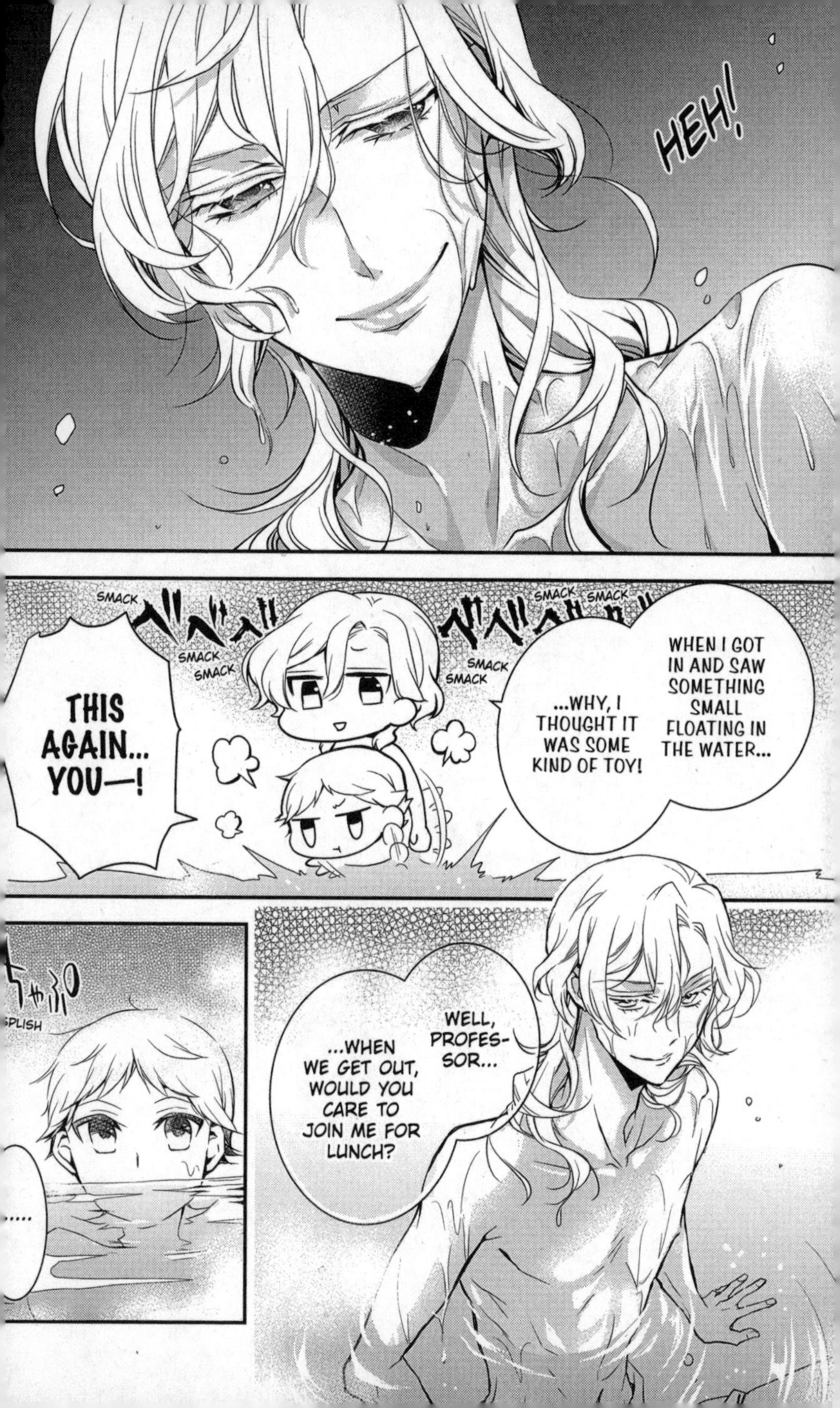
HEH!
SMACK SMACK
SMACK SMACK
WHEN I GOT IN AND SAW SOMETHING SMALL FLOATING IN THE WATER...
...WHY, I THOUGHT IT WAS SOME KIND OF TOY!
SMACK SMACK
SMACK
THIS AGAIN... YOU—!
WELL, PROFES-SOR...
...WHEN WE GET OUT, WOULD YOU CARE TO JOIN ME FOR LUNCH?
SPLISH
.....

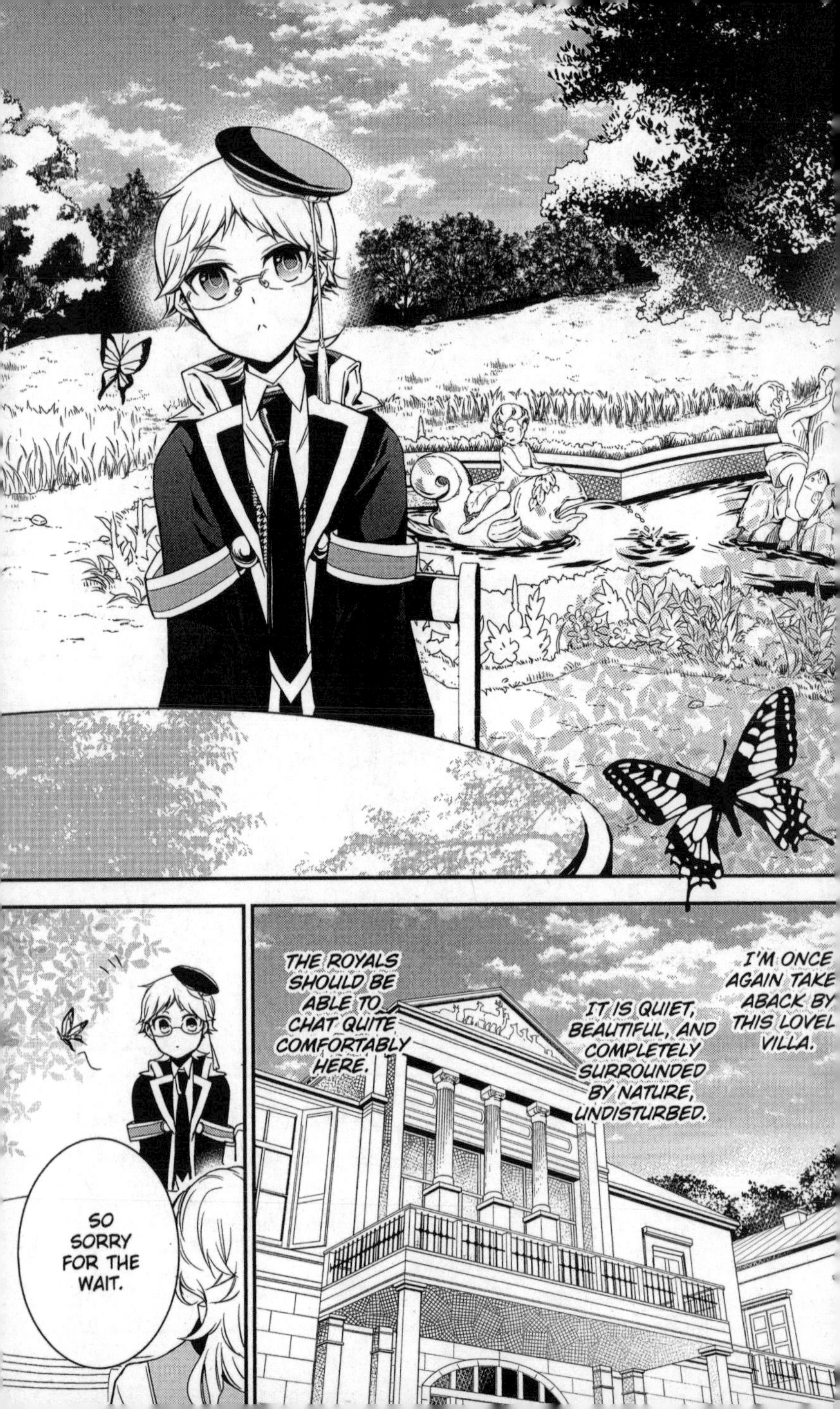
I'M ONCE AGAIN TAKE ABACK BY THIS LOVEL VILLA.
IT IS QUIET, BEAUTIFUL, AND COMPLETELY SURROUNDED BY NATURE, UNDISTURBED.
THE ROYALS SHOULD BE ABLE TO CHAT QUITE COMFORTABLY HERE.
SO SORRY FOR THE WAIT.

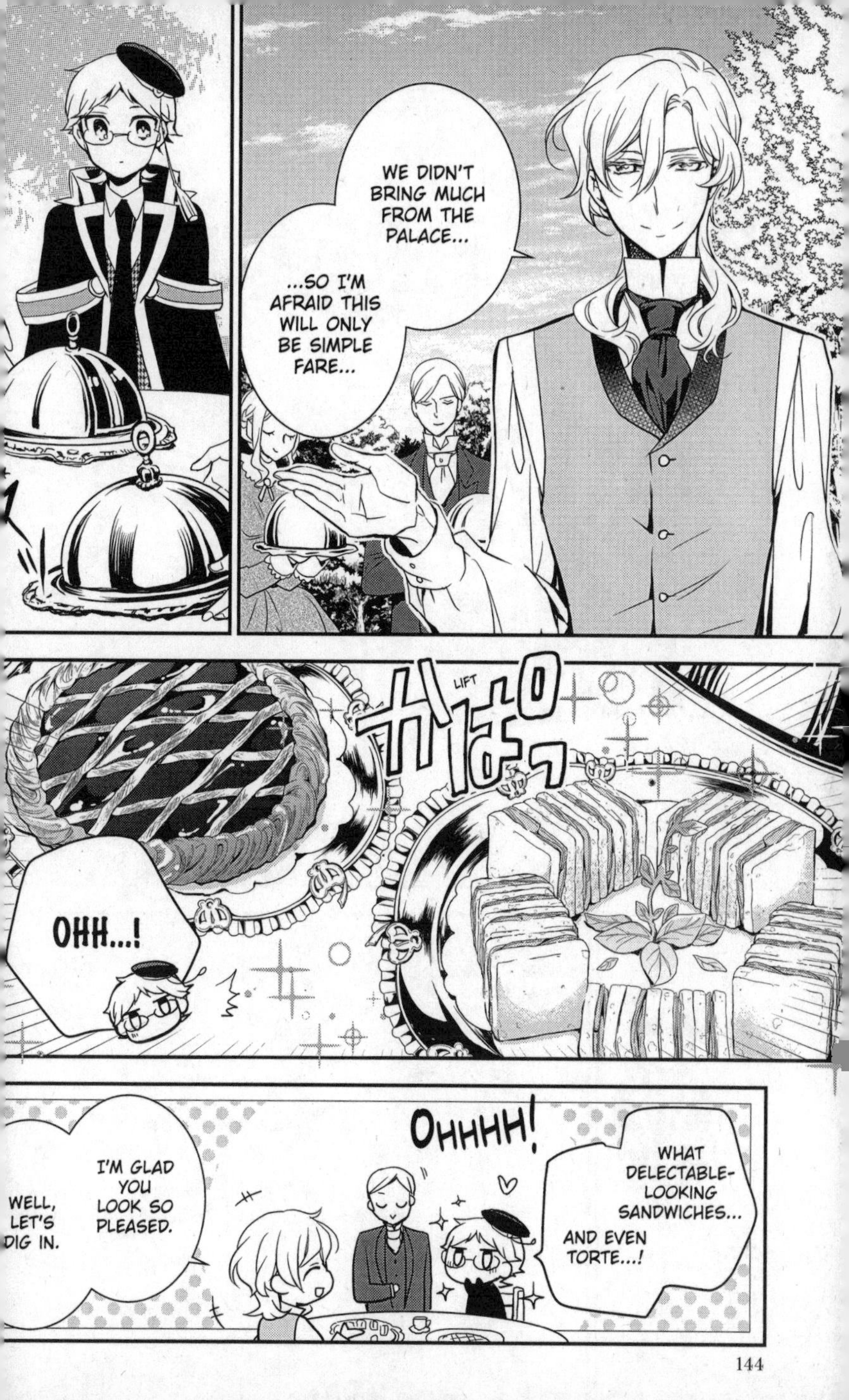
WE DIDN'T BRING MUCH FROM THE PALACE...
...SO I'M AFRAID THIS WILL ONLY BE SIMPLE FARE...
かぱっ
LIFT
OHH...!
WHAT DELECTABLE-LOOKING SANDWICHES...
AND EVEN TORTE...!
OHHHH!
I'M GLAD YOU LOOK SO PLEASED.
WELL, LET'S DIG IN.

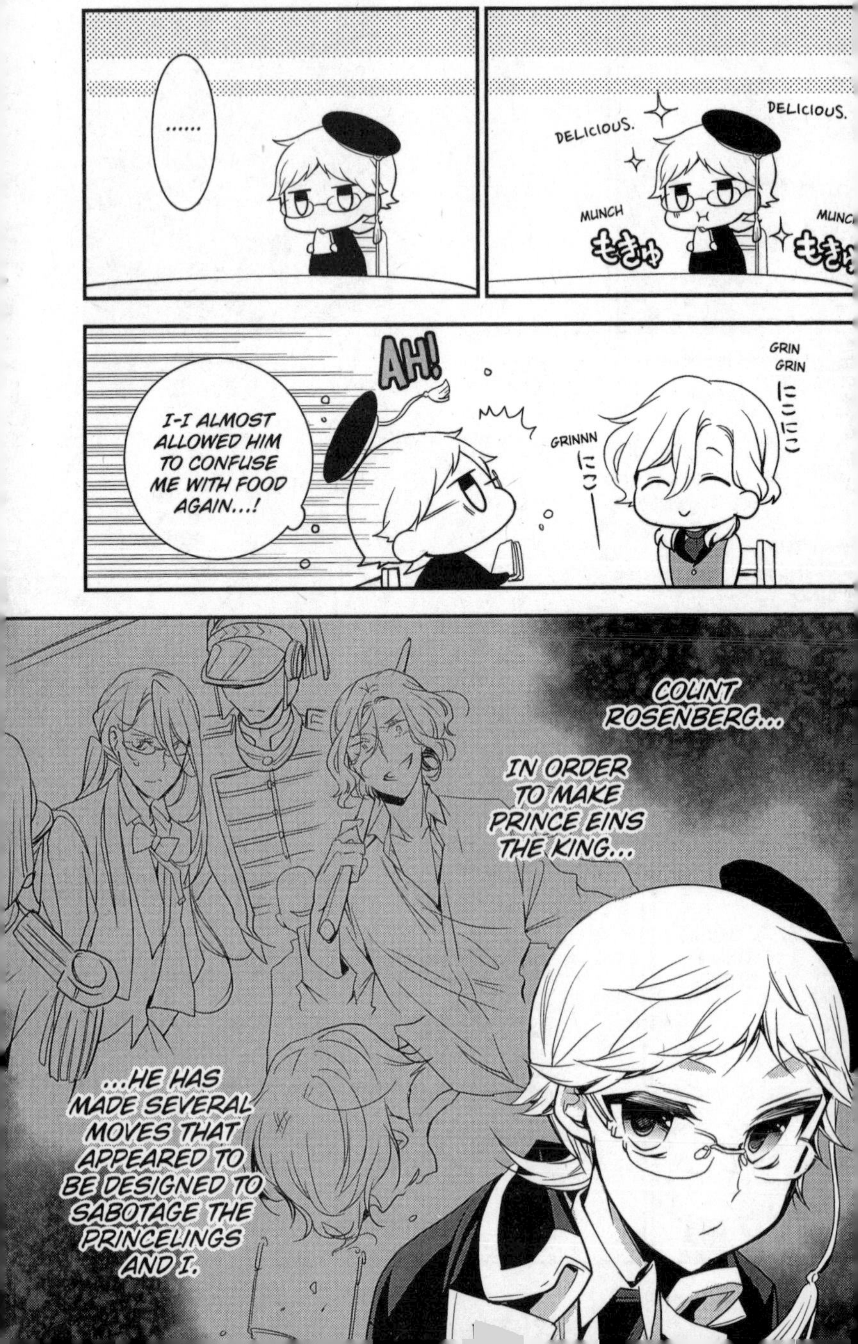
DELICIOUS.
DELICIOUS.
MUNCH
もきゅ
MUNCH
もきゅ
......
GRIN GRIN
にこにこ
GRINNN
にこー
AH!
I-I ALMOST ALLOWED HIM TO CONFUSE ME WITH FOOD AGAIN...!
COUNT ROSENBERG...
IN ORDER TO MAKE PRINCE EINS THE KING...
...HE HAS MADE SEVERAL MOVES THAT APPEARED TO BE DESIGNED TO SABOTAGE THE PRINCELINGS AND I.

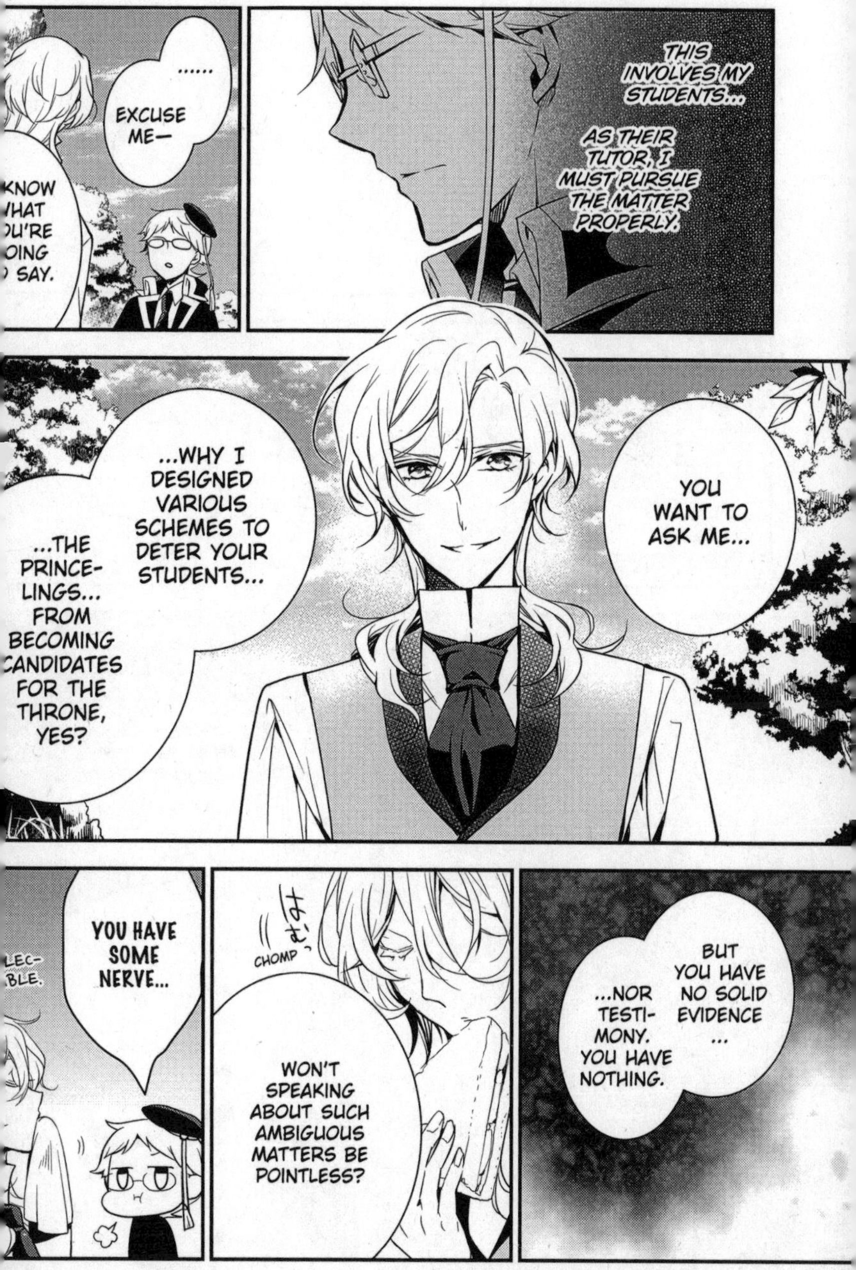
THIS INVOLVES MY STUDENTS...
AS THEIR TUTOR, I MUST PURSUE THE MATTER PROPERLY.
......
EXCUSE ME—
KNOW /HAT U'RE OING SAY.
YOU WANT TO ASK ME...
...WHY I DESIGNED VARIOUS SCHEMES TO DETER YOUR STUDENTS...
...THE PRINCELINGS... FROM BECOMING CANDIDATES FOR THE THRONE, YES?
BUT YOU HAVE NO SOLID EVIDENCE...
...NOR TESTIMONY. YOU HAVE NOTHING.
CHOMP
WON'T SPEAKING ABOUT SUCH AMBIGUOUS MATTERS BE POINTLESS?
YOU HAVE SOME NERVE...

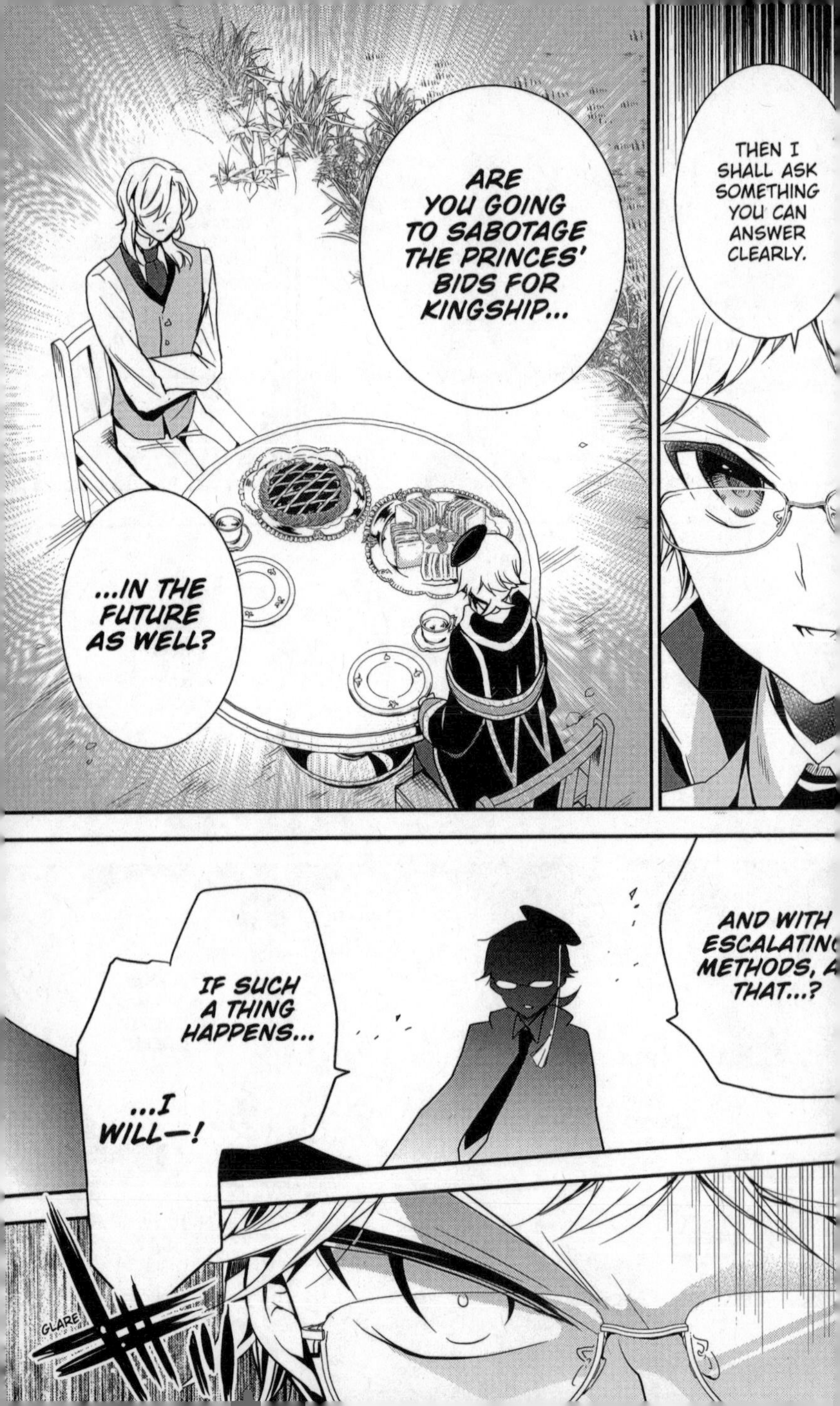
THEN I SHALL ASK SOMETHING YOU CAN ANSWER CLEARLY.
ARE YOU GOING TO SABOTAGE THE PRINCES' BIDS FOR KINGSHIP...
...IN THE FUTURE AS WELL?
AND WITH ESCALATIN METHODS, A THAT...?
IF SUCH A THING HAPPENS...
...I WILL—!
GLARE

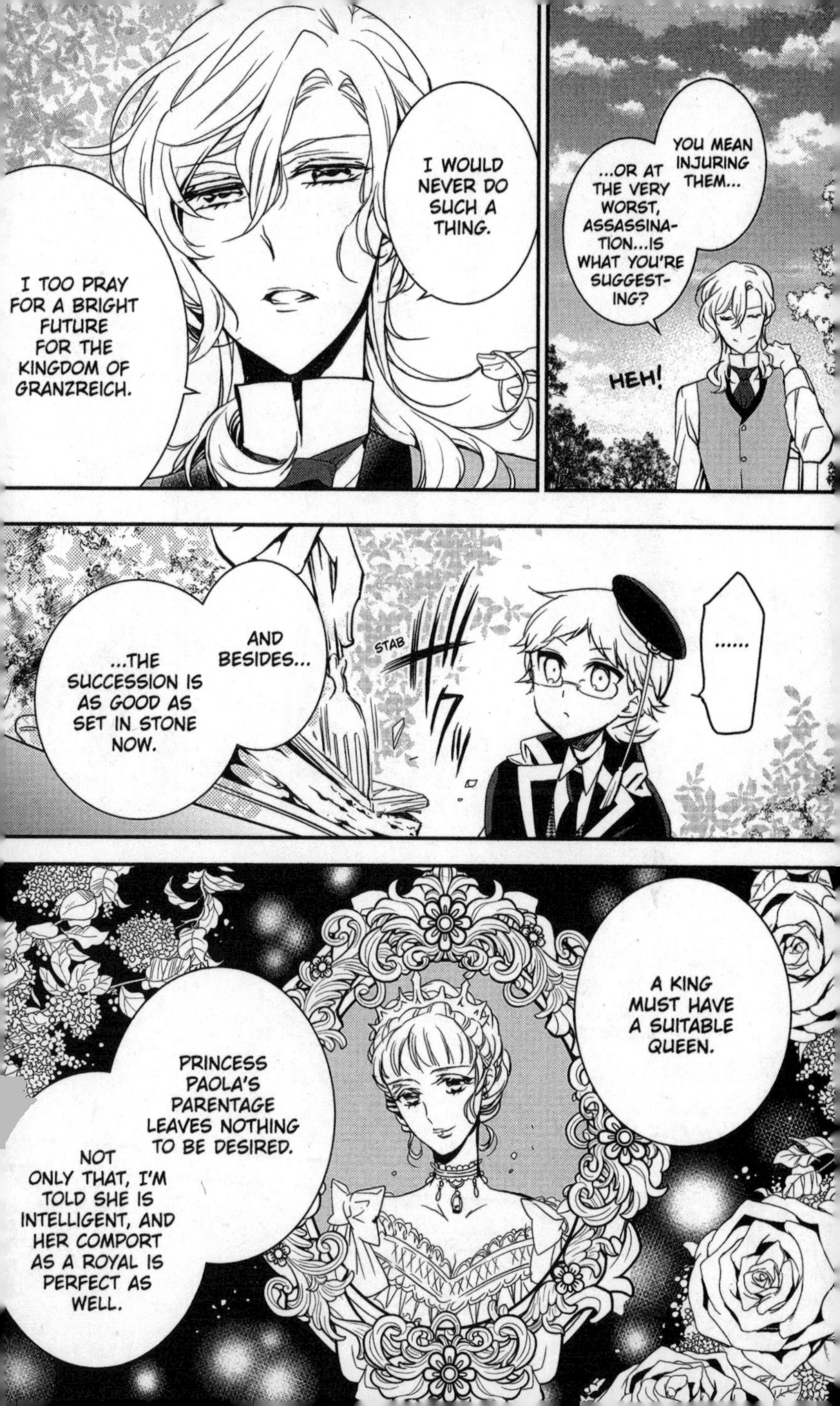
YOU MEAN INJURING THEM...
...OR AT THE VERY WORST, ASSASSINATION...IS WHAT YOU'RE SUGGESTING?
HEH!
I WOULD NEVER DO SUCH A THING.
I TOO PRAY FOR A BRIGHT FUTURE FOR THE KINGDOM OF GRANZREICH.
......
STAB
AND BESIDES...
...THE SUCCESSION IS AS GOOD AS SET IN STONE NOW.
A KING MUST HAVE A SUITABLE QUEEN.
PRINCESS PAOLA'S PARENTAGE LEAVES NOTHING TO BE DESIRED.
NOT ONLY THAT, I'M TOLD SHE IS INTELLIGENT, AND HER COMPORT AS A ROYAL IS PERFECT AS WELL.

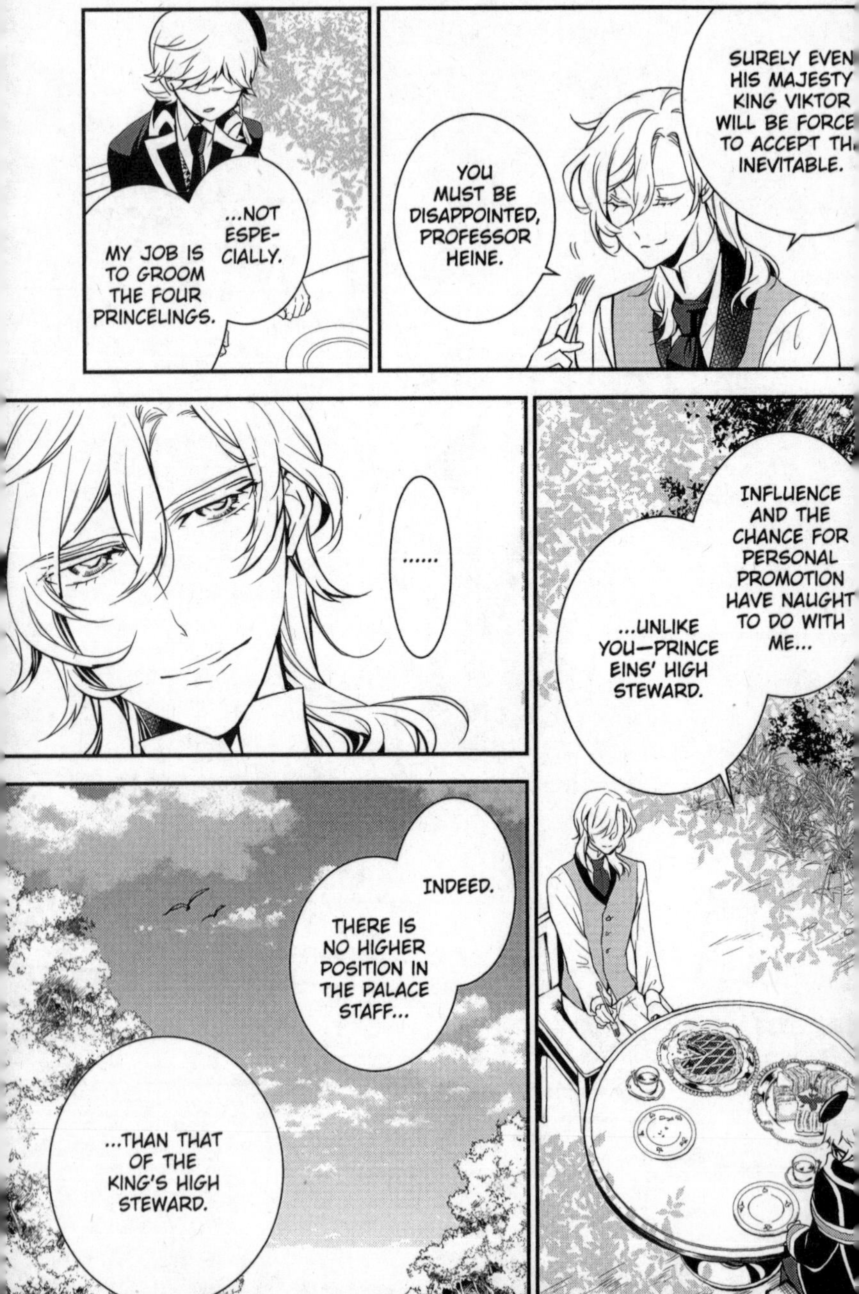
SURELY EVEN HIS MAJESTY KING VIKTOR WILL BE FORCE TO ACCEPT TH INEVITABLE.
YOU MUST BE DISAPPOINTED, PROFESSOR HEINE.
...NOT ESPECIALLY.
MY JOB IS TO GROOM THE FOUR PRINCELINGS.
INFLUENCE AND THE CHANCE FOR PERSONAL PROMOTION HAVE NAUGHT TO DO WITH ME...
...UNLIKE YOU—PRINCE EINS' HIGH STEWARD.
......
INDEED.
THERE IS NO HIGHER POSITION IN THE PALACE STAFF...
...THAN THAT OF THE KING'S HIGH STEWARD.

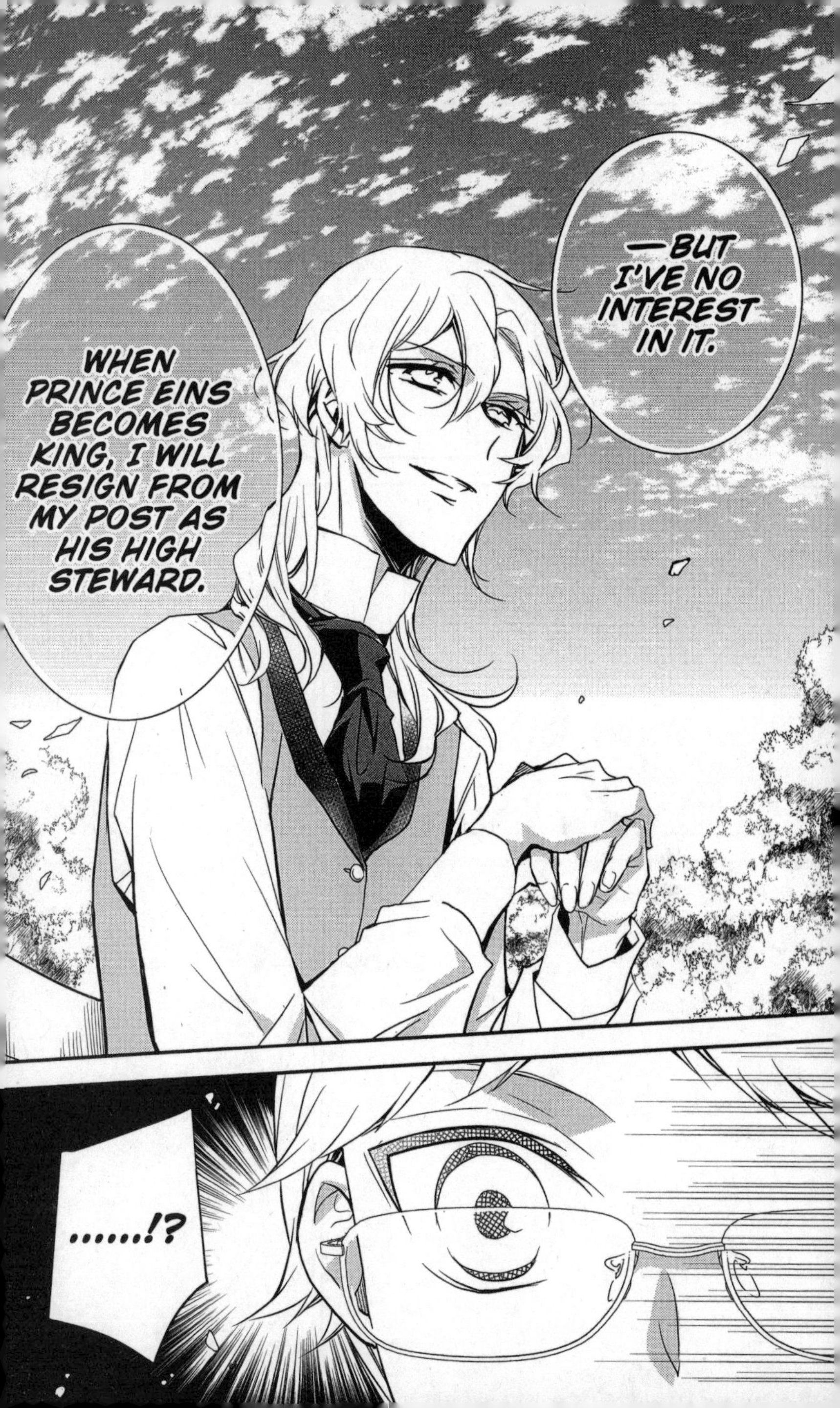
—BUT I'VE NO INTEREST IN IT.
WHEN PRINCE EINS BECOMES KING, I WILL RESIGN FROM MY POST AS HIS HIGH STEWARD.
......!?

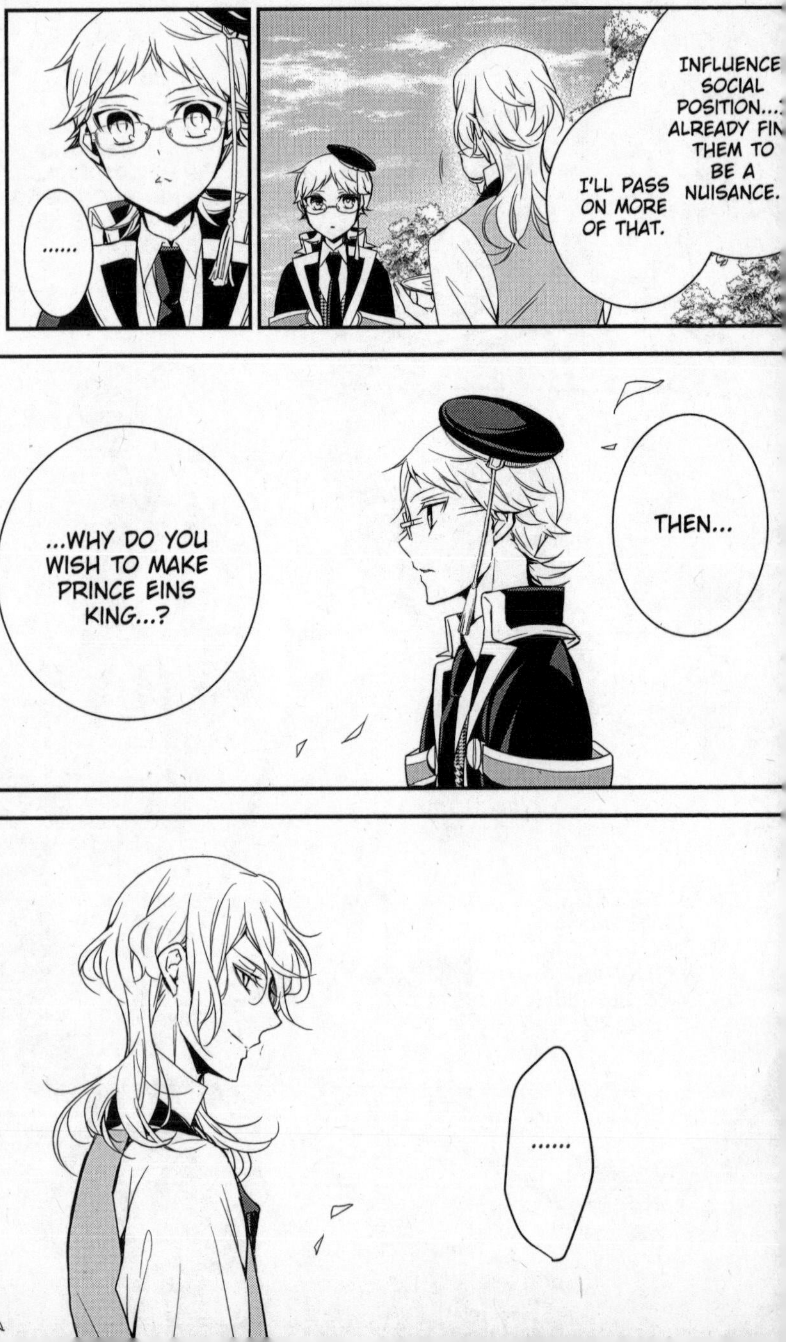
INFLUENCE SOCIAL POSITION... ALREADY FIN THEM TO BE A NUISANCE.
I'LL PASS ON MORE OF THAT.
......
THEN...
...WHY DO YOU WISH TO MAKE PRINCE EINS KING...?
......

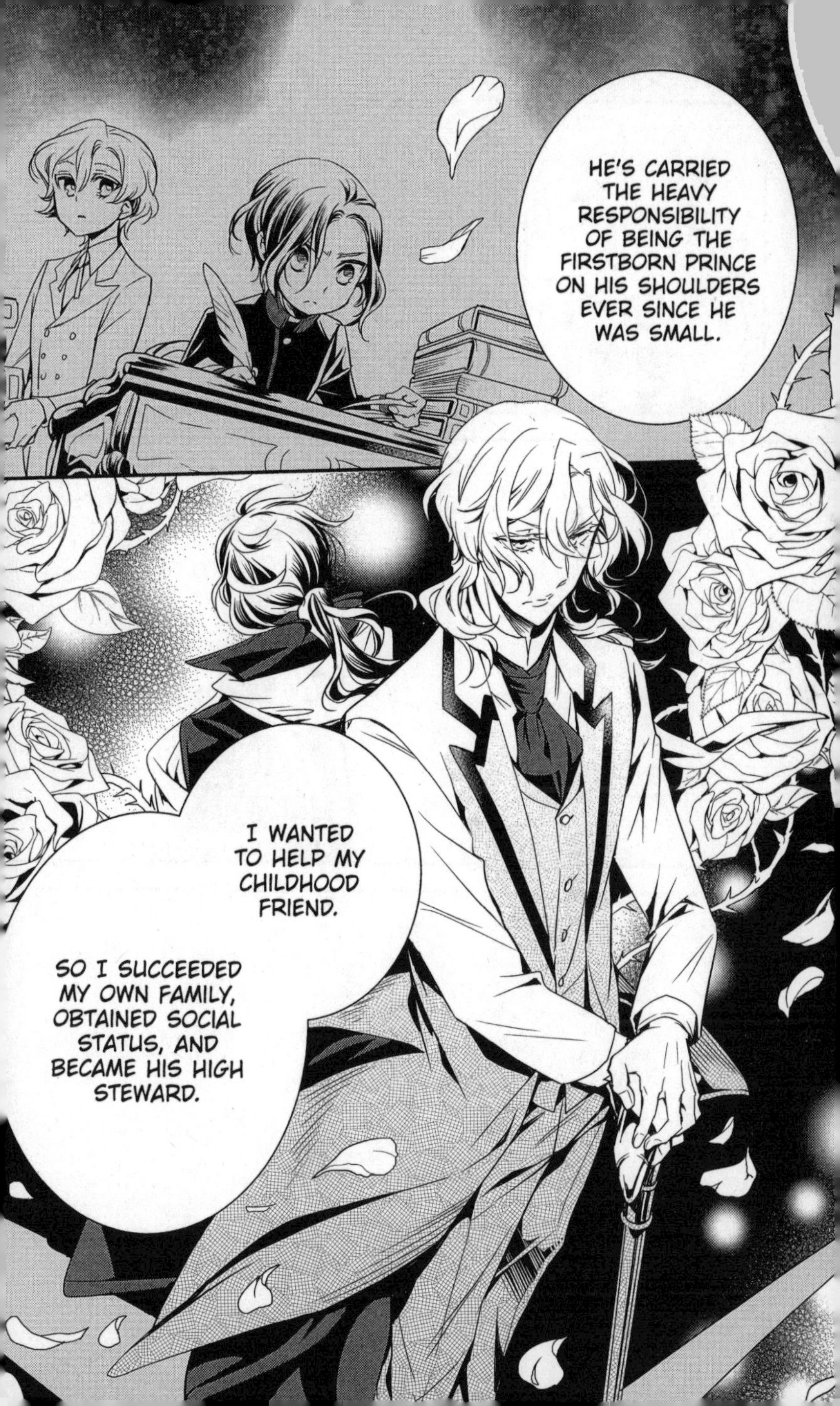
HE'S CARRIED THE HEAVY RESPONSIBILITY OF BEING THE FIRSTBORN PRINCE ON HIS SHOULDERS EVER SINCE HE WAS SMALL.
I WANTED TO HELP MY CHILDHOOD FRIEND.
SO I SUCCEEDED MY OWN FAMILY, OBTAINED SOCIAL STATUS, AND BECAME HIS HIGH STEWARD.

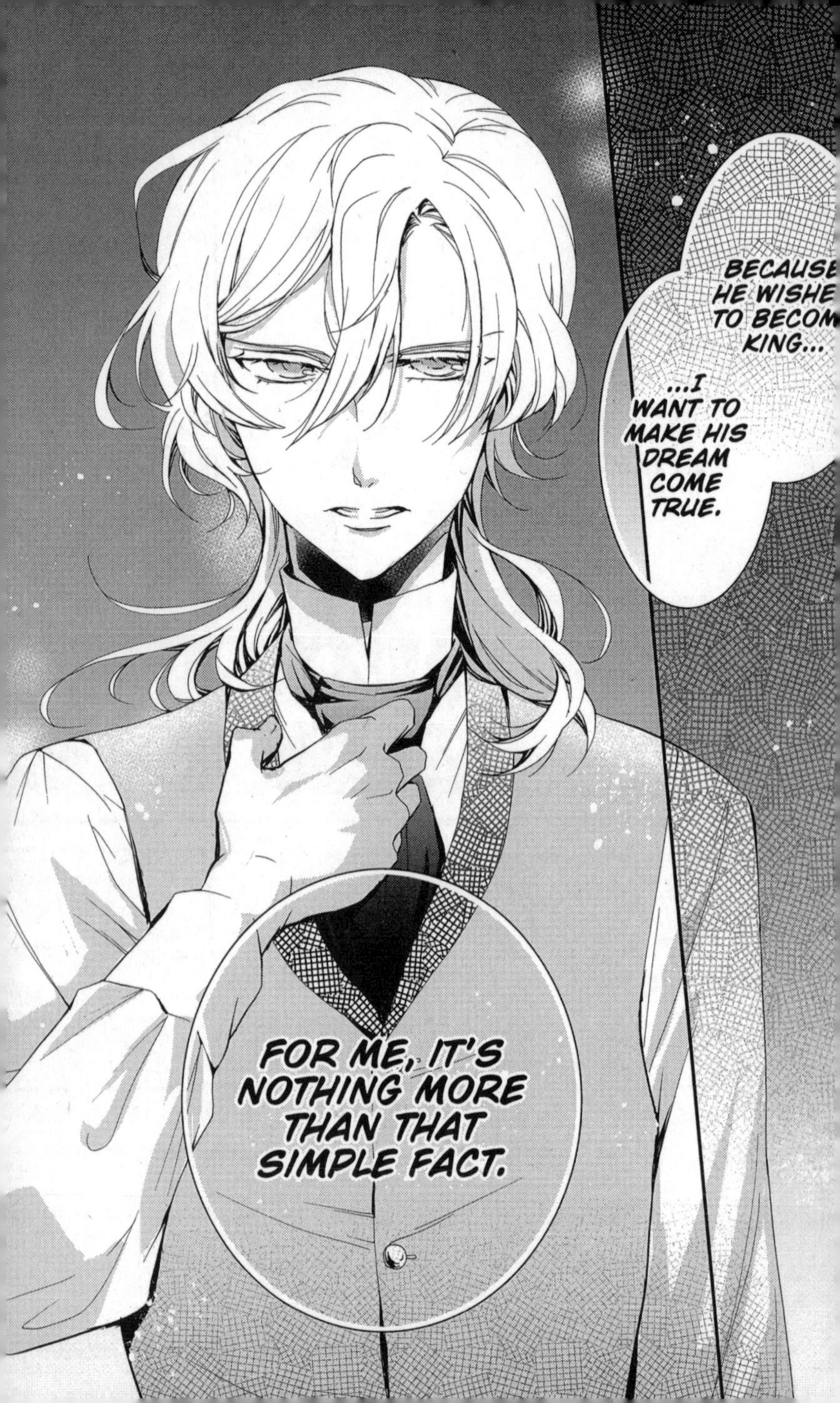
BECAUSE HE WISHE TO BECOM KING...
...I WANT TO MAKE HIS DREAM COME TRUE.
FOR ME, IT'S NOTHING MORE THAN THAT SIMPLE FACT.

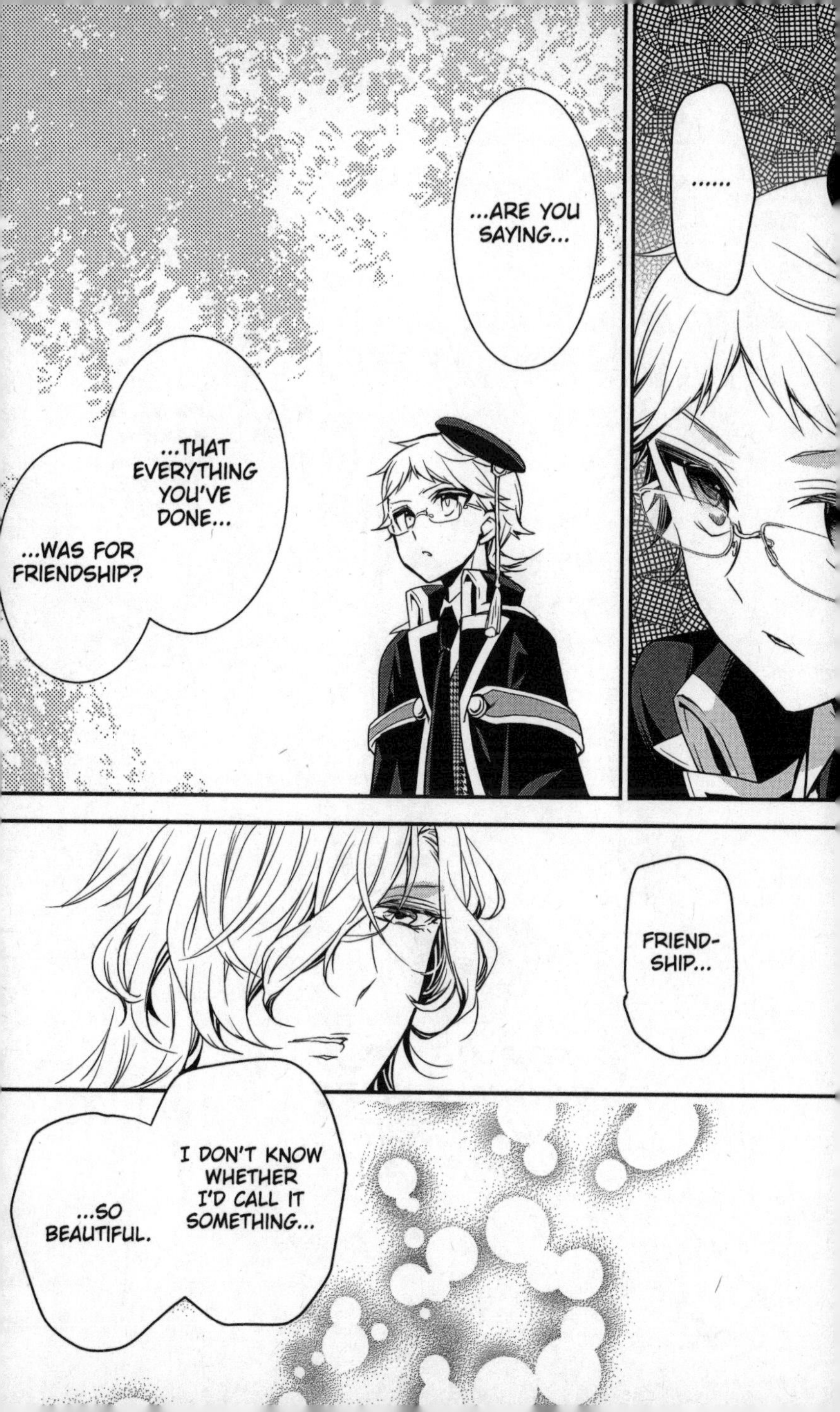
......
...ARE YOU SAYING...
...THAT EVERYTHING YOU'VE DONE... ...WAS FOR FRIENDSHIP?
FRIEND-SHIP...
I DON'T KNOW WHETHER I'D CALL IT SOMETHING...
...SO BEAUTIFUL.

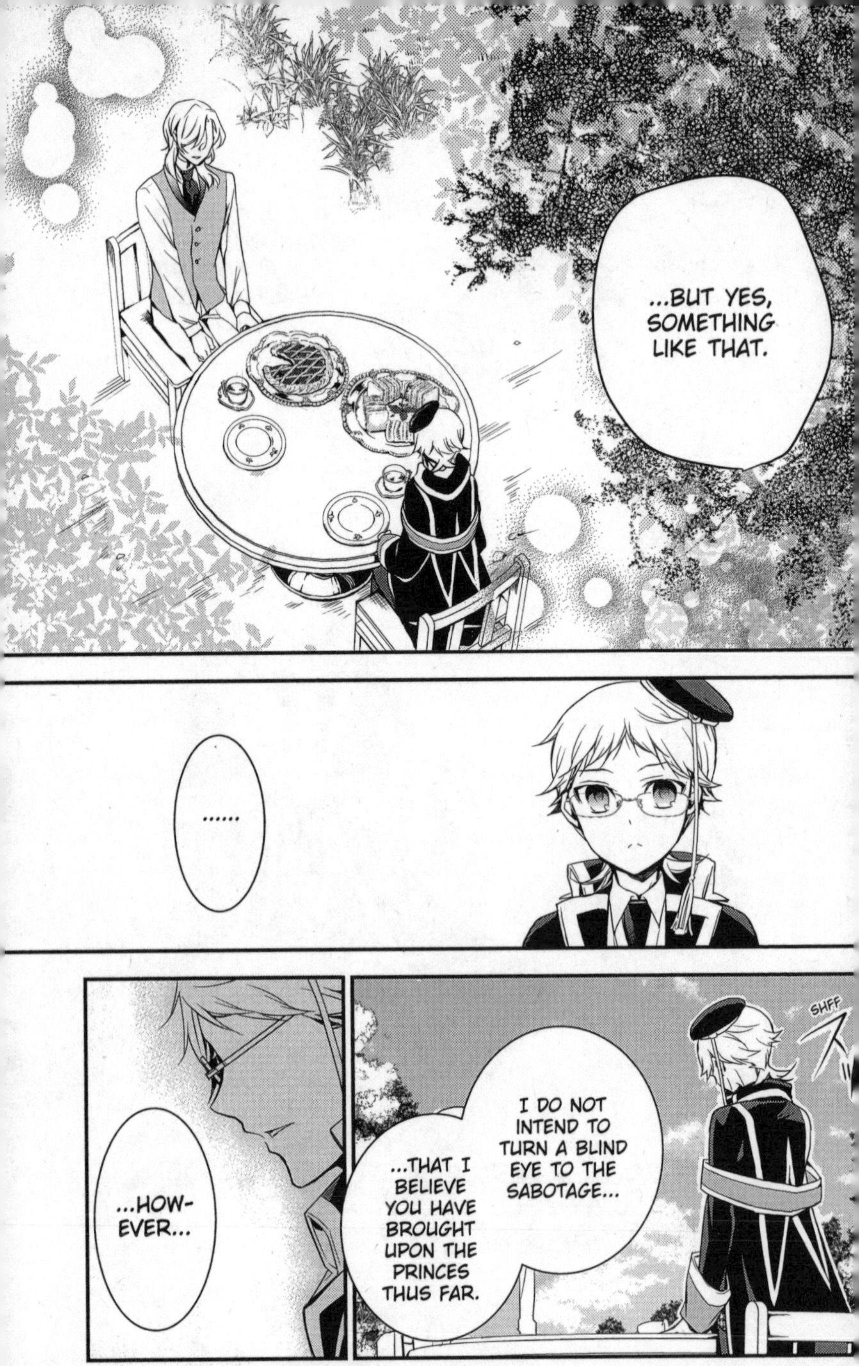
...BUT YES, SOMETHING LIKE THAT.
......
SHFF
I DO NOT INTEND TO TURN A BLIND EYE TO THE SABOTAGE...
...THAT I BELIEVE YOU HAVE BROUGHT UPON THE PRINCES THUS FAR.
...HOW-EVER...

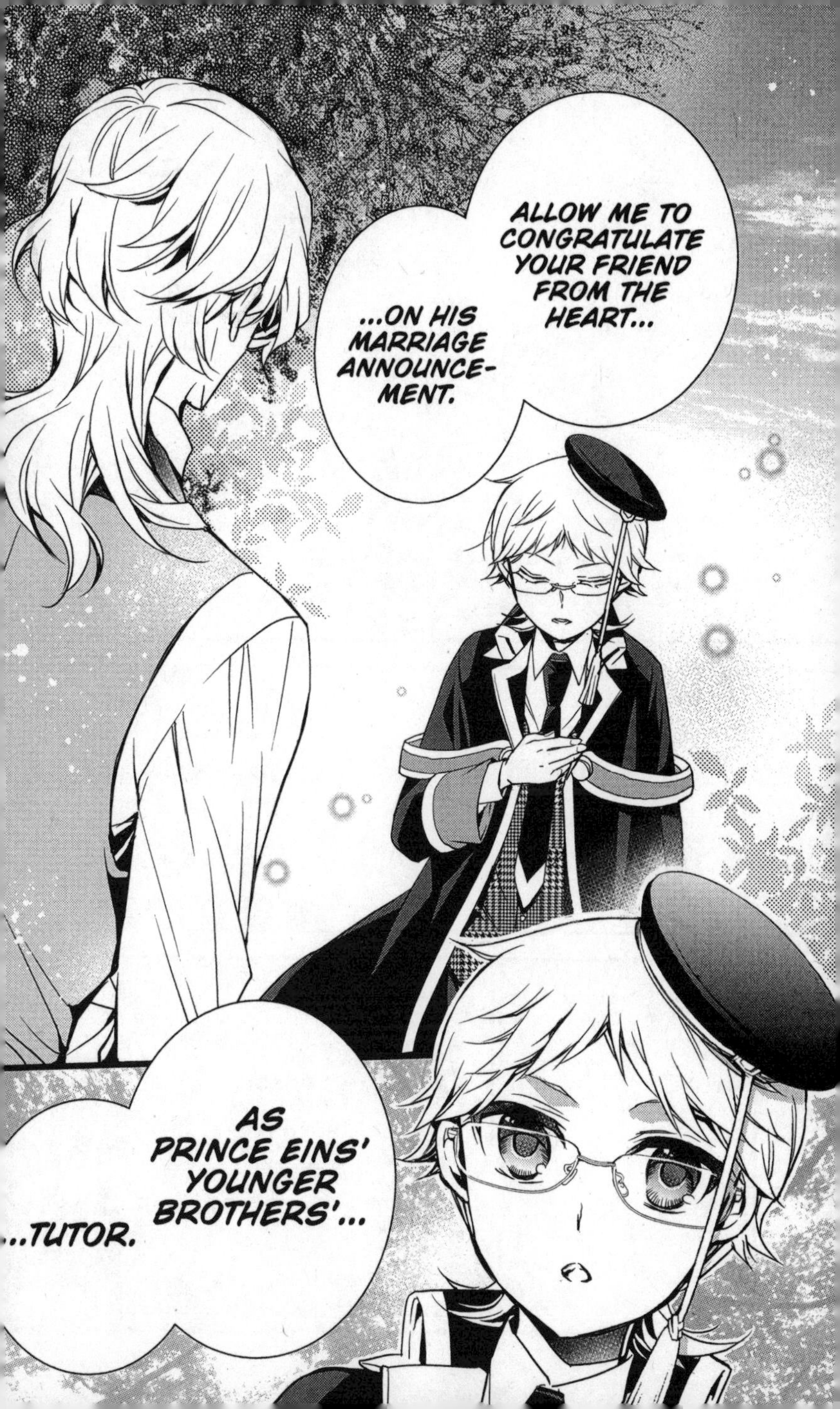
ALLOW ME TO CONGRATULATE YOUR FRIEND FROM THE HEART...
...ON HIS MARRIAGE ANNOUNCE-MENT.
AS PRINCE EINS' YOUNGER BROTHERS'...
...TUTOR.

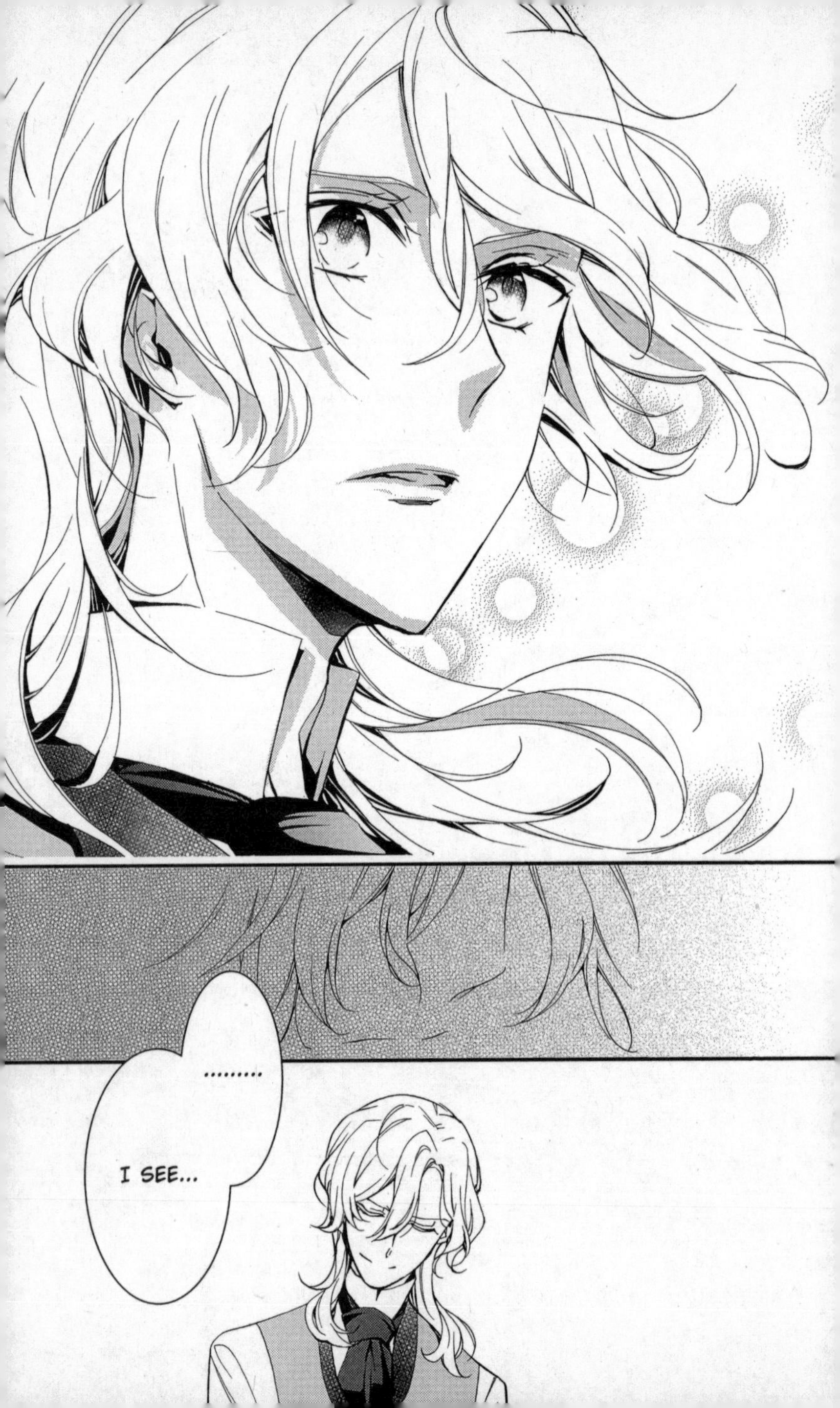
....
I SEE...

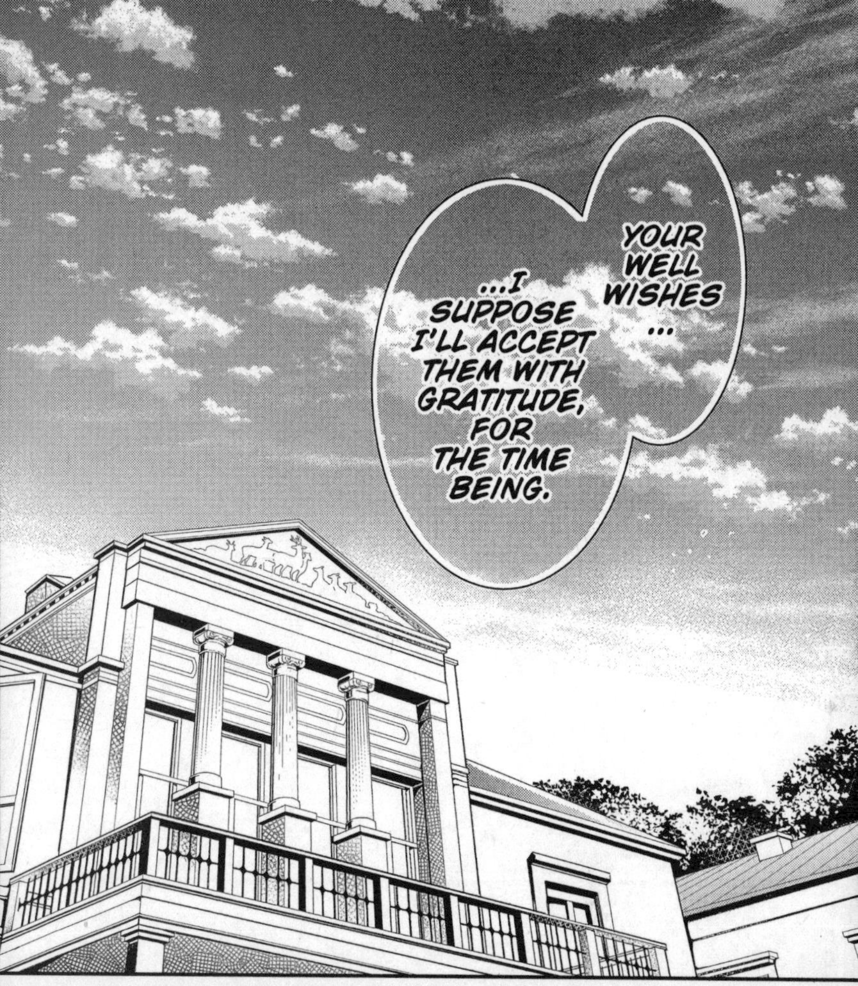
YOUR WELL WISHES... ...I SUPPOSE I'LL ACCEPT THEM WITH GRATITUDE, FOR THE TIME BEING.
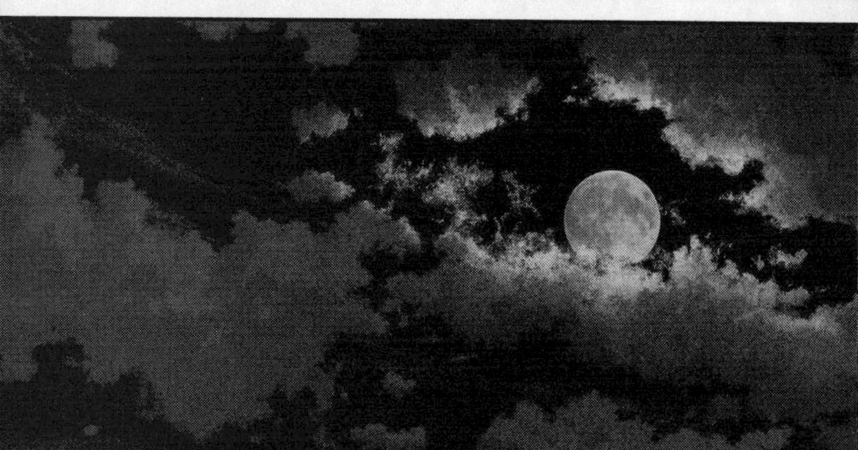

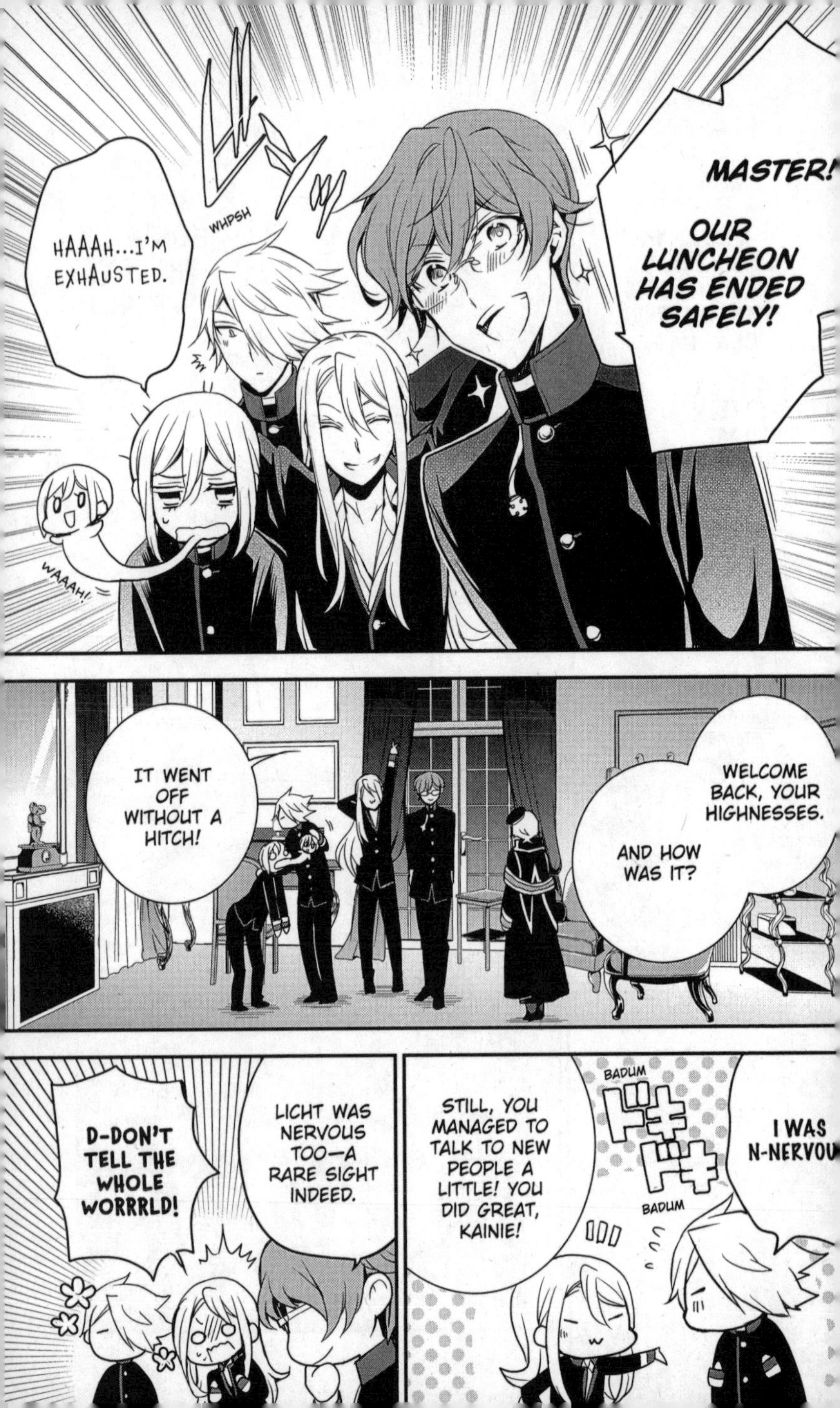
MASTER!
OUR LUNCHEON HAS ENDED SAFELY!
WHPSH
HAAAH...I'M EXHAUSTED.
WAAAH!
WELCOME BACK, YOUR HIGHNESSES.
AND HOW WAS IT?
IT WENT OFF WITHOUT A HITCH!
I WAS N-NERVOU
BADUM
BADUM
STILL, YOU MANAGED TO TALK TO NEW PEOPLE A LITTLE! YOU DID GREAT, KAINIE!
LICHT WAS NERVOUS TOO—A RARE SIGHT INDEED.
D-DON'T TELL THE WHOLE WORRRLD!

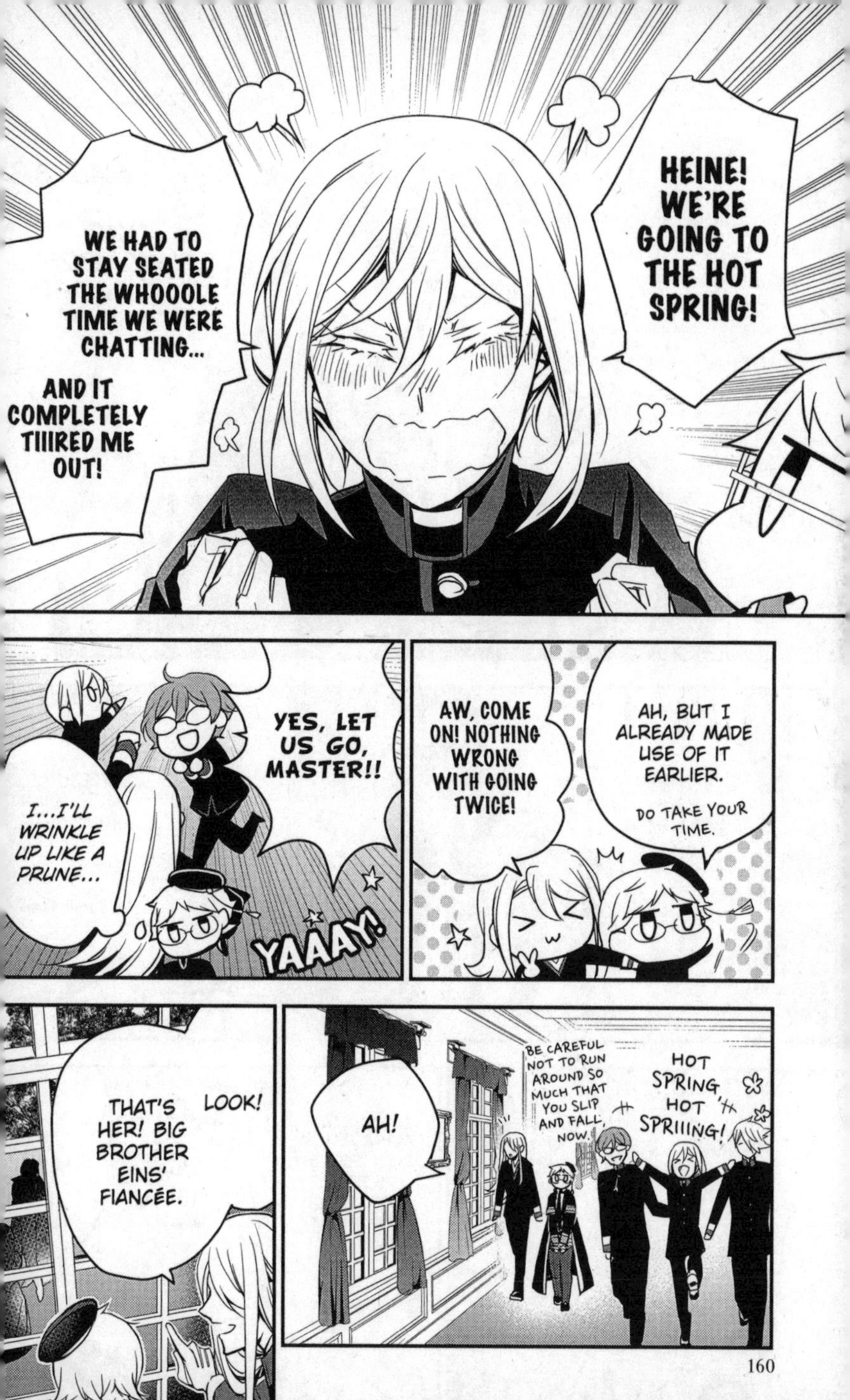
HEINE! WE'RE GOING TO THE HOT SPRING!
WE HAD TO STAY SEATED THE WHOOOLE TIME WE WERE CHATTING...
AND IT COMPLETELY TIIIRED ME OUT!
AH, BUT I ALREADY MADE USE OF IT EARLIER.
DO TAKE YOUR TIME.
AW, COME ON! NOTHING WRONG WITH GOING TWICE!
YES, LET US GO, MASTER!!
YAAAY!
I...I'LL WRINKLE UP LIKE A PRUNE...
HOT SPRING, HOT SPRIIING!
BE CAREFUL NOT TO RUN AROUND SO MUCH THAT YOU SLIP AND FALL, NOW.
AH!
LOOK!
THAT'S HER! BIG BROTHER EINS' FIANCÉE.

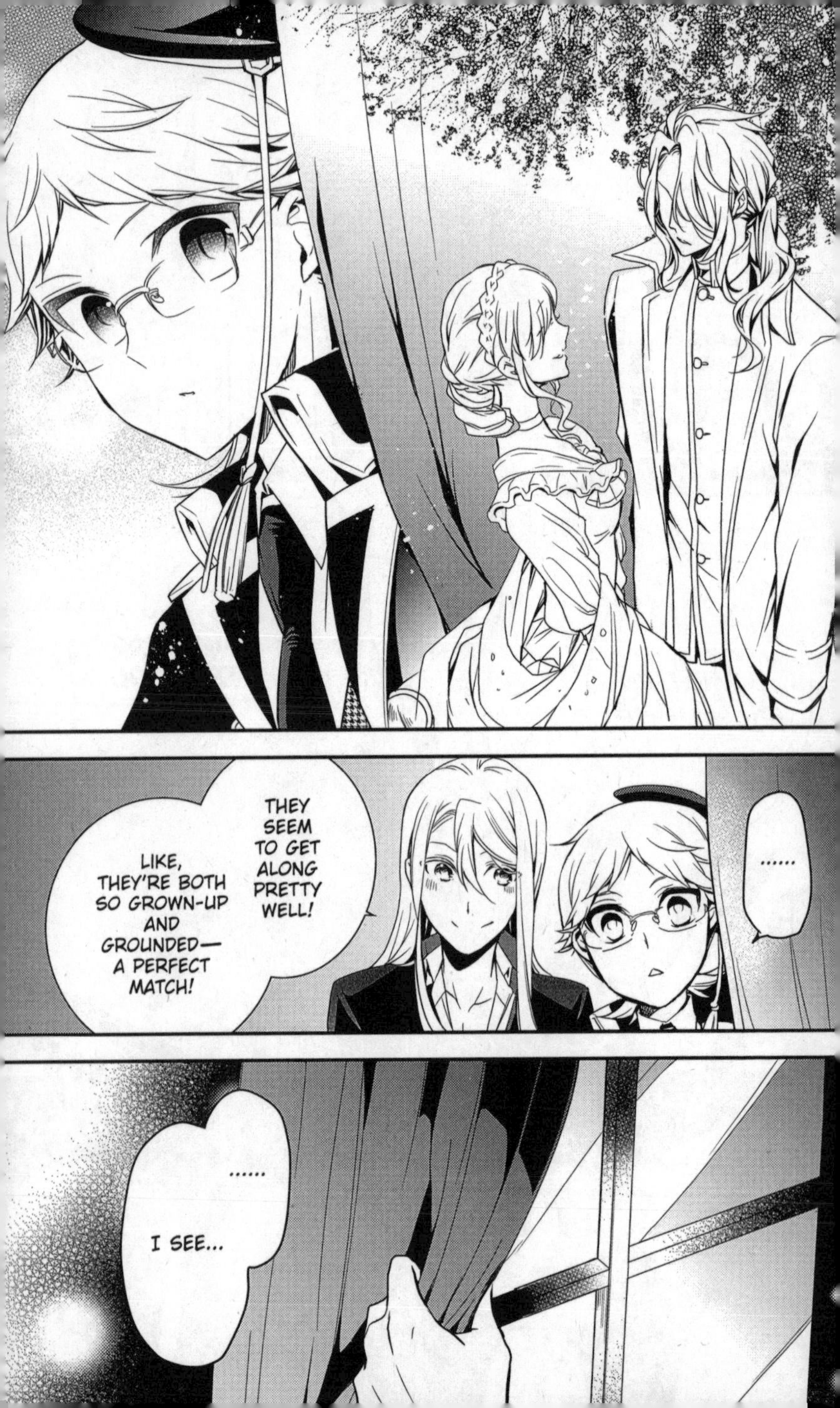
......
THEY SEEM TO GET ALONG PRETTY WELL!
LIKE, THEY'RE BOTH SO GROWN-UP AND GROUNDED— A PERFECT MATCH!
......
I SEE...

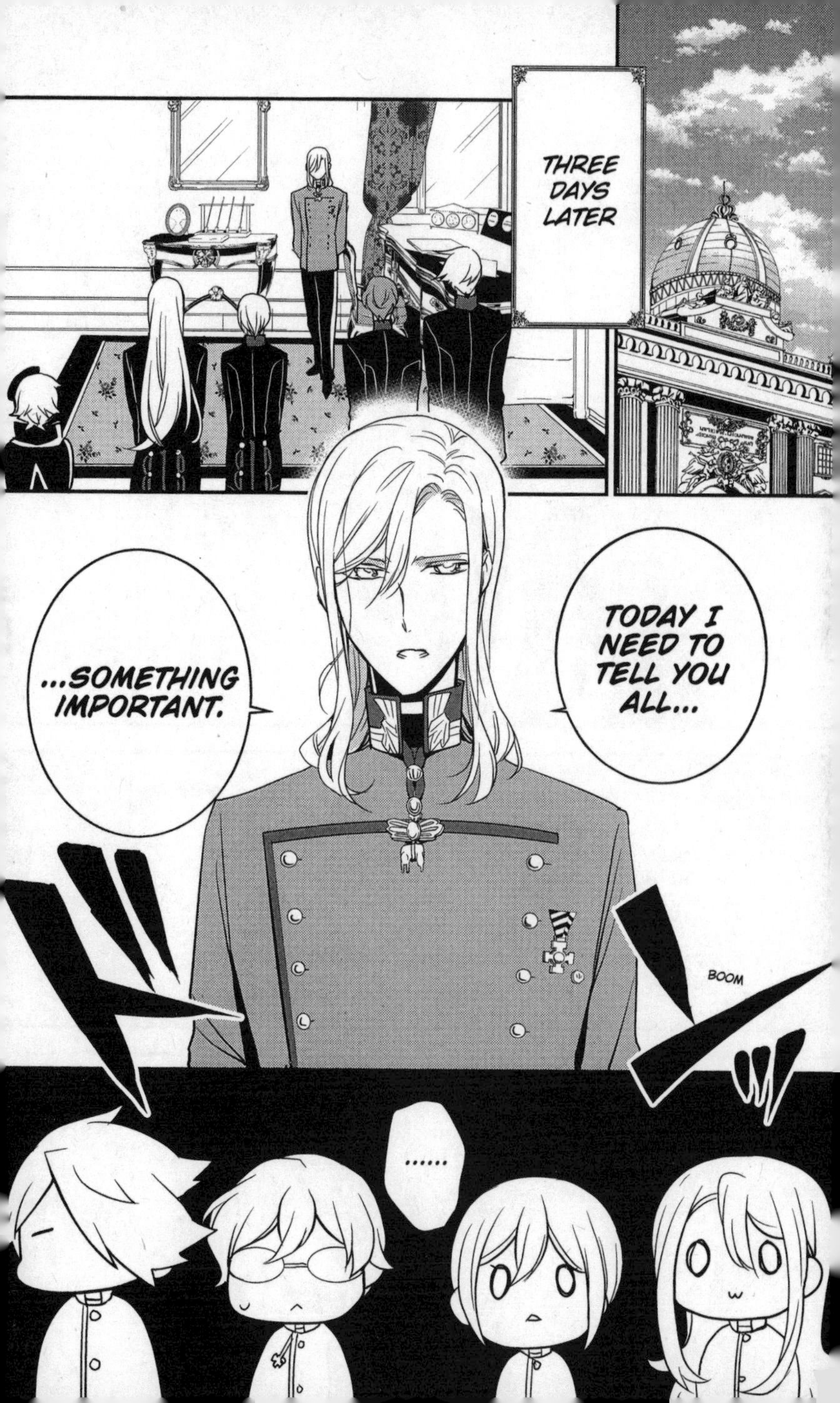
THREE DAYS LATER
TODAY I NEED TO TELL YOU ALL...
...SOMETHING IMPORTANT.
BOOM
......

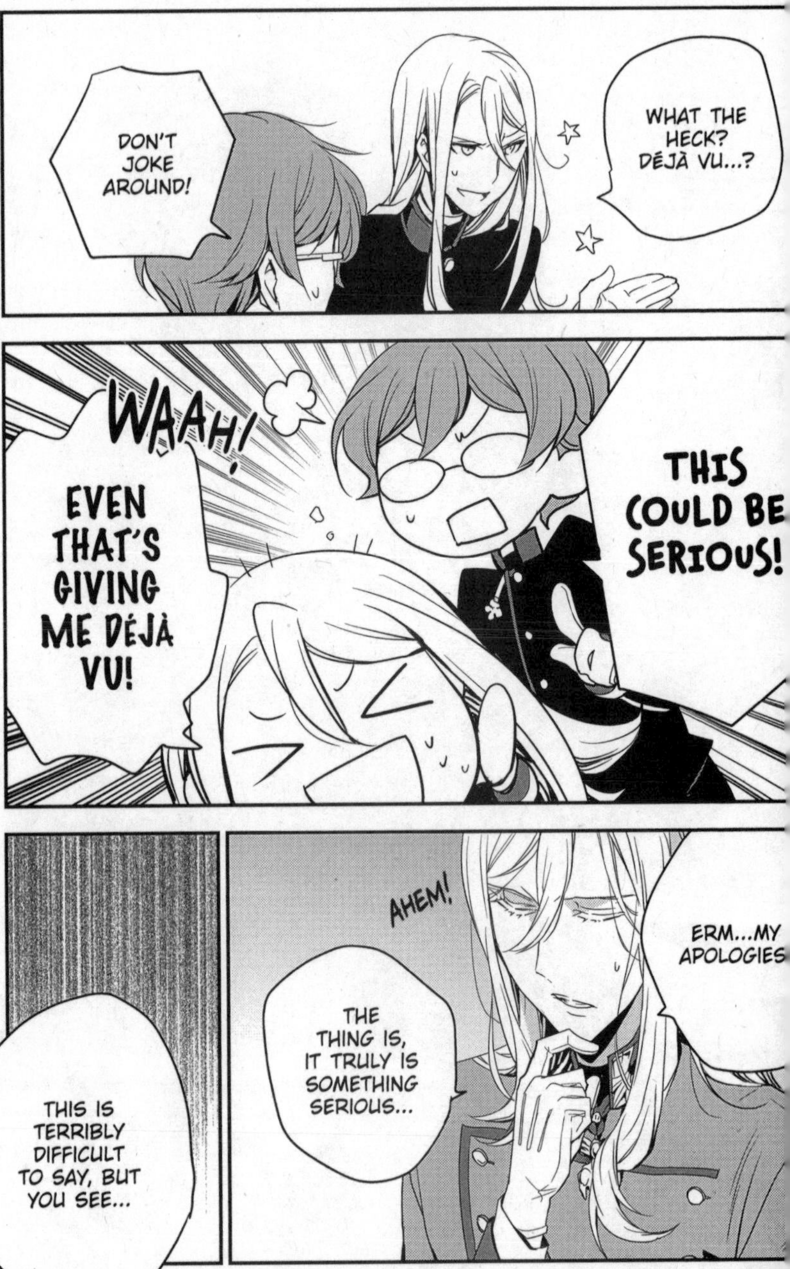
WHAT THE HECK? DÉJÀ VU...?
DON'T JOKE AROUND!
THIS COULD BE SERIOUS!
WAAH!
EVEN THAT'S GIVING ME DÉJÀ VU!
ERM...MY APOLOGIES
AHEM!
THE THING IS, IT TRULY IS SOMETHING SERIOUS...
THIS IS TERRIBLY DIFFICULT TO SAY, BUT YOU SEE...

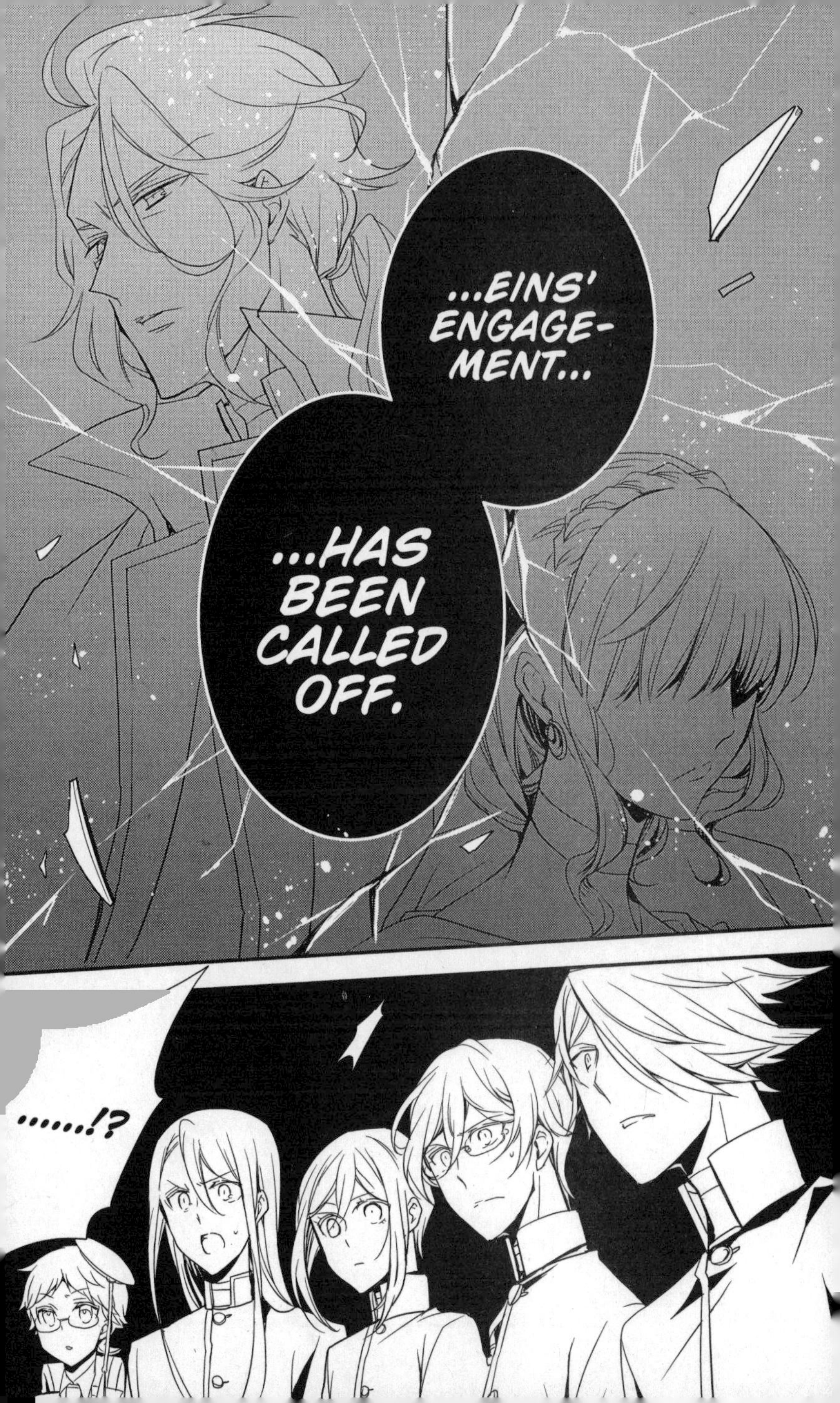
...EINS' ENGAGE-MENT...
...HAS BEEN CALLED OFF.
......!?

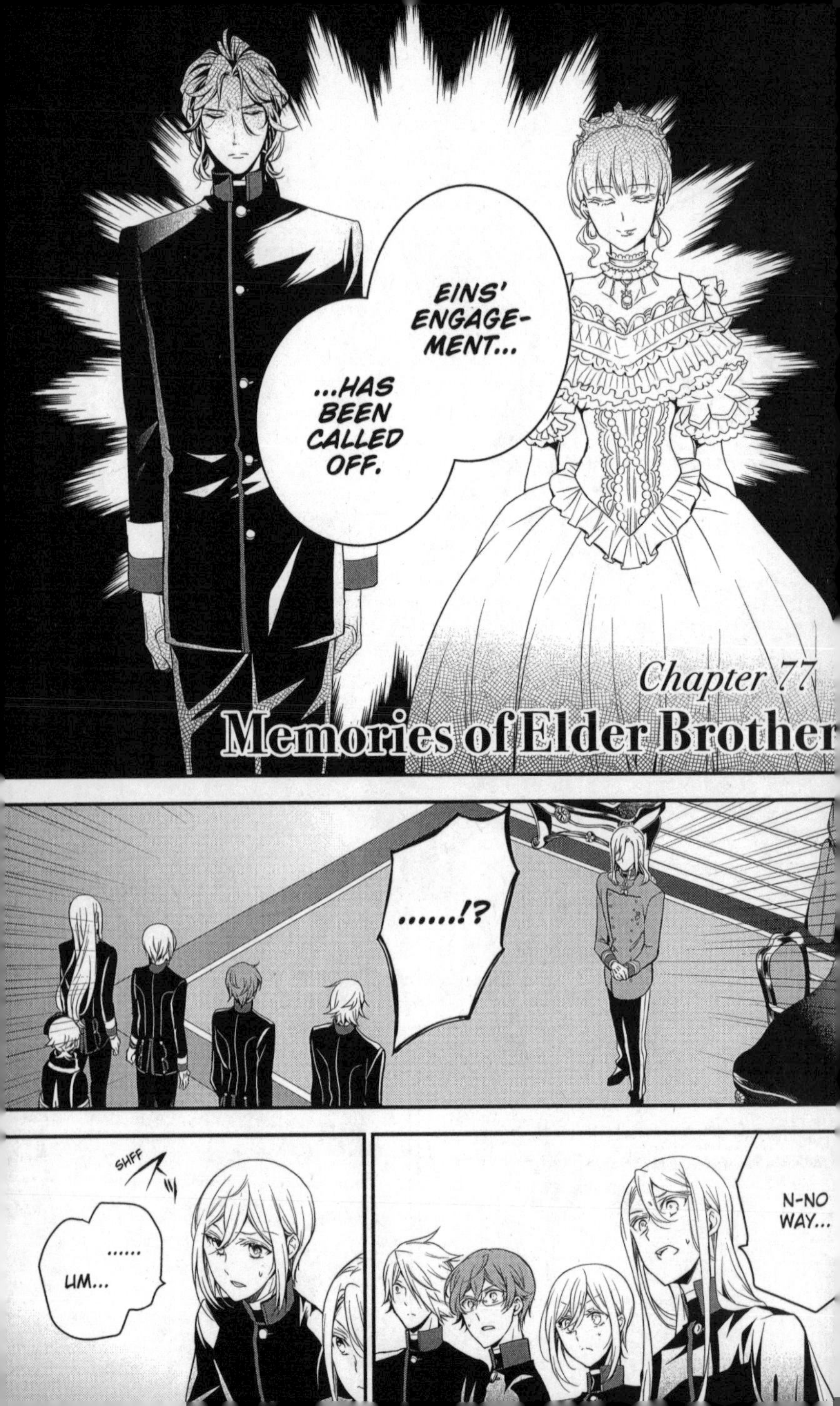
EINS' ENGAGEMENT... ...HAS BEEN CALLED OFF.
Chapter 77
Memories of Elder Brother
......!?
N-NO WAY...
SHFF
...... UM...

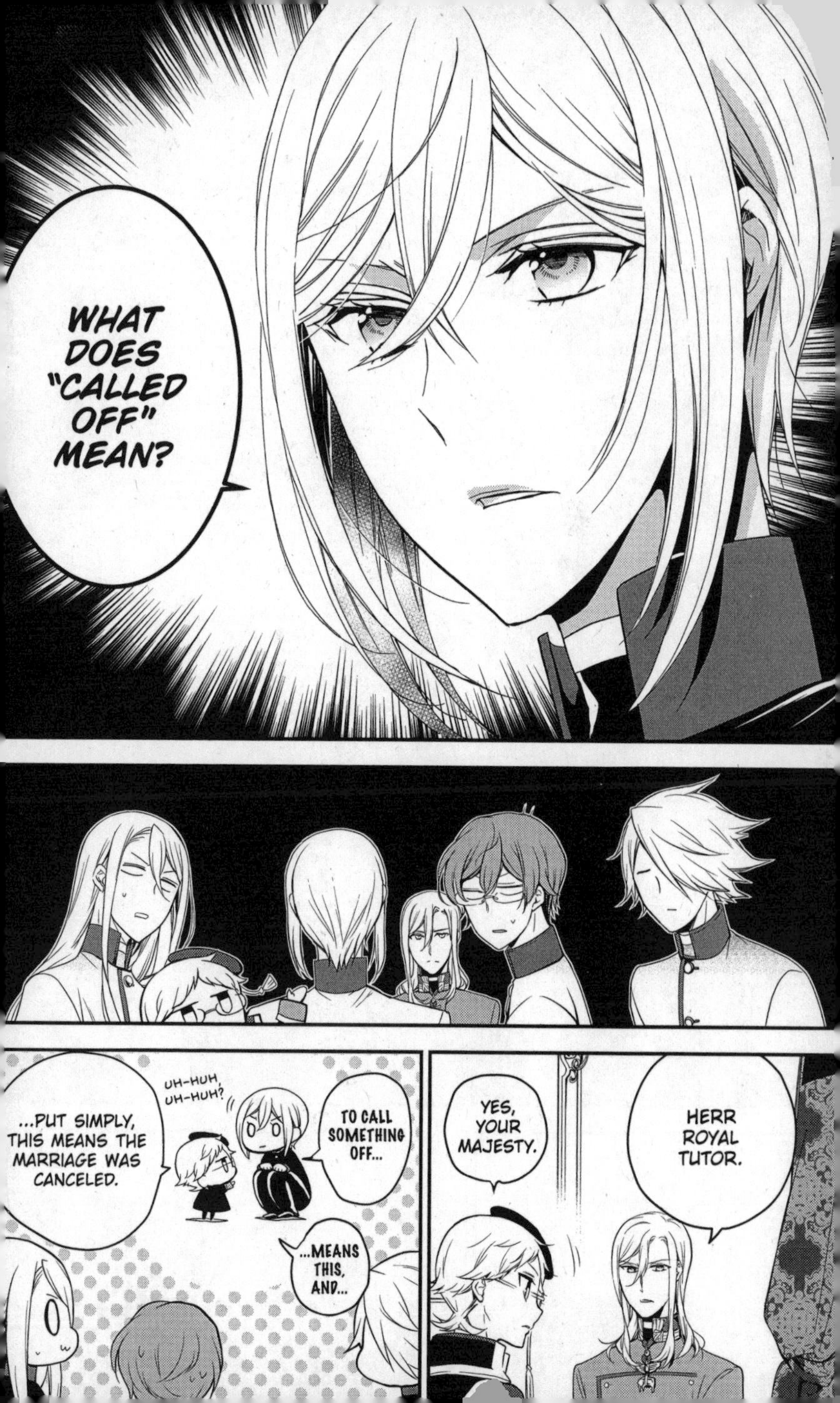
WHAT DOES "CALLED OFF" MEAN?
HERR ROYAL TUTOR.
YES, YOUR MAJESTY.
TO CALL SOMETHING OFF...
...MEANS THIS, AND...
UH-HUH, UH-HUH?
...PUT SIMPLY, THIS MEANS THE MARRIAGE WAS CANCELED.

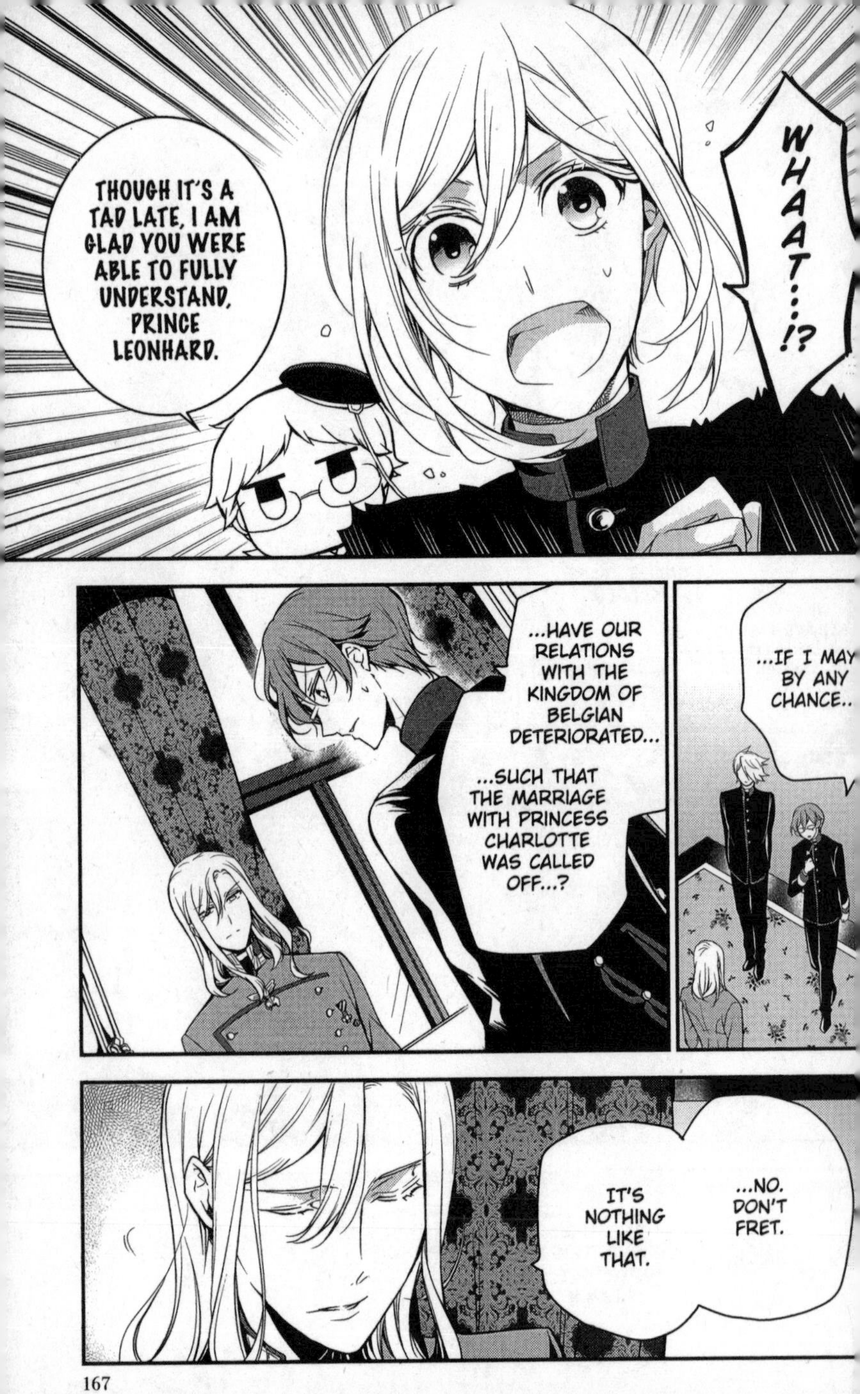
WHAAT...!?
THOUGH IT'S A TAD LATE, I AM GLAD YOU WERE ABLE TO FULLY UNDERSTAND, PRINCE LEONHARD.
...IF I MAY BY ANY CHANCE...
...HAVE OUR RELATIONS WITH THE KINGDOM OF BELGIAN DETERIORATED...
...SUCH THAT THE MARRIAGE WITH PRINCESS CHARLOTTE WAS CALLED OFF...?
...NO. DON'T FRET.
IT'S NOTHING LIKE THAT.

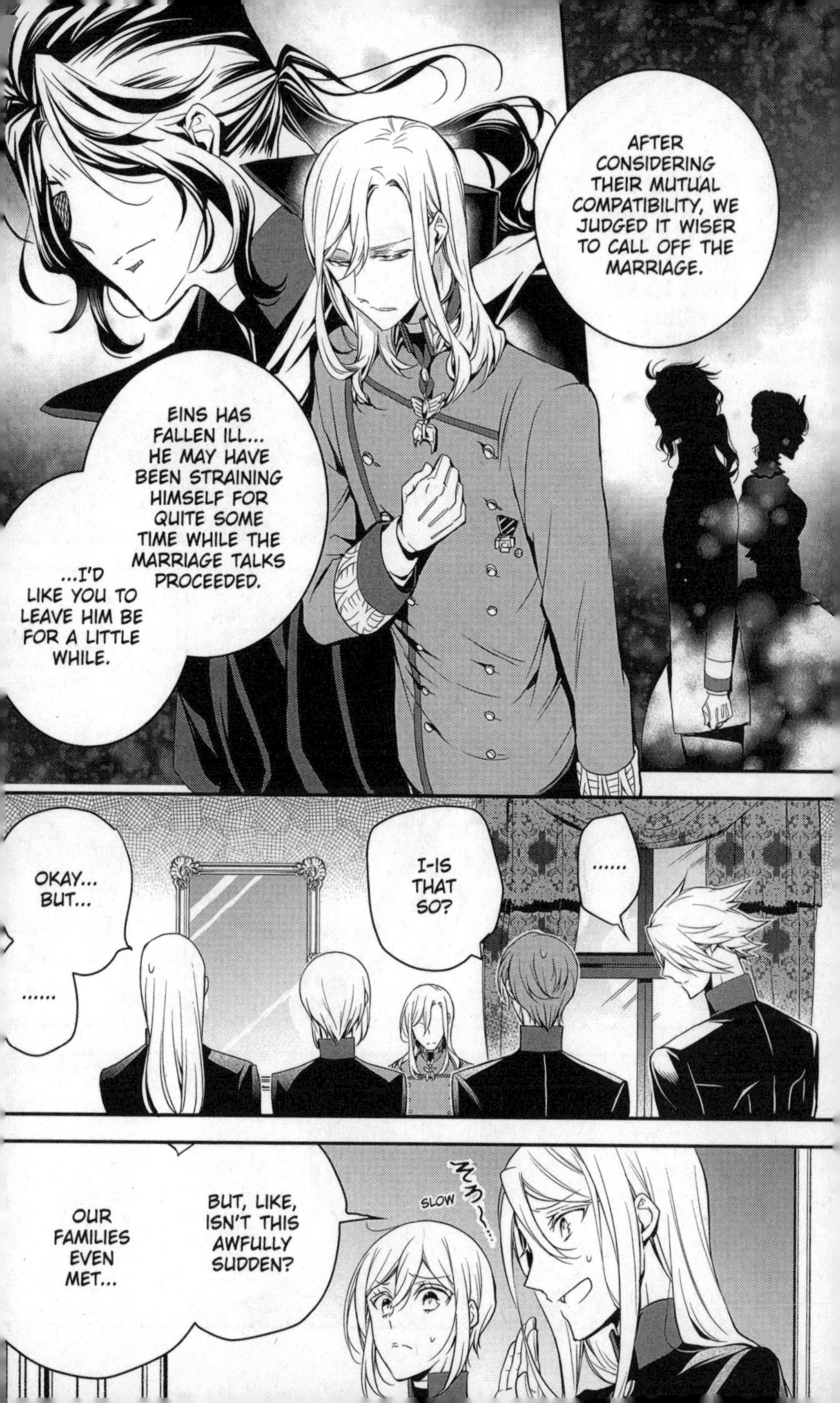
AFTER CONSIDERING THEIR MUTUAL COMPATIBILITY, WE JUDGED IT WISER TO CALL OFF THE MARRIAGE.
EINS HAS FALLEN ILL... HE MAY HAVE BEEN STRAINING HIMSELF FOR QUITE SOME TIME WHILE THE MARRIAGE TALKS PROCEEDED.
...I'D LIKE YOU TO LEAVE HIM BE FOR A LITTLE WHILE.
......
I-IS THAT SO?
OKAY... BUT...
......
SLOW
BUT, LIKE, ISN'T THIS AWFULLY SUDDEN?
OUR FAMILIES EVEN MET...

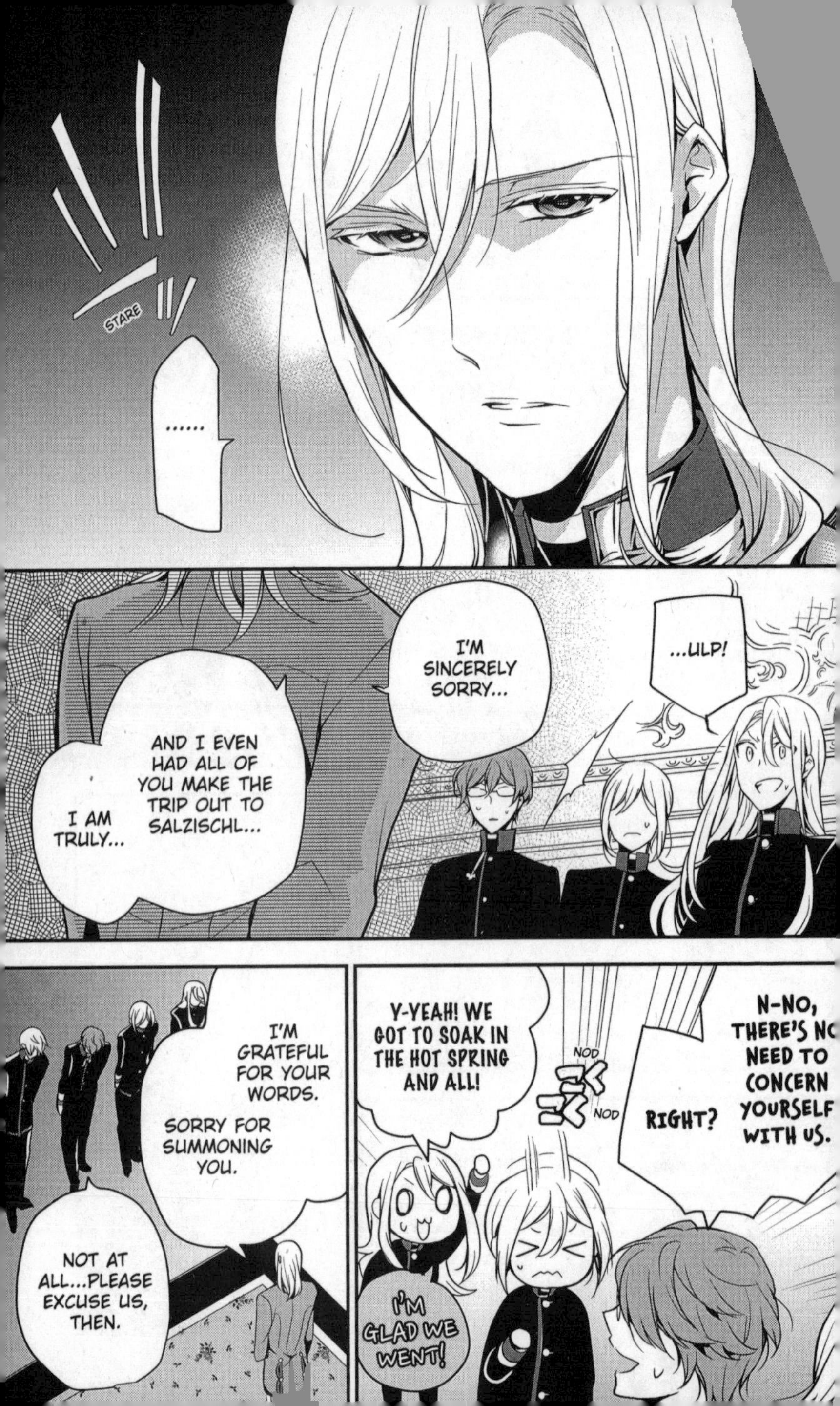
STARE
......
...ULP!
I'M SINCERELY SORRY...
AND I EVEN HAD ALL OF YOU MAKE THE TRIP OUT TO SALZISCHL...
I AM TRULY...
N-NO, THERE'S NO NEED TO CONCERN YOURSELF WITH US.
RIGHT?
NOD
NOD
Y-YEAH! WE GOT TO SOAK IN THE HOT SPRING AND ALL!
I'M GLAD WE WENT!
I'M GRATEFUL FOR YOUR WORDS.
SORRY FOR SUMMONING YOU.
NOT AT ALL...PLEASE EXCUSE US, THEN.

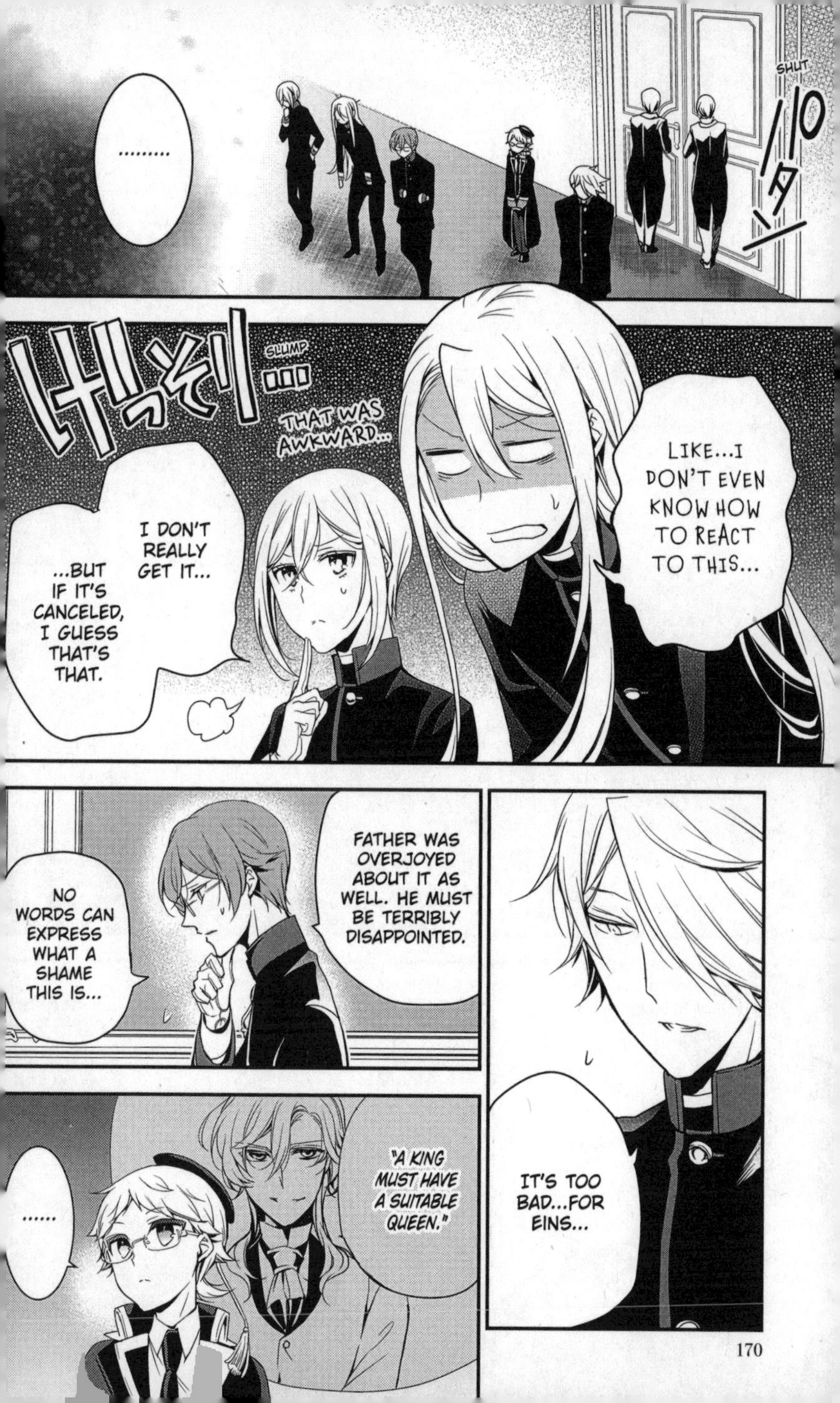
SHUT
....
SLUMP
THAT WAS AWKWARD...
LIKE...I DON'T EVEN KNOW HOW TO REACT TO THIS...
I DON'T REALLY GET IT...
...BUT IF IT'S CANCELED, I GUESS THAT'S THAT.
IT'S TOO BAD...FOR EINS...
FATHER WAS OVERJOYED ABOUT IT AS WELL. HE MUST BE TERRIBLY DISAPPOINTED.
NO WORDS CAN EXPRESS WHAT A SHAME THIS IS...
"A KING MUST HAVE A SUITABLE QUEEN."
......

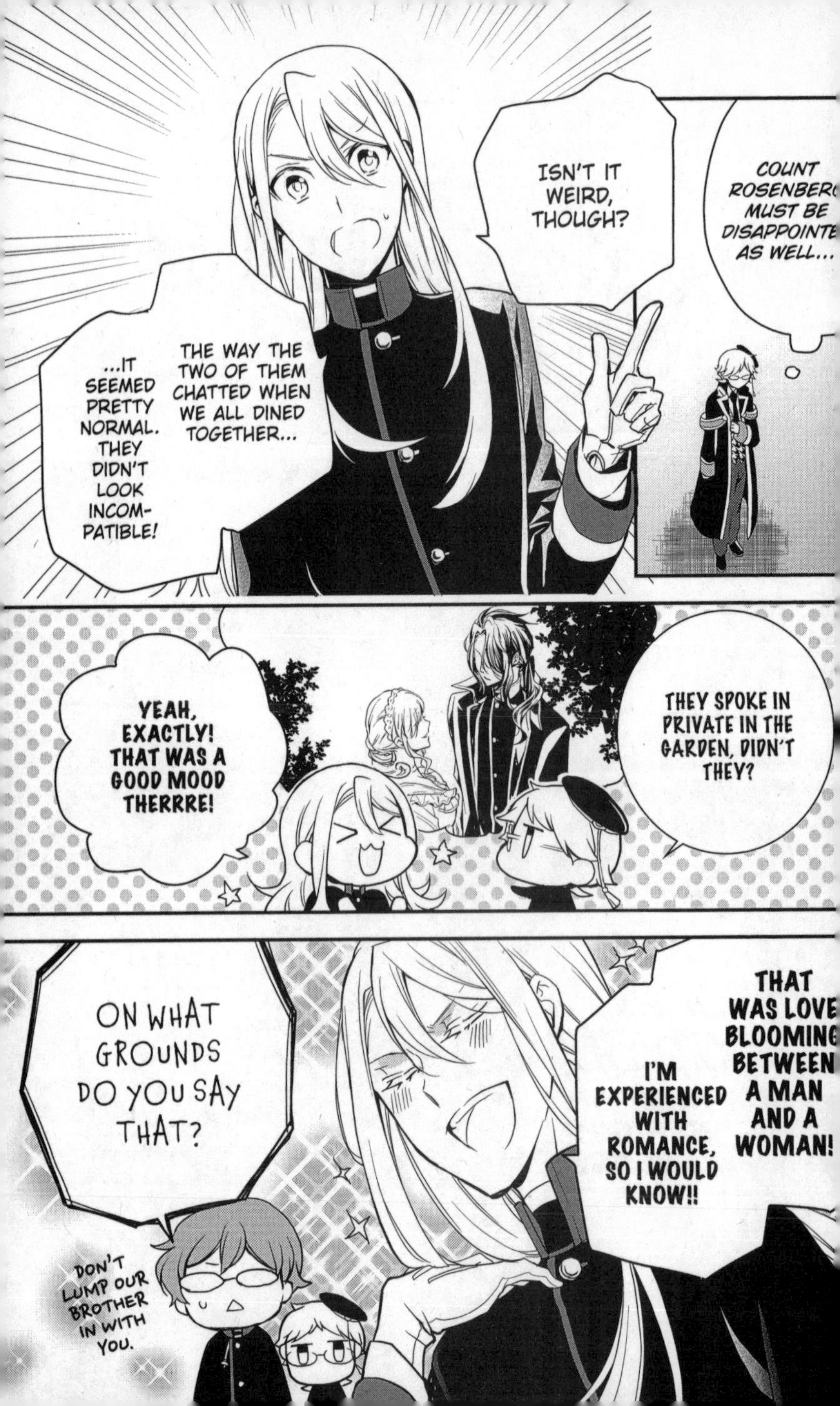
COUNT ROSENBER MUST BE DISAPPOINTE AS WELL...
ISN'T IT WEIRD, THOUGH?
THE WAY THE TWO OF THEM CHATTED WHEN WE ALL DINED TOGETHER...
...IT SEEMED PRETTY NORMAL. THEY DIDN'T LOOK INCOM-PATIBLE!
THEY SPOKE IN PRIVATE IN THE GARDEN, DIDN'T THEY?
YEAH, EXACTLY! THAT WAS A GOOD MOOD THERRRE!
THAT WAS LOVE BLOOMIN BETWEEN A MAN AND A WOMAN!
I'M EXPERIENCED WITH ROMANCE, SO I WOULD KNOW!!
ON WHAT GROUNDS DO YOU SAY THAT?
DON'T LUMP OUR BROTHER IN WITH YOU.

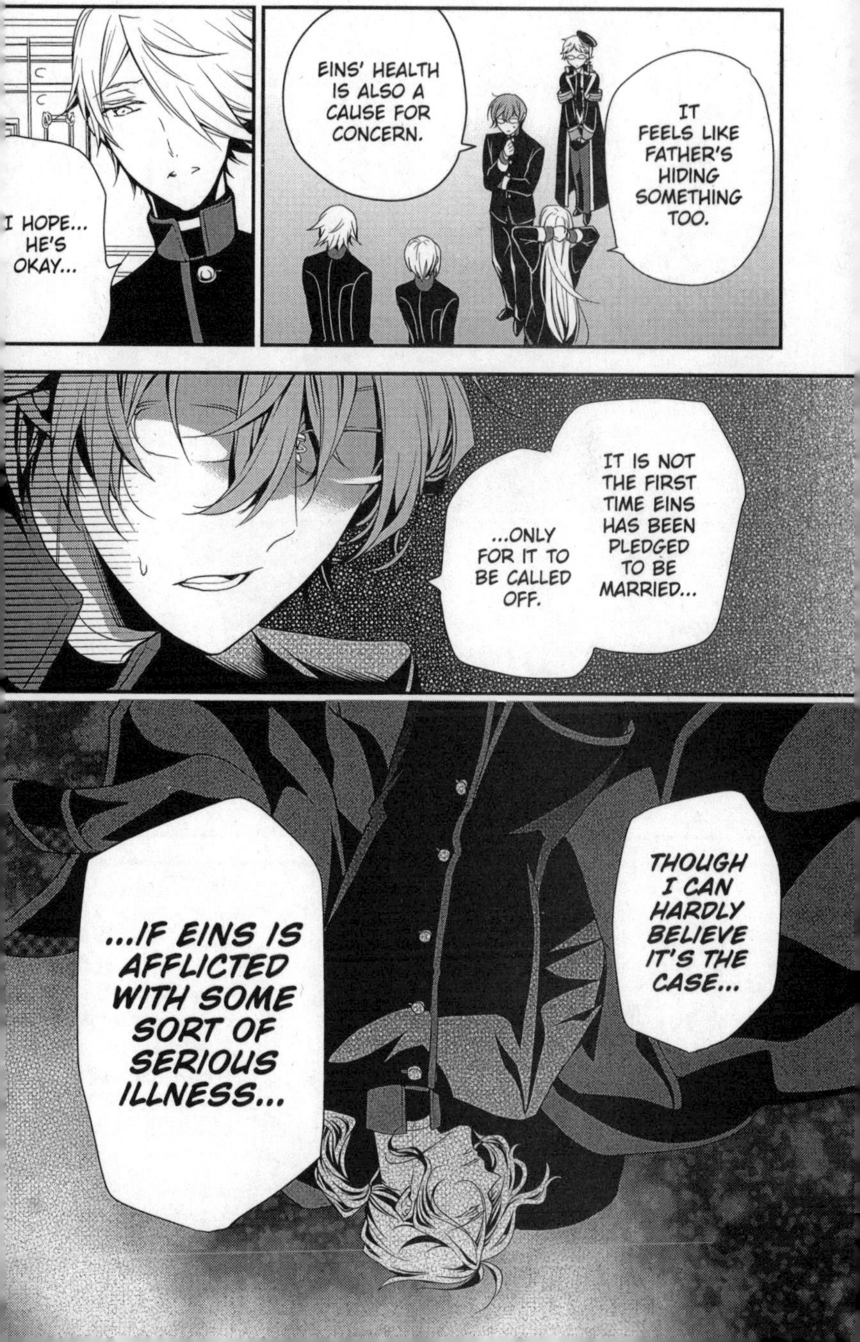
EINS' HEALTH IS ALSO A CAUSE FOR CONCERN.
IT FEELS LIKE FATHER'S HIDING SOMETHING TOO.
I HOPE... HE'S OKAY...
IT IS NOT THE FIRST TIME EINS HAS BEEN PLEDGED TO BE MARRIED...
...ONLY FOR IT TO BE CALLED OFF.
THOUGH I CAN HARDLY BELIEVE IT'S THE CASE...
...IF EINS IS AFFLICTED WITH SOME SORT OF SERIOUS ILLNESS...

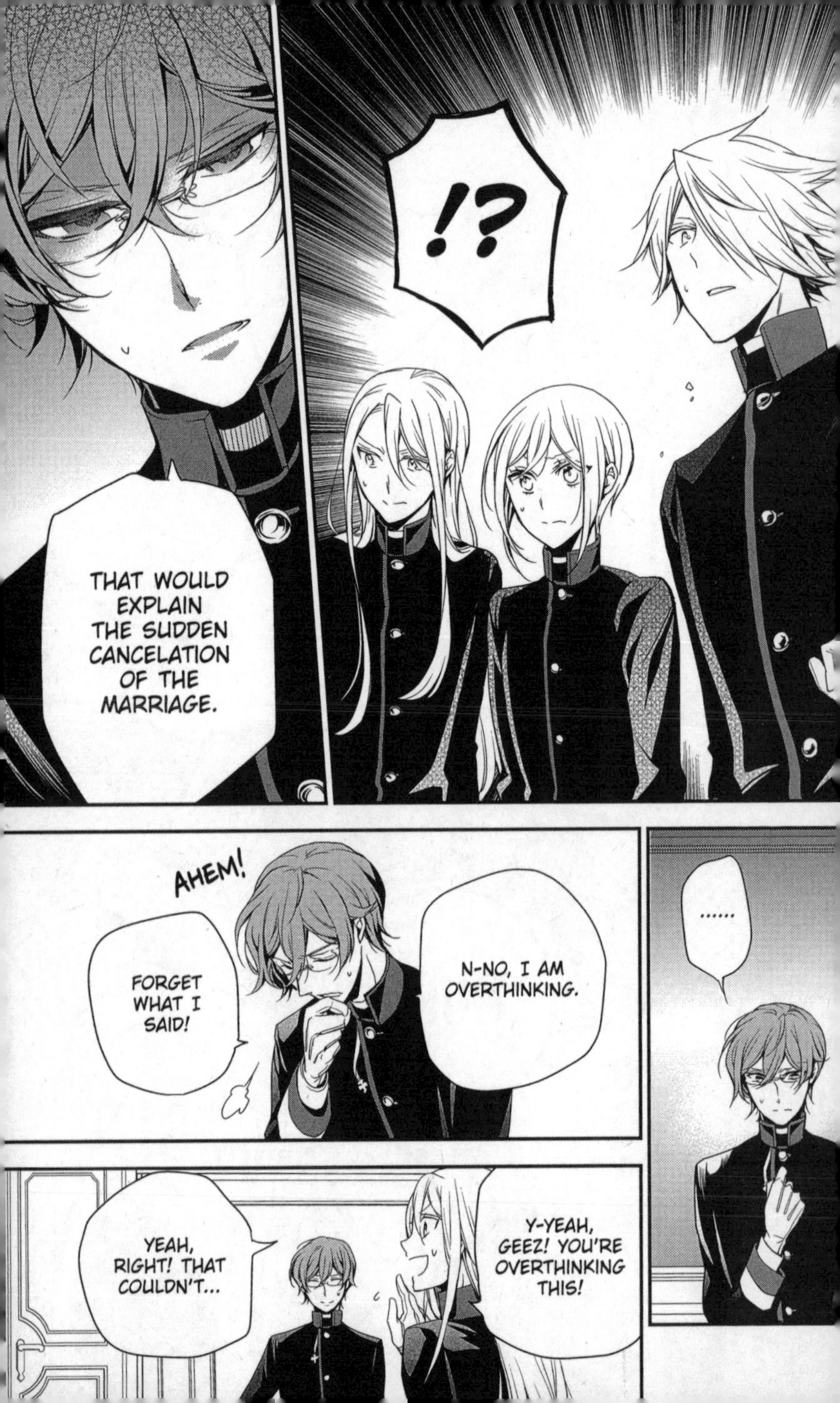
!?
THAT WOULD EXPLAIN THE SUDDEN CANCELATION OF THE MARRIAGE.
......
AHEM!
N-NO, I AM OVERTHINKING.
FORGET WHAT I SAID!
Y-YEAH, GEEZ! YOU'RE OVERTHINKING THIS!
YEAH, RIGHT! THAT COULDN'T...

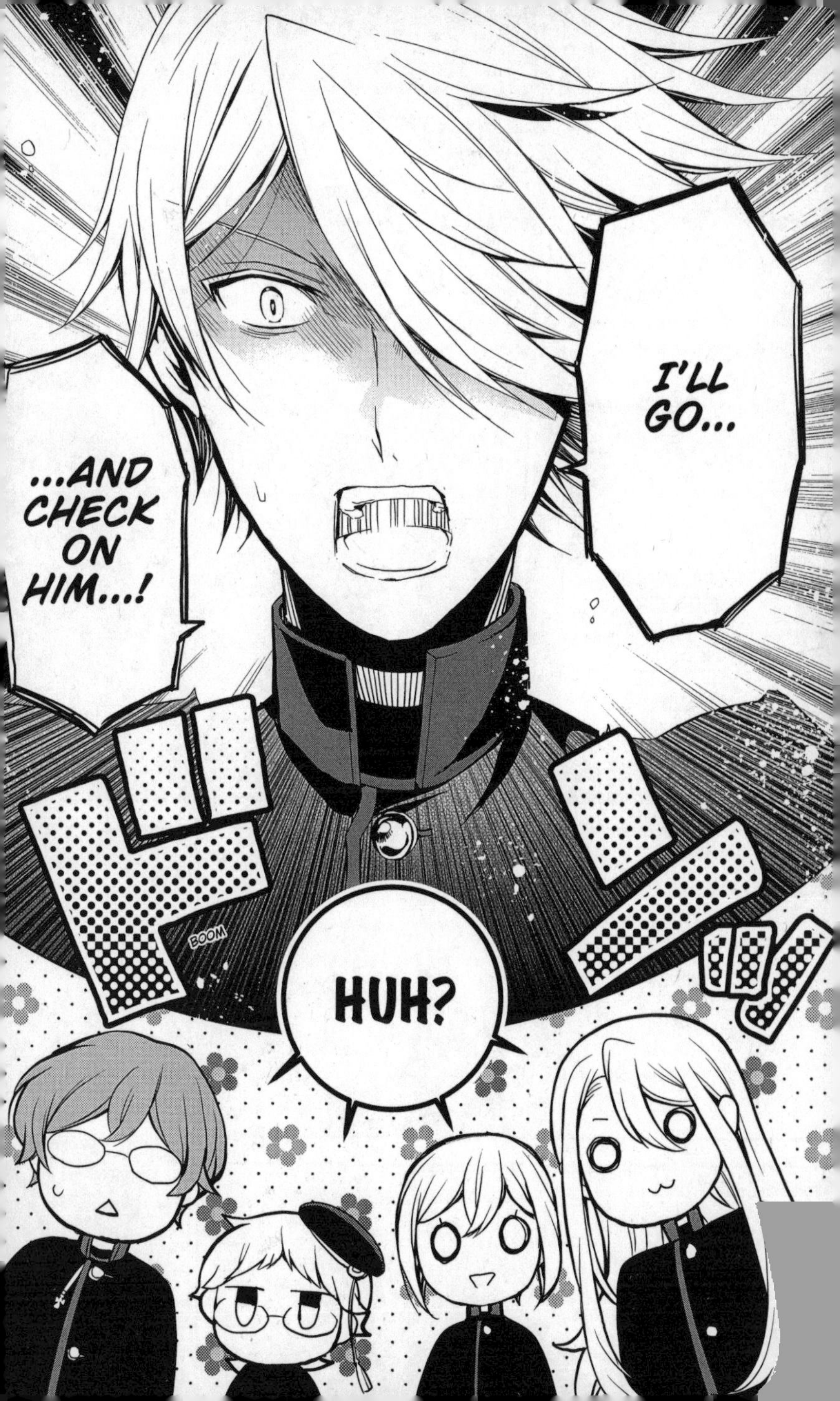
I'LL GO...
...AND CHECK ON HIM...!
BOOM
HUH?

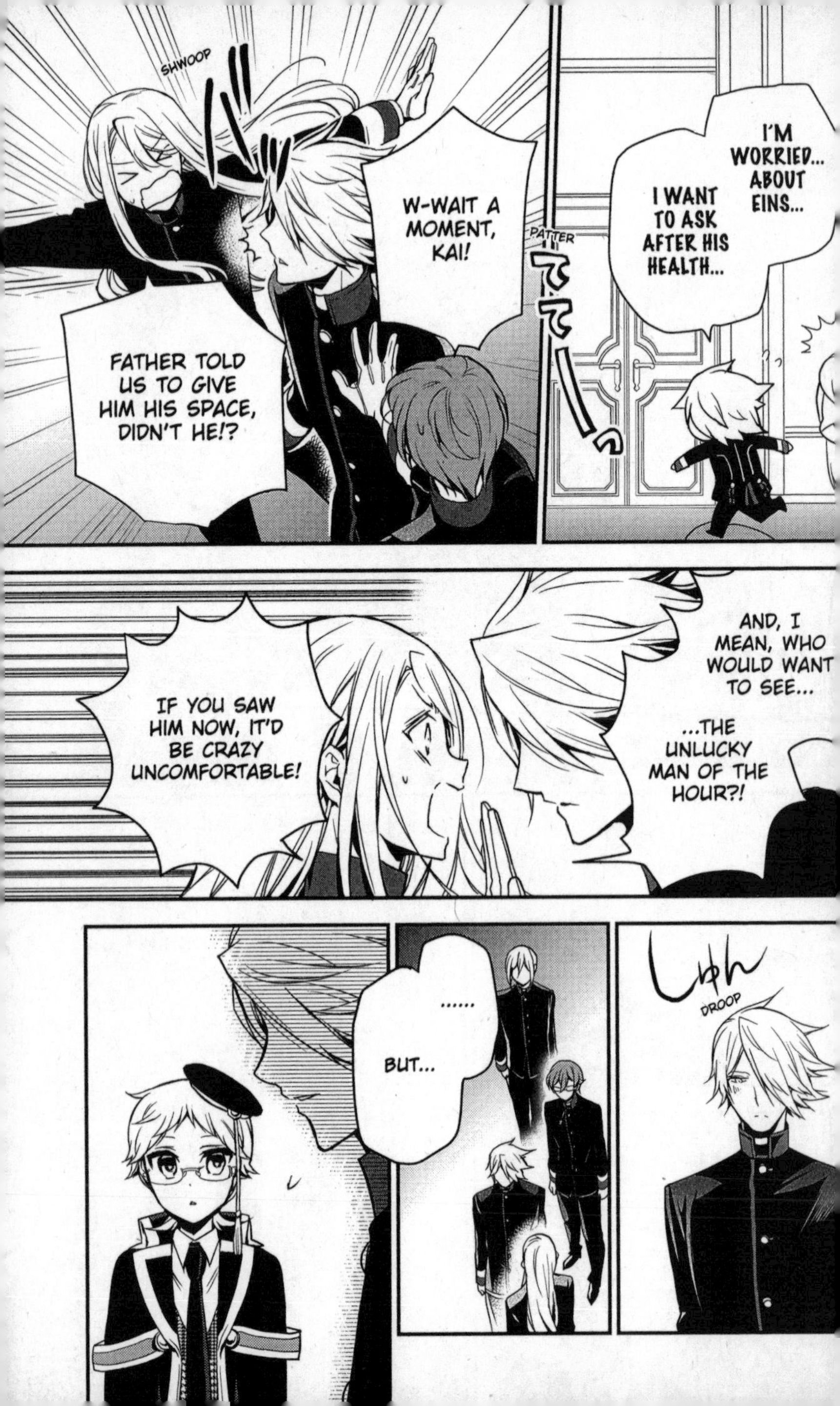
I'M WORRIED... ABOUT EINS...
I WANT TO ASK AFTER HIS HEALTH...
PATTER
SHWOOP
W-WAIT A MOMENT, KAI!
FATHER TOLD US TO GIVE HIM HIS SPACE, DIDN'T HE!?
AND, I MEAN, WHO WOULD WANT TO SEE...
...THE UNLUCKY MAN OF THE HOUR?!
IF YOU SAW HIM NOW, IT'D BE CRAZY UNCOMFORTABLE!
DROOP
......
BUT...

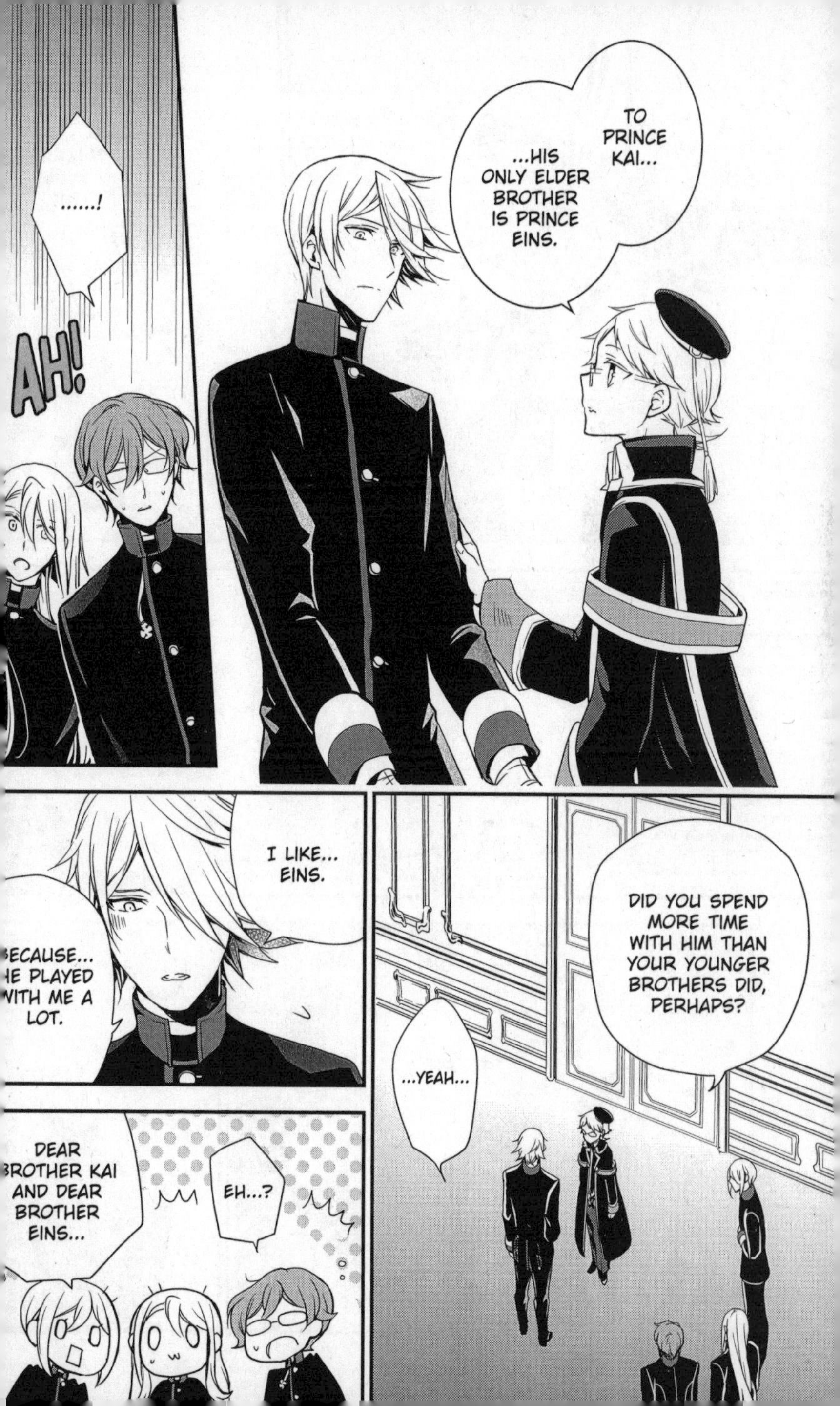
TO PRINCE KAI...
...HIS ONLY ELDER BROTHER IS PRINCE EINS.
......!
AH!
DID YOU SPEND MORE TIME WITH HIM THAN YOUR YOUNGER BROTHERS DID, PERHAPS?
...YEAH...
I LIKE... EINS.
ECAUSE... HE PLAYED WITH ME A LOT.
EH...?
DEAR ROTHER KAI AND DEAR BROTHER EINS...

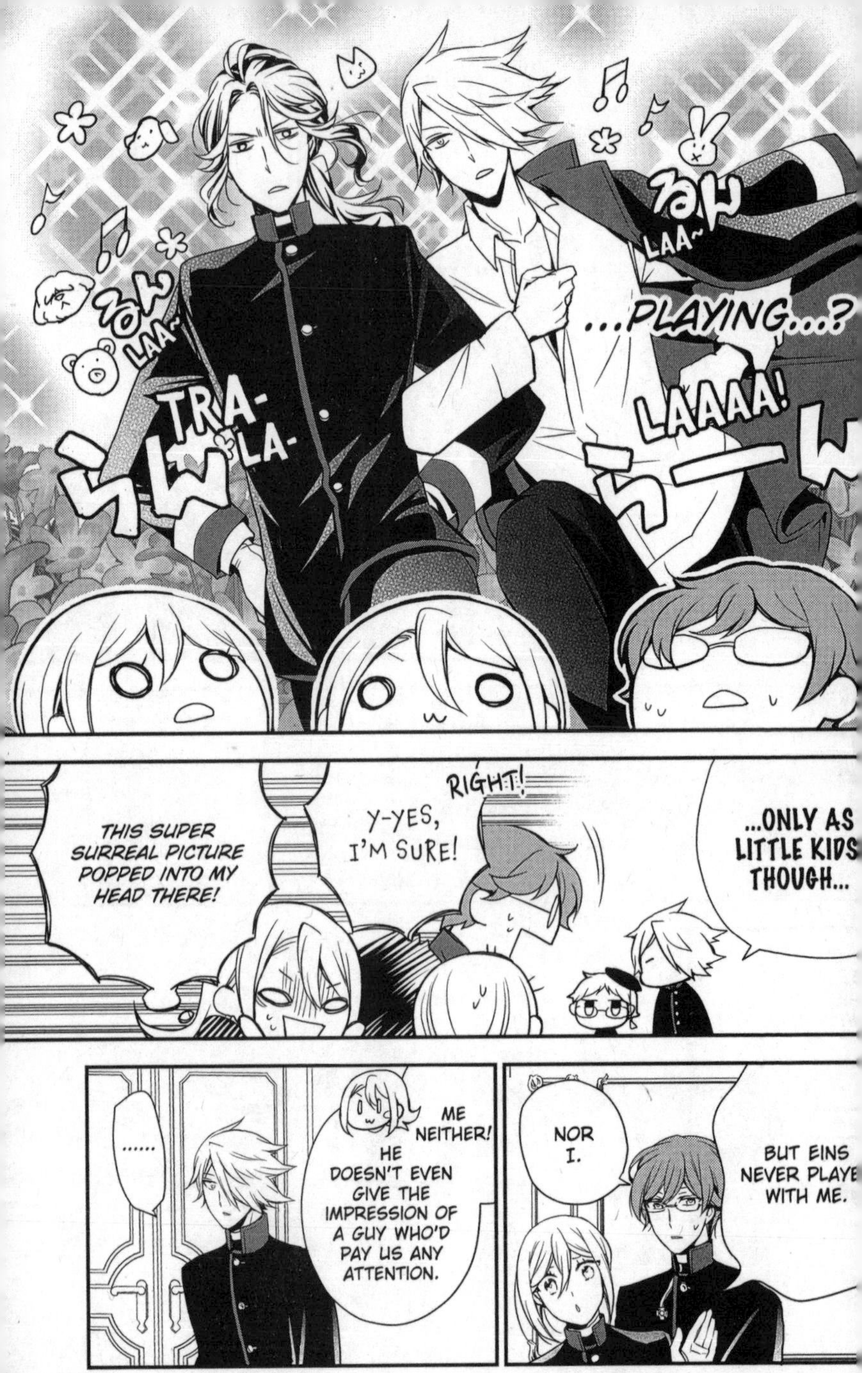
るん
LAA~
...PLAYING...?
LAAAA!
らーん
るん
LAA~
TRA-LA-
らん
...ONLY AS LITTLE KIDS THOUGH...
RIGHT!
Y-YES, I'M SURE!
THIS SUPER SURREAL PICTURE POPPED INTO MY HEAD THERE!
BUT EINS NEVER PLAYE WITH ME.
NOR I.
ME NEITHER! HE DOESN'T EVEN GIVE THE IMPRESSION OF A GUY WHO'D PAY US ANY ATTENTION.
......

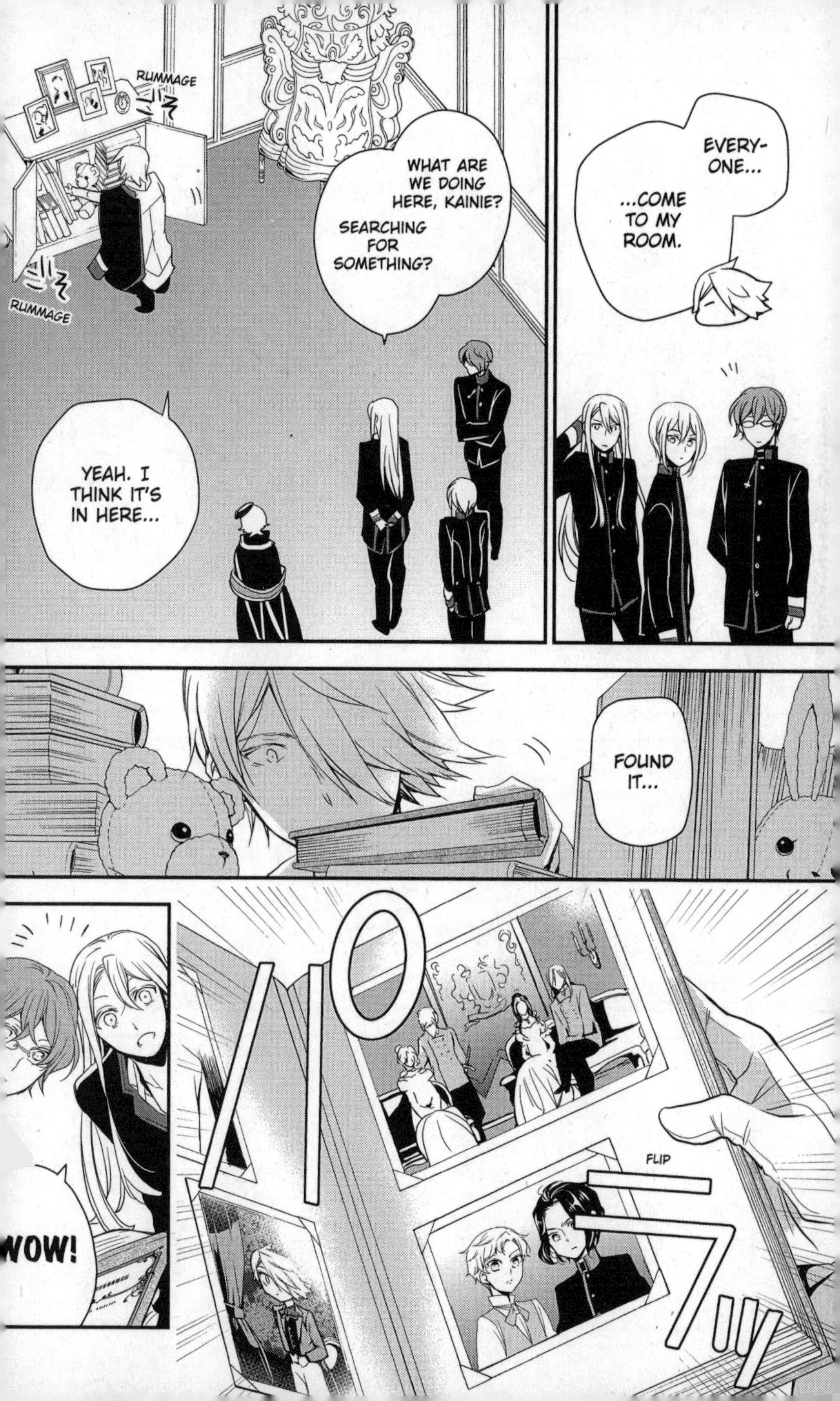
EVERY-ONE...
...COME TO MY ROOM.
WHAT ARE WE DOING HERE, KAINIE?
SEARCHING FOR SOMETHING?
RUMMAGE
RUMMAGE
YEAH. I THINK IT'S IN HERE...
FOUND IT...
FLIP
WOW!

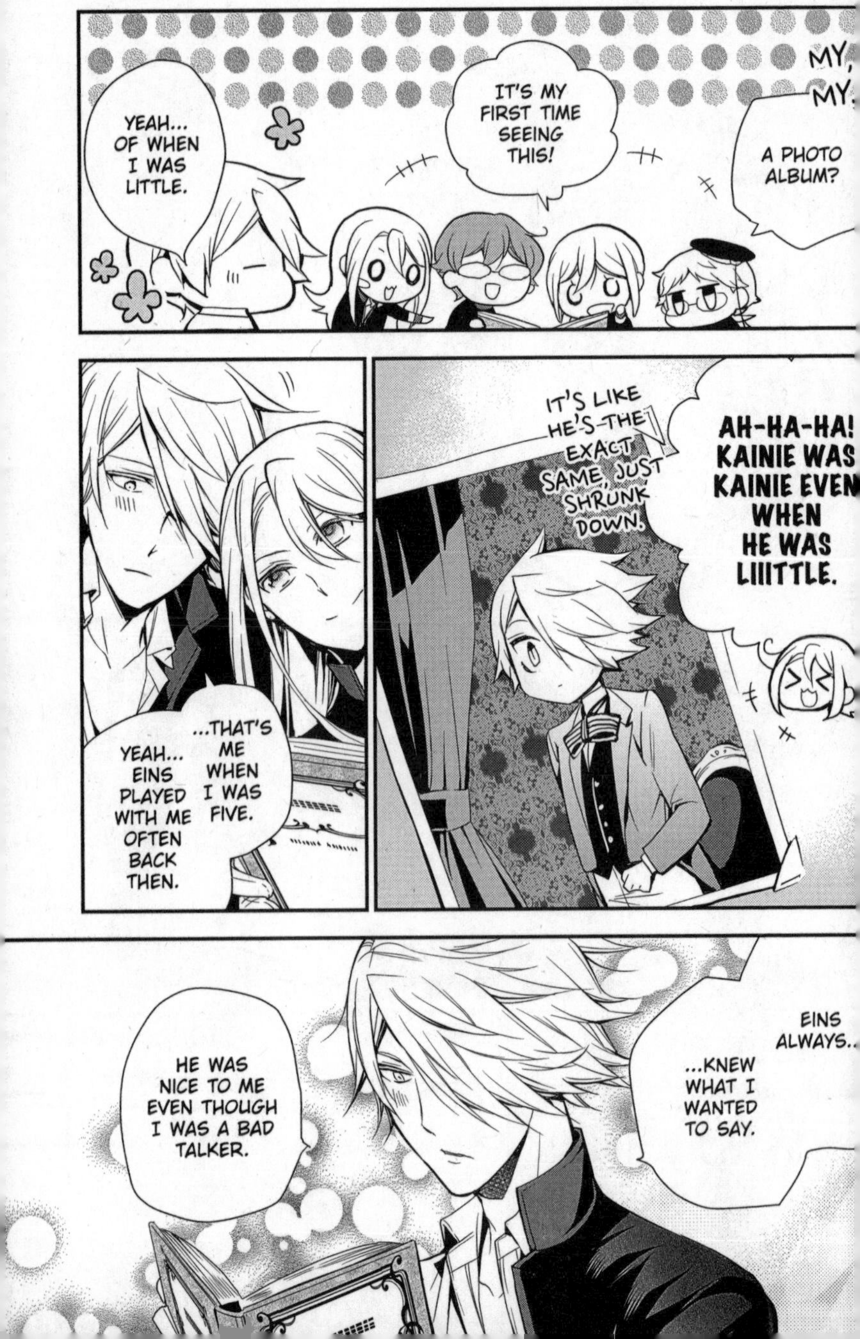
MY, MY.
A PHOTO ALBUM?
IT'S MY FIRST TIME SEEING THIS!
YEAH... OF WHEN I WAS LITTLE.
AH-HA-HA! KAINIE WAS KAINIE EVEN WHEN HE WAS LIIITTLE.
IT'S LIKE HE'S THE EXACT SAME, JUST SHRUNK DOWN.
...THAT'S ME WHEN I WAS FIVE.
YEAH... EINS PLAYED WITH ME OFTEN BACK THEN.
EINS ALWAYS...
...KNEW WHAT I WANTED TO SAY.
HE WAS NICE TO ME EVEN THOUGH I WAS A BAD TALKER.

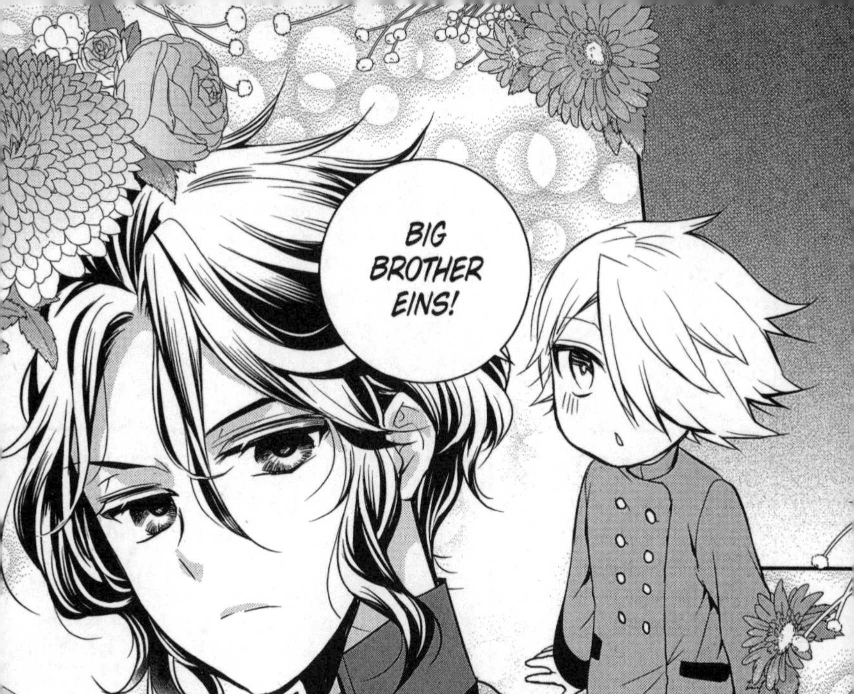
BIG BROTHER EINS!
EINS
11 YEARS OLD
KAI
5 YEARS OLD
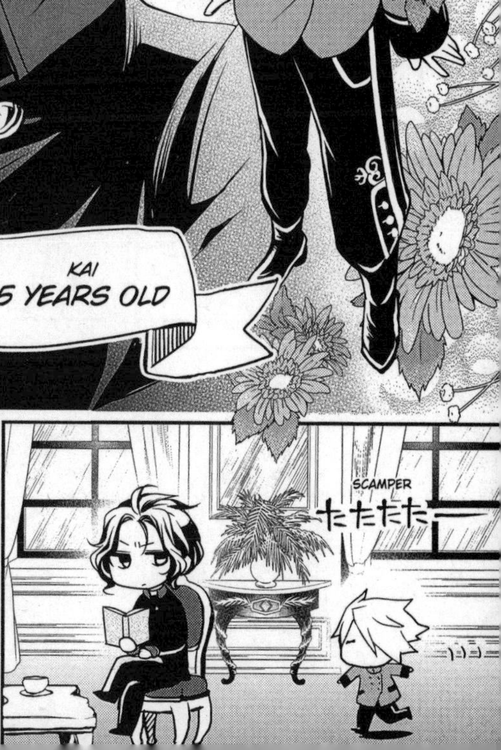
SCAMPER
たたたた—
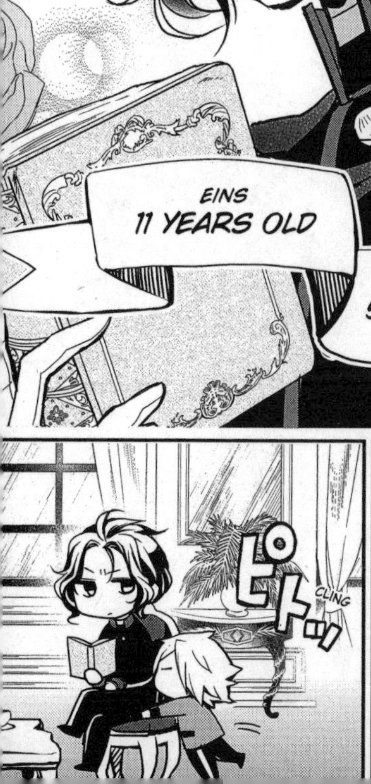
ピトッ
CLING

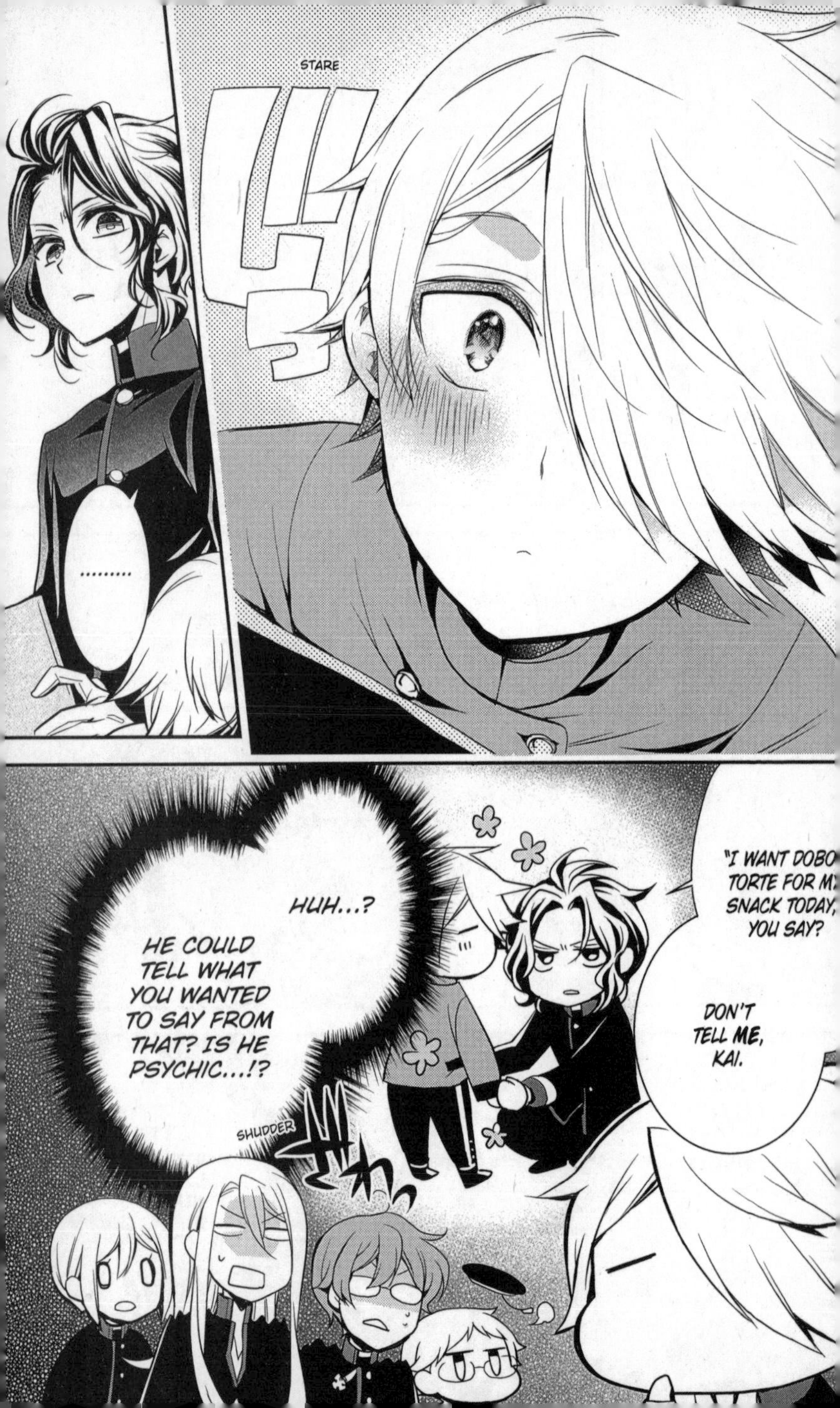
STARE
....
"I WANT DOBO TORTE FOR M SNACK TODAY," YOU SAY?
DON'T TELL ME, KAI.
HUH...?
HE COULD TELL WHAT YOU WANTED TO SAY FROM THAT? IS HE PSYCHIC...!?
SHUDDER

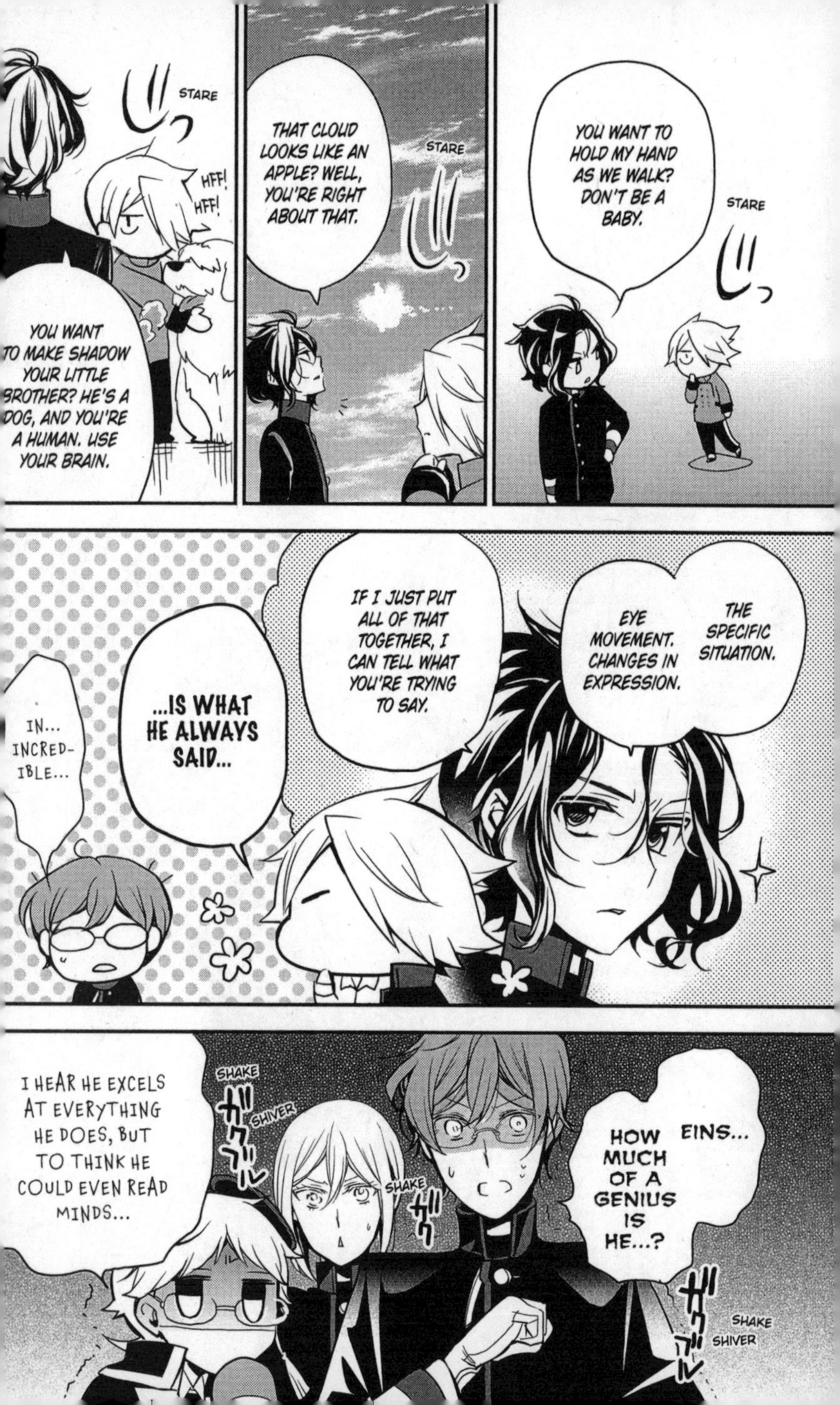
YOU WANT TO HOLD MY HAND AS WE WALK? DON'T BE A BABY.
STARE
THAT CLOUD LOOKS LIKE AN APPLE? WELL, YOU'RE RIGHT ABOUT THAT.
STARE
STARE
HFF! HFF!
YOU WANT TO MAKE SHADOW YOUR LITTLE BROTHER? HE'S A DOG, AND YOU'RE A HUMAN. USE YOUR BRAIN.
THE SPECIFIC SITUATION.
EYE MOVEMENT. CHANGES IN EXPRESSION.
IF I JUST PUT ALL OF THAT TOGETHER, I CAN TELL WHAT YOU'RE TRYING TO SAY.
...IS WHAT HE ALWAYS SAID...
IN... INCRED-IBLE...
EINS...
HOW MUCH OF A GENIUS IS HE...?
SHAKE SHIVER
SHAKE
SHAKE SHIVER
I HEAR HE EXCELS AT EVERYTHING HE DOES, BUT TO THINK HE COULD EVEN READ MINDS...

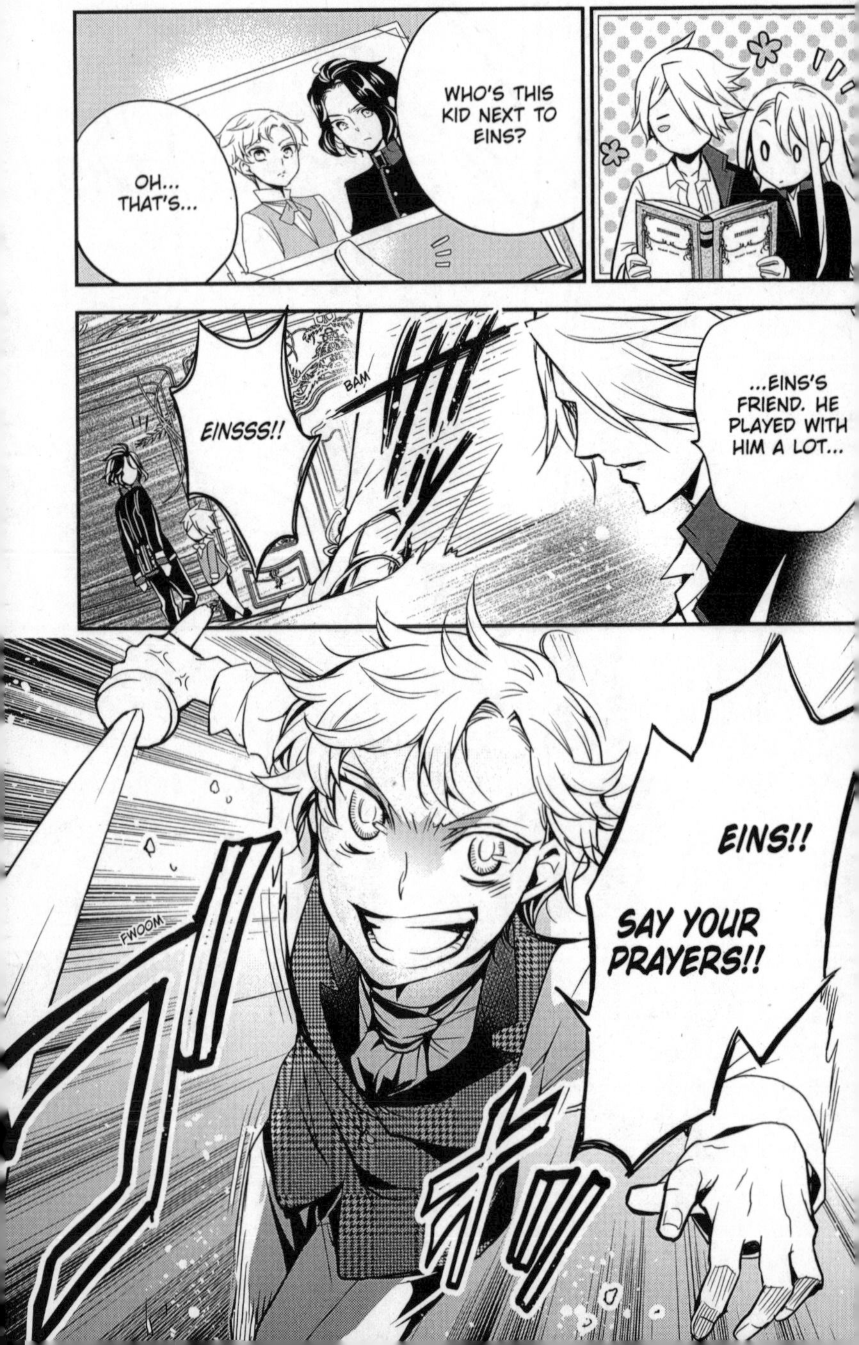
WHO'S THIS KID NEXT TO EINS?
OH... THAT'S...
...EINS'S FRIEND. HE PLAYED WITH HIM A LOT...
BAM
EINSSS!!
EINS!!
SAY YOUR PRAYERS!!
FWOOM

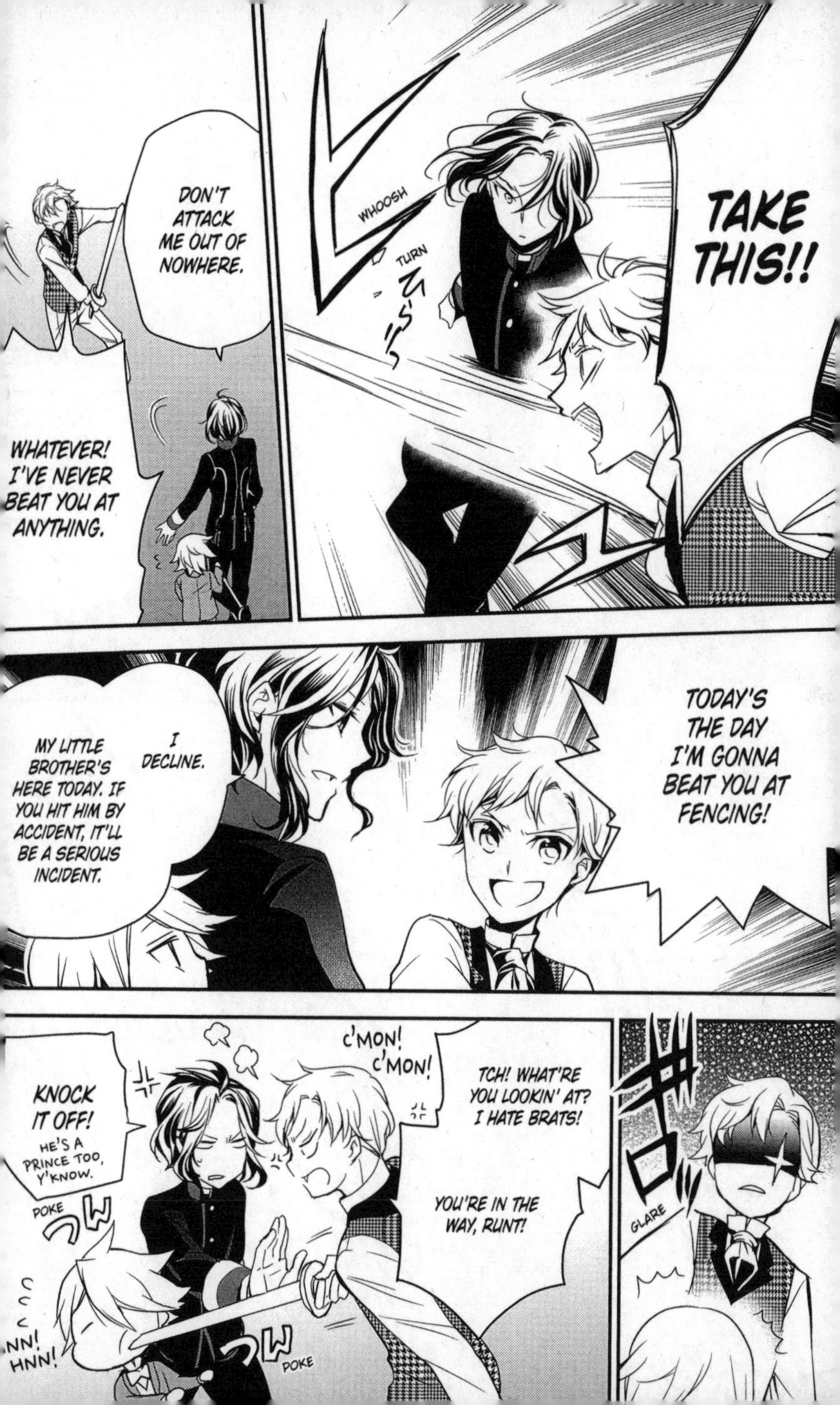
TAKE THIS!!
WHOOSH
TURN
DON'T ATTACK ME OUT OF NOWHERE.
WHATEVER! I'VE NEVER BEAT YOU AT ANYTHING.
TODAY'S THE DAY I'M GONNA BEAT YOU AT FENCING!
I DECLINE.
MY LITTLE BROTHER'S HERE TODAY. IF YOU HIT HIM BY ACCIDENT, IT'LL BE A SERIOUS INCIDENT.
GLARE
TCH! WHAT'RE YOU LOOKIN' AT? I HATE BRATS!
YOU'RE IN THE WAY, RUNT!
C'MON! C'MON!
KNOCK IT OFF!
HE'S A PRINCE TOO, Y'KNOW.
POKE
NN! HNN!
POKE

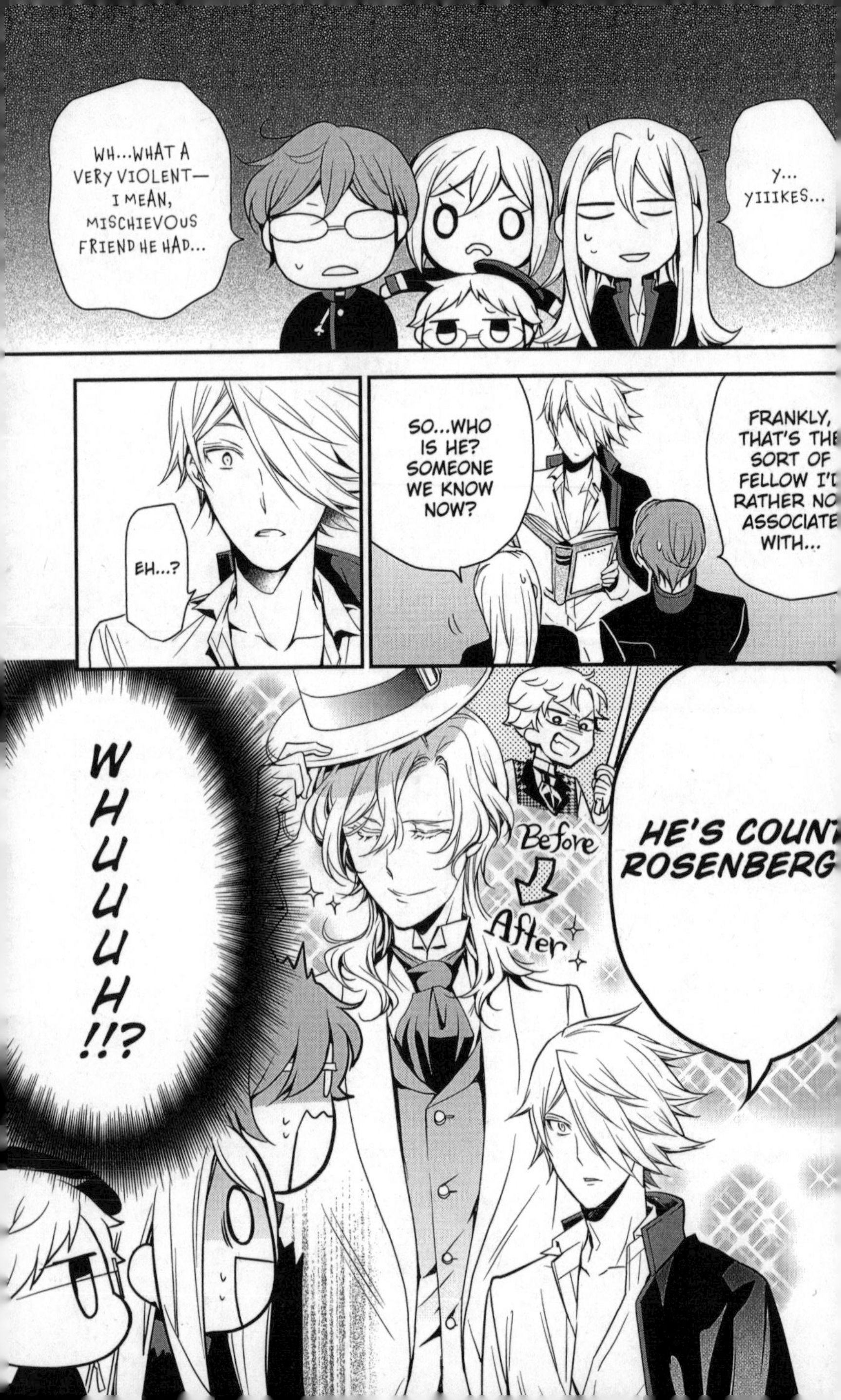
Y... YIIIKES...
WH...WHAT A VERY VIOLENT—I MEAN, MISCHIEVOUS FRIEND HE HAD...
FRANKLY, THAT'S THE SORT OF FELLOW I'D RATHER NO ASSOCIATE WITH...
SO...WHO IS HE? SOMEONE WE KNOW NOW?
EH...?
HE'S COUNT ROSENBERG
Before
After
WHUUUH!!?

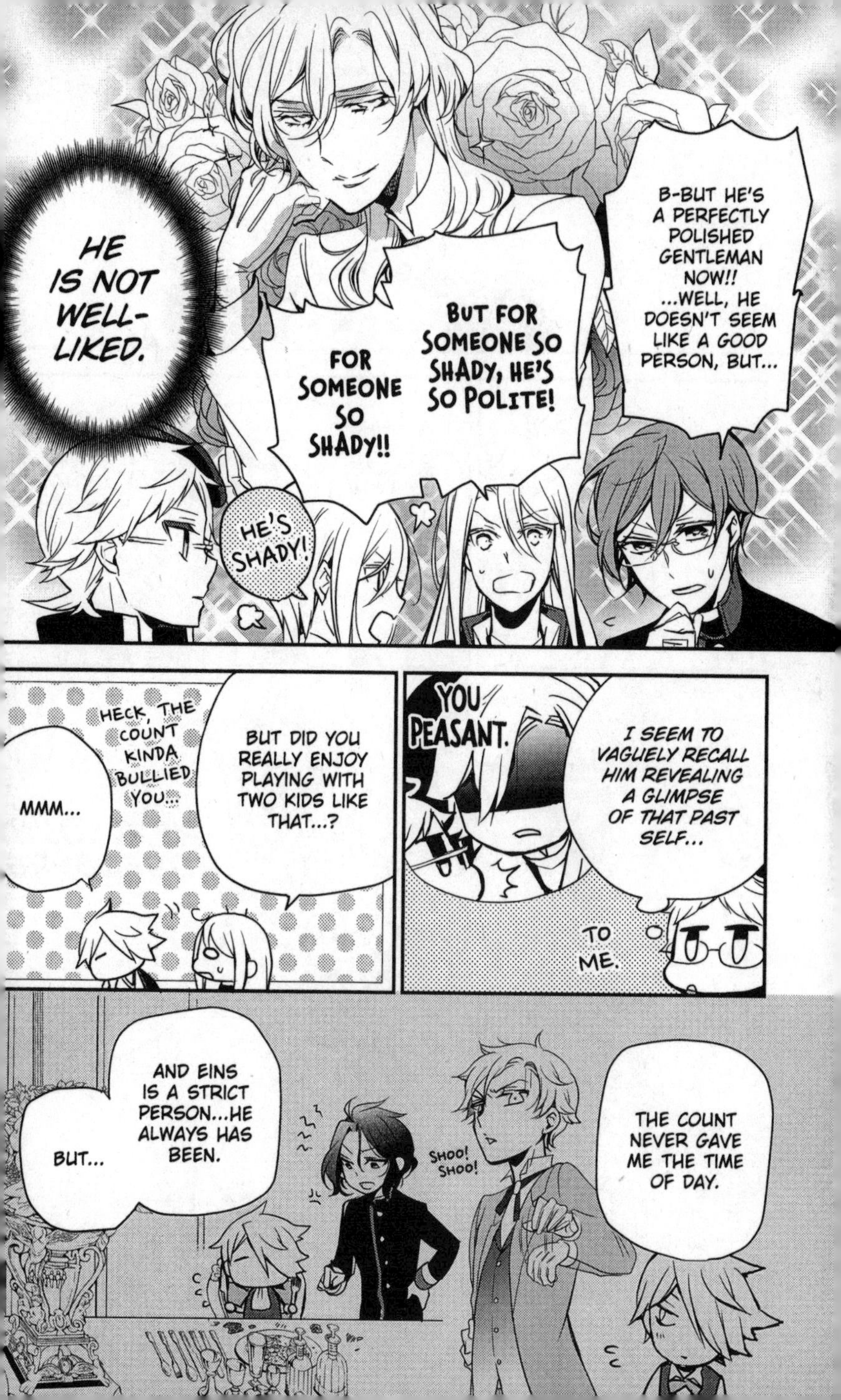
B-BUT HE'S A PERFECTLY POLISHED GENTLEMAN NOW!! ...WELL, HE DOESN'T SEEM LIKE A GOOD PERSON, BUT...
BUT FOR SOMEONE SO SHADY, HE'S SO POLITE!
FOR SOMEONE SO SHADY!!
HE IS NOT WELL-LIKED.
HE'S SHADY!
I SEEM TO VAGUELY RECALL HIM REVEALING A GLIMPSE OF THAT PAST SELF...
YOU PEASANT.
TO ME.
BUT DID YOU REALLY ENJOY PLAYING WITH TWO KIDS LIKE THAT...?
HECK, THE COUNT KINDA BULLIED YOU...
MMM...
THE COUNT NEVER GAVE ME THE TIME OF DAY.
SHOO! SHOO!
AND EINS IS A STRICT PERSON...HE ALWAYS HAS BEEN.
BUT...

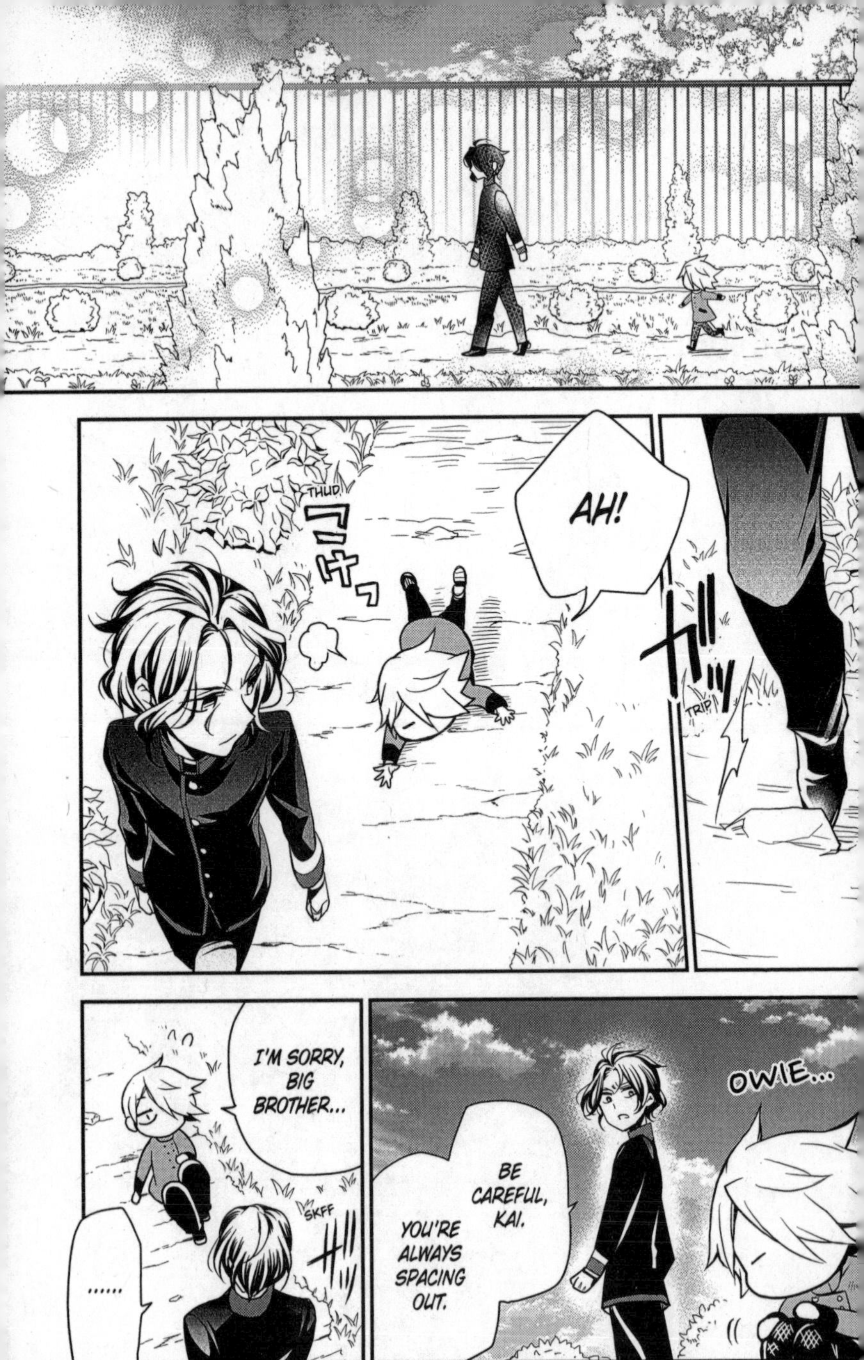
AH!
TRIP
THUD
I'M SORRY, BIG BROTHER...
......
SKFF
OWIE...
BE CAREFUL, KAI.
YOU'RE ALWAYS SPACING OUT.

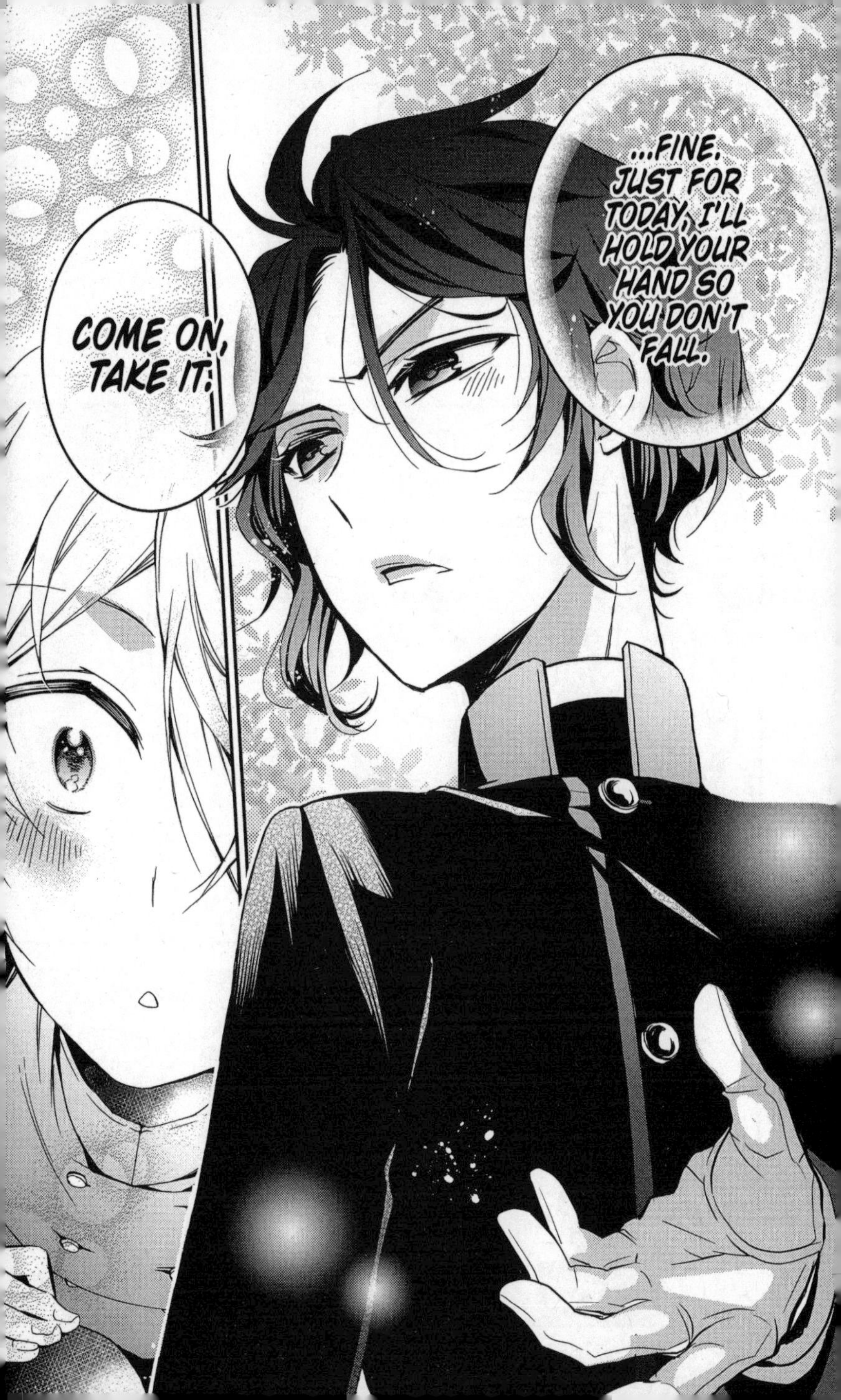
...FINE. JUST FOR TODAY, I'LL HOLD YOUR HAND SO YOU DON'T FALL.
COME ON, TAKE IT.

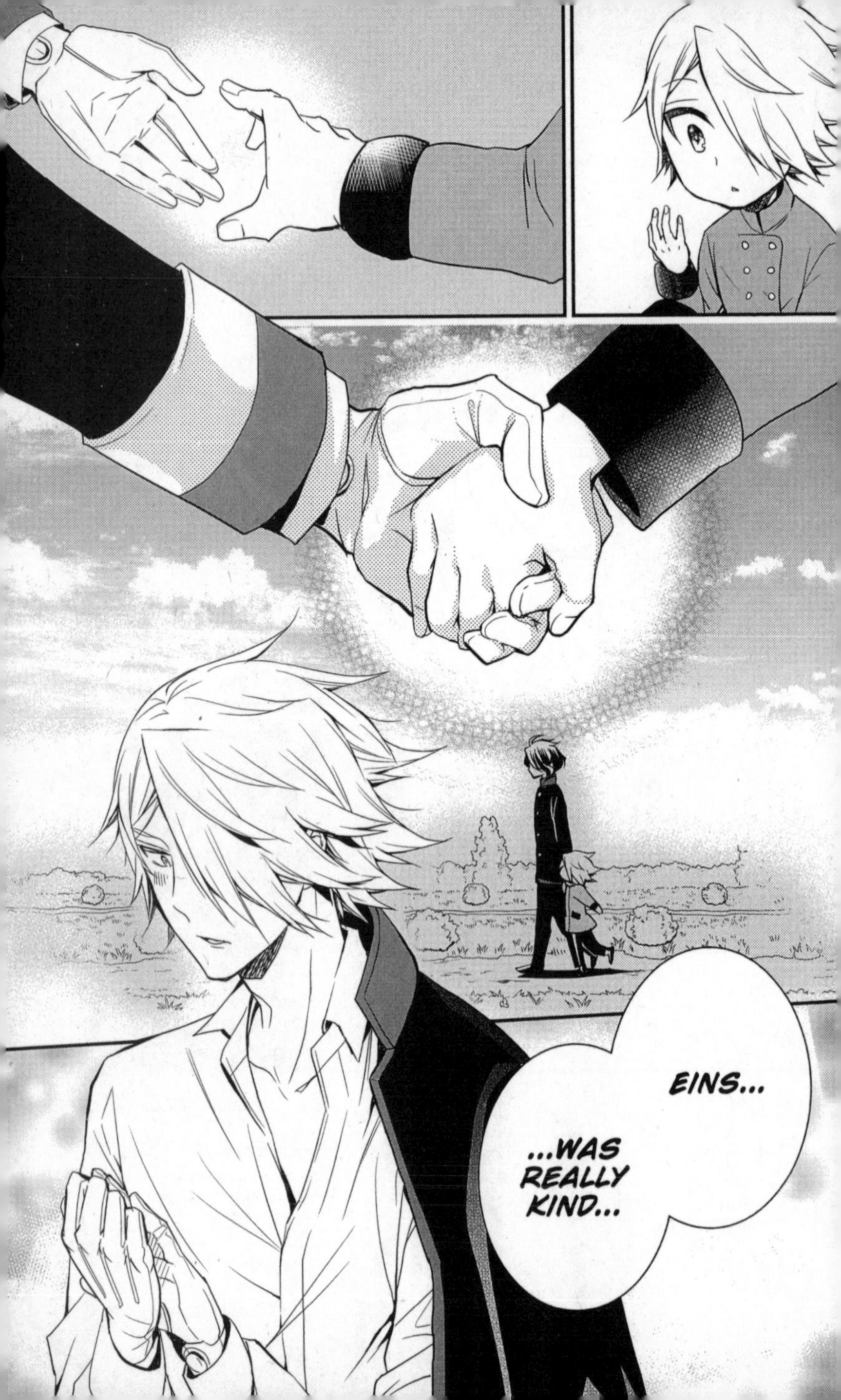
EINS...
...WAS REALLY KIND...

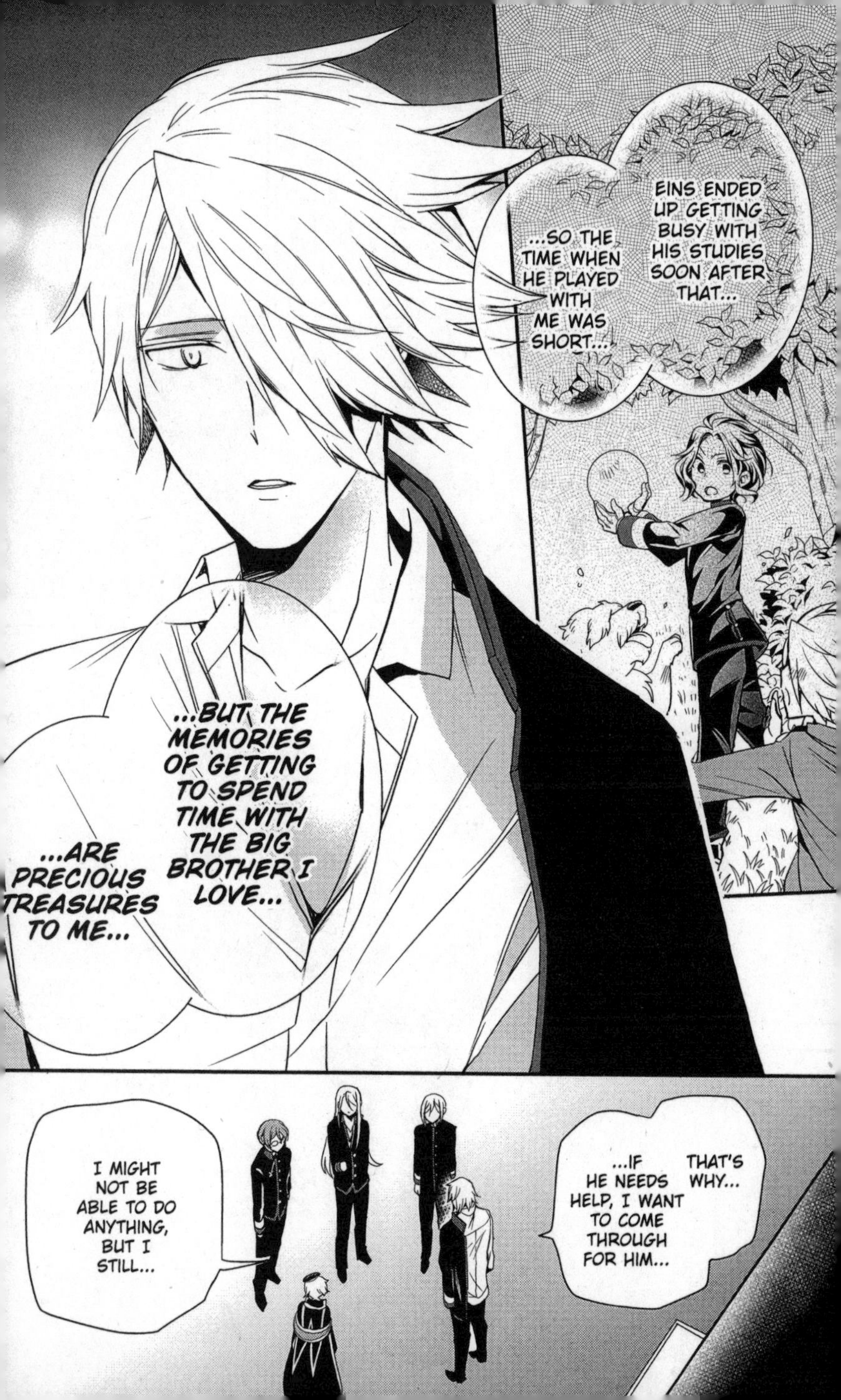
EINS ENDED UP GETTING BUSY WITH HIS STUDIES SOON AFTER THAT...
...SO THE TIME WHEN HE PLAYED WITH ME WAS SHORT...
...BUT THE MEMORIES OF GETTING TO SPEND TIME WITH THE BIG BROTHER I LOVE...
...ARE PRECIOUS TREASURES TO ME...
THAT'S WHY...
...IF HE NEEDS HELP, I WANT TO COME THROUGH FOR HIM...
I MIGHT NOT BE ABLE TO DO ANYTHING, BUT I STILL...

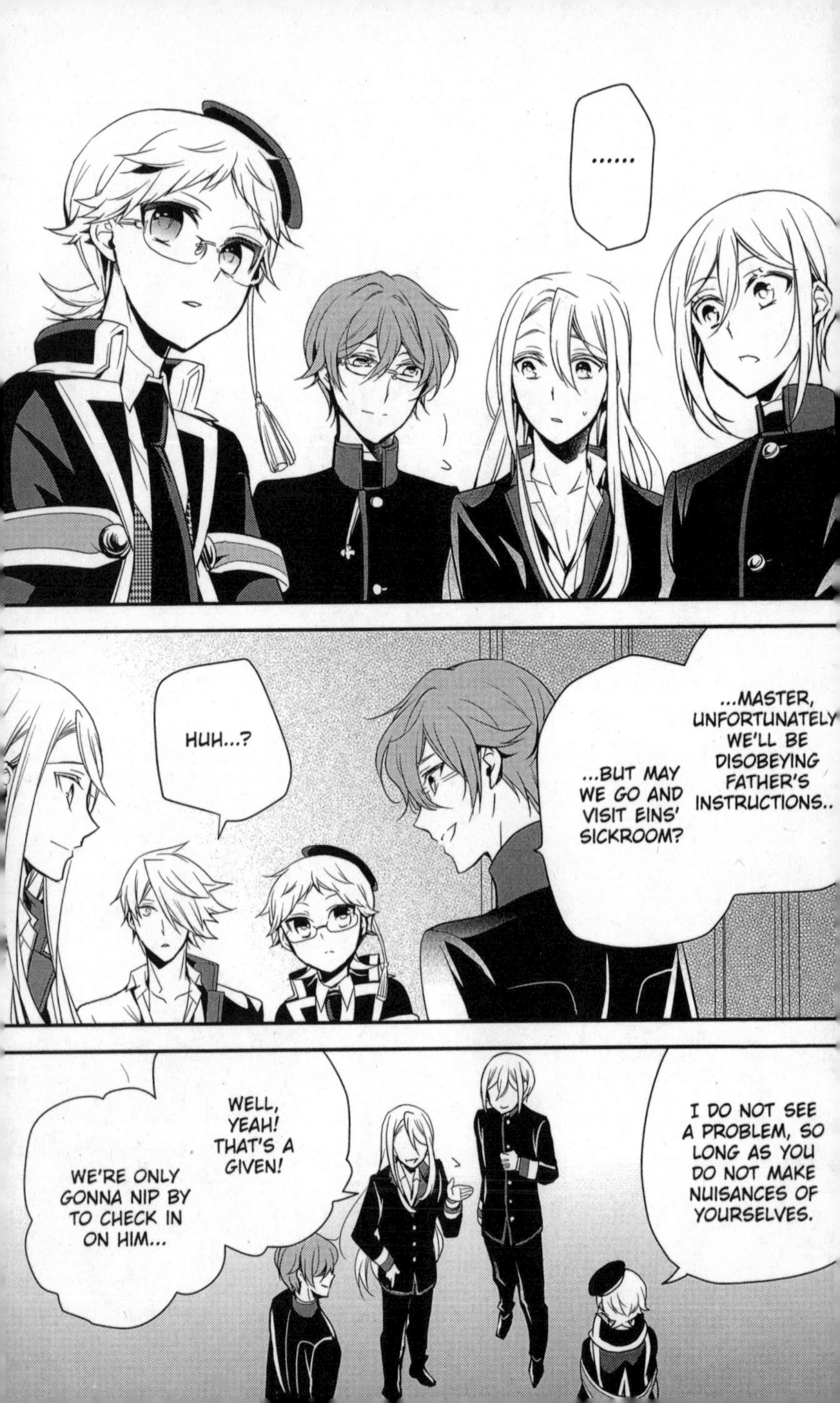

......
...MASTER, UNFORTUNATELY WE'LL BE DISOBEYING FATHER'S INSTRUCTIONS..
...BUT MAY WE GO AND VISIT EINS' SICKROOM?
HUH...?
I DO NOT SEE A PROBLEM, SO LONG AS YOU DO NOT MAKE NUISANCES OF YOURSELVES.
WELL, YEAH! THAT'S A GIVEN!
WE'RE ONLY GONNA NIP BY TO CHECK IN ON HIM...

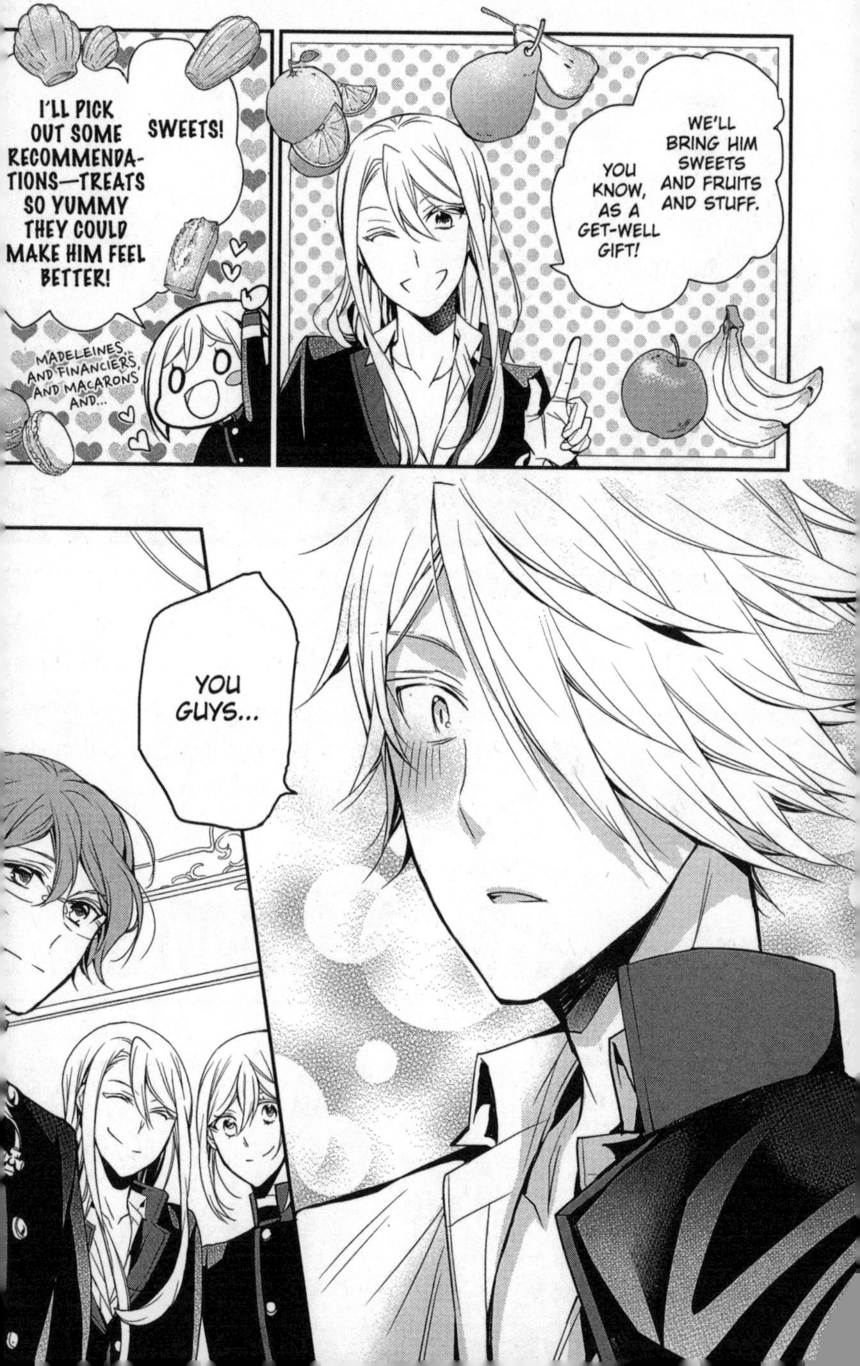
WE'LL BRING HIM SWEETS AND FRUITS AND STUFF.
YOU KNOW, AS A GET-WELL GIFT!
SWEETS!
I'LL PICK OUT SOME RECOMMENDA-TIONS—TREATS SO YUMMY THEY COULD MAKE HIM FEEL BETTER!
MADELEINES, AND FINANCIERS, AND MACARONS AND...
YOU GUYS...

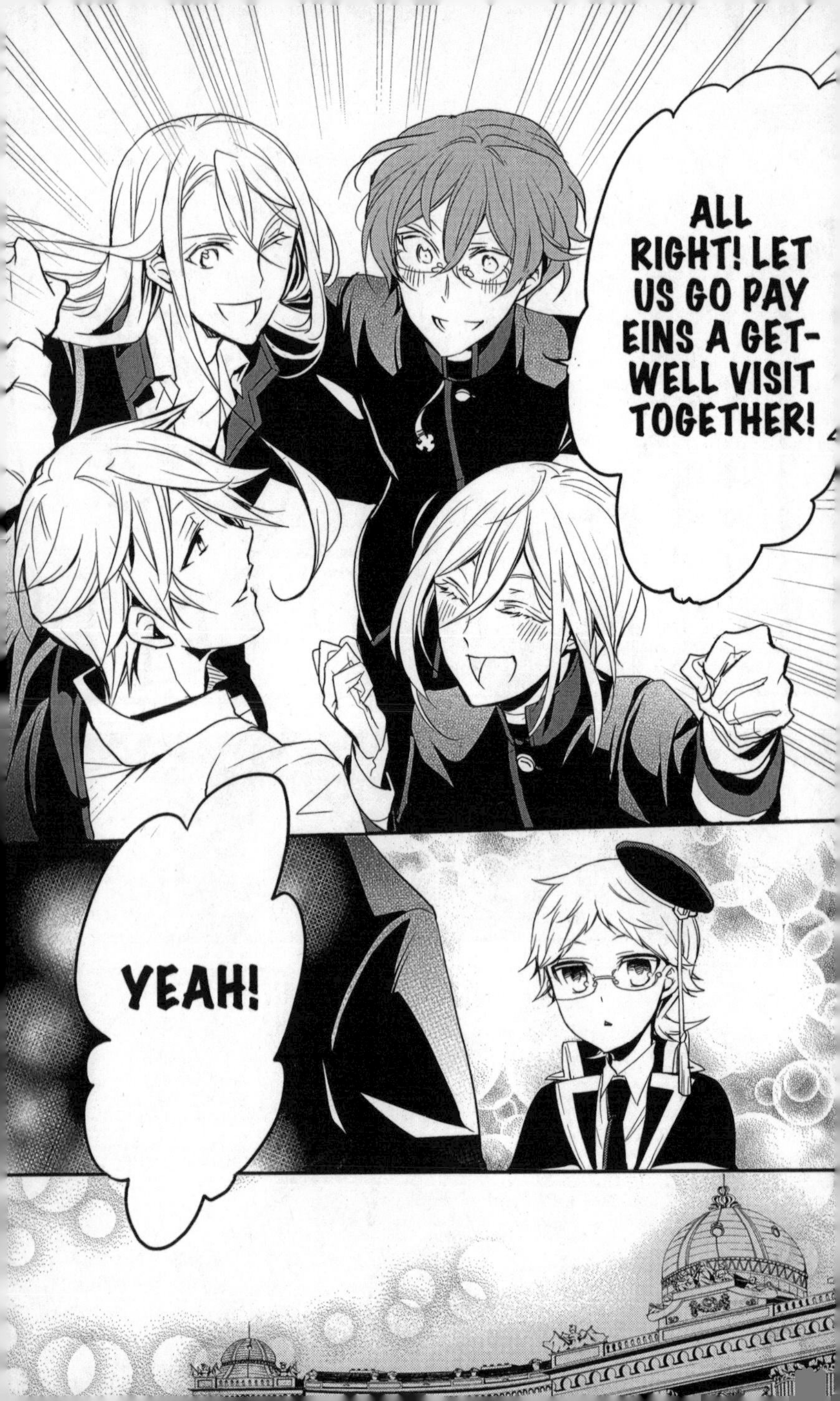
ALL RIGHT! LET US GO PAY EINS A GET-WELL VISIT TOGETHER!
YEAH!

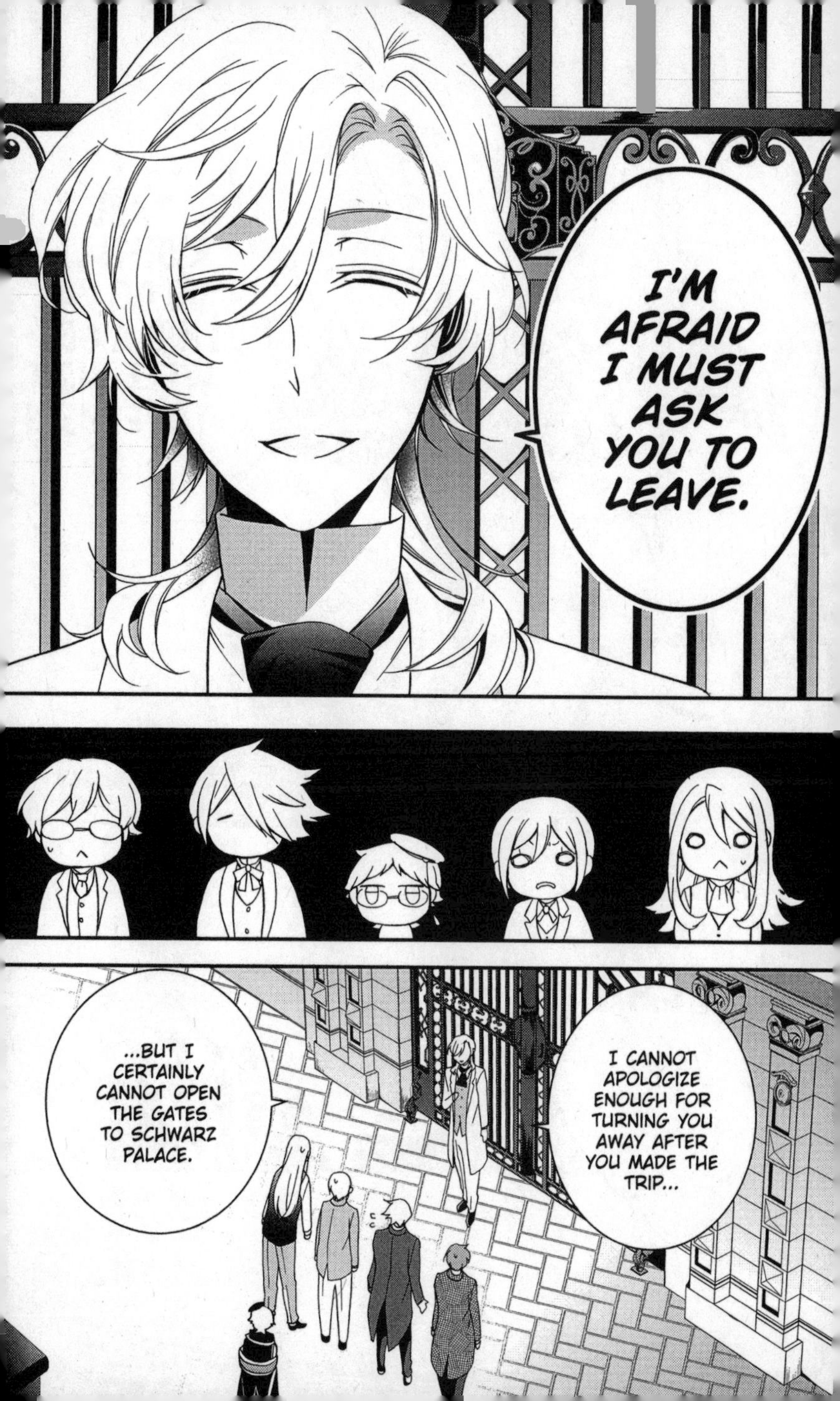
I'M AFRAID I MUST ASK YOU TO LEAVE.
I CANNOT APOLOGIZE ENOUGH FOR TURNING YOU AWAY AFTER YOU MADE THE TRIP...
...BUT I CERTAINLY CANNOT OPEN THE GATES TO SCHWARZ PALACE.

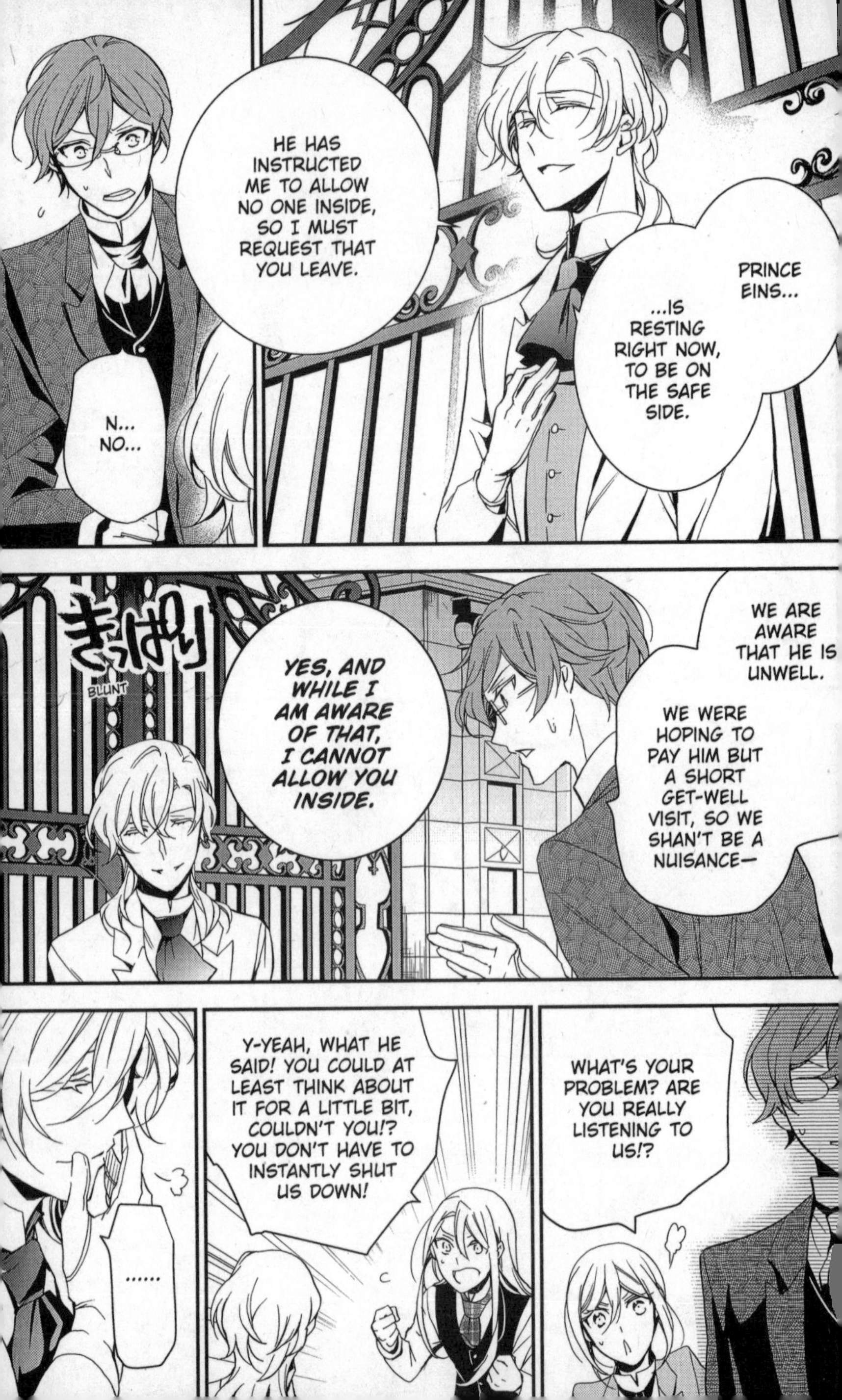
PRINCE EINS...
...IS RESTING RIGHT NOW, TO BE ON THE SAFE SIDE.
HE HAS INSTRUCTED ME TO ALLOW NO ONE INSIDE, SO I MUST REQUEST THAT YOU LEAVE.
N... NO...
WE ARE AWARE THAT HE IS UNWELL.
WE WERE HOPING TO PAY HIM BUT A SHORT GET-WELL VISIT, SO WE SHAN'T BE A NUISANCE—
YES, AND WHILE I AM AWARE OF THAT, I CANNOT ALLOW YOU INSIDE.
きっぱり
BLUNT
WHAT'S YOUR PROBLEM? ARE YOU REALLY LISTENING TO US!?
Y-YEAH, WHAT HE SAID! YOU COULD AT LEAST THINK ABOUT IT FOR A LITTLE BIT, COULDN'T YOU!? YOU DON'T HAVE TO INSTANTLY SHUT US DOWN!
......

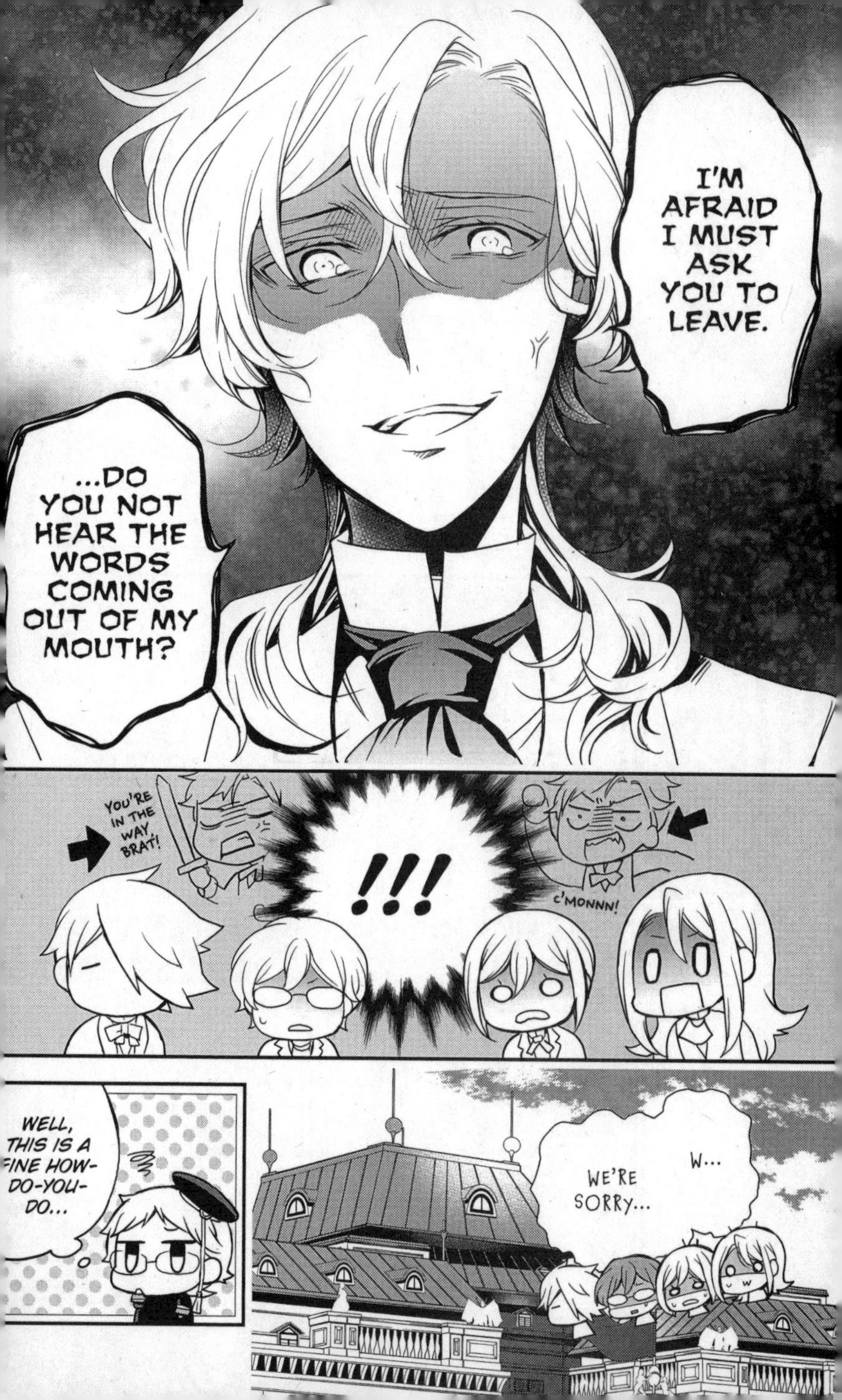
I'M AFRAID I MUST ASK YOU TO LEAVE.
...DO YOU NOT HEAR THE WORDS COMING OUT OF MY MOUTH?
!!!
C'MONNN!
YOU'RE IN THE WAY, BRAT!
W...
WE'RE SORRY...
WELL, THIS IS A FINE HOW-DO-YOU-DO...

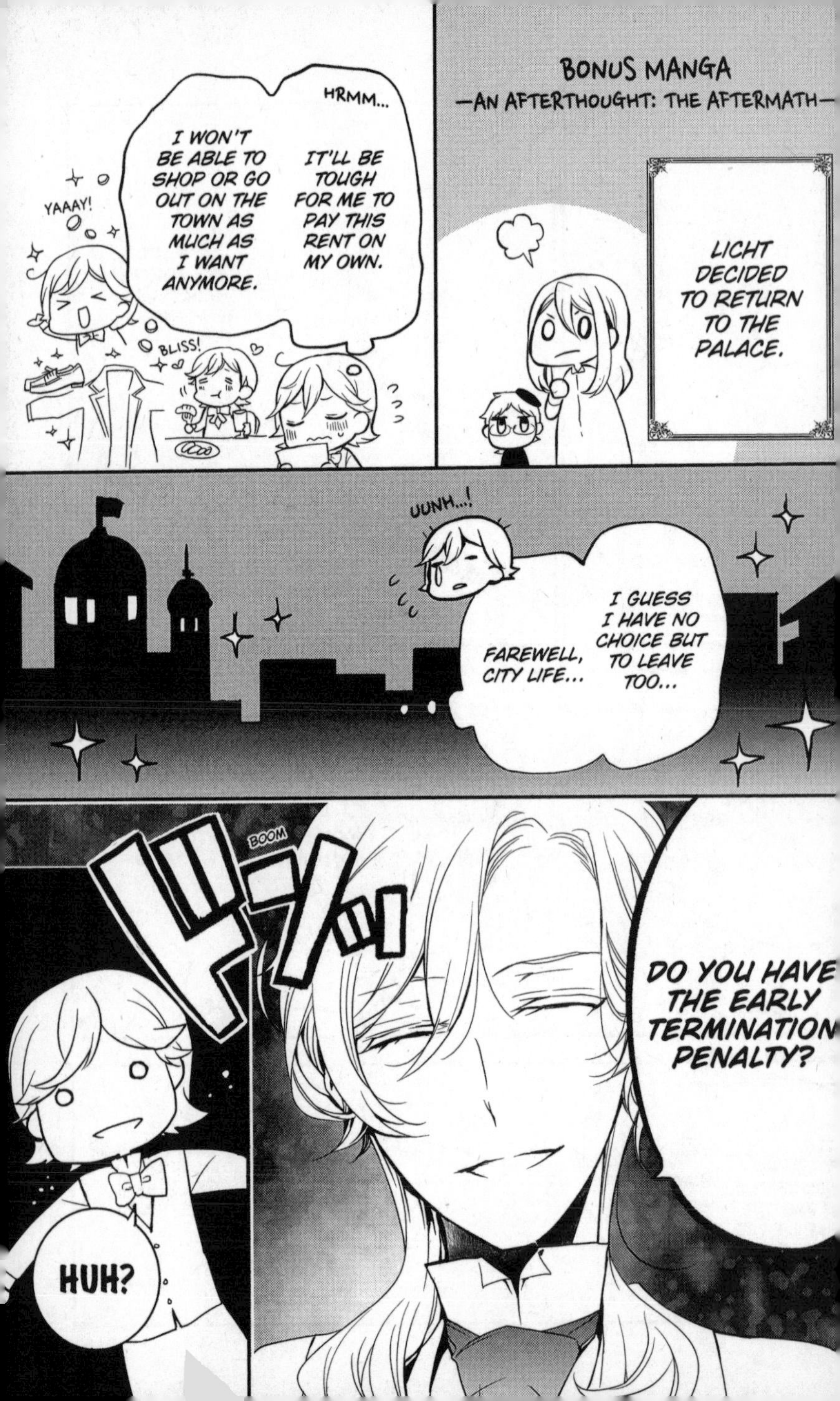

BONUS MANGA
—AN AFTERTHOUGHT: THE AFTERMATH—
LICHT DECIDED TO RETURN TO THE PALACE.
HRMM...
IT'LL BE TOUGH FOR ME TO PAY THIS RENT ON MY OWN.
I WON'T BE ABLE TO SHOP OR GO OUT ON THE TOWN AS MUCH AS I WANT ANYMORE.
YAAAY!
BLISS!
UUNH...!
I GUESS I HAVE NO CHOICE BUT TO LEAVE TOO...
FAREWELL, CITY LIFE...
DO YOU HAVE THE EARLY TERMINATION PENALTY?
BOOM
HUH?

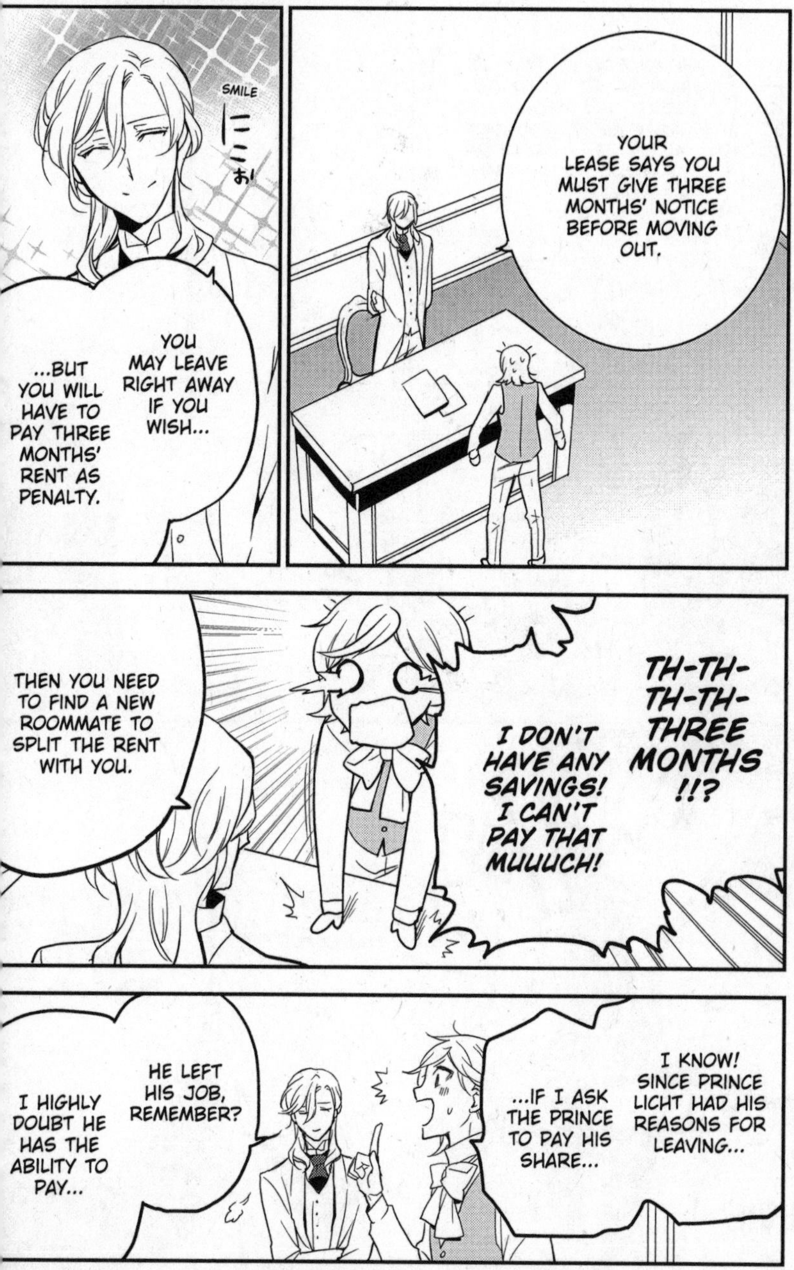
YOUR LEASE SAYS YOU MUST GIVE THREE MONTHS' NOTICE BEFORE MOVING OUT.
SMILE
YOU MAY LEAVE RIGHT AWAY IF YOU WISH...
...BUT YOU WILL HAVE TO PAY THREE MONTHS' RENT AS PENALTY.
TH-TH-TH-TH-THREE MONTHS!!?
I DON'T HAVE ANY SAVINGS! I CAN'T PAY THAT MUUUCH!
THEN YOU NEED TO FIND A NEW ROOMMATE TO SPLIT THE RENT WITH YOU.
I KNOW! SINCE PRINCE LICHT HAD HIS REASONS FOR LEAVING...
...IF I ASK THE PRINCE TO PAY HIS SHARE...
HE LEFT HIS JOB, REMEMBER?
I HIGHLY DOUBT HE HAS THE ABILITY TO PAY...

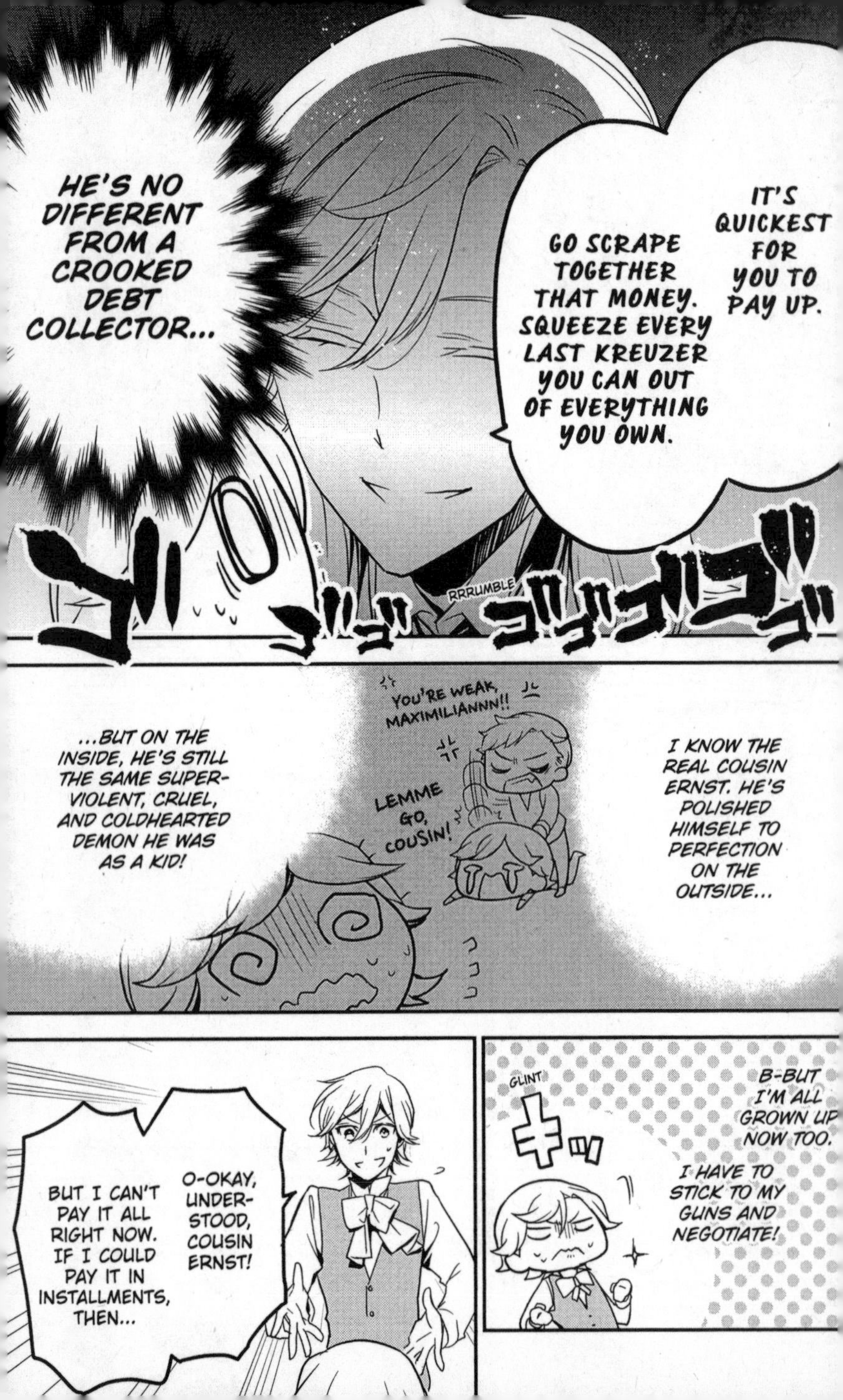
IT'S QUICKEST FOR YOU TO PAY UP.
GO SCRAPE TOGETHER THAT MONEY. SQUEEZE EVERY LAST KREUZER YOU CAN OUT OF EVERYTHING YOU OWN.
HE'S NO DIFFERENT FROM A CROOKED DEBT COLLECTOR...
RRRUMBLE
I KNOW THE REAL COUSIN ERNST. HE'S POLISHED HIMSELF TO PERFECTION ON THE OUTSIDE...
YOU'RE WEAK, MAXIMILIANNN!!
LEMME GO, COUSIN!
...BUT ON THE INSIDE, HE'S STILL THE SAME SUPER-VIOLENT, CRUEL, AND COLDHEARTED DEMON HE WAS AS A KID!
B-BUT I'M ALL GROWN UP NOW TOO.
I HAVE TO STICK TO MY GUNS AND NEGOTIATE!
GLINT
O-OKAY, UNDER-STOOD, COUSIN ERNST!
BUT I CAN'T PAY IT ALL RIGHT NOW. IF I COULD PAY IT IN INSTALLMENTS, THEN...

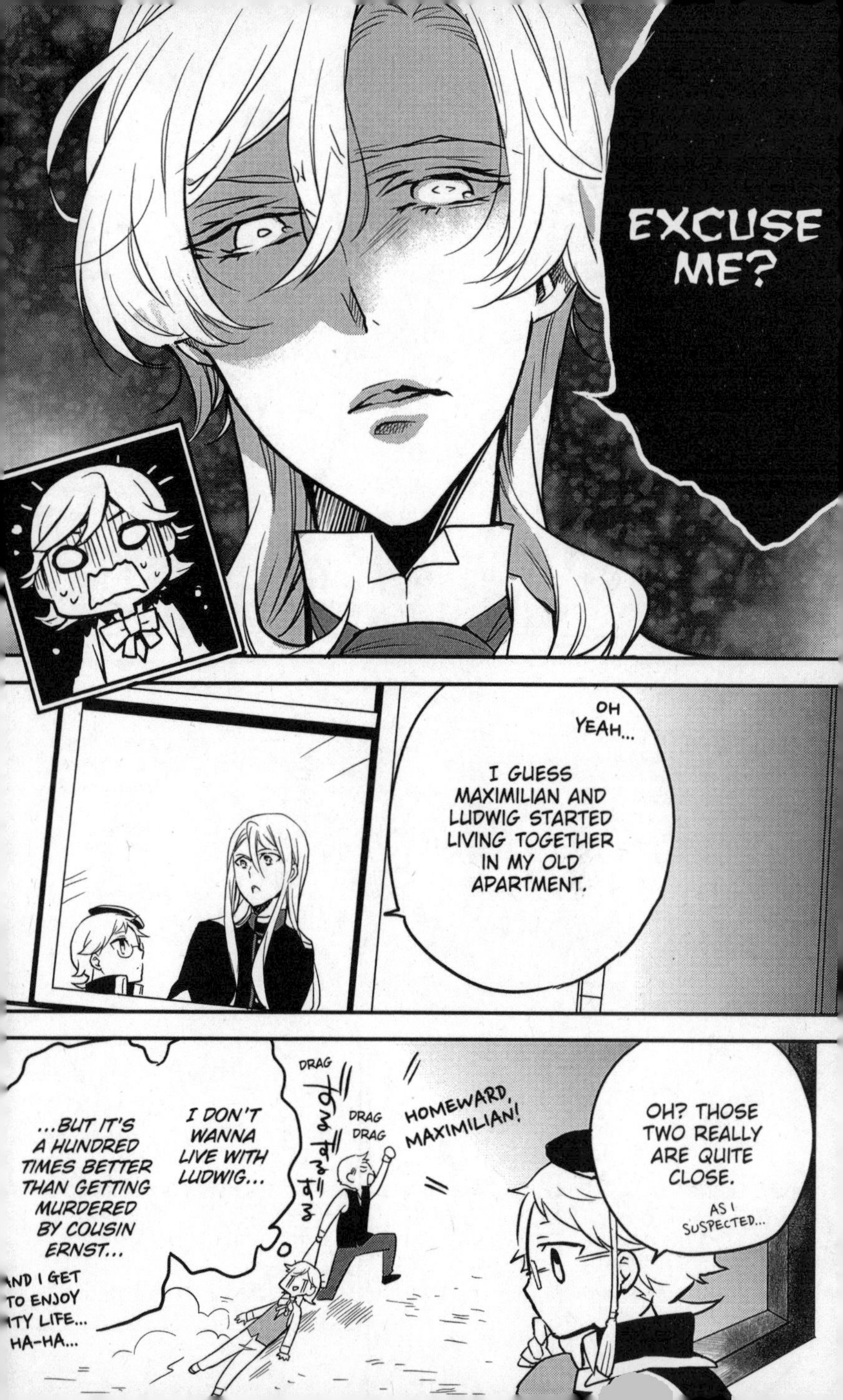
EXCUSE ME?
OH YEAH...
I GUESS MAXIMILIAN AND LUDWIG STARTED LIVING TOGETHER IN MY OLD APARTMENT.
OH? THOSE TWO REALLY ARE QUITE CLOSE.
AS I SUSPECTED...
HOMEWARD, MAXIMILIAN!
DRAG DRAG
DRAG
I DON'T WANNA LIVE WITH LUDWIG...
...BUT IT'S A HUNDRED TIMES BETTER THAN GETTING MURDERED BY COUSIN ERNST...
ND I GET TO ENJOY ITY LIFE... HA-HA...

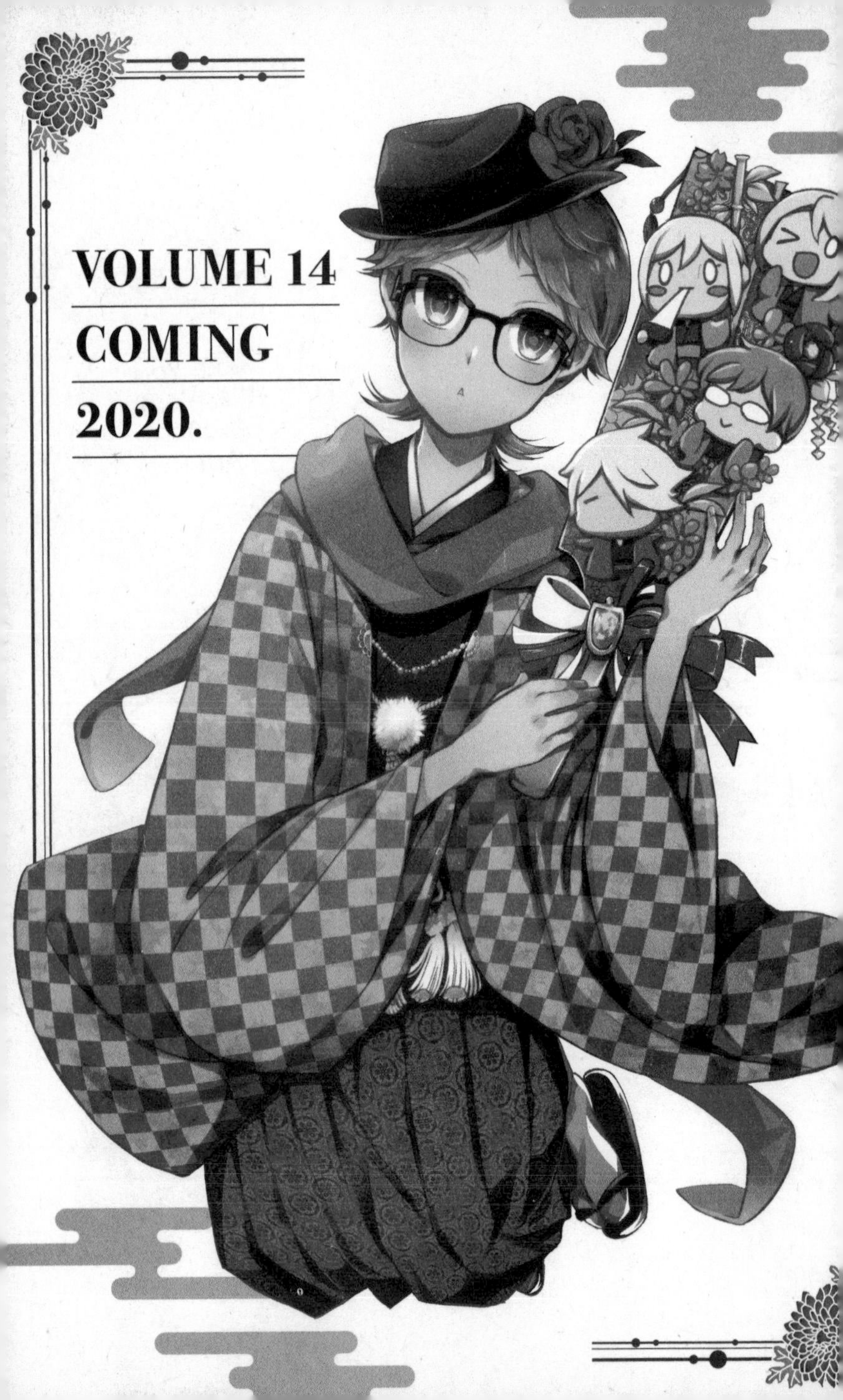
VOLUME 14
COMING
2020.

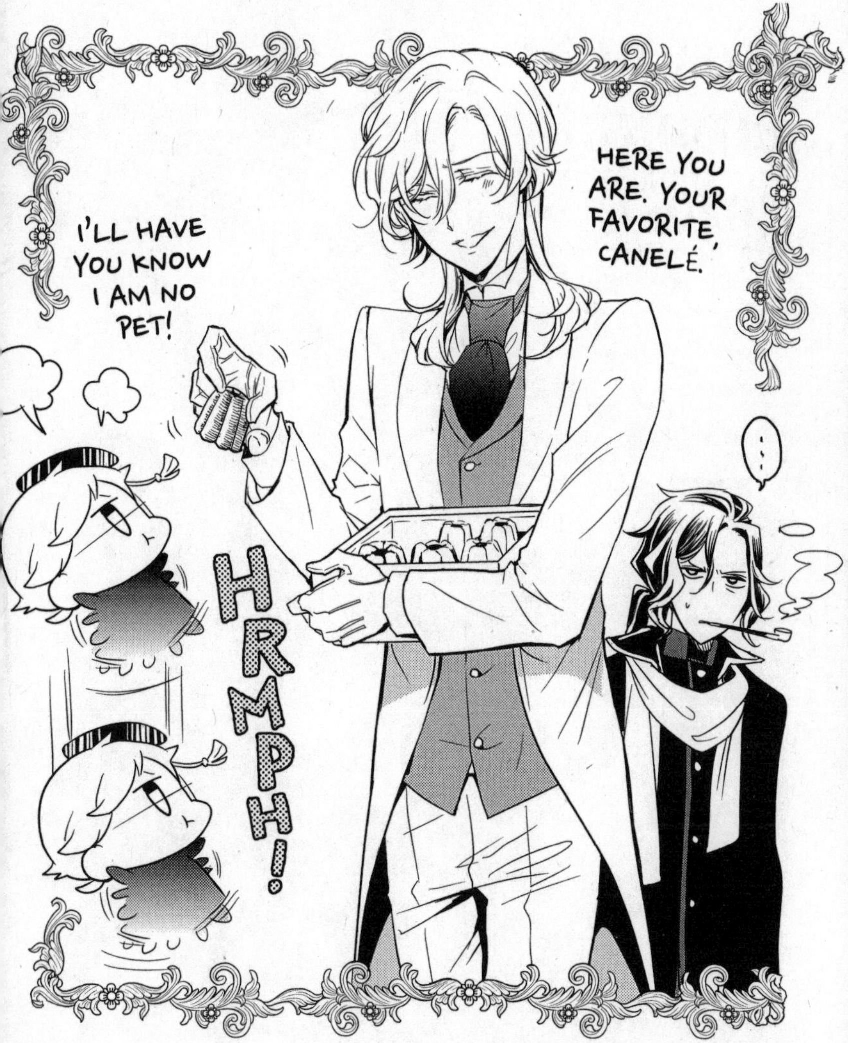
HERE YOU ARE. YOUR FAVORITE, CANELÉ.
I'LL HAVE YOU KNOW I AM NO PET!
HRMPH!
...

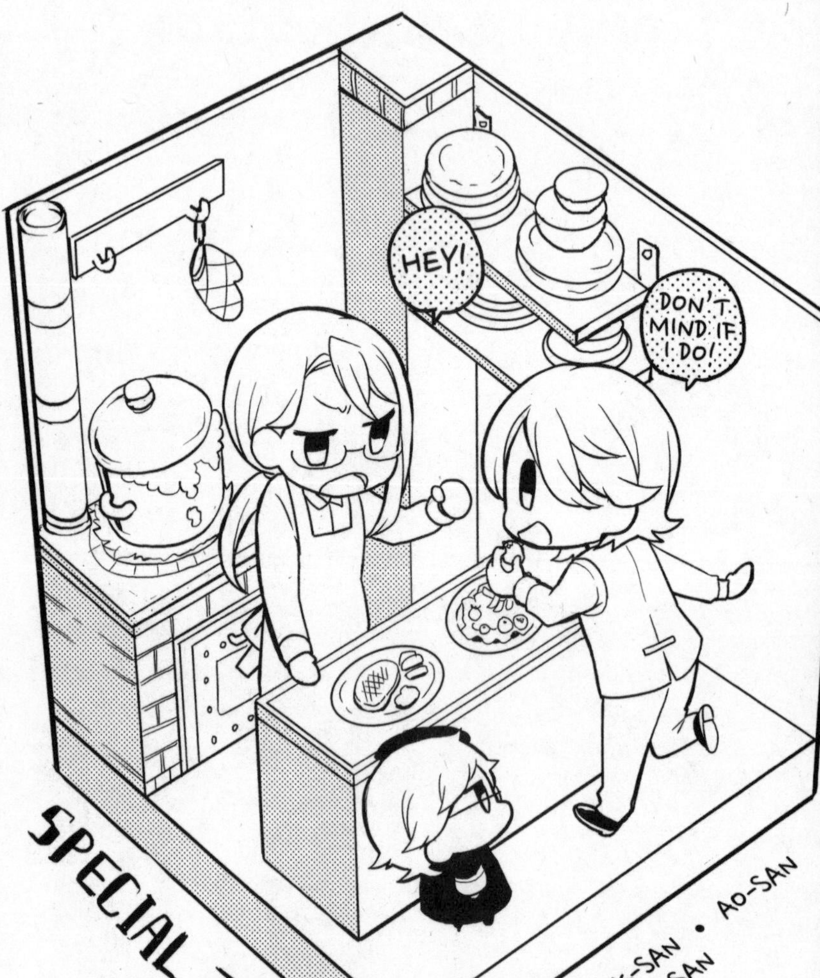
DON'T MIND IF I DO!
HEY!

SPECIAL THANKS

TSUCHIYA-SAN • K-SAN • AO-SAN
MY EDITOR, AKIYAMA-SAN

Now read the latest chapters of BLACK BUTLER digitally at the same time as Japan and support the creator!

The Phantomhive family has a butler who's almost too good to be true...

...or maybe he's just too good to be human.

Black Butler

YANA TOBOSO

VOLUMES 1-28 IN STORES NOW!

?ED IS THE NEW BLACK IN THIS 3LOODY, ACTION-PACKED SERIES ABOUT A GROUP OF RIGHTEOUS ASSASSINS!

eenage country bumpkin Tatsumi dreams of earning nough money for his impoverished village by vorking in the Capital—but his short-lived plans go wry when he's robbed by a buxom beauty pon arrival! Penniless, Tatsumi is taken by the lovely Miss Aria, but just when is Capital dreams seem in reach yet gain, Miss Aria's mansion is besieged y Night Raid—a team of ruthless ssassins who targets high-ranking embers of the upper class! As atsumi is quick to learn, appearances an be deceiving in the Capital, and his team of assassins just might be... e good guys?!

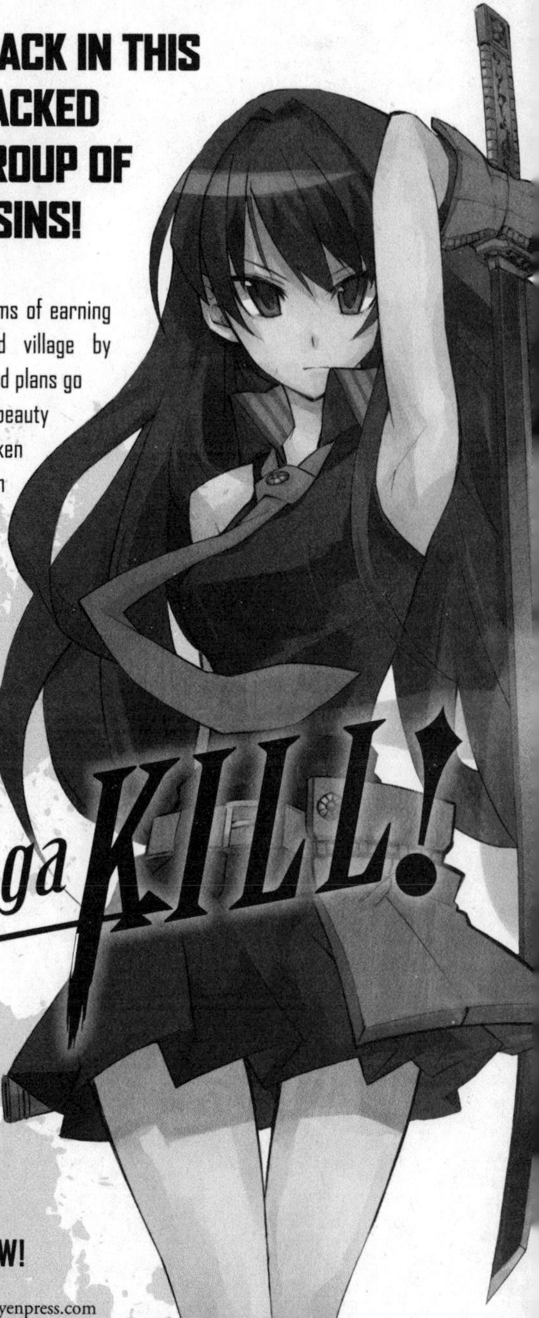

Akame ga KILL!

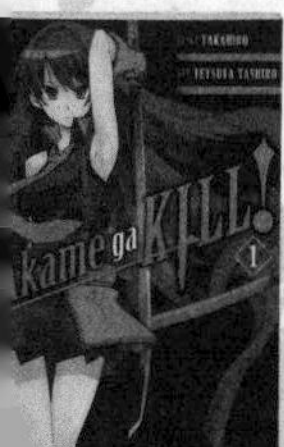

FULL SERIES AVAILABLE NOW!

For more information, visit www.yenpress.com

Yen Press

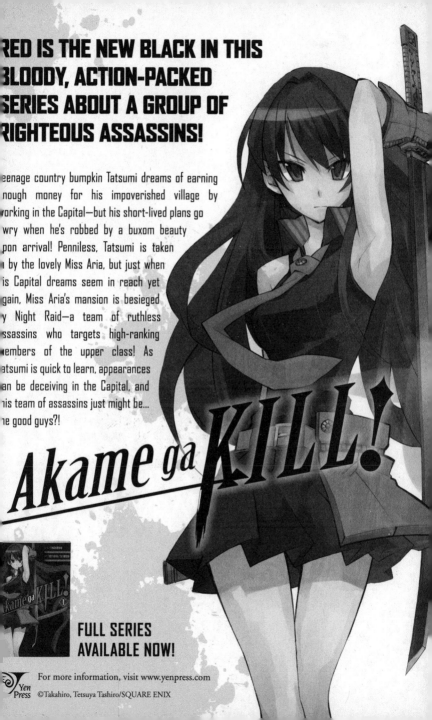

The Royal T

Translation: Amanda Haley • Lettering: Abigail Blackman

THE ROYAL TUTOR Vol. 13 © 2019 Higasa Akai / SQUARE ENIX CO., LTD. First published in Japan in 2019 by SQUARE ENIX CO., LTD. English translation rights arranged with SQUARE ENIX CO., LTD. and Yen Press, LLC through Tuttle-Mori Agency, Inc., Tokyo.

English translation © 2020 by SQUARE ENIX CO., LTD.

Yen Press
150 West 30th Street, 19th Floor
New York, NY 10001

Visit us at yenpress.com
facebook.com/yenpress
twitter.com/yenpress
yenpress.tumblr.com
instagram.com/yenpress

First Yen Press Print Edition: February 2020
The chapters in this volume were originally published as ebooks by Yen Press.

Yen Press is an imprint of Yen Press, LLC.
The Yen Press name and logo are trademarks of Yen Press, LLC.

The publisher is not responsible for websites (or their content) that are not owned by the publisher.

Library of Congress Control Number: 2017938422

ISBNs: 978-1-9753-0789-9 (paperback)
       978-1-9753-0788-2 (ebook)

10 9 8 7 6 5 4 3 2 1

BVG

Printed in the United States of America